Daughters of Light

DAUGHTERS OF LIGHT

Quaker Women Preaching and Prophesying
in the Colonies and Abroad, 1700–1775

R E B E C C A   L A R S O N

Alfred A. Knopf

NEW YORK

1999

THIS IS A BORZOI BOOK
PUBLISHED BY ALFRED A. KNOPF, INC.

www.randomhouse.com

Knopf, Borzoi Books, and the colophon are registered trademarks of Random House, Inc.

Library of Congress Cataloging-in-Publication Data
Larson, Rebecca, [date]
Daughters of light : Quaker women preaching and prophesying in the colonies
and abroad, 1700–1775 / Rebecca Larson. — 1st ed.
p.   cm.
Includes bibliographical references and index.
ISBN 0-679-43762-2 (alk. paper)
1. Quaker women—United States—History—18th century.   2. Women clergy—United
States—History—18th century.   3. Society of Friends—United States—Clergy—History—
18th century.   4. Society of Friends—Missions—History—18th century.   I. Title.
BX7636.L37   1999
289.6′73′082—DC21   98-42459   CIP

Manufactured in the United States of America

First Edition

To my mother,

Virginia Ellen Andreas

*And it shall come to pass
afterward, that I will pour out
my spirit upon all flesh; and
your sons and your daughters
shall prophesy, your old men
shall dream dreams, your young
men shall see visions:*

    *And also upon the servants
and upon the handmaids
in those days will I pour out my
spirit.*

Joel 2:28–29

Contents

Appendixes

Daughters of Light

Introduction

W H E N Sarah Kemble Knight made the daunting journey by horseback from Boston to New York in 1704, she encountered a talkative female tavernkeeper along her route. The Puritan traveller satirically claimed that her loquacious hostess spoke for such "a long time, that I began to fear I was got among the Quaking tribe, beleeving [believing] not a Limbertong'd [limber-tongued] sister among them could out do Mad[a]m. Hostes[s]."[1] The New Englander's portrayal of nimble-tongued women was a witty allusion to Quaker women's innovative, public activity as preachers. Knight's mocking description mystifies most present-day readers because she referred to a role for women largely overlooked in historical accounts of early America.[2]

On October 23, 1704, only a few weeks after Knight's departure from Boston, two "limber-tongued sisters" of "the Quaking tribe," Esther Palmer of Flushing, Long Island, and her travel companion, Susanna Freeborn of Newport (a city where half of the white population were Quaker), set out from Rhode Island on a journey in "ye Love of Truth" that, for Palmer, would extend 3,230 miles. Travelling across colonial America, where diverse peoples mingled and created a strange, new hybrid of indigenous North American, enslaved African, and metropolitan European cultures, the Quaker women ministers stressed an experiential religion, seeking "Comfortable times of refreshment" when an overwhelming sense of the presence of God filled their gatherings for worship.[3] The women rode through snake-infested swamps and crossed swiftly moving rivers in canoes, in order to preach the Gospel in courthouses, residences,

3

and Quaker meeting-houses, asserting that the Holy Spirit had been planted in the hearts of all humans to inwardly teach them. Their message deeply affected some colonists who were "Much brocken [broken] and very tender & pres[s]ed us to visit them again."[4]

Believing they were providentially led, with almost a magnetic force (as one Quaker described, "the Spirit which led me forth, was to me like a needle of a compass, touched with a loadstone; for so it pointed where I ought to go, and when I came to the far end of the journey"), the female preachers witnessed the range of North American life in eight colonies: from the rolling farmlands of Pennsylvania, to the Algonquian-speaking Indians' village of Askiminikansen on the Eastern Shore of Maryland, with its low, bark-covered dwellings, smoke emerging from roof-holes, and the new capital of Virginia where they "Call'd at ye Governours at Williams Burrough (at his request) who treated us Kindly." In Williamsburg, the Anglican governor, Colonel Francis Nicholson, presented the Quakers with coconuts, lemons, and other fruit to take with them. The women travelled in "ye unity of ye Spirit" as far southward as the remote Albemarle Sound region of North Carolina before Palmer returned to her Long Island residence in January 1706.[5] During Esther Palmer's fifteen-month journey, more "limber-tongued sisters" had joined her, replacing Susanna Freeborn (who returned to Rhode Island) for stages of the trip: including Mary Lawson, a Philadelphia preacher, and Mary Bannister, a visiting London minister (whose ministerial companion from York, England, Mary Ellerton, was en route to Barbados). These visible female figures on the colonial American landscape, the travelling Quaker ministers, were the legacy of the previous century's religio-political upheaval, across the seas, in the "mother country" of England.

Although the Puritan model of female submission to male ministerial authority has shaped our views of women in early America, in 1700 Quakerism was one of several religious alternatives for colonial Americans and "possibly the most potent religious movement in the colonies outside Puritan New England."[6] Women's participation in the ministry, traditionally a masculine prerogative, sprang from Quaker belief in both genders' capacity to be guided by the Holy Spirit in inspired preaching. Quakers rejected "hireling priests," a paid, trained clergy, in an attempt to return to the genuine, Spirit-filled Christianity of the apostles. Eighteenth-century Quakers (unlike many present-day Quakers) formally distinguished an individual who possessed a "gift" in the ministry, whether male or female, as one whom God had "called & chosen, raised up & gifted, for His great work. . . ."[7] All had access to the Holy Spirit; but eighteenth-century Quakers believed that there were differing spiritual gifts, and God qualified certain "instruments" to voice His messages. Frequent preaching by an individual was not permitted without recognition by the Quaker meeting (usually recommendation to a select meeting of ministers and elders). In an eighteenth-century Quaker meeting, ministers typically sat at the front of the meeting-house facing the other worshippers. In the ministers' gallery, women and men sat on opposite sides of the same raised platform. Eighteenth-century Quakers viewed the now obscure Quaker preacher Rachel Wilson and John Woolman (the Quaker minister famed for his devotional journal and abolitionism) as equal religious authorities. Both were spiritual exemplars, "That like a Woolman or Wilson Shines," stated a Friend's poem of the period.[8]

This book explores the lives of Quaker women preachers between 1700 and 1775. During the first half of the eighteenth century, adherents of Quakerism formed their highest proportion of the American population and reached the peak of their secular power in the colonies. Unhampered by the legal disabilities they suffered in the British Isles as dissenters from the Church of England, Quakers dominated the colonial governments of Pennsylvania and Rhode Island, as well as served in the New Jersey and North Carolina governments in significant numbers. In a period characterized by one historian as "the Golden Age of Quakerism in America," Quaker governors held office for thirty-six successive terms in Rhode Island; a Quaker majority existed in the Pennsylvania Assembly until 1756; New Jersey Quakers served as governors, assemblymen, and councillors; and, before oaths were required to hold public office, Quakers controlled half the seats in the North Carolina Assembly in 1703. The contributions of eighteenth-century Quaker female preachers, as religious leaders of a significant colonial group, form a rich chapter in the history of women in America: from Catharine Payton advising the Quaker members of the Pennsylvania Assembly to withdraw from political office during the French and Indian War, and Ann Moore obtaining permission from General James Abercromby to preach to the British military forces in New York in 1758, to Susanna Hatton preaching to the Delaware Indians during governmental treaty negotiations at Easton in 1761, and Rachel Wilson visiting Patrick Henry in support of his promotion of religious toleration in the Virginia Assembly.[9]

Painting of Gracechurch Street Meeting in London,
c. 1770, by an unknown artist. Sophia Hume, a native of
Charleston, South Carolina, sits among her fellow ministers
in the "gallery" (third woman from the left, her hand partly
covering her face). Hume (1702–1774) was the daughter of
an Anglican official who served as attorney general and
secretary of South Carolina. She returned to the faith of her
grandmother Mary Fisher, a pioneer Quaker missionary to
America. The aged, bent woman, her face averted, seated
directly below the Friend preaching, wears a green apron,
customary for Quaker women a quarter of a century earlier,
when white aprons were fashionable in the world. *Reproduced with permission of the Library Committee of the Religious Society of Friends in Britain*

Quaker women in colonial America have entered the collective memory as seventeenth-century "enthusiasts," their image formed by the first encounters of Quaker missionaries with New England magistrates, when they were perceived as a serious threat to social order, members of a scorned sect on the margins of Puritan society. In the 1650s and 1660s, harsh laws were passed in Massachusetts to exclude such Quaker "heretics" with threats of whippings, ear croppings, and, eventually, execution. But Quakers returned to protest the injustice of these severe measures, resulting in the martyrdom of four, including one female Quaker who was killed in 1660 on Boston Common, before King Charles II ordered the revocation of the Massachusetts death sentence on Quakers. By 1677, Quakers had established a regular meeting for worship in Boston. One hundred years after Mary Dyer, the early Quaker "witness" against unjust laws, was executed in Boston, Rachel Wilson (whom the *Boston-Gazette* of 1769 identified as "an eminent preacher among the friends") arrived in the metropolis. The *Gazette* recorded the Quaker woman minister's visit in a laudatory fashion, noting that she "preached to a large audience and gained applause," and displayed "that general benevolence, which is the distinguishing characteristic of the true christian."[10]

Even before Quaker colonization efforts in the 1670s and 1680s, travelling Quaker missionaries had found receptive audiences in different sections of the colonies. Quakerism had flourished early in Rhode Island, a refuge in the seventeenth century for those alienated from the Puritan establishment in Massachusetts. Quakerism also had taken hold in peripheral New England areas among settlers with separatist leanings: on Nantucket Island, in southern Massachusetts, and the Piscataqua region of New Hampshire. In New York, the governor had complained of the religious diversity in 1687: "Here bee not many of the Church of England; few Roman Catholicks; abundance of Quakers preachers men and Women especially. . . ."[11] Long Island, settled in part by English colonists who had fled the Puritan north, had a large Quaker population by 1700.

Quakerism, with its unpaid, travelling ministry, "requiring no church building, a minimum of organizational apparatus, and offering a faith shorn of liturgy, sacraments, and an intricate theology" was uniquely suited to colonial American circumstances.[12] In the southern colonies, long distances between settlements and a lack of ordained clergy weakened attempts, for a time, to create a powerful Anglican establishment. Maryland, founded as a haven for English Catholics, already had a tradition of dissent, and by 1672, a Quaker yearly meeting had been organized there. In the Anglican colony of Virginia, Quakerism had made inroads, establishing a yearly meeting by 1673. Successful Quaker itinerancy prompted Thomas Bray, in the 1690s, to create a proselytizing arm of the Church of England, the Society for the Propagation of the Gospel in Foreign Parts, to compete for the loyalties of the English settlers.[13] The Church of England struggled to gain a foothold in North Carolina in 1700, where Quakerism had been the only form of organized religion for the previous twenty-five years.

The Middle Colonies became the region of greatest Quaker strength in North America, where Quaker colonization, rather than the extension of the faith through evangelism, began in 1674, with the purchase of West Jersey by English Quakers for settlement. When William Penn obtained the huge land grant of Pennsylvania in 1681 for his "holy experiment," a commonwealth to be governed by Quaker principles, thousands of additional Quaker immigrants were drawn by the promise of religious freedom and economic opportunity. Between 1675 and 1740, the largest group migration from the British Isles to the American colonies was that of the Quakers.[14]

The prosperity and religious pluralism of the Quaker-founded colony of Pennsylvania greatly enhanced the reputation of the religious group (eventually known as the Society of Friends). By the eighteenth century, Quakers were being admired by French philosophers, like Voltaire, as paragons of Enlightenment virtue—tolerant, peaceable, and benevolent.[15] In cities such as Philadelphia and Newport, Friends were among the political and economic leaders. Although the Church of England had increased in strength and the Congregational way dominated in New England, in 1750, Quakers were the third largest religious group in colonial America. Quakers had 250 meetings for worship, narrowly surpassed by the Anglicans (289 churches), and more distantly behind the Puritan/Congregationalists (465 churches). Quaker meetings extended the length of English settlement: from Casco Bay (in present-day Maine) to Charles Town (Charleston), South Carolina.[16] Eighteenth-century Quakers in British North America were also part of the larger, transatlantic Society of Friends, their influence augmented by their coreligionists in London who lobbied the imperial government against unfavorable colonial legislation or political appointments.

A transatlantic perspective will be taken in this book to achieve a fuller understanding of Quaker women in British North American life: the illuminating experiences of British Quaker female preachers who visited the colonies are included, as well as those of colonial American ministers who travelled overseas. The American colonies did not form a separate nation before the American Revolution, but were part of the British empire, not only politically, under British government, but culturally, as "part of the expanding periphery of Britain's core culture."[17] Pre–Revolutionary War Quakers especially viewed themselves as linked in one transatlantic community: no colonial religious group had closer transatlantic ties. American Quaker meetings for church business were supreme within their own jurisdictions, but all were attuned to the guidance of the important London Yearly Meeting in England which established separate committees of correspondence with each colonial yearly meeting. Travelling preachers, male and female, circulated on both sides of the Atlantic, unifying Friends in faith and practice. Their religious principles specified distinctive language, dress, and patterns of behavior shared by Quakers in every region. Friends formed a tight-knit sectarian network, in part, to contend with hostility or sufferings for their religious testimonies. As a dissenting minority in many areas, Quakers were penalized for refusing to pay tithes to maintain the established church, for refusing to swear oaths, and for not performing military service (except in Pennsylvania, New Jersey, and Rhode Island). Frequent emigration, Quaker intermarriage, and strong business ties further blurred the regional divisions between Friends during this period.

The life of Esther Palmer illustrates the seamlessness of this transatlantic Quaker culture. Born to a New York Quaker family, Palmer travelled through the colonies with Quaker women from other parts of the British world, including Susanna Freeborn of Rhode Island, Mary Lawson of Pennsylvania (who had emigrated from Cumberland, England), and Mary Bannister from London, England (who eventually moved to the American colonies). Palmer herself voyaged on religious service to the British Isles in 1710 and subsequently married Richard Champion, a Quaker merchant of Bristol, England. Champion, a leading partner in the Bristol Brass Company and short-term financier of the Coalbrookdale Ironworks, where Abraham Darby was experimenting with the coke-smelting of iron, was among the British Quakers who helped lay the foundations of the Industrial Revolution. Esther (Palmer) Champion, minister, wife, and mother, had successfully navigated the North American wilderness, but contracted smallpox in the bustling urban port of Bristol, England, dying there in 1714. The native New Yorker was memorialized by English Friends as "a virtu-

ous woman, of a sound judgment, and very quick understanding," who
expressed "her great grief when there was . . . want of true love in any
church, meeting, or family, where she travelled."[18]

Participants in the Quaker transatlantic culture with its ministerial role
for women were more similar to other members of the Society of Friends
throughout the English Atlantic world than to nearby neighbors of another
faith. Recapturing the religious diversity in British North America reveals
female lives that strikingly diverge from standard portrayals of eighteenth-
century women. Colonial American women have been characterized "as
wholly domestic beings whose influence in the world was confined to their
immediate families."[19] Quaker female preachers, however, were designated
"Public Friends" by their community (as were Quaker male preachers),
encouraged by Quaker tenets to bear public testimonies to the workings of
God's Spirit. Long before nineteenth-century women reformers pioneered
in the secular realm, challenging social convention as females delivering
public lectures, Quaker women ministers in colonial America were routinely speaking in public before "mixed audiences" (composed of both
men and women). Ann Moore, a Maryland Quaker preacher, for example,
presented "a noble & worthy testimony" before "the Governor the
Recorder many of the Councill Aldermen severall [non-Quaker] Ministers
(of other persuasions) many Lawyers, & a great number of Merch[an]ts &
Private Gentlemen . . ." in Philadelphia in 1763.[20]

In contrast to Puritan/Congregationalist women who gave accounts of
their conversion experiences, but were expected to remain silent before
clergymen's scriptural interpretations, Quaker women explicated Scriptures in oral sermons and published writings. Female Quakers were supported to enter public space not only through preaching, but through
authorship and travel. When Sarah Kemble Knight ventured on a five-
month trip from Boston to New York to help settle an estate on behalf of
her cousin's widow, she had displayed "an independence and resilience
that, at the time, was remarkable for her sex." A Puritan woman like Knight
might be disparagingly labelled a "gadder" for leaving the household, the
central scene of her duties, for extended lengths of time.[21] Travel was perceived to be a primarily masculine activity (usually an occupational necessity, as it was for Knight's husband, a ship captain). Yet for numerous
Quaker female preachers, like Esther Palmer, such intercolonial travel was
characteristic. After Esther Palmer's journey in 1704, she travelled to New
England in the ministry in 1706, visited Pennsylvania on religious service in

Eighteenth-century Quaker woman preaching. From *The Ceremonies and religious customs of the various nations of the known world . . . [by J. F. Bernard], and illustrated, with a large number of folio copper plates . . . designed by Bernard Picart . . . Faithfully translated into English, by a gentleman some time since of St. John's College in Oxford* (London, 1733–39). *Courtesy Department of Special Collections, University Research Library, University of California, Los Angeles*

1707, returned to New England in 1709, and then sailed across the Atlantic to preach in the British Isles in 1710. While travelling, Quaker women preached not only in Quaker meeting-houses, but in town halls and in courthouses, places usually reserved for men in public action. In their gospel labors, Quaker women ministers acted independently of their husbands and children. Journeying in pairs, with "Public Friends" from different regions, they created a transatlantic network of women who shared a similar "calling."

Quakers created a unique transatlantic culture, embracing both mysticism and rational capitalism, female spiritual leaders and shrewd male merchants, as they attempted to balance, in historian Frederick Tolles's words, the cultivation of the outward plantation and "the inward plantation" of the spirit. Recognizing no dividing line between the religious and the secular, Friends infused their spiritual values into their commercial and political worlds. Since Quaker preachers' oversight was not limited to a religious realm separated from the rest of life, the women's ministerial role was a wedge into eighteenth-century men's monopoly of societal leadership. In Pennsylvania, William Smith, an Anglican priest, tried to dislodge Quaker men from governmental power in the 1750s by exciting alarm over the influence wielded by Quaker women ministers: "Each Saint in Petticoats foretells our Fate," Smith wrote, "And fain wou'd guide the giddy Helm of State."[22]

A different understanding of religion led to a different social reality for these eighteenth-century women. Colonial American newspapers detailing the activities of these Quaker women portrayed them as public figures: preachers, authors, and travellers. Notice of Sophia Hume, a native South Carolinian, appeared in the *Virginia Gazette* of 1767: "Yesterday, Mrs. Hume (the celebrated writer and preacher lately arrived from England) delivered an exhortation to a numerous body of people, of all professions [of various religious affiliations], at the Quakers meeting house."[23] Studies of women in early America have made creative use of nonliterary sources such as needlework, paintings, and gravestones, since few non-Quaker colonial women (whose hands were often thought better suited for needle and thread than the pen) left writing in any form. But a substantial collection of written sources (women's correspondence, diaries, church business meeting records, and published treatises, as well as literature written about these women) survive for Quaker female preachers.

In restoring Quaker women ministers' biographies to the historical account of the period, we gain insight into the religious complexity of colonial America and a more refined understanding of eighteenth-century women's constraints and possibilities. Who were the eighteenth-century women acknowledged as Quaker preachers? How did their ministerial role affect their families? How did these women cope with the dangers and difficulties of eighteenth-century travel? What ideas and practices did they transmit across the Quaker transatlantic community? What was the response to the Quaker women ministers in the larger society? At the heart of this book are the reconstructed lives of women who crossed the Atlantic on religious service from the American colonies, England, or Ireland between 1700 and 1775 (among the best-documented eighteenth-century Quaker women ministers' lives), supplemented with material on other preachers who travelled only regionally. Seventeenth-century English missionaries had carried Quakerism to the colonies, and by 1700, American Quaker ministers were paying reciprocal visits to the British Isles. The chronology of this book concludes approximately seven decades later, in

1775, when trips originating on either side of the Atlantic ceased temporarily. The American Revolutionary War would forever alter the once thriving transoceanic Quaker culture.

The first section of this book, "Beginnings," sets the stage for the stories of the eighteenth-century women ministers in the succeeding chapters. This initial chapter provides the historical background: Quakerism's origins in mid-seventeenth-century England and the theological justification for women's preaching. Chapter 2 describes how eighteenth-century Quaker women experienced "callings" to preach and presents a composite portrait of these spiritual leaders. The third chapter examines how these women felt "leadings" to travel in the ministry and the means by which they accomplished their journeys. The fourth chapter explores the effects of the ministerial role on the women's private lives: their marriages, child-bearing, and child-rearing practices. The impact of the female preachers' travels on the transatlantic Quaker community is the subject of the fifth chapter. The Quaker women ministers as public figures in the larger, non-Quaker culture is the topic of chapter 6. The afterword summarizes how Quaker spiritual egalitarianism translated into the lives of these eighteenth-century women.

One

BEGINNINGS

Y O U that cannot own [acknowledge] the prophesying of the daughters, the woman-labourers in the gospel, you are such as the apostle speaks of . . . which serves not the Lord," George Fox wrote in 1656, referring to the majority of his Christian contemporaries.[1] The Quaker leader's inclusion of women in the ministry challenged fundamental assumptions of established Christianity. "Your sons and your daughters shall prophesy," according to the biblical verse Joel 2:28. But "that kind of prophesying which consists in interpreting Scripture . . . cannot bee meant in this place," argued a seventeenth-century Anglican priest, giving the traditional interpretation, "because in that kind of prophesying the daughters of God have no part nor fellowship with the sons of God; for God hath excluded them."[2]

Origins of Quakerism

Quakerism emerged during a turbulent era in English history, when political, social, and religious upheaval created "a world turned upside down." "Bold impudent huswives" and uneducated laborers preached on stools, spreading "new and strange blasphemies."[3] Civil war and regicide heightened the intensely apocalyptic atmosphere. Attacks on the authority of both church and state generated a creative ferment of ideas in mid-seventeenth-century England. Traditions were repudiated or reexamined. Conflicting biblical interpretations were fiercely debated in pamphlet wars. Diverse sects and movements arose in the absence of a controlling orthodoxy: including the Ranters, the Diggers, the Levellers, the Muggletonians, the Grindletonians, and the Fifth Monarchy Men. The Quakers were one of the few sectarian groups from this heady period to survive the restoration of the monarchy in 1660.

The Protestant Reformation, over a century earlier, initially had released forces of dissent. In accepting the Bible (the revealed Word of God) as a sufficient guide to salvation, Protestants promoted individual scriptural interpretation: "a priesthood of all believers." The Protestants' rejection of the Roman Catholic Church as mediator between God and humankind placed every man and woman in a direct relationship to the Divine Being. When Martin Luther posted his ninety-five theses on the door of the Wittenberg church in Germany in 1517, he stimulated a reforming zeal to purge Christianity of corruption and practices not based on Scriptures.

The Reformation had proceeded in a distinctive manner in sixteenth-century England, paving the way for future religious conflicts. King Henry VIII's desire to break with Rome had been fueled less by Protestant convictions than by his aim to establish the state's authority over the church, and his need for a divorce. Rejecting papal authority, the Church of England had retained most of the Catholic ecclesiastical organization and ceremonial forms. English Protestantism divided into two factions: Anglicans (those who supported the Church of England as established) and Puritans (those who wanted further reformation). Puritans sought to replace the bishops, whose authority, like that of the pope, supposedly derived from Saint Peter, with a presbyterial or congregational form of church government in which all clergymen were of equal rank. Many reformers wanted to purify the church of other vestiges of Catholicism, including priestly garments, statues, and elaborate rituals, construed as symbols of idolatry or superstition. They endeavored to recapture the simplicity of early Christian worship.

The cruel measures adopted by William Laud, King Charles I's archbishop of Canterbury, to enforce religious uniformity in the 1630s exacerbated these disputes within English Protestantism. Laud's persecution of Puritans angered those who perceived his exalted view of episcopal authority as crypto-Catholic. Popular fears that a design existed "to alter the kingdom both in religion and government" by returning it to Catholicism and erecting a despotism were stimulated by Charles I's ineptitude and his devotion to his Catholic queen. Alarmed Protestants viewed the pope as the Antichrist who had led believers astray and plunged the church into spiritual darkness with his deviations from God's Word.

Archbishop Laud, "that Arch-enemy of our Prosperity and Reformation," was impeached by the Long Parliament in December 1640 and sent to the Tower. Antiprelatical feeling was so widespread that even vendors in the streets of London "lock'd their Fish up, / And trudg'd away to cry No Bishop." The imprisonment of Laud led to the almost total collapse of ecclesiastical authority in England. Puritans in Parliament debated the proper form of church government, liturgy, and teachings, unable to settle the "Church Question." As John Milton wrote in "The Reason of Church Government Urged Against Prelaty" (1642), people were seeking "to inform their understanding in the reason of that government which the church claims to have over them." Milton lamented that "whether it ought to be presbyterial or prelatical [church government by bishops], such endless question, or rather uproar, is arisen in this land. . . ."[4]

In the unaccustomed fluidity of national religious practice, sects representing a variety of theological opinions mushroomed. Disorder increased with the outbreak of civil war in 1642 between the parliamentary army and forces supporting Charles I. The catastrophic events convinced many that the Millennium, the thousand-year-period predicted in the Bible when Christ will reign on earth, was imminent. A "Babelish confusion" of contending voices proposed to redeem the nation from its spiritual and political ills during the revolutionary fervor surrounding the execution of the king in 1649.[5]

George Fox and Quaker Theology

Participating in the period's widespread spiritual seeking and unrest was George Fox (1624–91), a shoemaker's apprentice. Journeying from the English Midlands in the turbulent 1640s, Fox spoke with people professing a multiplicity of beliefs, from those who "held women have no souls . . . no more than a goose," to others who "relied much on dreams." Accelerated change and the disruption of traditional certainties had created a vacuum of trusted authority. In the midst of this external chaos, George Fox had a revelation—one could look inward for God's guidance to truth. Fox described the religious experience he had in 1647: "And when all my hopes in them [teachers of religion] and in all men were gone so that I had nothing outwardly to help me, nor could I tell what to do; oh! even then I heard a Voice which said 'There is one, even Christ Jesus, that can speak to thy condition'; and when I heard it my heart did leap for joy, then did the Lord let me see why there was none on earth that could speak to my condition . . . and this I knew experimentally [by direct experience]."[6]

In Fox's changed understanding of religion, the Spirit of God was within, yet people were expecting divine truth to be revealed to them by external authorities: Christ Himself was "their teacher to instruct them, their counsellor to direct them, their shepherd to feed them, their bishop to oversee them, and their prophet to open Divine mysteries to them."[7] Each person possessed this Inward Teacher since Christ was "the true Light which lighteth every man that cometh into the world" (John 1:9). Before the historical Christ departed the world, he had promised: "The Comforter, which is the Holy Ghost, whom the Father will send in my name, he shall teach you all things, and bring all things to your remembrance, whatsoever I have said unto you" (John 14:26), "the Spirit of truth" which "will guide you unto all truth" (John 16:13). George Fox concluded that this Inward Christ, or universal capacity for divine revelation, had become obscured by worldly corruptions and man-made superstitions.

"Hireling priests" (professional clergy) were relied upon, and the gift of preaching by the Holy Spirit had been lost. The "world's" churches, Protestant, as well as Catholic, had degenerated from the power and purity of religious experience in early Christianity. The goal of the Reformation, returning to the genuine religion of the apostles, had not been achieved. Yet it was not by "man's arts and parts, and knowledge and wisdom" that one rightly interpreted the Bible, but rather by the immediate inspiration of the Holy Ghost. Since "the light is the same in the male and female, which cometh from Christ," Fox believed that, by the power of the Spirit, women had the same capacity as men to voice the Word of God.[8]

George Fox travelled around the Midlands and Yorkshire for several years, convincing some Baptists and other sectarians of his beliefs, and establishing contact with people who had independently reached similar conclusions. But a Quaker movement really coalesced around Fox's journey to the northwest of England in 1652, when he connected with the Seekers of Westmorland, Cumberland, Lancashire, and Yorkshire. His account of inward divine guidance, God speaking within the individual soul, powerfully appealed to these seventeenth-century separatists who prayerfully waited in silence, uncertain of the validity of any church ordinances, and oppressed by the forced maintenance of priests. Fox's vision during this northwestern visit, "of a great people in white raiment by the river side, coming to the Lord," appeared to be prophetic as the crowds that gathered to hear his words formed the first substantial Quaker following. Fox and other early Quakers preached in the open air to residents of the northwestern hills and dales who wept when they heard "that the steeple house [the church] and that ground on which it stood were no more holy than that mountain." The body was the temple of the Holy Spirit (1 Cor. 6:19) and the church was "a spiritual household" of believers, not "an old house made of lime, stones, and wood." Religious affiliation with the national church had been obligatory; all inhabitants, regardless of personal beliefs, had been tithed for the priests' salaries. The Quaker message that "Christ was come, who ended the temple and the priests and the tithes" had revelatory force to men and women already estranged from "the false teachers" of the Church of England, in search of authentic religious practice.[9]

Those "convinced" of the Quaker tenets gathered to worship as a community of equals. They rejected all outward sacraments ordinarily performed by a priest in favor of immediate divine guidance. Unlike other Protestant reformers who retained the rituals of baptism by water and Communion, the Quakers insisted that Christ had drawn people from "all outward dependence" to be baptized in the Spirit. They believed that such external forms were hollow exercises. Quakers attempted to recapture the power of early Christianity by waiting in silence, ceasing their outward, "carnal" talk so that God's voice could speak within them. Those attentive to their inward spiritual experience could be led by the Holy Spirit in a spontaneous vocal ministry. Contemporaries were shocked by the radical gender egalitarianism observable in Quaker meetings for worship: "Sometimes girls are vocal in their covenant, while leading men are silent."[10] The Quakers viewed social identities, gender attributes, and human appetites as superficial layers covering the "Seed," or "Light," of God's voice within each person. Since Quakers believed that *inspired* words came from the same source, the indwelling Spirit of God, it was irrelevant who actually preached at the meeting.

Quakers repudiated individual pretensions (deferential social gestures, scholarship, and rational speculation) in order to achieve an authentic experience of God. Their intensity of focus sometimes resulted in involuntary physical quaking and weeping. When George Fox told an English magistrate to "tremble at the Word of the Lord," the judge contemptuously called Fox a "Quaker," and the name, originally a term of disparagement, labelled the movement.[11] The Quakers called themselves "Children of Light" (Eph. 5:8, "For ye were sometimes darkness, but now are ye light in the Lord: walk as children of light"), and "Friends in the Truth" (John 15:15, "Henceforth I call you not servants; for the servant knoweth not what his lord doeth: but I have called you friends; for all things that I have heard of my Father I have made known unto you.").

Women as Preachers

Leaders of the Protestant Reformation had proclaimed a theoretical universal "priesthood," with each individual interpreting the Bible on the basis of a direct relationship to God. But in practice, most Protestants deferred to a male minister as an ordained, educated professional. The clergyman was not truly of a different "order" than the laity, but he conducted worship services and administered sacraments. In Quakerism, since an authentic ministry rested solely on the "charismatic" authority of divine inspiration rather than on the "traditional" authority acquired through academic training and ecclesiastical ordination, women's religious leadership was legitimized on the same basis as men's. Most Protestants argued that such direct revelation by the Holy Spirit had ended with the apostles. The Bible, therefore, was the final authority in matters of theological truth. But to Quakers, the Scriptures were "only a declaration of the fountain, and not the fountain itself." More importantly, God's "immediate speaking never ceased in any age."[12] Since God "from whom each private revelation came was forever *one*, there could be no final disharmony" between the inspiration given to one person and that of any other truly enlightened individual, including "the apostles who recorded their revelations in the Bible."[13] Through the guidance of the indwelling Light ("the inward Word"), all human beings could receive new revelations and deepened understandings of earlier revelations. This tenet justified the Quaker practice of a lay ministry: a literal "priesthood of all believers."

The Quaker interpretation, however, opposed powerful gender ideology embedded in Western thought. Historically, Christians had believed that women were barred from positions of ecclesiastical authority by divine judgment. Their assumption that women were to be excluded from the priesthood was based primarily on passages in Genesis, and the New Testament writings of Apostle Paul. According to early Church leaders' reading of the Creation story, woman was created from the rib of man for man's needs. Therefore, she was an afterthought, innately inferior to man. For these Christians, Eve's role in the fall from God's grace proved that a woman was intellectually weaker, unable to resist Satan's argument, and dangerous in her power to seduce man. A woman's teaching had drawn man away from God. Consequently, she had to be placed in a position that prevented her from undermining man's relationship to the Divine. She also had to be protected from her own frailty. After the Fall, the female connection to the Creator would be mediated by man.[14]

In the New Testament, Apostle Paul wrote that women should be veiled and silent in church. Church governance and doctrinal instruction were reserved to men: "But I suffer not a woman to teach, nor to usurp authority over the man, but to be in silence" (1 Tim. 2:12). Again, Paul stated, "And if they will learn any thing, let them ask their husbands at home: for it is a shame for women to speak in the church" (1 Cor. 14:35). He further asserted in 1 Cor. 11:3, "But I would have you know, that the head of every man is Christ; and the head of the woman is the man; and the head of Christ is God."

The dangerousness of Eve, as well as the subordination of females to males, became codified in the early Christian church. A celibate male ecclesiastical order was established, based on the presumed heirs of Christ's authority: the twelve male disciples chosen by Christ to preach the Gospel to the world. These apostles had consecrated replacements by the laying on of hands, creating an "apostolic succession." Eventually, most Protestants abandoned the principle of "apostolic succession" as the unbroken historical sequence through which religious authority was transmitted (the Catholic hierarchy of an infallible church). Protestant reformers also rejected clerical celibacy, but they maintained the creed that women's exclusion from the ministry was scripturally sanctioned.

Quakerism's Unity of the Genders

In contrast to the early Christian church's hierarchical ordering by gender, Quaker belief in the shared aspect of God contained within each human stressed the unity of the genders. George Fox focussed on the account of Creation in Genesis that described man and woman as both having been created in the image of God. Woman's subjection to man did not reflect the moral perfection of the Great Chain of Being. Instead, this was an unnatural relationship brought about by the fall from grace. According to a seventeenth-century Quaker epistle, Satan had sowed dissension between the sexes to create a hierarchy, in order to separate them from God, "so he would still keep them there, and make a difference, and keep a superiority one over another, that Christ the head should not rule in male and female . . . and then they are fit for his temptations." To have Christ reign, rather than Satan, humans needed to understand that men and women were in the same position, both utterly dependent on God, as in Gen. 1:27, "Here God joyns them together in his own Image, and makes no such distinctions and differences as men do; for though they be weak, he is strong."[15]

Since the sexes had existed in a state of equality before original sin, George Fox contended that after rebirth in Christ, this relationship was restored: "For man and woman were helpsmeet, in the image of God and in Righteousness and holiness, in the dominion before they fell; but, after the Fall, in the transgression, the man was to rule over his wife. But in the restoration by Christ into the image of God and His righteousness and holiness again, in that they are helpsmeet, man and woman, as they were before the Fall." Eve's curse could be overcome by women who experienced the presence of Christ within. "An evangelical and saving light and grace [existed] in all," so the possibility of spiritual rebirth was extended to everyone.[16]

Early Friends were convinced that Apostle Paul's injunctions that women remain silent in church had been taken out of context by theologians. The Quakers noted that Apostle Paul had dismissed the hierarchical order he had emphasized in other passages when he described spiritual rebirth: "There is neither Jew nor Grecian: there is neither bond nor free: there is neither male nor female: for you are all one in Christ Jesus" (Gal. 3:28). Patriarchal order remained unchanged in the natural, "fallen" world, but for those who spoke "in the Light," there was neither male nor female. When the Holy Spirit filled the early Christians at Pentecost, Apostle Peter had asserted, "But this is that which was spoken by the prophet Joel; / And it shall come to pass in the last days, saith God, I will pour out of my Spirit upon all flesh: and your sons and your daughters shall prophesy . . ." (Acts 2:16–17). According to Margaret Fell's tract, *Womens Speaking Justified* (1666), Apostle Paul must have, therefore, been referring to only the vain, confused women in the specific congregations he was addressing and not to all women, certainly not to those who "have the Power and Spirit of the Lord Jesus poured upon them."[17] In the same letter in which Paul had commanded silence, he had written that "every woman that prayeth or prophecieth bareheaded, dishonoreth her head: for it is even one very thing, as though she were shaven." The Quakers reasoned that Paul would not have been concerned about women covering their heads during prayer and prophesy unless some were allowed to speak in church.

Since the same Holy Spirit that had directed Apostle Paul could direct later writers, the Quakers felt free to metaphorically interpret the other Pauline passages in support of their position. They argued that Paul was condemning human frailty in his prohibitions. He referred to weakness (symbolized in Christian orthodoxy by Eve) that was not specific to women but shared by all humankind. Playing on the traditional inferiority of females in Western thought, in which the body equalled "woman," while the mind (or spirit) was represented by "man," Richard Farnsworth argued in *A Woman forbidden to speak in the Church* (1654) that Paul had meant "the flesh" or carnal wisdom when he wrote "women." Therefore, "the woman or weakness whether male or female, is forbidden to speak in the Church." Edward Burrough also advised both male and female preachers ("Male and Female-man," since both had access to the Spirit) to overcome the "Wo-man," or the nonspiritual talker, in themselves:

> Let [the Word] dwell richly in you, which will cast down,
> and wholly root out the whorish Wo-man within your
> selves, which is not permitted to speak in the Church . . . the
> Wo-man, the unprofitable talker, the vain babbler,
> boasts . . . O Male and Female-man, wherefore keep thine to
> within, in thy Head, and the Head of every man
> [humankind] is Christ Jesus.[18]

In another revision of Paul's stricture that women should not usurp men's authority by speaking in church but, instead, should ask their husbands at home, a Quaker author insisted that "Christ is the Husband to the Woman as well as the Man, all being comprehended to be the Church." The bride of Christ was the church: the body of believers, both male and female. After learning from their husband Christ, therefore, both men and women were permitted to preach. Those who would usurp authority over the Man (metaphorically transformed into the husband Christ) were those "who would not have Christ Reign, nor speak neither in the Male nor Female. . . ."[19]

Finally, the Quakers argued that Christ had not despised, but rather encouraged, the ministry of women, as in the Woman of Samaria story (John 4:7–39). The disciples marvelled that Christ had talked with the woman, but many Samaritans believed because of her testimony: "He told me all that ever I did." Fell's tract, *Womens Speaking Justified*, noted all the occasions in the Old and New Testaments when "God made no difference, but gave his good spirit, as it pleased Him, both to Men and Women." In addition to citing biblical prophetesses such as Deborah, Margaret Fell suggested that women had a special role in the redemption of humankind. Although Christ's disciples were male, women were the first to convey the news of Christ's resurrection: "It was Mary Magdalene, and Joanna, and Mary the mother of James, and the other women that were with them, which told these things unto the apostles" (Luke 24:10). Fell warned: "Mark this, you that despise and oppose the message of the Lord God that He sends by women; what had become of the redemption of the whole body of mankind if they had not cause to believe the message that the Lord Jesus sent by these women, of and concerning His resurrection?" Satan triumphed when half of humankind was prevented from voicing the Word of God. For Margaret Fell and other early Quakers, women's preaching signalled that the Millennium was near at hand: the end of the era of the "false Church" and evidence for all to see of the arrival of "the true Church."[20] These were the last days of human history, predicted by the biblical verse Joel 2:28–29, which, for Quakers, clearly justified women's activity.

Spread of Quakerism

Quakerism spread quickly to other parts of the British Isles after Fox's dynamic visit to the northwest of England in 1652. Many "convinced" men and women moved outward from the north to publish the "Truth" to a darkened world. "About this time did the Lord move upon the spirits of the many, whom He had raised up, and sent forth to labour in His vineyard, to travel southwards, and spread themselves in the service of the gospel to the eastern, southern and western parts of the nation . . . ," George Fox wrote of this zealous Quaker missionary movement.[21]

Early Friends conceived of their evangelizing in apostolic terms: "The command to me is, what is revealed to thee in secret, that preach thou on the house tops . . ." (Matt. 10:26–27). Like the first apostles, they were unpaid laypeople, "freely ye have received, freely give" (Matt. 10:8). Filled with religious fervor to disseminate God's message, they journeyed thousands of miles, preaching against the reliance on "hireling" (or paid) priests. Their primary goal was to turn people "to that inward light, spirit, and grace, by which all men might know their salvation, and their way to God."[22] In the millennial optimism of the mid-seventeenth century, Quakers anticipated the establishment of the Kingdom of Heaven on earth. They sought to sweep away the errors and corruptions in the "world's" religions that had distanced people from Christ.

As "soldiers" in the "Lamb's War" against "the beast and false prophet which have deceived the nations," Quakers entered steeplehouses, "the world's churches," to rebuke priests for profiting from God's Word, and to challenge their legitimacy. Men who preached without a "divine calling" "were not lawful ministers of Christ . . . but were deceivers and antichrists, and such whom the Lord never sent."[23] The "false church" had made university training a prerequisite for voicing the Word of God, and in the reforming battle waged against it, two women were the first Quaker missionaries to challenge the all-male clergy training grounds at Oxford and Cambridge. The activities of female preachers had special significance in seventeenth-century culture as a demonstration of the sufficiency of God, and not man, in qualifying people, even such "weaker vessels," for the ministry.

Working outside of any institutional framework, the itinerant Quakers preached wherever crowds collected: at public markets, fairs, and in the streets, to gather a community of believers. At times, like aggressive Old Testament prophets, they warned people of the need for repentance. Occasionally they resorted to symbolic behavior (sign performances) to rouse the culture from spiritual lethargy. Sarah Goldsmith, for example, wore sackcloth and ashes through the streets of Bristol as a sign against the pride of the city. Some early Quakers briefly even went naked (or in loincloths) to symbolize the spiritual nakedness of the unconverted.[24]

Under the conviction that they were suffering for the cause of "Truth," the missionaries endured beatings, whippings, and stonings. Using the method of passive resistance relied upon by subsequent generations of activists, early Friends submitted to brutal treatment to "witness" against unjust laws, appealing to people's consciences. Prompted by "the Spirit of the Lord," they sought confrontations to illustrate the unenlightened condition of their antagonists, exhibiting little fear of worldly authorities.

Their attack on the hypocrisy of the "world's ways" included distinctive "testimonies" for Truth. Living according to God's will required congruency of principle and practice, consistency between rhetoric in the meeting for worship and behavior outside of it. Quakers insisted on truth-telling at all times in order to "walk in the Light." In their attempt to return to genuine Christianity, they rejected the customary seventeenth-century forms of deference and politeness as inconsistent with Truth's simplicity. Usage of the pronoun "you" in the singular was the established mode of address to a social superior in seventeenth-century England. Testifying against the "fleshly" pride that exacted such vain honor when all were equal in God's eyes, Quakers addressed individuals of every social rank with the familiar forms of "thee" and "thou," reserving honor for God alone. They refused to use flattering titles such as "your excellency" and "your grace," and would not confer "worldly" honor on people by bowing or taking off their hats. Quakers numbered the days of the weeks and the months, rather than use pagan-based names: for example, Sunday was "first day," Monday "second day." They refused to take oaths, because the practice implied a double standard of truth-telling as well as violated the biblical prohibition of swearing.

Convinced that they were ushering in the Millennium, early Friends conceived of their mission in worldwide terms, transcending racial and national boundaries. George Fox had advised supporters: "Be obedient to the Truth, and spread it abroad, which must go over all the world, to professors, Jews, Christians, and heathen, to the answering the witness of God in them all. . . ." Since God had implanted the seed of grace in every human being, Friends expected that authentic preaching, prompted by the Light within, would reach this inner "witness" to Truth in others, resulting in mass conversions. The Quaker approach to evangelism was epitomized in a letter of a man "convinced" by the ministering of Elizabeth Harris in 1658: "I salute thee in the tender love of the Father, which moved thee toward us and I do own thee to have been a minister by the will of God to bear the outward testimony to the inward word of truth in me and others."[25]

A remarkably energetic spiritual campaign led Quaker missionaries to France, Italy, the Palatinate, Holland, Denmark, Surinam, and other overseas locations. An early missionary, Mary Fisher, even tried to convert the sultan in Turkey. Quakers trusted the Holy Spirit to work "on Some hearts to Edification where all the words were not understood," when interpreters were unavailable.[26] At least sixty preachers crossed the Atlantic to the American colonies between 1656 and 1662. After the first flush of missionary activity from the mid-1650s to the early 1660s, Quaker converts could be found in England, Scotland, Wales, among the Protestant settlers in Ireland, the West Indies, the American colonies (particularly in areas, like Cape Cod and Rhode Island, settled by Separatist Puritans), and on the European continent (in Germany and Holland).

The Quaker appeal to religious conscience was more successful in drawing adherents than the claims of any other seventeenth-century radical sect. Quakerism attracted about sixty thousand converts in its first decade of existence.[27] Friends' anti-institutional emphasis on returning to the authentic power of early Christianity, and their convention-defying insistence on integrity in both words and actions, within and outside of the meeting, were especially persuasive. The Quaker movement, rejecting an ecclesiastical hierarchy, augmented the spiritual authority of the laity, but, particularly, expanded women's role. Females, as fellow "servants of God," preached, travelled on religious service, and published their prophecies. Men outnumbered women as early Quaker ministers (12 of the 66 "Publishers of Truth" who were active by 1654 were female), but female missionaries often pioneered in new areas. Quakerism was introduced to New England by Mary Fisher and Anne Austin. Elizabeth Harris carried the Quaker message into the southern colonies. In an era of few female authors, Quaker women penned most of the published works by women in seventeenth-century England. Of the approximately 300 women who preached and published during the Interregnum (the period between the reigns of Charles I and Charles II), 220 were Quakers.[28]

Critics of Quakerism

But most "respectable" Christians of the period, moderate Puritans as well as Anglicans, viewed "the arrogance and presumption of the Quakers" with astonishment. It was outrageous, as well as blasphemous, that Quakers believed they could be divinely inspired to preach and prophesy. Critics were offended by Friends' assertion that "what they speak and write is really a declaration of the word and mind of God, as authentic as any part of Scripture." Popular opinion held that Quakers were woefully deluded in their belief "that the light of Christ was sufficient for salvation with little outward help from Scripture, books, teaching, or even a professional clergy. . . ."[29]

Many Quaker actions, designed to confront corruption, were deeply shocking to their seventeenth-century contemporaries. Quakers frequently evoked hostility and physically violent reactions. In 1653, Robert Withers, a Quaker preacher, "was moved to go to Coldbeck steeple house" in Cumberland, England. He entered the church and spoke "to priest Hutton, when he was in his high place, and the rude people, the priest's hearers, threw Robert down among the seats, and dragged him forth into the yard, and threw him down upon the ground, and punched and beat him until the blood gushed out at his mouth. And he lay for dead some time, but a woman took pity of him, and held up his head till his breath came to him again (as some said who stood by)." When a newly "convinced" Quaker servant began addressing his mistress with the nondeferential "thou," "she took a stick and gave me such a blow upon my bare head, that made it swell and sore for a considerable time; she was so disturbed at it, that she swore she would kill me; though she would be hanged for me; the enemy [Satan] so possessed her, that she was quite out of order; though beforetime she seldom, if ever, gave me an angry word."[30]

Quakers' insistence on an Inward Light was often interpreted as a proclamation that Friends were "above reason and Scripture, not subject to control," with a total contempt for external authority. Their doctrine of perfection while "speaking in the Light" equated, in many observers' minds, with antinomianism: a rejection of the need for moral law. A later generation of French Enlightenment thinkers would embrace the Quakers' trust in an inner guide to Truth and Friends' dismissal of authoritarian institutions. At this period, however, Quakers appeared to be advocating anarchy by relying on individual "leadings." Their sign performances prompted accusations of immorality and lunacy. Their refusal to adhere to customary forms of deference suggested an antagonism to social rank and civil government.

Such Quaker "enthusiasts" seemed to threaten the entire system of hierarchies: in the family, the church, and the state, that kept seventeenth-century society "well-ordered." One fundamental sign of disorder was women's preaching. The Puritan leaders in New England, forewarned of

Quaker activities in the British Isles, dreaded the arrival of their missionaries, and the Quaker "infection" that would not only lead listeners astray religiously, but erode the fabric of society with levelling attitudes. The Massachusetts establishment had already banished one of their own, Anne Hutchinson, for her presumed antinomianism. Hutchinson, who had criticized most of the colony's clergy, taught the covenant of God's grace in religious meetings held at her home. She was told: "You have stepped out of your place, you have rather been a husband than a wife, and a preacher than a hearer; and a magistrate than a subject. . . ."[31]

Back in England, growing alarm at the rapid increase in the number of radical sectarians (not only Quakers, but others), and their behavioral excesses, contributed to a changing political climate. Reaction to the social and religious disorder hastened the reestablishment of the monarchy in 1660. The restoration of Charles II disappointed millennial expectations by initiating intensified persecution of religious dissenters. Oliver Cromwell (who died in 1658) had afforded Quakers a precarious protection under his government, although local magistrates and priests were usually antagonistic to them.

Quaker Movement Transformed

Between 1660 and 1700, the Quaker movement transformed in significant ways, in response to external and internal pressures. The 1660s was a decisive decade in determining the future of Quakerism. During Charles II's reign, the Quaker Act of 1662 and the Conventicle Acts of 1664 and 1670 were imposed. This legislation dealt harshly with Quakers who had been seized at their prohibited meetings for worship. Friends' sufferings from 1660 to 1680 included an estimated 12,000 imprisonments and 366 prison-related deaths.[32] Controversy within Quakerism also plagued the movement, dividing an already fragile community.

A sensational episode had badly discredited the Quakers in 1656. James Nayler, a charismatic preacher among the Friends, rode into the city of Bristol astride a donkey while enthusiastic followers spread garments before him, singing, "Holy, holy, holy." Nayler was tried before a parliamentary committee, convicted, and brutally punished for his blasphemous re-creation of Christ's entrance into Jerusalem. Nayler claimed that his reenactment was only intended as a prophetic sign of the second coming of

Christ. Some of his supporters apparently viewed Nayler himself as Christ come again. Nayler's extravagant behavior offended many Quakers, underscoring the problem of distinguishing the leadings of "truth from Imaginations."[33]

Another schism was triggered by the Quaker minister John Perrot when he became convinced, in 1660, that God had commanded him to keep his hat on while praying. The Perrotians insisted that even gathering to worship should be done only at the "immediate promptings of the Spirit" and meetings should not be scheduled in advance. Such dissension in the movement damaged the credibility of the Quaker message, since the doctrinal foundation of Quakerism was the essential unity of Truth even when expressed through different human "instruments."

The vigor of the Quaker movement had been largely directed into mystical inward experience and missionary activity, because Quaker leaders had considered themselves to be prophets of a message, not "the founders of a new sect."[34] But the Nayler and Perrot episodes highlighted the need for an external means of testing the validity of an individual's "divine leading" and for an organizational structure to prevent the movement from fragmenting into a hundred different sects. Since the basis of legitimate spiritual authority for Quakers was inward (the Light of Christ within each person), the only possible reference point by which to gauge the soundness of an individual's "leading" was the unity of a group of Friends adhering to the Inward Light. A corporate spiritual authority could be created in Quakerism by intersubjective agreement to discern an individual's departure from "Truth." Quakers asserted this new form of authority in a circular letter in 1666 drafted in response to the Perrot schism. Those who stood "not in unity with the ministry and body of Friends, who are steadfast and constant to the Lord and his unchangeable Truth" did not have a true spiritual right to preach in meetings. If they did not submit to "the judgment of the Spirit of Christ in his people," they would be publicly proclaimed as not in unity with the Quakers.[35] This measure was taken to preserve people from error and uphold the reputation of "Truth."

The struggle for survival in an adverse political environment required pragmatic provision for outward, material needs as well. Before 1666, Quakers simply had responded to the exigencies of particular circumstances. Swarthmoor Hall in Lancashire, England, the residence of Margaret Fell, had served as an informal center of correspondence and support for the widely dispersed missionaries. Fell, who converted to Quakerism in

1652, was known as the "nursing mother" of the movement. Her wealth, education, and social status, as the wife (then widow) of Judge Thomas Fell, enabled her to negotiate with magistrates on behalf of suffering Quakers. In addition to being a powerful preacher and author herself, Margaret Fell administered the Kendal Fund to assist Quakers "in the service of Truth," whether they were travelling on religious service or imprisoned for their principles. Some early meetings "for the good government and well ordering of the affairs of Friends in outward things" also were established in London to supplement the meetings for worship.[36] To provide for the many London Friends suffering from imprisonment and poverty, Sarah Blackborrow, a minister, had begun meeting weekly with a group of women (known as the Box Meeting) in 1659. They inquired into the necessities of widows, orphans, and the sick, placing contributions into a box.

But increased governmental persecution in the 1660s resulted in an alarming number of confiscations and arrests. The preservation of the movement demanded an overall system of meetings that could provide social welfare for the Quaker community as well as monitor members' behavior so they continued to "walk in the Light." As dissenters, Friends opposed the Church of England's formal monopoly of religion. Consequently, marriages, burials, and other traditional social practices had to be performed within the separate Quaker community of faithful believers.

System of Meetings: Extension of Quaker Women's Authority

George Fox proposed an ingenious system of meetings for church business, suitable for a religion of the laity, which encouraged the broad-based participation of members. The meetings were organized in a pyramidal framework of increasing authority and territorial jurisdiction. At the local level, in addition to a meeting for worship, a preparative meeting met which sent representatives to a monthly business meeting. Most duties relating to the oversight of the membership were done at the monthly meeting level: the disciplining of errant members, the recording of births and deaths, the authorization of marriages, and the relief of the poor. Quarterly meetings were composed of representatives from a larger area, sometimes from all the monthly meetings in a county, and served as a court of appeal for disputes within these meetings. Yearly meetings represented a significant region or served as a national meeting; they dealt with larger policy questions of the newly organized Society of Friends. Fox labored to settle the meetings in the British Isles during the late 1660s and early 1670s. From 1671 to 1673, he visited North America to establish the Quaker organizational structure among colonial Friends. George Fox's journey, along with the efforts of William Edmundson and other travelling companions, in the West Indies, the southern colonies, Long Island, and New England, not only set up meetings for church affairs, but led to a new period of Quaker expansion, as many were "convinced" in areas such as North Carolina, where Quakerism had not previously existed. The Quaker governor of Rhode Island, Nicholas Easton (whose wife, a Quaker missionary to America, had been a servant at Margaret Fell's Swarthmoor Hall), escorted Fox on part of his religious expedition.

The Quaker establishment of separate women's meetings for business at each level, as a counterpart to the men's meetings, was an unprecedented inclusion of females in church government. Margaret Fell (who had married George Fox in 1669) encouraged this formation of women's meetings. Fell also contributed ideas for regularizing Quaker marriage procedures so that Friends' marriages could be legally recognized.[37] George Fox (advisor in settling the earlier Box Meeting) believed that "for civility and modesty's sake," members of the Society of Friends ought to watch over others of their own gender.

Women were "to look into their own selves and families, and to look to the training up of their children; for they are oft times more amongst them than the men." As part of their oversight of members, the approval of women's meetings was required before a marriage could take place. Couples who proposed to marry had to appear twice before the women's meeting and then twice before the men's meeting before permission was granted. The women's meeting examined their clearness from other commitments, parental consent, provisions made for children of prior marriages, and reported to the men's meeting. George Fox envisioned that women would take a prime role in poor relief, as "women many times know the condition of poor families, and widows, and such as are in distress, more than the men, because they are most conversant in their families, and about such things."[38]

But Quakers were by no means unified in support of these innovations. The creation of an organization seemed to contradict the fundamental principles of the Quaker movement: "to deprive us of the law of the Spirit and to bring in a tyrannical government; it would lead us from the rule within to subject us to a rule without." In the British Isles, John Wilkinson and John Story led a Quaker separatist movement in opposition to George Fox's ecclesiastical structure, which divided the Society in the 1670s. The schismatics particularly objected to the establishment of separate women's meetings, labelling such gatherings a "frivolous government of women." They feared "the world would laugh at it, as indeed well they might, having never heard before, that a meeting of women must be advised with, before marriage. . . ." These separatist Friends were not "against a woman's declaring in a religious meeting, what God had done for her soul" but strongly opposed women meeting "monthly for government."[39]

Justification for women's visionary preaching had rested on their transcendence of gender. But the gathering of women to conduct Quaker church business challenged seventeenth-century assumptions about the unsuitability of women for authoritative positions while "in the body" (in their gendered social identities). Some early Friends distinguished between a woman's capacity to speak in church as an individual and as a minister inspired by God. A 1674 tract written by George Keith, who later converted to Anglicanism, argued that when neither men nor women were "moved by the Lord," only men still had the authority to speak. George Fox responded in his 1676 epistle, "An encouragement to all faithful women's meetings": "some of them say, the women must not speak in the church, and if they must not speak, what should they meet with them for? But what spirit is this, that would exercise lordship over the faith of any?" Disputants especially believed that the men's meeting alone should grant permission to marry, since the Society's proposed marriage procedure obligated men to submit to the authority of the women's meetings. One disgruntled Friend described the procedure as "a thing never heard of . . . except the Government of the Amazons." Some Quakers also objected to collecting money for the women's treasury and felt that women's meetings should not discipline members.[40]

Quaker women's new authority was based on the extension of their parental role into the public sphere and the necessity (it was argued by Fox) of their specifically "feminine" sphere of knowledge: "women that are the wise orderers of families" should have a part in the Quaker marriage procedure. "Elder men" should be treated as fathers, "and the elder women as mothers," for "there were mothers in the Church as well as fathers." But in order for women to carry out their complementary duties in the Quaker organizational structure, Fox had advocated innovations in their role. Women's meetings were to have their own financial stock to dispose of: "no believing husband, will hinder his believing wife, being heirs of life, to administer some of their temporal things to them that are in necessity."[41] Each monthly meeting of women Friends, like the men's counterpart, appointed a treasurer who kept the accounts and a clerk who recorded the minutes. In Quaker meetings for discipline, as in meetings for worship, Friends sat in silence before proceeding, waiting to experience God's guidance. In church business decisions, the clerk recorded the resulting "sense of the meeting." Many women in Stuart England, and the colonies, had not been taught to write, since the domestic routine to which females were confined did not require this skill, but the Quakers' inclusion of women in the ministry and church business meetings encouraged female literacy.

In lieu of a highly educated, ecclesiastical order, the Society of Friends had to depend on the widespread involvement of a literate laity of both sexes. Written communications would link the far-flung Quakers into one religious community. Epistles were to be regularly sent from the men's and women's monthly meetings to report the state of affairs to quarterly and yearly meetings. To protect the reputation of the Society and ensure its survival, important decisions were to be recorded in writing: misbehavers presented a paper of acknowledgment for wrongdoing or the meeting drafted a paper of disownment. Certificates of removal were to be written for all members who changed residence. Clerks generally drafted these certificates but dozens of members were to add their signatures attesting their unity with them. In addition, female, as well as male, representatives, were obligated to travel to attend the ascending levels of their respective business meetings.

Quaker women were aware that their activity in separate women's business meetings conflicted with not only social, but legal conventions. Women's subjection to their husbands was maintained by English common law. Although a single woman or a widow could own property, enter into contracts, and receive wages, a married woman's possessions, including her own person, belonged to her husband, who performed all legal functions for her. The minister Judith Boulbie mimicked popular ridicule in her epistle of encouragement to women's meetings: "W[ha]t will These Silly Quakers Doe There Setting up men & womens Meetings Their pr[e]scribing laws & Statutes Edicts & Decrees To w[ha]t purpose is womens Meetings ye men can Doe ye business The women must be Subject to their Husbands. . . ." But Boulbie continued in her own words, citing the example of the Old Testament prophetess Deborah, "My D[ea]r Sisters let nothing Discompose yo[u]r minds or make y[o]u unfit for God's Service, but go on in ye name & pow[er] of ye L[or]d: & all come to Deborah's Sp[ir]it for Tho[ugh] She was but a woman She served ye Lord in h[e]r Day. . . ."[42]

Those in favor of female assistance in the organizational structure emphasized the traditional conception of the church as the Mystical Body of Christ (composed of the body of believers, both male and female, who were joined to Christ through faith). To disregard women's service would be to dismember the "Body of Christ" (or the church). James Lancaster wrote, in 1675, "You that stumbles at Women's Meetings and think yourselves sufficient as being men: what was and is it that makes thee sufficient? Is it not the grace of God, and hath not that appeared to all men and to all women? . . . Thus being members of the Church, Christ Jesus being the head, male and female, all one in him, therefore, dismember not the Body . . . look on them [women] to be meet helps."[43]

Quaker Survival in the World

With the establishment of the business meetings, in the 1670s, Quaker leadership shifted away from the rather isolated north of England to London. The London Yearly Meeting, a national meeting composed of male ministers and representatives of the men's quarterly meetings, developed primary legislative importance in the Society through its queries and epistles of advice to subordinate meetings. Although George Fox had stressed that authority in the organization was to be shared equally between men and women: "God said to them 'have domination,' he did not say to them, 'do thou have dominion without thy wife,' but said to them, 'have domination' . . . ," at this highest level of English Quaker church government, no women's counterpart to the London Yearly Meeting was established. In spite of the early establishment of women's yearly meetings in the American colonies (a Maryland women's yearly meeting in 1672, and one for Pennsylvania / New Jersey in 1681), English Friends would not establish a women's yearly meeting for another century. Originally, the distinction between men's and women's meetings was intended to be functional instead of a matter of status, but women's meetings developed a more limited authority (although there were variations by locality).[44]

The growing Quaker preoccupation with survival in the world, rather than transformation of it, brought people with different strengths and emphases to the forefront. Many of the first "Publishers of Truth," such as Edward Burrough, Richard Farnsworth, James Nayler, and Martha Simmonds, were now either dead or imprisoned. The decease of so many radicals who had been products of the revolutionary milieu of the mid-seventeenth century contributed to a change in the tone of Quakerism. They were replaced by people, less millenarian than earlier Friends, who focussed on the long-term preservation of the movement. The new leaders "were pragmatists who realized that organization, lobbying, and legal tactics were imperatives . . . in a hostile political and legal environment."[45]

The pressures of persecution in the British Isles, including the confiscation of property (for forced payment of priests' salaries) and imprisonments for not worshipping at the Church of England, prompted Friends to wage a struggle for governmental toleration. They established the all-male Meeting for Sufferings in 1676, which provided access to legal counsel. This meeting developed into "a sophisticated legal defense organization," collecting records of the sufferings endured by Friends throughout the country, then lobbying Parliament and the monarchy on their behalf. The Meeting for Sufferings became the dominant executive body of the Society since "it controlled the policy which determined the Quakers' action when challenged by the state after 1675."[46]

Organization of the Quaker movement tended to promote male government, but Quaker development was paradoxical in that Friends had established separate women's business meetings and continued to affirm the importance of "charismatic" experience. To achieve toleration in Restoration England, other radical sects which had permitted preaching by females as a temporary expedient during the upheaval of the Interregnum ended this practice under the reign of Charles II. But the tenet of a universally shared Inward Light led Quakers to specifically advocate female preaching on the basis of theological principle. During this period of retrenchment, many of the Quakers' first formal defenses of women's preaching were published. Rather than eliminating their prophetic ministry, Quakers sought to gain toleration by more carefully overseeing the activities of both men and women preachers. Their meeting system allowed Friends to supervise entry into the ministry, enabling them to restrict preaching to those "rightly called." Ministerial authority still rested on the "charismatic base of divine leading," but "a form of speaking by an individual originally responsible only to God" now required human corporate legitimacy.[47] Approval by the monthly meeting was needed for frequent preaching, and certificates were now necessary for travel on religious service.

A new strategy to highlight the "peaceable" and "inoffensive" spirit of Quakerism was reflected in meeting directives against extravagant behavior. In 1672, the London Yearly Meeting advised those in the ministry to "avoid all imagined, unseasonable and untimely prophesyings; which tend not only to stir up persecution, but also to the begetting airy and uncertain expectations, and to the amusing and affrighting simple people from receiving the Truth: for this practice, God's wisdom neither leads to, nor justifies."[48] The sign performances which had brought Quakers notoriety in the 1650s and early 1660s, had largely disappeared from Quakerism by the mid-1670s.

"In an effort to standardize Quaker doctrine in the face of a hostile world," London Yearly Meeting founded an editorial committee in 1672 (later transferred to the Second Day's Morning Meeting which was devoted to the oversight of Friends in the ministry).[49] No Quaker work could be printed without the approval of this meeting. Ministering (and other) Friends' writings were revised, politically sensitive statements were deleted, inaccuracies were corrected, or the works were rejected, in order to present a unified Quaker message. Some of the most learned male ministers and elders served as editors, including William Penn, George Whitehead, Stephen Crisp, and Thomas Ellwood. During this period, Quaker beliefs were systematized, most notably in Robert Barclay's *An Apology for the True Christian Divinity being an Explanation and Vindication of the Principles and Doctrines of the People Called Quakers* (1678).

At the same time Quakers worked to gain toleration in England, another plan for long-term survival was implemented: the creation of a haven in the American colonies where Friends could worship freely, labor in their occupations without harassment, and escape the corrupt atmosphere of Restoration England. William Penn (1644–1718), the son of one of England's most influential naval officers, was among the proprietors of the first Quaker "refuge" of West New Jersey (1674), contributing to the colony's liberal charter which guaranteed religious liberty. The Oxford-educated Penn had converted to Quakerism as a young man in 1667. A familiar and respected figure at the court of Charles II, Penn managed to maintain his high-level contacts, even though he was imprisoned several times for his Quaker beliefs. When Penn received the land grant of Pennsylvania from Charles II in 1681, as the payment of a debt owed his father, the Quaker gained authority to govern a large territory. Penn designed the colony's Frame of Government to establish a "just and righteous" system, incorporating such Quaker ideals as freedom of worship. Pennsylvania, well located and advertised, drew thousands of English and Welsh Quakers seeking religious freedom. The province rapidly increased in both population and prosperity, strengthening the Friends' political power. The patrician William Penn was also crucial in moderating the strident Quaker public image, and moving it toward respectability. Penn called Quakerism "Primitive Christianity Revived," asserting the truth of the Scriptures and a belief in the historical Christ, in response to accusations that Quakers were not Christian and had desacralized the Bible with their emphasis on the Inward Light.

Achievement of Political Toleration

Quaker claims of being orthodox and Protestant enabled the Society of Friends to qualify for the Toleration Act of 1689. The Toleration Act was a major triumph for Protestant dissenters from the established church in the British Isles, legalizing Quaker meetings for worship if they were properly registered with the authorities. The Church of England remained state supported, however, and the Toleration Act did not exempt Quakers from the payment of tithes for the maintenance of Anglican priests. Nor did Friends' new tolerated status remove their obligations under the Test Acts. Friends' refusal to take oaths of allegiance to the government and receive Communion according to the Church of England, consequently, barred them from political office and university attendance.

After limited toleration was granted in 1689, the Quakers tried to preserve their privileges, as well as gain more freedom regarding oaths and tithes, by monitoring their members' actions and publications. Judith Boulbie, a minister of an earlier generation, who had previously published *A testimony for truth against all hireling priests* [1665], *To all justices of the peace, or other magistrates* [1667], and *A few words to the rulers of the nation* [1673], was notified, in 1690, that the editorial committee had rejected one of her efforts as not fit for publication. The editors considered it unwise to print further attacks against magistrates in "this time of peace." Such political pragmatism prompted some Quakers to accuse the committee of "stopp[in]g the Passage of the Spirit" (although rejected writings were sometimes allowed to circulate in manuscript within the Society.)[50]

The uninhibited, ecstatic, confrontational Quaker preacher of the mid-seventeenth century was evolving into the more introspective quietist of the eighteenth century. Quaker meeting leaders encouraged conservatism, warning against activities that might jeopardize Friends' achieved status. The change in approach was reflected in a 1692 epistle issued by the London Yearly Meeting: "And show forth your affection to Christ, to His kingdom and government, by a quiet life and peaceable subjection unto the higher powers that God is pleased to set over us . . . let all study to be quiet and mind their own business, in God's holy fear, and none to be meddling or exercising themselves in things too high for them." By 1700, the Second Day's Morning Meeting was cautioning Friends against "forwardly" going into the churches of the "world's people" (a common practice of "soldiers" in the "Lamb's War" of the 1650s), without first advising the meeting, "soe none . . . may bring a Suffering upon ffriends and have a Tendency to deprive Us of the pr[e]sent liberty w[hi]ch through the Lords Goodness and the Governm[en]ts favour we enjoye."[51]

A hierarchical element, absent in the earliest days of Quakerism, was injected by the system of graduated meetings and assertion of corporate control over the prophetic ministry. The Society's increasingly rigid distinction between ministers and nonministering Friends was visibly expressed in the construction of ministers' galleries in meeting-houses (the building of which took place rapidly in England after the Toleration Act of 1689 permitted Quakers to freely gather for worship). Yet women, as "charismatic vessels," were included in the new hierarchy: designated as qualified ministers, separated from what had been an assembly of equals. Female, as well as male, preachers sat on a raised platform at the front of the meeting facing the other worshippers. At the close of the seventeenth century, Quaker women, like Elizabeth Webb of Gloucestershire, continued to be recognized as "gifted" ministers: "Her Service for the Lord hath been great where She hath Travelled, he haveing been pleased to furnish her w[i]th wisdome, holy zeale, dilligence, & Patience in his worke Soe that the word of Live [Life] declared by her hath been made Effectuall and the heartes of People reached, & I w[i]th many more have Cause to Blesse the Lord on her behalfe."[52]

The Second Day's Morning Meeting, in 1700, however, seemed to depart temporarily from even ministerial gender egalitarianism when it noted that it was "a hurt to Truth for women ffriends to take up soe much Time as some doe in our publick Meet[ing]s: when severall publick and Serviceable Men ffriends are present and are by them prevented in their Services—It's therefore advised that the women ffriends Should be tenderly Cautioned agst. taking up Soe much time in our Mixt publick Meetings." But a 1702 epistle reminded "the Brethren" to "have Charity toward the Women & not to discourage them in their respective Service." In the maturing Society of Friends, tensions remained between "speaking in the Spirit," when there was no male or female, and life in the gendered body. But the trend toward quietism, requiring passive meditation on God, increasingly benefitted Quaker women. Quietist reluctance to dilute the purity of the ministry with any hint of human will enabled preachers to reassert a "divinely inspired," rather than male-deferential, order of speaking. Catharine Payton, a minister of a later generation, would write in 1757: "Although this meeting was attended by several able ministers of the male sex, it pleased the wise Master of the solemnity to employ them but little, and to lay the weight of the service upon the females; who, though the weaker vessels by nature, are at times rendered strong through his Divine power: and our brethren rejoiced that it was apparently so. . . ."[53]

An Emerging Quaker Transatlantic Culture

Quakerism had changed dramatically since its birth in the millennial atmosphere and reforming zeal of mid-seventeenth-century England. By the late seventeenth century, with political pragmatism, effective lobbying, and the demonstration of orderly self-government, Friends had achieved toleration. The survival strategies of the Friends, while encouraging conservative tendencies, had enabled their unique tenets to endure. A new role for women in Western religion had been created by the Quakers' desire to not hinder the workings of the Inward Light. The Society of Friends had additionally expanded the authority of women's traditional familial role by including females in church government.

Through evangelism and emigration, Quakerism had spread outward, from its seeds in northwestern England, to every part of the British empire: Wales, Scotland, Ireland, the West Indies and colonial America (where Quakers not only worshipped without penalties, but held governmental offices, in Rhode Island, New Jersey, Pennsylvania, and for a time, North Carolina). Friends had transferred their belief in a religious leadership based on "charismatic" authority ("gifts of the Spirit") and their system of church business meetings to every region where they resided. From his outpost on the colonial fringe of the English Atlantic world, William Gordon, a Church of England representative in North Carolina, angrily reported that John Archdale, the Quaker governor from 1694 to 1696, had "uncovered his head to hear a foolish woman make an unaccountable clamour [pray] before meat at his own table, but when he subscribed his oath [affirmation] to be taken for putting in execution the laws of trade he did it with his hat on which is an error no Barclay has made an 'apology' for!"[54] Governor Archdale ("convinced and separated from his father's house by the preaching of George Fox") had demonstrated in the New World his faith in the "prophesying of the daughters, the woman-labourers in the gospel," by removing his hat when a female preacher prayed at mealtime, and keeping it on for temporal authority.

From Charleston to Dublin, "Children of Light" identified themselves as members of one community linked by shared beliefs, instead of geographical boundaries. Quakers' failure to evoke worldwide conversion increased their determination to be a faithful "remnant of Israel": the Lord's people gathered out of many "nations, tongues, kindreds, and peoples. . . ." The widely dispersed Quakers, a dissenting minority in many communities, maintained powerful connections with their distant coreligionists, forming one "household of faith." "We have Reseaved [received] many Episels [epistles] from our dear friends in London and of late a P[a]rcell of Books as a token of true love," the women's yearly meeting of Maryland wrote, for example, in 1678; "it is agreed upon . . . to wright [write] a Lett[e]r . . . to ye Womens Meeting in London and to send it with two hhd. [hogsheads] of tobacco."[55] The Society of Friends pioneered in transatlantic church communications, shipping epistles (formal letters), books, and ministers, to preserve this spiritual fellowship.

Since "it was the way of the world to forget God," Quakers tried to avoid the ever-changing "customs, fashions, and words of ye world," to remain attuned to the eternal, in "ye truth that changeth not." Beginning in the late seventeenth century, "testimonies" that had originated as spontaneous "witnesses" to "the leadings of Truth" were formalized into a specific code of conduct. This codification of Quaker attitudes, the discipline, provided a moral ideal, a guide for living in accordance with "Truth." Yearly meetings were supreme within their own limits, but "all paid great respect to the letters of George Fox and the official epistles of London Yearly Meeting." George Fox had written, "Be patterns, be examples . . . that your carriage and life may preach; then you will come to walk cheerfully over the world, answering that of God in every one." No matter where Friends settled, certain "testimonies to Truth," including the participation of women in the ministry, expressed their separateness as the Lord's people, distinguishing them from their neighbors. Quaker principles affected all aspects of a Friend's life: the use of food and drink, clothing, furniture, family roles, work, leisure, and politics. Plainness and moderation, the stripping away of superfluity and carnal indulgence, consistent with "Truth," were the guiding tenets of Quaker material life. Whether Friends lived in Wales, Barbados, or New Hampshire, they shared common attitudes such as the disapproval of "frivolous diversions": the theater, music, dancing, and hunting for sport ("Let our leisure be employed in serving our neighbour, and not in distressing the creatures of God for our amusement").[56]

The spiritual work of salvation was still of the greatest importance, but "the Farmer, the Tradesman, and the Merchant, do not understand by our Lord's Doctrine, that they must neglect their Calling, or grow idle in their Business. . . ." With the postponement of millennial hopes, obedience to God included diligence in a vocational "calling": "for the Honour of God and Good of Mankind." The political achievement of toleration in the British Isles in 1689 and Quaker immigration to North America gave Friends unprecedented opportunities in "outward Trades and Callings." With expanding markets and newly settled lands, Quakers were now engaged in "outward cultivation," forming businesses and establishing farms, as well as "inward cultivation" of the Spirit, their energies released with the diminishment of religious persecution. William Penn had insisted that "true Godliness dont turn Men out of the World, but enables them to live better in it, and excites their Endeavours to mend it."[57]

The close ties of British Quakers with those in the American colonies and the West Indies, particularly after the large Quaker immigration to Pennsylvania, encouraged Friends to embark on long-distance trading ventures. Seventeenth-century Quakers had been of largely humble origin, residing in the economically depressed northwestern counties of England, but, increasingly, Friends' capitalist enterprise, assisted by a sectarian network that functioned "in matters of commerce as well as conscience," and their early purchase of fertile lands in the colonies, resulted in their rise to the middle and upper social classes. Friends' religiously based tenets of industry, integrity, and frugality were noted even by William Gordon, the Anglican representative of the Society for the Propagation of the Gospel in Foreign Parts, who confirmed that his rivals in North Carolina, the Quakers, "In their way of living . . . have much the advantage of the rest, being more industrious, careful, and cleanly."[58] A recognizable Quaker transatlantic culture was emerging by the eighteenth century, a culture that would encompass the "Celebrated Mrs. Drummond" and Fellows of the Royal Society, Barbados sugar merchants and industrialists of the English Midlands, antislavery reformers and avid botanists, Rhode Island governors and Pennsylvania farmwives.

Two

"CHOSEN INSTRUMENTS": IDENTIFYING THE WOMEN MINISTERS

O N a wintry first day (a Sunday to the "world's" people) in 1738, worshippers filled the Gracechurch Street Meeting in London. Some figures sat with hands clasped, ankles crossed, heads bowed, while others looked straight ahead, arms folded across their chests. Here and there a hand half covered a face in rapt inward concentration. Calm expectancy pervaded the meeting-house.

In one-half of the room, men wearing broad-brimmed hats sat on the long, wooden benches. They wore collarless coats, waistcoats, and knee breeches with matching stockings. The suits ranged from somber grays and browns to lighter hues like peach. Small silver shoe buckles were their only ornamentation. Across the center aisle of the meeting-house, the benches were occupied solely by women. Black silk hoods over white caps framed their faces with a nunlike effect. Many wore old-fashioned green aprons over their simple gowns.[1] The lack of embroidery, lace, or other decoration on their costumes created a unifiedly plain appearance.

The natural light of the December day, unfiltered by stained-glass windows, slanted across the wooden floor. Facing the congregation, at the front of the unadorned meeting-house, other soberly dressed men and women sat on a raised platform. Lydia Lancaster, a visitor from northwestern England, was among those in the ministers' gallery. After a stay of several weeks in London, this was Lydia's farewell meeting before returning to her Lancashire residence. Her reputation as a preacher probably swelled the number of worshippers. (A rare copy of the sermon delivered by Lydia on this seventeenth day of December has survived because a listener transcribed it in shorthand.) Non-Quaker onlookers would have been distinguishable from most of the Quaker congregation by the ladies' elaborate coiffures or the swords worn by the gentlemen.

Silence engulfed the meeting-house for some time before Lydia preached. No empty liturgical form was allowed to substitute for the spontaneous expression of God's Spirit. Several others may have been "moved" to speak before Lydia stood in the gallery. Perhaps, as in one eighteenth-century description, an elderly man in the front pew broke the gathering's silence by suddenly standing and removing his hat. He spoke quietly and so haltingly that several minutes elapsed between sentences. He half-sang the words, ending each cadence of a few syllables with a kind of sob: "My friends" (pause), "put in your mind" (pause), "we" (pause), "do nothing" (pause), "good of our selves" (pause), "without God's" (pause), "help and assistance." The Friend used no text; instead, he appeared to wait for inward direction as he spoke. Eventually, he began to talk louder and faster, his words flowing more easily. Then he abruptly stopped in midsentence, as if all inspiration had ceased. He sat down and replaced his hat.[2]

When Lydia finally stood in the quiet meeting, she was a striking figure, "her gesture awful" (both "reverential" and "awe-inspiring"), "her Voice solemn, and all her demeanor in the exercise of her gift becoming the dignity of the Gospel ministry." At fifty-five, she was a highly experienced minister, having preached in meetings for over thirty years, throughout the British Isles and the American colonies. Lydia, "favoured above most with an excellent utterance," was probably a natural orator who spoke with a clear voice, projecting well. She began slowly, perhaps like another Quaker woman minister, standing up "with one hand in her pocket, which she always took out when the flow of matter came on."[3]

Lydia consulted no notes as she spoke, but quoted from the Scriptures throughout her discourse. At times, she explicated a Bible verse: "We find in a certain place, how this kingly Prophet David was excessively concerned to be establish'd a Member in the Church of God . . . for I take the House of God to be the Church of God, and the Church of God are such as are born of God." At other moments, she directly questioned the congregation, "Are you willing to open to him? May he have Room in your Hearts that he may Rule there, and put down all Authority, and all the Powers of Darkness, and bring to naught all the Kingdom of Antichrist?" Lydia strove to preach "in the power of the Holy Spirit" to reach the Light of God within her listeners. The text of her sermon reveals a deliberate "want of rhetoric or a fine way of Speaking," and an unstudied eloquence in Lydia's usage of ordinary language.[4] Some worshippers may have had their hearts "melted into tenderness" by a sense of the Lord's living presence. Lydia stood for perhaps an hour, preaching extemporaneously, her voice the primary sound in the meeting-house.

Following her sermon, Lydia knelt to deliver a prayer (which the shorthand-writer recorded verbatim). The female preacher was known to be "signally favoured in Supplication, having near access in Spirit to the throne of majesty and grace, before which she worshipped with calm rejoicing and awful reverence." The congregation stood when Lydia began to pray. The male listeners at last removed their hats in deference to the Creator, hats that were never doffed to human authorities. Her prayer no doubt concluded the powerful meeting. On this day in 1738, Lydia prayed for more inspired preachers of God's Word, a living ministry: "For the Furtherance of the Glory of thy Kingdom, and for the Gathering in of the Nations, raise up a Number of such as shall run to and fro like Sparks amongst the Storms. . . ."[5] An elder, seated among those facing the worshippers, signalled the meeting's termination by shaking hands with the person next to him.

Women Ministers Throughout the Transatlantic Quaker Community

Lydia Lancaster was considered to be "a woman of extraordinary qualifications" by her Quaker peers: a minister "of the first ranck."[6] As a "Public Friend," or Quaker preacher, Lydia embraced a role that was unusually public and influential for an eighteenth-century woman. Traditionally, a virtuous woman did not engage in public speaking, but modestly remained silent, particularly in church, where she was not to usurp men's authority. Yet in the eighteenth-century transatlantic Quaker culture, the ministerial role had become a customary one for women. The names of female, as well as male, preachers pepper the eighteenth-century Quaker meeting records. From Long Island to London, from Wales to the West Indies, wherever

SERMONS

Of several of the

PEOPLE

CALLED

Q U A K E R S.

Taken in Short-Hand,

As they were spoken in their *Meeting-Houses*,
and made publick to prevent the Clamour
and Misunderstanding of many People, about
their Manner and Method of Preaching.

By *J. A.*

And Nathanael *said unto him, Can there any good Thing com
out of* Nazareth? Philip *saith unto him, Come and see.* John
i. 46.

LONDON:

Printed for *Joseph Ady,* and Sold by *John Ady,* Comb-Maker,
over-against the *South-Sea-House* ; and at *Joseph Ady's* in
Marshal-Street, the *Bank-Side, Southwark.*

(Price 1 s. 6 s.)

Lydia Lancaster's *Farewel* Sermon *at* Gracious-street, Dec. 1 7, 1 7 3 8, *concerning the Great Love of God, in sending
Christ into the World to redeem and save
it.*

 E have the State and Warfare of
the Christian described and set forth
to be far different from that of this
World.

When the Prophet speaks after
this manner, *Every Battle of the Warrior is
with confused Noise, and Garments roul'd in Blood.*
But this, says he, *shall be with Burning, and
with Fewel of Fire*; *for unto us a Child is
born, unto us a Son is given, and the Government shall be upon his Shoulders*; *his Name shall
be called Wonderful, Counsellor, the Mighty God, the
Everlasting Father, the Prince of Peace*; *of the Increase of his Government and Kingdom there shall be
no End.* Thus this holy Prophet sets forth, in an
holy Triumph, the Kingdom and Government of
Grace ; how it shall purify and purge the Consciences of Mankind ; for we must know, that
the Fire purifieth, and taketh away the Dross ;
there the Gold, as that's try'd in the Fire, so are
acceptable Men in the Furnace of Adversity ;
                                                    they

Lydia Lancaster's farewell sermon at Gracechurch Street Meeting (also called Gracious-
Street Meeting) on December 17, 1738, was published in Joseph Ady's *Sermons of
several of the people called Quakers . . .* (London, 1738). The collection included the
sermons of Deborah Bell and Benjamina Padley, as well as those of two Quaker men.
Lydia Lancaster (1683–1761) travelled in the American colonies, from New England
to North Carolina, 1718 to 1719, where she left "many seals of her ministry." *Courtesy
William Andrews Clark Memorial Library, University of California, Los Angeles*

Quakers resided, eighteenth-century women rose to speak in meetings and were recognized as preachers by Friends.[7]

Behind the formulaic descriptions of ministers as "chosen instruments" or "gifted vessels" distinctive to Quaker worship, were a spectrum of flesh-and-blood women. Jane Fenn of the American colonies, an indentured servant singled out from obscurity because of her "gift," Catharine Payton of England, an intellectual with literary accomplishments, from a middle-class family, and Abigail Craven of Ireland, the wife of a "gentleman" landowner, reflect the diversity of women who shared a ministerial vocation in the transatlantic Quaker community. The stories of these three women, with markedly different personalities, from varied social classes, as well as geographical origins, illustrate the range of females acknowledged as eighteenth-century Quaker preachers.

JANE FENN

In 1718, a turning point occurred in Jane Fenn's life at a crowded Quaker meeting in Chester, Pennsylvania. The meeting-house was filled with worshippers drawn by the presence of John Danson, an English preacher on a religious tour of the American colonies. Jane remembered, "I sat about the middle of the house, under much exercise of spirit, insomuch that the Friend [Danson] was sensible of it, though at that distance." The twenty-four-year-old maidservant was struggling with "giving up" to her ministerial "calling," a weighty commitment, although she had occasionally spoken a few "inspired" words in past meetings. As soon as worship ended, Danson signalled a prominent Friend, David Lloyd, the chief justice of Pennsylvania and former speaker of the assembly: "Stop that young woman [Jane Fenn], who sat in such a place. I have something to say to her, from the Lord." In response, the Lloyds invited her to their residence, where Danson was to dine after the meeting.[8]

When Jane arrived at the imposing mansion in Chester, she tried to go among the servants ("not thinking myself worthy"). Many important Quakers were already visiting with the noted English preacher. But Danson took the maidservant's hand, encouraging Jane in the work for which he believed the Lord was preparing her. The visiting Englishman advised the Lloyds to assist Jane in the development of her ministerial "gift": "Take this young woman; make her your adopted child; and give her liberty to go wherever Truth leads." Wealthy and powerful, David Lloyd had been temporarily eclipsed in Pennsylvania politics by the success of his opponents in a rival faction. Although Lloyd had briefly retired from his controversial leadership of the antiproprietary party, both he and his wife were active in the Quaker religious organization. Danson promised that "the blessing of God" would attend the couple for supporting Jane's religious service. The Lloyds, heeding the English preacher's instructions, employed Jane as their housekeeper, entrusting her with all the keys, plate, and linen of their socially distinguished family.

After Jane entered the Lloyd household, she began to preach frequently in meetings, receiving Friends' formal recognition as a minister. She noted of her public role as preacher: "Many eyes were upon me." Seated at the front of the meeting-house, facing the other worshippers, Jane commented: "I was become like a city set on an hill which could not be hid." When the young woman asked herself, "Will the Almighty engage a poor unworthy creature [Jane] in so great a work?" the "divine word" to her was, "Trust in my sufficient power, that shall properly qualify thee for every service." Whenever Jane felt "concerned" to travel on religious service, the Lloyds released her from her housekeeping duties. At times, she spoke prophetically on her preaching tours, which included journeys to Maryland, Virginia, North Carolina, Long Island, New England, Barbados, and the British Isles. Jane reflected in her memoir, "I admired at the ordering of Providence, in thus providing for me. . . ."[9]

Six years earlier, Jane Fenn had arrived in Pennsylvania destitute, estranged from her family, and not a Quaker. Born in London, she had been raised by pious Anglican parents. But, at sixteen, she experienced a near-fatal illness: "The terrors of the Almighty took hold of my soul, and then was brought into my remembrance all my sins and mispent time." Jane made a covenant with God: if He should spare her a little longer, she would dedicate her remaining days to His service. Then, she recalled, "it was as though it had been spoken to me, 'if I restore thee, *go to Pennsylvania.*' "

Jane endeavored to stifle this "witness of God" in herself, with reasonings and amusements, until she became convinced that emigration was a divine requirement ("like thunder to my soul"). Her parents vehemently opposed her plan. "The girl has a mind to turn *Quaker,*" Jane's father asserted, insisting that he would never consent to the move. Although "his will was a law to me," Jane defied her earthly father, believing she was acting in obedience to divine will. She arranged to travel by ship with a Welsh family immigrating to America. She contracted with her Welsh shipmate without the usual indenture (which bound a person as a servant for a specified period), promising to pay him for her passage after she earned the sum in the colonies.[10]

When Jane landed in Pennsylvania, she found a position among her fellow Anglicans in Philadelphia. The Welshman, however, reneged on their agreement, insisting that Jane sign a four-year-indenture to his considerable financial advantage. When Jane refused, he had her imprisoned. After her situation became known, several offers of assistance came to the young Englishwoman. But not until some Plymouth residents sought a sober schoolmistress to instruct their children in reading did Jane feel divinely directed to accept a place. She bound herself by indenture to them for the term of three years to pay for her Atlantic ship passage. Since her new employers were Friends, Jane began attending Plymouth Quaker meetings "though at first, only as a spy." But the Quakers' "solid, weighty and tender frame of spirit" made a deep religious impression on Jane, as she asked herself, "Why is it not so with me?"

Concluding that Friends were truly God's people, Jane laid aside all superfluity in her apparel, and began diligently attending Quaker meetings. One day, while Jane was seated in a meeting, a "call" arose in her mind: "I have chosen thee a vessel from thy youth to serve me, and to preach the Gospel of salvation to many people; and if thou wilt be faithful, I will be with thee unto the end of time, and make thee an heir of my kingdom." Jane trembled, inwardly protesting, "Lord, I am weak and altogether incapable of such a task, I hope thou wilt spare me from such a mortification." Jane had previously criticized the practice of female preaching. In great anguish of mind, Jane rebelled, refusing "to stand up in a meeting and speak the words he bid me." She avoided attending Quaker meetings for a time, but after her acquaintances' repeated urging, Jane went to a gathering again. She had not been seated long when "the concern to stand up and speak a few words" came powerfully upon her. After praying to the Lord to "take away the fear of man," Jane "felt the aboundings of heavenly love towards God and his people," and rising to her feet, she spoke. The Plymouth Quakers were "sensibly affected" by her public testimony, "and as many said afterwards it was a time not to be forgotten."[11]

David and Grace Lloyd had first encountered Jane in Haverford, after completion of her Plymouth indenture. At that time, they had experienced "a near sympathy" with her, reflecting "this young woman is or will be a preacher." In spite of having arrived in the colony as an impoverished Anglican, Jane was perceived by the Quakers to have a spiritual "gift," and the ministry of such a "gifted vessel" was highly valued by Pennsylvania Friends. When Jane was formally recognized by the meeting as a "chosen instrument" of God, her circumstances in the Quaker community were altered greatly. Although she was "but in the station of a servant" in the Lloyd household, as a minister, Jane was "taken notice of" by eminent Friends who visited the residence, and permitted to join their company. Instead of dining with the other servants, Jane sat with her master and mistress at the table, engaging in edifying conversation. When David Lloyd died in 1731, he left a legacy to the preacher. After his death, Jane no longer lived as a hired servant, but stayed with Grace Lloyd, at her request. Jane wed Joseph Hoskins, a prosperous Quaker merchant of Chester, in 1738, remaining active in the ministry until her death in 1764.[12]

CATHARINE PAYTON

In contrast to Jane Fenn, Catharine Payton was born into a family that had been Quaker for several generations. Both her father, Henry Payton, and her aunt, Sarah Payton (later, Baker), had been well-esteemed ministers in Dudley, Worcestershire, England, and had travelled on religious service to the American colonies. "Thus descended," Catharine wrote, "it may be supposed I was in the way to receive religious instruction from infancy. . . ." When Catharine's father was disabled by a paralytic disorder from further ministerial travel, her mother hoped that at least one of their children, daughters or sons, might receive a "calling" to preach. Familial expectations were fulfilled in Catharine, the youngest child, whom her mother "as freely dedicated . . . to the Lord as Hannah did Samuel." Catharine recalled that her mother "was always ready to put me forward in his work; yet was weightily concerned that I might not run before my true guide."[13]

In spite of Catharine's parentage, there had been some doubt as to whether she would become a Quaker preacher. Catharine's older brother, Henry (her father's son by his first wife), had also been raised as a Friend but had "strayed from the path of peace and safety" after he fell in with bad company. Henry rejected his Quaker affiliation and "addicted himself to pleasure and to the gratification of his natural appetites." During a period of deep distress in Catharine's early adulthood, she, too, questioned the religious principles received from her Quaker upbringing, "nor could I attain to . . . [a convincement of Quaker tenets] by the testimony of others." Only a personal spiritual experience, "from the deep ground of divine revelation," could enable her to truly worship as a Friend.[14]

Catharine had been religiously inclined as a child. Travelling preachers frequently lodged at her parents' home in Dudley. Payton recalled, "I loved their company when very young, and their tender notice of me I commemorate with gratitude." Her religious tendencies had been further encouraged by the Quaker books she read. She explained, "I could read well when very young, and spending much time with my afflicted father, I read to him; and the experiences and sufferings of the faithful martyrs, and of our worthy friends, with the accounts of the glorious exit of such as launched out of time in full assurance of everlasting bliss, made profitable impressions upon my mind; my spirit being often tendered thereby, and my love of virtue and piety strengthened."

But Catharine's intelligence and love of reading were also, according to her, the sources of dangerous temptations. A relative (perhaps Henry) who had fallen away from religion and kept a house in town, provided Catharine with the opportunity in adolescence "of obtaining plays and romances, which I read with avidity . . . so that my state was indeed dangerous, & but for the interposition of divine Providence, I had been left to pursue courses which must have terminated deplorably." She continued, "I also read history, was fond of poetry, and had a taste of philosophy; so that I was in the way to embellish my understanding . . . and become accomplished to shine in conversation; which might have tended to feed the vain proud nature, render me pleasing to those who were in it, and make me conspicuous in the world."[15]

Catharine was educated primarily at home because of "the afflicted circumstances" of her family. Her father was an iron merchant, but his illness had led to financial hardship for the Paytons. After Catharine's mother took over her father's business affairs with some success, Catharine was sent, at age sixteen, to a London boarding school directed by Rachel Trafford, a Quaker preacher and family friend. When Catharine returned from the school after only a few months, she experienced a spiritual awakening. Her sins appeared clearly before her, and in great brokenness of heart she asked God to receive her into covenant with Himself.

Following her "convincement," Catharine decided that she was divinely required to "desist from these publications and studies, and pursue the one necessary business, viz. working out the salvation of my immortal soul. . . ." It may have been proper to study natural and cultural history in moderation, but Catharine's "attention was now powerfully attracted to higher subjects." After leaving the school, Catharine "read but little, save religious books." Her literary interests continued in the form of poetry writing and "several small tracts, all of a religious nature" composed between the ages of eighteen and twenty-two.

Despite early indications of a ministerial "calling," Catharine waited in a state of earnest prayer, "that I might not be suffered to move before the proper time." In her twenty-second year, she began preaching in her local meeting. Soon after, she gave up poetry writing. Although Catharine did not consider this sacrifice to be a divine requirement, she was concerned that "it might have engaged my attention too much, or tended to make me popular . . . for I was early afraid of my mind and services being tarnished with vanity."

After embarking on her ministerial career, Catharine forbade herself to read even religious books "except the Scriptures: all which I believe was in divine Wisdom, that I might not minister from what I had gathered from religious writings; but might receive the arguments I was enabled to advance on behalf of the Truth, by the immediate revelation of the Holy Spirit."[16]

The year following her entrance into the ministry, Catharine began travelling on religious service. She journeyed throughout England, Wales, Scotland, Ireland, Holland, and the American colonies during the course of her lifetime. Among the important accomplishments of Catharine's ministry was her conference with the Quaker members of the Pennsylvania Assembly during the colonial crisis of 1755. Her remarks encouraged Friends to withdraw from political office rather than relinquish their pacifist principles.

At least one male Quaker criticized Catharine for deviating sharply from normative female behavior—which he attributed to a habit of authority she had developed as an "instrument" of divine communication. James Jenkins believed that when Catharine had become a minister as a young woman, she "was so fondled by Friends of the foremost rank, as to be spoiled by them; for even in her juvenile days, she assumed a great deal of consequence; often asserting, and maintaining authority to which she had no rightful claim, and which was, in some instances, unusual for women to exercise." At a circular yearly meeting in 1778, Jenkins reported indignantly

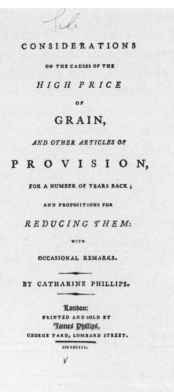

CONSIDERATIONS

ON THE CAUSES OF THE

HIGH PRICE

OF

GRAIN,

AND OTHER ARTICLES OF

PROVISION,

FOR A NUMBER OF YEARS BACK;

AND PROPOSITIONS FOR

REDUCING THEM:

WITH

OCCASIONAL REMARKS.

———

BY CATHARINE PHILLIPS.

London:
PRINTED AND SOLD BY
James Phillips,
GEORGE YARD, LOMBARD STREET.

Title page of a pamphlet by Catharine (Payton) Phillips (1726–1794). Many eighteenth-century Quaker ministers became published authors; written material was another expression of religious inspiration. Ministerial authorship for Quaker women broadened in the eighteenth century to include Phillips's reasoned treatise on economics, which one eighteenth-century Quaker observed was "spoken of, with considerable approbation." *Courtesy the Library Company of Philadelphia*

that Catharine had acted as "the Lady-president." He thought it was outrageous that when "a council of procedure was held, with respect to the distribution of ministers to the different places of meeting . . . she not only assisted at the Council-table, but sat at the head, in the chair of sovereignty." In spite of Jenkins's dislike of Catharine, he admitted, "Independent of all these things, she was an extraordinary woman who possessed no common gift in the ministerial allotment, as well as of natural abilities. . . ."[17]

Intellectual and literary, Catharine returned to writing when increasing paralysis prevented her from travelling on religious service late in life. In the introduction to a tract, Catharine wrote, "When active minds are confined in decrepid bodies, they naturally 'muse on many things.' This is my case. . . ." James Jenkins noted that Catharine's pamphlets on methods to reduce the high price of grain and the reasons Quakers could not join with the Methodists on missionary work were "spoken of, with considerable approbation."[18] Her later poems and treatises demonstrated both wide reading and experiential knowledge, derived from her ministerial travels and her family's dealings with farmers (her brothers were maltsters). A life-long preacher, Catharine continued to promulgate Quaker principles through her writings (at times indirectly). Catharine's suggestions for redressing economic woes, for instance, targeted tithes and extravagances frowned upon by Quakers. Catharine lived with her aged mother until 1772. She then married William Phillips, a Friend, who was an agent for a copper company in Cornwall. She died in 1794.

ABIGAIL CRAVEN

Abigail (Craven) Boles, a forty-five-year-old married woman, had been a Quaker preacher for seventeen years when she received the following poem in a letter:

> As the apple-tree among the wood,
> Beautiful and good for food,
> Is this dear creature, whom the Lord
> Green preserves, & fills with th' word,
> Amongst much wood, that is not good,
> Liveth this plant of great renown,
> Bows to the root, well fill'd with fruit,
> Of love and life, by some unknown.
> Little valued by the proud the wicked,
> Ever making Zion's sinners afraid,
> Sweet milk to babes she minist'red,
>   And to strong men the living bread.
> Remember me dear soul, our mutual love
> I hope is fixt, surpassing nature cannot move.

This spiritually themed acrostic verse, written in Abigail's honor in 1729, spelled her name with the letters beginning each line. The approximate initials of the author were in the final two lines of the composition. Robert Jordan, an American preacher visiting Ireland, referred to Abigail Boles, the subject of his poem, as his "dear sister . . . one of my principal friends I have now left in the world, & a true yoke-fellow in the work of the gospel." Abigail, beloved by Quaker ministers of both genders, was known as a true "nursing mother" in her ability to dispense advice and give encouragement. Robert Jordan wrote to Abigail that he had been "sometimes so low I fear my faith and patience will quite fail me, the seed [the Light within] being oppress'd with many things." His poem expressed gratitude to Abigail for her recent letter "which being full of experience and instruction yields me fresh comfort."[19]

Abigail's own spiritual struggles enabled her to be an effective "Mother in Israel" or spiritually nurturing woman (Quaker male counterparts were called "Fathers in Israel" or "nursing fathers"). Abigail was the eleventh child in a large Quaker family. Thomas Loe, the itinerant English minister who convinced William Penn of Quaker principles, preached at her parents' marriage in Cork, Ireland. Like most Irish Quakers, the Cravens were of English ancestry; Abigail's forebears probably had emigrated as part of the Protestant "plantation" of Ireland. Abigail described herself as "having had . . . more learning than some others of our sex"—suggesting that the Cravens were well situated socioeconomically.[20]

Abigail progressed from her Quaker upbringing to a personal covenant with God only after youthful temptations had led her to a spiritual crisis. Abigail recalled, "Though it was my parents' care to educate me soberly in the way I now walk . . . contrary to their knowledge, I associated my self with such company as led me into many youthful vanities, but the Lord was pleased to follow me with his judgments, & brought sorrow and affliction upon my mind in the midst of my jollity & merriment, so that I have been made to weep in secret, & when the Lord's hand was upon me I was ready to promise that if he would be pleased to pass by & forgive, I should be more careful."

While serving as a companion to a notable Irish minister, Elizabeth Jacob, on a religious visit to England in 1712, Abigail began to preach in meetings. When she first appeared in the ministry at age twenty-eight, Abigail was pained by her inability to use her educational attainments to persuade the crowd. She struggled to depend solely on "divine" inspiration: "I would have expressed myself also in finer language, & learned expressions . . . which I thought might make it more acceptable to the auditory, especially other people [those who were not Quakers], to whom I found my concern was very much;—but I found it would not do;—it was but the snares of my proud Enemy, who sought my destruction, who endeavours to hinder the work of God . . . so, finding all my own parts, &

abilities, & wisdom, was to be laid aside, & that nothing would do but the Cross, I was enabled to bear it."[21]

Abigail continued to travel on religious service after her marriage, in 1719, to a Quaker farmer and landlord of County Tipperary, Ireland, John Boles, who served as clerk of the County Tipperary Friends' meeting. The local meeting for worship met at his home on alternate first days. His spiritually "gifted" wife was a valuable addition to the Quaker community at Cashel. An observer of Abigail's visit to England in 1722 wrote: "Her Service was extraordinary . . . she was instrumental in quickning of us to a livelier Zeale in going to meetings for where she did go, at those places our Meetings were much larger yn[than] at other times, besides others not of our Society were many of them reached."[22]

A religious visit to the American colonies in 1725 enlarged Abigail's influence and her circle of correspondents. After her return to Ireland in 1727, Abigail's visit was still on people's minds. A long, hot summer in Pennsylvania during which many inhabitants died prompted one Friend to write: "Thy warning at Philad[elphi]a. Not to put ofe [off] Repentance to adieing bead [a dying bed] & how Suddanly Some wer[e] taken way is Now Rem[em]brd & talked of by many." One correspondent was Grace Lloyd of Chester, Jane Fenn's employer. Grace, an elder of the Pennsylvania meeting, had accompanied Abigail on her journey to New England during the Irish preacher's American tour. "My dear Abe," she wrote, "for thou art daily in My Minde, Noe fr[ien]d. Nor Relation in ye world I Should So glad to See Espesaly in my Sickness I wo[u]ld have given aboundance to have one hours time wth. thee . . . being brought, as I thought, very Near to ye Grave. . . ." Jane Fenn also became acquainted with Abigail, serving as her travel companion on a visit to the southern colonies, and sailing with the Irish minister on her return Atlantic crossing, to fulfill her own "concern" to visit Ireland.[23]

Although Abigail resided in Ireland, she enjoyed an extensive network of friendships because of her travels in the ministry and hosting of visiting preachers. Through her letters and encounters at meetings, Abigail influenced the development of ministers in every part of the Quaker transatlantic community. When Abigail and her companion, Elizabeth Hutchinson, visited England in 1733, Abigail helped launch a young woman on her ministerial vocation, in a situation that paralleled her own entrance into the ministry several decades before. Mary Weston recalled that the two preachers, "having a tender Sympathy with me, in my infant State of the Ministry, considering the Difficulties I had struggled through in giving up to that Weighty Work, being poorly in Health, proposed my going with them to a few Meetings in Kent & Sussex." Years later, Weston, who resided in London, wrote to Abigail, "Alas I long for such a mother in Israel in our great Citty To Unbosome my Self to on Various Subjects, but thou knows how I am situated on yt account haveing Abundance of ffr[ien]ds, tho few Intimates I think none yt could So freely oppen my heart to as thy Dear Self." Weston claimed that "no mortal has been so helpful to me in the times of distress as thy-self, both by word & writing. . . ." Abigail sent letters of support to Mary Weston when the Englishwoman made a religious tour of the American colonies in 1750.[24]

Abigail's sympathetic interest in assisting other "Public Friends" recognized no geographical boundaries. When Elizabeth Hudson, a young American preacher, travelled to Ireland on religious service in 1748 with Jane Fenn (now Hoskins, after her marriage), she noted in her journal that she had "Contracted an Intimacy wth. [Abigail] wch. proved to my advantage She being one of the few nurceing Mothers that Our Israel is favoured wth. . . . I Esteem'd her one of Our first rank female warriours." Elizabeth Hudson observed that after her encounter with Abigail, she was "divers times favour. wth. Instructing Consolatory letters from her Some of wch. are living Testimonys of her Sincere regaird for me as well as good will to the Cause I was Engaged in, And had oft to wade through deep baptisms in wch. States She truely Sympathized."[25]

Mary Peisley, who later accompanied Catharine Payton (the English preacher from Dudley, Worcestershire) on her religious visit to the American colonies in 1753, was another recipient of Abigail's advice. Peisley, a young Irish minister, had already received much popular acclaim when she wrote to Abigail, "I am oblige'd to thee, for the Caution, and for all thy good Counsil . . . whom I Look upon as A well trained Disciplined Soldier, on whome the Lord has put his Armour and Sent forth in the Spiritual warfare haveing known the wiles and Subtility of that grand Enemys Such A One is Surely fit to instruct A poor Yo[u]ng raw Unskilfull Striplin[g] as I am." Peisley hastened to assure Abigail, "It was not to please the Ears of men that I first became A fool (nor are men to be my rewardars) it was for the sake of that p[e]ace which the world Can neither give nor take Away. . . ." Abigail's own preaching career had been beset by similar temptations.[26]

After Abigail's husband died in 1731, she married Samuel Watson of Killconner, County Carlow, Ireland. Watson was an extensive landholder, "his Circomstances . . . being very Considerable in ye world." He was listed as a "gentleman" in his will. Samuel Watson was very active in Quaker business meetings for discipline as an elder and, at times, accompanied his wife on her religious visits. As she aged, Abigail continued to travel even though she became so physically weakened that on a visit to England in 1748, she had to deliver her sermons while remaining seated. Elizabeth Hudson was inspired by the way Abigail's "doctrinial appearence Manifested a S[u]periour Authority Over The weekness [weakness] of her declining nature . . . wch. She Seem[s] to prefer to natural life wch. was freely given up and devoted to the Noble Cause." In Abigail's final days, her husband carried her downstairs so that she could attend the meetings for worship which were held in their home. Friends remembered her as being "of a frank disposition, and a courageous spirit; not afraid to reprove those who deserved it, of what rank soever. Simplicity and humility were conspicuous in her character: she desired not applause; was ready to give way to others, and to prefer them to herself." She died in 1752 at the age of sixty-eight.[27]

The Acknowledgment of Eighteenth-Century Quaker Ministers

Despite their apparent differences, Jane Fenn, Catharine Payton, and Abigail Craven were strongly linked by their vocation and Friends' recognition of their ministerial "gifts." Their stories exhibit many similarities, including an inward assurance, the centrality of preaching in their lives, and authority in the Quaker community. Although particular women and men were acknowledged as preachers by eighteenth-century Friends, Quakers still believed that every individual potentially could give voice to the Word of God. "I am of the same universal mind in that respect that Moses was of: I wou'd to God that all the Lord's people were Prophets," wrote Abigail (Craven) Boles in 1723. But a stricter division was maintained in the eighteenth century between Quakers seated in the ministers' gallery and the largely silent worshippers filling the benches. "Qualified" preachers were viewed as having been selected by God to bear a public testimony to the "Truth": "called & chosen, raised up & gifted for His great work. . . ."[28]

The appearance of new preachers among the Quakers was thought to be the immediate result of divine activity: "the Lord is certainly arising in power & might in some places . . . divers[e] have been lately convinced in the east of Yorkshire, & some have come forth with publick testimony," noted a Quaker in 1737. Friends frequently cited the biblical verse John 3:8 to describe this rippling of inspiration: "The wind bloweth where it listeth [likes], and thou hearest the sound thereof, but canst not tell whence it cometh and whither it goeth. . . ." The ongoing development of a spiritual leadership for the Society was uneven and unpredictable. Some Quaker meetings could count no preachers among their members. In other places there were accounts of "remarkable visitations" sweeping through meetings when a number of people suddenly felt "called" to the ministry. During one such period, between 1732 and 1734, one hundred new ministers came forth in Philadelphia Yearly Meeting.[29]

Since true Gospel ministers were mysteriously made, by "the Spirit from on high being poured upon them," the Friends' community could only recognize, not create, an authentic ministry. Quakers believed that no human selection process or training (the "traditional authority" acquired through education and ordination) could initiate genuine spiritual leadership. They requested those not "rightfully called" to be silent in meetings, since a speaker preaching from the human, "carnal" will, rather than by guidance of the Holy Spirit, generated speech that was corrupt and misleading. An eighteenth-century Friend noted, "silence in our solemn meetings is far preferable," unless the Lord favored them with "a truly living baptizing ministry." Theoretically, aspiring ministers were not rejected on the basis of gender, age, wealth, or education. The Lord could choose any "instrument" through which to utter His voice and work His purposes. The Quakers were famous for their diversity in manner of preaching: "and it may be said, what perhaps could not be asserted of the same number of preachers of any other society in the world;—not any two were alike with respect to their mode of address, for each had their own exclusive tone."[30]

If one were speaking from the Inward Light, Quakers believed that "the words would reach to the Spirit of God in those who received them because the Spirit was the same in all people."[31] When testimony resonated with the "witness of Truth" in another, this often resulted in the "convincement" (or conversion) of the listener: "the seal of a ministry." Conversely, "the Seed" or the Light within each person was "oppressed" by a false minister's testimony, which was "lifeless, dry, dead," and "burdening." Those who spoke "in the form, but not in the power" brought "evil, darkness" and sowed "divisions." Quakers across the transatlantic community developed a common terminology to distinguish a legitimate ministry from a false one. A good minister was "weighty," "solid," "sound," and "orderly." The edifying preacher, by speaking "plainly, simply, nakedly," brought "refreshment" and created "unity."

In evaluating prospective preachers, Friends watched for those who were unduly "forward" (eager to speak), suspecting them of going forth in their own will rather than waiting until "put forth by ye Power of ye Lord." Quakers considered "travailing" in silence (inwardly struggling, testing the "promptings") before finally speaking, a mark of legitimacy. Since the purest ministry was one in which the human vocalist functioned as a "channel" of God's message, Friends noted "all affectation in Speech, Tones, Sounds & Gestures" by speakers seeking popularity for themselves. Displays of human learning also indicated that an individual was not ministering out of divine inspiration. When Friends spoke before their "guide," the Holy Spirit, they brought "forth what they may have heard from others, or in the heat of their own spirits, . . . [which was] far from Edifieing." Those that depended on the "inticeing Words of Man's Wisdom," the "floating Notions" of scholarship, were "out of the Innocency" and "never could be Serviceable in bringing People to Christ." Ministers were to rely only upon the "Immediate revelation of the Spirit of God." An approved minister, Elizabeth Hudson, described the spontaneity of Quaker ministry: "I did not know that I should preach for some time after I sat down in meeting much less what I should say which was not shown me untill I was on my feet, and that when I had delivered one sentence I knew not the next. . . ."[32]

Doctrinal error in testimony ("Unscripturall" meanings) or immorality in conduct, such as drunkenness or adultery, were strong indications that an individual was not attuned to the Inward Light. Worshippers were advised to remain seated and keep their hats on when such a "disorderly speaker" preached. Friends spoke to the offender "in the spirit of Wisdom & meekness" afterwards, but if a "false" preacher persisted in disturbing the meeting, they publicly proclaimed their lack of unity with the ministry. Meetings protected the vocalizations of a "rightfully called" minister. John Scarbrough, whose own preaching efforts had been silenced by Friends for not being "in the Light," interrupted an approved woman minister during worship. Consequently, Scarbrough was disciplined by the Quaker men's

Elizabeth Hudson (later Morris) (1722–1783), of Philadelphia, wrote this account of her first appearance in the ministry: "On wch [which] day it pleas'd the Lord to open my mouth the first time in Publick wch was in prayer . . . at the Bank meeting-House a day I trust never to be forgot by me. . . ." Although Hudson had experienced a "calling" to the ministry when she was fifteen years old, she first spoke in the meeting at age twenty-one. Most eighteenth-century Quaker preachers kept journals, or spiritual autobiographies, similar to this one. *Courtesy Quaker Collection, Haverford College Library, Haverford College* meeting in Middletown, Pennsylvania, for "disorderly Speaking" to Ann Chapman, "w[he]n. She was declaring truth in ye pow[e]r. of it."[33]

Piety alone did not qualify a Quaker to be a preacher. Many exemplary Friends never felt they received a "gift" in the ministry. Quaker ministers, as evidenced by their "inspired" preaching, were considered to be especially sensitive to "divine influences." Telepathic knowledge, premonitions, and visions were viewed as "dispensations" of the Holy Spirit by eighteenth-century Friends, additional confirmation of an authentic ministerial "calling." With the assistance of divine revelation, "gifted" preachers were thought to have the capacity to unerringly address the spiritual conditions of worshippers without prior information: "opening to me my State & Condition, declaring the very matter & things that had rested a considerable time before in my mind" as if they had known them. Such "spiritual gifts" fill the memoir (entitled "Concerning my experience of the dealings of the Lord with me from my Youth") of Margaret Ellis, an eighteenth-century Quaker minister who immigrated to Pennsylvania from Merionethshire, Wales. Margaret described praying at the bedside of a sick neighbor: "Unexpectedly I was indued, with such Power & fervency of Spirit as I never felt before & prayed for a long time . . . scarce knowing whether I was in the Body or out of it. . . ." In her trancelike state, Margaret had a vision concerning the woman's fate "& saw one arrayed in white cloathing coming to tell me that Woman would dye soon, whereupon I was just like One coming out of a Trance, & I acquainted the sick Woman's Daughter of it . . . ac[c]ordingly she did dye in a short time afterwards."

In another episode, Margaret felt compelled to preach against "Peoples deriding the Spirit & making a Mock at it . . . [since] what People made a mock at was really the Spirit of the Lord more than at his People." Prior to her arrival, unbeknownst to Margaret, strangers attending the Quaker meeting out of curiosity had made a mocking disturbance, "urging one & another of the Friends to Preach saying what don't the Spirit move you yet now that we come on purpose to hear." At the conclusion of the meeting, the visitors who had ridiculed the Quaker belief in a Spirit-led ministry approached Margaret and apologized. They confessed that what the woman minister had preached must have been revealed to her by the Holy Spirit "or else I could not have known what had been done there in the Meeting before I came in."[34]

Friends' formal recognition of a Quaker preacher came after the individual had spoken several times in the meeting for worship. The monthly meeting of church business inquired how the Friend's preaching was received by others, and decided whether the meeting was in unity with the ministry. An approved preacher typically was recommended to be a member of the select meeting of ministers and elders. Elders, appointed to watch for "any weakness . . . or miscarriage" of ministers, including the misquoting of Scriptures or the outrunning of their "gifts," also encouraged developing preachers.[35]

There were an estimated thirteen hundred to fifteen hundred women ministers active in the transatlantic Quaker community during the first three-quarters of the eighteenth century. Friends kept no formal membership records during this period, but preachers have been identified in monthly meeting minutes (which noted recommendations of ministers, approval of religious travel, and memorials to deceased preachers), lists of "Public Friends" visiting specific meetings, and certificates of removal (which often indicated a member's ministerial "gift"), as well as by descriptions in Quaker diaries. These records were often incomplete and fragmentary, and given the unpredictable nature of the Quaker ministry, there may have been more female participants, but not substantially less. One source noted the deaths of 834 female ministers between 1700 and 1799 within the compass of the London Yearly Meeting alone. (Six yearly meetings existed in the American colonies.) Male preachers initially outnumbered female preachers on the London Yearly Meeting list, but as the eighteenth century progressed, the number of women ministers equaled or exceeded the number of men in later decades.[36]

Patterns in the Women Ministers' Identities

The lives of Quaker women who travelled across the Atlantic on religious service were among the best-documented of Quaker female preachers' lives. Ministers' memoirs recounting transatlantic journeys were likely to be published or preserved. Their travels also resulted in extensive correspondence and meeting activity. A group portrait of these transatlantic travellers can serve as a window on the eighteenth-century Quaker ministerial experience. A collective biography reveals trends across regions in the identities of the women who participated in the ministerial role: enabling us to discover, for example, whether most transatlantic preachers were wealthy or poor, educated or illiterate, converts to Quakerism or from

Quaker families. Only two points inherently distinguished the transatlantic religious travellers from all other eighteenth-century Quaker women ministers: (1) they experienced a "concern" to cross the Atlantic on religious service; and (2) approval of their transatlantic visit indicated the Society of Friends' high level of trust in the ministers' qualifications.

Quakers believed that there were varying degrees of "gifts" in the ministry: "Though but small in comparison of others," each "gift" could be of service, "and had great Beauty in it." A person with a small "gift" might speak only a few words occasionally in meetings. Individuals determined the level of their "gifts," to some extent, by submitting to or resisting "the leadings of the Spirit." The preacher Samuel Bownas described a Quaker woman who had "something to say, tho' but little, as a Minister, and her Husband thought she did not give way to her Gift as she ought." Another minister, Lydia Mendenhall, "being preserved in faithfulness and humility . . . increased in her gift."[37] Some preachers, usually those with smaller "gifts," never experienced a "concern" to travel "in the service of Truth." But at least two-thirds of female preachers listed in the "Dictionary of Quaker Biography," did travel on religious service. Many eminent ministers with large "gifts" journeyed extensively in different regions, yet never felt the "concern" to make the transatlantic journey.

The religious visit across the Atlantic was considered to be the most demanding journey a Quaker preacher could undertake, generally lasting several years and requiring prolonged separation from family members. A minister who "found an Engagement on her Mind to travel abroad" presented her "concern" before not only the monthly meeting to which she belonged but also the national meeting of ministers and elders (the foremost Friends in the nation) in order to receive a certificate of unity with her undertaking. Most transatlantic religious travellers, including Lydia Lancaster, Jane Fenn, Catharine Payton, and Abigail Craven, were well-respected preachers whom the Society of Friends recognized as "the first rank," possessing large "gifts" in the ministry. However, preachers with relatively small "gifts," but overwhelming "drawings on their spirit" to make the religious visit abroad, also were approved by the Society.[38]

About sixty women, nearly half from the British Isles (twenty-four from England, four from Ireland), and the remainder (twenty-nine) from the American colonies, received approval to travel "beyond the seas in the service of Truth" between approximately 1700 and 1775.[39] Most of these women were acquainted, even across generations (as the biography of Abigail Craven illustrated), with the other female transatlantic preachers, as they hosted, accompanied, and corresponded during travels. American travellers came from Quaker meetings in Massachusetts, New Hampshire, New York, and Maryland. But they emerged predominantly from Pennsylvania and New Jersey meetings. Visitors from the British Isles came from a spectrum of meetings as well: from northern Ireland to London. A significant number travelled from northwestern England, the traditional area of Quaker strength.

RELIGIOUS BACKGROUND

The majority of women providing spiritual leadership in the eighteenth-century transatlantic ministry were, like Catharine Payton and Abigail Craven, the children of Quakers—reflecting the change in the Society's membership. By the eighteenth century, Quakerism had a fifty-year history, and, for the first time, a majority of its followers were the products of Quaker families. As a result, the experience of most of the eighteenth-century female transatlantic ministers was essentially different from that of the first generation of Quaker missionaries "who were turned out of their places and families for Truth's sake."[40] In contrast to the earliest "Publishers of Truth" whose religious commitment often meant a radical break from their upbringing, these eighteenth-century Quaker women were proponents of the principles inculcated by their families, and participants in a well-approved ministerial role.

Most of these transatlantic preachers, as second- and third-generation Quakers, were descendants of people who had suffered greatly for their beliefs. Some women were, in fact, descended from "The Valiant Sixty": the Quaker missionaries who began their service between 1652 and 1654. Lydia (Rawlinson) Lancaster, the eminent preacher visiting Gracechurch Street Meeting in London, was the daughter of Thomas Rawlinson, a leader in the dynamic Quaker movement of the 1650s. After his conversion, Thomas Rawlinson "underwent great afflictions." He was "banished from his father's house for many years."[41] Sophia (Wigington) Hume was the granddaughter of Mary Fisher, the pioneer Quaker missionary to New England. Among the many distresses Mary Fisher endured in the Puritan Massachusetts Bay Colony were imprisonment and deportation. The parents of Ann (Waln) Sibthorp had been among the first converts to Quakerism in Yorkshire, England. Barbara Bevan's father, after his "convince-ment," had hosted the first Quaker meetings in Treverigg, Wales. Such early Friends had been repeatedly fined and jailed for their Quaker wor-ship before the passage of the Toleration Act in 1689.

The parents of thirteen transatlantic female ministers were acknowl-edged Quaker preachers (their mothers in five cases). Sarah Morris jour-neyed in the ministry to the British Isles fifty-seven years after her father's similar voyage. Her father, Anthony Morris, served as the clerk of both the Philadelphia Monthly and Yearly Meetings, as well as treasurer, and as an overseer of the press. Some women had siblings in the ministry. Susanna (Heath) Morris and three of her sisters were well-esteemed ministers, although she alone made the transatlantic visit. Sarah (Goodwin) Worrell travelled in the ministry across the Atlantic a year before her sister Mary (Goodwin) James made the trip, and ten years before her brother Thomas Goodwin felt a "concern" to go abroad. Most of the women transatlantic travellers, however, were the only ones in their childhood families to have recognized ministerial "gifts."

The eighteenth-century female preachers generally were the offspring of devout Quakers who were "pillars" of their monthly meetings in rural areas rather than major figures at the yearly meeting level. At least two-thirds of the "birthright" Quakers in this group came from families active in the Quaker meeting. Many relatives who were not "gifted" in the min-istry served in appointed offices: as overseers, elders, and representatives. But not all of the Quaker women ministers' parents were in good standing with the meeting. In Ireland, Mary Peisley's father was imprisoned for debt and cautioned by his meeting. A few months later, her brother was "fraud-ulently gone off in Debt to several Persons" and boarded a privateer.[42] Dur-ing Elizabeth (Levis) Shipley's childhood, her father was threatened with disownment for refusing to remove his hat while an approved male preacher was in prayer. He was involved in a property dispute with the man. Although Elizabeth's father, Samuel Levis, finally reconciled, he no longer attended the meeting for business.

Following the Quakers' achievement of toleration in the British Isles and their colonization efforts in America, prosperity seemed to pose a larger threat to religious integrity than did persecution, as some transatlantic trav-ellers had more worldly minded Quaker parents. The parents of Mary (Pace) Weston were respectable London Quakers, but she recalled that "through the Multiplicity of Business, and a close Confinement to the

Shop, [they] neglected the Strict Education of us in various Branches of that Christian Testimony." Weston noted that her parents' absorption in commerce "made hard Work for me, when it pleas'd the God of Truth graciously to visit my Soul; and discover the Self denying Path I was to walk in if I would obtain Eternal Life. . . ."[43] Sophia Hume's ministry was an effort to return to the earlier purity of Friends' principles from which her family had declined. The granddaughter of the zealous Quaker missionary Mary Fisher had been raised as an Anglican in Charleston, South Carolina, after her mother had violated Quaker discipline by "marrying out" to a wealthy member of the Church of England. Many of the third-generation Quakers in this group would contribute to the mid-eighteenth-century reformation of the Society of Friends.

Adding to the diversity of this transatlantic group were nine women, including Jane Fenn, who previously had been affiliated with the Church of England. Even so, Friends had found their ministerial "gifts" convincing. Ann (Lewis) Roberts, for example, arrived in Pennsylvania in conflict with her father and unknown to the Quaker community. Although Ann had been raised as an Anglican, she quickly became a highly respected minister: "Such indeed was the Divine savour, which usually accompanied her discourse and conversation, one could rarely be an hour with her without sensible edification."[44] A Quaker heritage of religious intensity may have contributed to many women's dedication to their ministerial "calling," and familial Quaker activism may have increased the likelihood of the meeting's approval of their ministry. But women were still recognized as eminent preachers even when their families were in conflict with the meeting, or when they were converts from non-Quaker backgrounds. The spectrum of familial situations suggests that the eighteenth-century Quaker ministry continued to be a role which rested on the individual's demonstration of "gifts of the Spirit."

WEALTH AND SOCIAL STATUS

"On male and female Rich and Poor / on Maids and Servants too / My Holy Spirit I will Pour / and wonders to them show," stated a Quaker poem of 1756. The Quaker ministry was a largely classless grouping in which disparities of wealth and status were superseded by the unity of those "gifted" with preaching and prophecy. Despite widely differing social backgrounds, the transatlantic women ministers travelled together as companions "in gospel labour." Elizabeth Hudson, a Philadelphia heiress, journeyed with Jane (Fenn) Hoskins, a former indentured servant, as spiritual equals. An Irish maidservant, Susanna Hudson, travelled on religious service with her employer, the preacher Ruth Courtney. In spite of her functions as a servant, young Susanna Hudson was perceived by attenders at Quaker meetings for worship to be clothed with "Divine authority and dignity" when she preached.[45]

Friends believed that no one should profit financially from preaching God's Word, but did not want to limit religious service to the wealthy. Servants had been among the earliest Publishers of Truth, and eighteenth-century preachers who needed financial assistance to perform a journey were aided by the meeting in the same way that poor Quakers were charitably relieved. Quaker religious travellers were cautioned "to Avoid an Idle life but Apply themselves to some Lawfull Employment, when they Return from their Service." A number of transatlantic ministers, like Jane Fenn, had to labor to sustain themselves. Fenn asserted that "In all the journeys I went, whilst he lived," her employer, David Lloyd, had "cheerfully supplied me with the necessaries requisite." Elizabeth Whartnaby, of Philadelphia, made a livelihood from her shop on Market Street, in between her ministerial trips. Her advertisement in 1724 offered various remedies, such as "the Spirit of Scurvy-grass" to treat scurvy, and "Elizabeth Whartnaby's right and genuine Spirit of Venice Treacle, truly and only prepared by her in Philadelphia, who was the original and first promoter of it in this city."[46] Elizabeth Ashbridge, who had arrived in Pennsylvania as an indentured servant, supported herself during her widowhood as a seamstress and teacher, when not travelling on religious service.

In response to the "concern" of Margaret Paine (a single woman of Bedfordshire, England) to visit America, her monthly meeting "Considering her Circumstance did Allowe her ten pound out of this Meeting Stock."[47] Mary Ellerton, a widow in Yorkshire, England, and Mary Kirby, a widow in Norfolk, England, were among the women who frequently received charity from their meetings, yet were regularly approved for extensive ministerial travels. The husband and children of Comfort Hoag of New Hampshire were financially assisted during her absence on religious service. In contrast, Elizabeth (Hudson) Morris, the wealthy Philadelphian, was discouraged by the Quaker meeting from travelling in the ministry when she had fallen into a spiritual depression after marriage and childbirth.

The display of wealth, especially after the mid-eighteenth-century Quaker reformation, could hinder approval of a ministry. Luxurious living almost prevented Elizabeth Smith from receiving a certificate of unity with her "concern" to voyage to Great Britain. "When I signed thy certificate, expressing thee to be exemplary, I had regard to the state of thy mind as it appeared to me," the notable preacher, John Woolman, wrote to Smith, "but many times since I signed it I felt a desire to open to thee a reserve which I then, and since, have often felt, as to the exemplariness of those things among thy furniture which are against the purity of our principles." Woolman warned the Burlington, New Jersey, preacher about her opulent residence: "Friends from the country and in the city are often at thy house, and . . . the minds of some . . . are in danger of being diverted from . . . attention to the light."[48]

The socioeconomic level of Quakers was greatly affected by where they lived, whether in urban or rural areas, and whether they resided as a penalized religious minority, or in Quaker-governed colonies. Among Quaker families of the transatlantic preachers, nine could be clearly classified as wealthy. Mary (Pace) Weston's parents "carried on a considerable Branch of Business in the Linnen Drapery Way and brought up their Six Children in a very handsome manner" in London, England.[49] In Pennsylvania and New Jersey, seven other women were, like Elizabeth (Hudson) Morris, raised among the colonial Quaker elite, the daughters of rich assemblymen and members of the Provincial Council. Elizabeth Smith of Burlington came from a proprietary family (among the first settlers of West Jersey). Her father, Richard Smith, a merchant, owned and built vessels for his extensive trade with the West Indies. Elizabeth's grandfathers, father, and brothers were West Jersey assemblymen. Among her brothers were Samuel Smith, historian and treasurer of the province, John Smith, merchant, founder of Pennsylvania Hospital, and Richard junior, lawyer, delegate to the First Continental Congress. Smith was habituated to the wealth and social leadership of her Quaker family in religiously tolerant New Jersey. Her father's handsome town house had a high observatory on the roof from which the approaches of his returning ships could be seen. Nearby were the family-owned wharves and warehouses where the cargo they shipped to the West Indies and received from the islands (sugar, rum, and other tropical products) was stored. The Smiths also owned a country house, Green Hill (the former estate of a New Jersey governor).

Most "birthright" Quakers came from families of more moderate means.

Their fathers were yeomen farmers, glaziers, carpenters, and mariners. Rachel Wilson came from the town of Kendal, England, which had a well-established woollen industry, surrounded by the Westmorland sheep farms, where Quakers were predominantly tanners (as were Rachel's family members), weavers, wool combers, or small-scale farmers. Respectable and middle-class Quaker artisans in the English Lake District, like the Wilsons, were subject to tithes and barred from political office. The father of Elizabeth (Beck) Rawlinson was a skinner and glover in Lancashire, England, "a trade in which he prospered," but he also "suffered distraint on his goods repeatedly" for refusal to pay tithes.[50]

But at least four of the Quaker women ministers were from impoverished situations. After Susanna Hudson's father died, her Quaker family had lived in limited circumstances in northern Ireland. At the age of thirteen, she was placed out as a maid to a Quaker minister. An observer wrote that Hudson's mistress "made her not only wash their linens constantly, but supply with her own hands the horses with hay and oats, and rub them with straw several times a day, and would let no other Friends' servants intermeddle." Hudson was still a servant when the Quaker meeting recognized her ministerial "gift." Mary Peisley, also of Ireland, apparently experienced poverty throughout her childhood. She wrote that God "left me no inheritance on earth but his own Providence." Peisley was employed in others' households, entrusted with the care of the children. In spite of her father's indebtedness, Peisley was considered to be one of the finest Quaker preachers of her generation. Converts to Quakerism also came from a range of socioeconomic circumstances. Sophia Hume was the daughter of a wealthy Anglican landowner and colony official of South Carolina. Elizabeth Ashbridge wrote about her parent, an English ship's surgeon, "Though my father was not rich, yet, in his house I lived well. . . ."[51]

A significant number of the female transatlantic preachers were from privileged backgrounds, but, again, this was a widely varying group. The acknowledgment of poor servants indicates that the "charismatic" Quaker ministry was a viable role for those without "traditional" authority in the culture. Ministerial status in the Quaker community remained consistent even when financial circumstances altered. Susanna Hudson was a single woman employed as a maid when her first visit to America was approved by Grange Monthly Meeting in 1737. She was the widow of Joseph Hatton, who had been testified against by the meeting for his bankruptcy, when her second overseas trip received support from Waterford Six Weeks Meeting in 1760. In 1763, she married Thomas Lightfoot, a wealthy elder of Uwchlan Monthly Meeting in Pennsylvania, and continued her religious travel in the colonies.

SPIRITUAL DEVELOPMENT

The female transatlantic travellers, experiencing an "inward calling," had each initiated their own ministries by speaking in the meeting for worship. Their accounts of the experiences that led to their preaching had common themes.[52] "Birthright" Quakers shared with non-Quakers the need for a personal "convincement" of Friends' tenets. Most female preachers had been religiously oriented as children; as Catharine Payton had reported, "early in the morning of life, I knew the Lord to be a God nigh at hand." Barbara Bevan was soberly educated by her Quaker parents, "and when she was but six years of age, diligently kept to Friends' meetings." Through her Anglican mother's teachings, Elizabeth Ashbridge had "an awful [reverent] regard for religion and religious people." Elizabeth Webb was educated in the ways of the Church of England but, "in those days I looked on the ministers to be like angels, that brought glad tidings to the children of men."[53]

But in adolescence, the world's vanities and amusements obscured earlier spiritual inclinations. A crisis usually precipitated a more lasting spiritual awakening. A fall from her horse which nearly ended Mary Peisley's life caused her "solidly to consider the dismal consequence of being hurried off the stage of mortality in an unprepared state." Peisley recalled: "Had not Infinite Goodness arrested me in my headlong race " toward vain and carnal pleasures, "it would have . . . terminated in my utter ruin both of soul and body." Margaret Ellis, raised as an Anglican, at fourteen first felt "the call of the Lord . . . when seeing some of my Companions carried to the Grave, a concern came over my mind . . . whither their Souls were gone & where mine would be if I should then be taken away." Sophia Hume, in her tract arguing against smallpox inoculations, "did not confine the visitations of Providence to a sick bed, nor any peculiar disease," but noted the effectiveness of physical illness in prompting spiritual growth. Hume recalled: "My first awakening was in my youth, when I languished under a great degree of infection from the small pox, in what is stiled the natural way.—In that season of great affliction, a light shone out of obscurity, the like of

A Quaker woman preaching in an eighteenth-
century Quaker meeting in London. Among those
standing below are a few worldly (non-Quaker)
onlookers, the men wearing swords. Some people
display the effects of the minister's preaching,
apparently "reached" with the power of God's
Spirit. One description of a Quaker ministry
referred to the seizings of souls, when some fell to
the ground under a sense of the opening of their
spiritual states. From *The Ceremonies and religious
customs of the various nations of the known
world . . . , Written originally in French [by J. F.
Bernard], and illustrated, with a large number of
folio copper plates . . . designed by Bernard
Picart . . . Faithfully translated into English, by a
gentleman some time since of St. John's College in
Oxford* (London, 1733–39). *Courtesy Department of
Special Collections, University Research Library,
University of California, Los Angeles*

which I never before had beheld, and discovered in my soul the hidden things of darkness: it set my sins in a clear manner before my view, and I was summoned to judgment by the Judge both of quick and dead."[54]

Concern about what happened after death, particularly the fear of future punishment and the consequent desire to guarantee salvation, fueled the women's religious quests. Mary Weston wrote of "the dreadful Apprehension of being cast into the Lake that burns with Fire and Brimstone . . . knowing I had lived too much in Forgetfulness of God . . . gratifying my vain Mind in the Delights, Pleasures & pastimes of a deluding World." A near-death experience or sudden awareness of mortality was usually accompanied by a "dying to this world": a sense of the illusoriness and instability of life's enjoyments, and the desire for more secure, enduring values. When Sarah Morris fell ill, she "had so near a prospect of eternity" that she seemed just entering it: "O then, the emptiness and vanity of the world, and all the pleasures and friendships of it, appeared in a clear and strong light: nothing but the hope of an entrance into the kingdom of heaven seemed of any value. . . ."[55]

Converts to Quakerism had grown increasingly anxious about the validity of their religious tradition, unconvinced that its rituals ensured salvation. Often, their unease was connected to hypocrisies they had witnessed within their church. Elizabeth Webb noticed grave discrepancies between the doctrine and practice of Anglican clergy. Observing that most priests seemed to forget the perils of sinful behavior after they had finished their devotions, she worried about the afterlife: "I was much afraid of hell, and wanted an assurance of a place in the kingdom of heaven." Webb eventually concluded that ministers who were paid for their preaching were not messengers of Christ. Elizabeth Ashbridge was mistreated by her Anglican master when she was an indentured servant: he "appeared to be a religious man, praying in his family, taking the sacrament so called, but as she knew him to be a wicked man, his profession made her loath his pretended religion."[56]

The converts' criticism of their childhood religion was frequently coupled with some early exposure to Quaker principles. Elizabeth Webb, at age twelve, had been taken by her mother to a Quaker meeting, "and the doctrine of one man that preached there, proved to me (as the wise man terms it) 'like bread cast upon the waters, for it was found after many days.' . . ." Elizabeth Ashbridge had been sent by her mother to live with a Quaker relative in Ireland after her father refused to receive her (she having eloped with a man who died shortly thereafter). At this early time in her life, Ashbridge rebelled against the strictness of her Quaker relative, who disapproved of her singing and dancing. Sophia Hume had been educated as an Anglican (her father's religion), but her mother was the child of Quakers. Hume recalled, "When I was (by Marriage) remov'd from my Mother's Care and Direction, I continued in my Father's Profession of Religion, for no other Reason that I remember, but that it allow'd me most Liberty in Dress and Recreations, tho' my Father, as well as my Mother, did not fail to inculcate a just Abhorrence of the Evils the moral Law condemns."[57] In later moments of spiritual crisis, both Ashbridge and Hume returned to the security of the Quaker discipline which they had previously rejected.

After reaching a sense of their sins, in a state of despair and anxiety about their souls, the women entered into a covenant with God, promising obedience to His will. Following her near-death experience, Sarah Morris "thought I saw a great deficiency, [in my past conduct] and desired of the Lord, that if it was his will to restore me, he would enable me to live more closely attentive to his teachings, and to follow him more fully than I had hitherto done. But in order to [do] this, I saw that a work of greater mortification than I had ever experienced, was necessary." Elizabeth Webb wrote that, at nineteen, she had promised the Lord that "I would answer his requirings, if it were to the laying down my natural life."[58]

There was a dramatic change in appearance and behavior following a "conversion" experience, particularly for women from non-Quaker backgrounds. When Elizabeth Ashbridge encountered a family who had known her "before her Convincement" they were extremely surprised "to See Such a Change in her dress and deportment. . . ." Even a Quaker could change from being a less observant Friend to becoming a devout one following a personal revelation. New converts began to dress plainly and use plain language (addressing an individual with "thee" and "thou" instead of "you"). They no longer sang, danced, or played cards. Sophia Hume was convinced that she had to renounce the frivolities she had previously enjoyed: plays, balls, fine clothes and jewelry. Conversion for non-Quakers inevitably created conflict with their relatives and former acquaintances. Sophia Hume recalled, "Thus I became singular, and consequently despicable to my Children, and some of my Acquaintance and Friends; who not only profess'd a Dislike, but a Concern that I should appear in so contemptible a Manner, and so very different from what I usually had done."[59]

For women raised in the Church of England, converting to Quakerism involved the additional tension of deviating from traditional gender roles. Converts defied male ecclesiastical authority to reject their religious upbringing. The Quaker emphasis on inward religious experience encouraged the women's spiritual autonomy. Margaret Ellis's father invited three Anglican priests to their residence to dissuade her from joining the Society of Friends. Ellis justified her conversion to Quakerism with this Bible verse (I John 2:27): "But ye anointing wch. ye have received of him abideth in you, & ye need not that any Man teach you, but as ye same anointing teacheth you of all things & is Truth & is no Lye." Earlier, Margaret Ellis had been asked to pray at a sick neighbor's bedside, but found that she had forgotten to bring the Church of England's Book of Common Prayer. Suddenly Ellis felt "divinely inspired" in prayer. When the neighbors reported "they never had heard the like before," her family demanded to know from which book Ellis had extracted the prayer. She responded that she "had learnt it out of no Book at all, for indeed it was through the Inspiration of the Holy & Divine Spirit."[60]

The non-Quaker women's religious quest challenged patriarchal authority in their families as well. The Quaker theological understanding supported the women's sense of a direct connection to God, which empowered them to bypass human authority. When Elizabeth Ashbridge converted, she found inner peace, but her husband refused to let her go to meetings. Ashbridge responded, "That as a dutiful wife, I was ready to obey all his lawful commands; but when they imposed upon my conscience, I could not obey him . . . God, who was nearer than all the world to me, had made me sensible that this was the way in which I ought to go."[61] Her enraged husband threatened to cripple Ashbridge to prevent her from attending meetings. She went in spite of his threats.

THE CALL TO THE MINISTRY

The "call" to appear in public testimony was characterized as one more step in the mortification of the natural will (begun for the Quaker or the convert by adhering to plain language and clothing, and abstaining from various amusements) required by a covenant-making God. An emergent minister often trembled observably in meetings—resisting the call to speak. As Sarah Morris described the process, "Consultations with flesh and blood began; doubts, fears, and reasonings increased, so that great darkness and distress came upon me." Quakers characterized Satan as "the Reasoner," seeking to thwart "the leadings of the Spirit" with false rationalizations. The typical struggle of developing ministers was "marked by a period of self-doubt, resistance, and confusion . . . followed ultimately by a spiritual breakthrough into the ministry."[62]

Many women's memoirs cited visiting ministers' predictions, that new preachers would emerge from their meeting, as having strengthened their sense of a "calling." Susanna Lightfoot remembered, "John Hunt prophesied of me, before he knew me in the meeting I belonged to, that there was some there who would not be concerned for Purse or scrip nor two Coats [Matt. 10:9–10] but would go forth and publish the glad tidings of the Gospel, and friends remarked there was no body for it but Susy, which exceedingly humbled me." Other preachers were often crucial in encouraging those struggling with "giving up to that Weighty Work." But it was primarily an internal experience that gave the women the certainty that they had been divinely chosen. Sophia Hume claimed, "I could have been content to have sat in silence . . . but . . . the word was gone forth 'Obey my voice.' " When the women tried to ignore this "call," they found they had no peace of mind and their relationship with God was severed. Margaret Ellis at first resisted the call to preach, contrary "to what the Lord seemed to appoint for me," then, she found "darkness surrounded me . . . no comfort at all could I meet with."[63]

"Birthright" Quakers often sensed their vocation early but described waiting years before "giving up" to their ministerial "calling." Lydia Lancaster was fourteen when "she had a view of the will of Providence to engage her in the ministerial service; under which concern she continued about ten years, growing in wisdom and experience, that she might come forth in the right time, endued with proper qualifications." Elizabeth Hudson believed she had a "calling" to the ministry at age fifteen, but deferred for six years. Hudson was unwilling to accede for a long period—fearing both the demands of such a vocation and the consequences of being mistaken about her "calling." Hudson wrote: "What bore principle weight w[i]th me was my unfitness for such an awfull undertakeing And fear of my being misstaken respecting my being Call'd theirto & the Ill Consequence atending Such mistakes was Continually before my Eye with many Other discouraging Considerations, wch Induced me to put of[f] every appearance of it in my mind, and by one means or other diverted it from properly takeing hold of me. . . ."[64]

Although Quaker women, like Elizabeth Hudson, were fulfilling familial expectations when they became ministers, they were very conscious of the serious implications of asserting a "call" to the ministry. These women were torn between the hazards of resisting a true "calling" ("It is dangerous and criminal to withhold the word of the Lord") and rushing into a false ministry. Jane Fenn had been raised as an Anglican, but she articulated this fear: that she had deceived herself and others by claiming to preach by the guidance of the Holy Spirit. Fenn described her initial preaching efforts: "I had not long enjoyed Divine peace, before the old accuser [Satan] began again, telling me I had blasphemed against the Holy Ghost, in that I had deceived the people, in pretending to preach by Divine influence, which he insinuated was a positive untruth; and for me to make a show of worshipping Him whom I had thus belied, was a sin never to be forgiven."[65]

Quakers realized that the commitment to adhere to the "gift" was a lifelong responsibility. An acknowledged minister shouldered the burden of being a spiritual exemplar for the community. Mary Rogers, a "Public Friend," wrote a testimony "to Cleare ye pure truth from my owne Impurity," condemning her frailties, "O how much have I dishonored ye way of truth & caused ye weake to Stumble." A preacher was subject to the pressure of intense public scrutiny and critical evaluation of her adherence to the "Truth." Elizabeth Hudson, after becoming depressed, had to bear the "Various Conjectures" upon her silence in meetings, while she hoped for better days. Margaret Ellis, although a Quaker convert, was also reluctant to preach at first because "I thought the way was to[o] hard & narrow for me, to be exposed & under the Censures of every Body. . . ."[66]

For those women who had been educated as Anglicans, the primary difficulty was the practice of female preaching itself. Women who spoke in a public manner not only disrupted traditional social mores, but their ministering apparently contravened the Scriptures. When Elizabeth Ashbridge first heard a woman preach, she "looked upon her with pity for her ignorance, and contempt for her practice." Some females hesitated to even join the Society of Friends for fear they might experience a "calling" to preach. Benjamin Ferris, a "convinced" Quaker minister, wrote that his wife Phebe (not a transatlantic traveller, although, eventually, a Quaker preacher) was raised among the Presbyterians, who "believed it to be Heresy for a

Woman to preach to a congregation of People." He observed, "that from the first of her going to Friends Meetings She was afraid She Should be called to preach, and it was a great exercise to her 'till She had strength given to her to give up to what was required at her hands."[67]

The converts' memoirs revealed a strong connection in eighteenth-century Anglo-American minds between Pennsylvania, Quakers, and women preaching. Non-Quakers repeatedly expressed the fear that a woman's move to Pennsylvania inevitably meant that she would become a Quaker and begin to preach. Elizabeth Ashbridge converted to Quakerism after visiting relatives in Pennsylvania. When she began to attend meetings, her non-Quaker neighbors started "to revile me with the name of Quaker; adding, that they supposed I intended to be a fool, and turn preacher."[68] When Ashbridge's husband went to an Anglican priest for advice, the priest's remedy was that he move her out of Pennsylvania and settle where there were no Quakers, as if Quakerism were contagious and women were particularly susceptible.

For many of the converts to Quakerism, the "call" to the ministry occurred soon after their "convincement." In Elizabeth Ashbridge's case, a "call" came before she had even joined the Society as a member. When Ashbridge became convinced that Quakerism was the true religion, "it was required of me in a more public manner, to confess to the world what I was. I felt myself called to give up to prayer in meeting . . . I begged to be excused till I had joined, and then I would give up freely. The answer was, 'I am a covenant-keeping God, and the word I spake to thee when I found thee in distress, even that I would never forsake thee if thou wouldst be obedient to what I should make known unto thee, I will assuredly make good. If thou refusest, my spirit shall not always strive . . . but be faithful, and I will give thee a crown of life.' " After her conversion to Quakerism, Sophia Hume felt a divine "call" to return to her native South Carolina, where she had once lived as a lady of fashion, to preach to the misguided populace. She embarked on her urgent errand before she was officially recognized as a minister by her Quaker meeting in England. Hume recalled, "a concern I had often had for the inhabitants of my native country revived in my soul for their eternal happiness; whither I was to return . . . declaring what God had done for my soul . . . this discovery of the divine will gave me the greatest uneasiness I think I ever felt, the greatest cross I had ever had to bear . . . my unwillingness [was] to become a fool, to go and abase myself in my native country, where I had long lived in pride and exaltation of mind, and forgetfulness of God my Creator and preserver."[69]

The public nature of the testimony, to be "a fool for Christ," was part of the cathartic, transformative religious experience for the women, particularly for converts who were breaking out of traditional social constraints. Elizabeth Webb gave a mystical account of the alteration in her experience: "I was constrained, under a sense of duty, to kneel down in the congregation, and confess to the goodness of God . . . and I remember after I had made publick confession to the goodness of God, my soul was as if it had been in another world, it was enlightned and enlivened by the divine love, that I was in love with the whole creation of God, and I saw everything to be good in its place . . . so everything began to preach to me, the very fragrant herbs, and beautiful innocent flowers, had a speaking voice in them to my soul. . . ." After her public statement of inward spiritual change, Webb recalled that "things seemed to have another relish with them than before: The judgements of God were sweet to my soul and I was made to call to others sometimes, to come and taste and see, how good the Lord is."[70]

The direct impulse to preach was characterized as an "exercise" within. Elizabeth Hudson felt compelled to stand in a meeting "from the weight of the pressure of (y)e Word." Ministers needed "to clear" themselves: divine messages were as "something [that] lay as a burthen to be delivered. . . ." The "inspired" message was often described in physical terms, as a heaviness or "a fire," uncomfortable if only partially released. After venting in a meeting the "concern" she had been given, Elizabeth Wilkinson apprehended she was not quite clear: "but thro' fear & asking Counsel where I should not, omitted two remarks which afterwards made me feel heavy & it so increased that I could not be easy without mentioning it." At another meeting, when Wilkinson believed she was required to pray, she "had such a hard struggle to give up thereto that I thought the meeting would have concluded in Silence; but the Concern became so heavy that I may truly say it was as a fire & I no longer durst refuse but gave up thereto . . . I thought I witnessed more peace afterwards than I had for several days."[71]

A minister's first preaching attempts were usually painful and halting as she attempted to wait for divine inspiration rather than rely on human learning. "When the Lord brought me forth in the ministry," as Abigail Craven had recalled, "after many years great exercise . . . [it] was in a very simple, stammering manner, as I apprehended, though attended with some zeal and power:—but I did not like it, but fretted, and brought trouble upon myself, & thought if it were delivered like such a one, or such a one, I should be easy; but to make a fool of myself appeared very hard to me. . . ." As the person in the "infant" state of the ministry adhered to the dictates of the Inward Light, the "gift" might increase. Rachel Wilson, for example, preached for nearly two hours at a meeting in 1771.[72]

Theoretically, a person could receive a "gift" in the ministry at any age. Most of the eighteenth-century female transatlantic travellers (both "birthright" Quakers and converts) first preached in the meeting for worship as young adults. Six "birthright" Quakers came forward between the ages of sixteen and nineteen. But most began to preach in their twenties. Some of the women who came forth in the ministry later in life (for instance, in their forties) had only recently converted to Quakerism. Since most of the women were ministers prior to marriage, the meeting's recognition of their capacities was not connected to the status of their husbands. After identifying their "calling," the ministerial "gift" became central to these women's self-definition and a crucial organizing principle of their lives. Mary Peisley wrote, "For I am resolved by the blessed assistance of Israel's God, not to bury that talent which he has given me (in the earth) nor to quit the occupying it for any outward employment . . . For I am sure, to drudge for the sustenance of the body, as do the beasts, and to live for no nobler ends, then to eat, drink and sleep, such a life is not worth living for."[73]

Most converts in this group of transatlantic travellers emigrated from the British Isles to Pennsylvania, where they could situate themselves among people with similar beliefs. Colonial Pennsylvania was a land of opportunity for an enterprising young man (most famously, in Benjamin Franklin's "rags-to-riches" *Autobiography*), but the colony was also a refuge for young, devout women who had converted to Quakerism against their families' wishes. These converts could receive community support for their defiance of non-Quaker patriarchal authority, and rise in the world on the basis of their own "divinely inspired" talents. After the death of Margaret Ellis's sympathetic mother, her father had proposed to the young Quaker preacher in Wales "to let me go twice a year only to the Quakers' Meeting and the rest of the time either to go to church or stay at home." Upon consideration of her father's arrangement, Ellis asked permission to go to

Pennsylvania, where, she noted: "I understood there were many Friends & that I could work for my livelyhood." Ellis's father responded bitterly "[that] if I chused to live like a Fool & be buried like a Dog [without the Anglican rituals] I might go where I would, this also was very hard for Flesh & Blood to bear from so near & dear a Relation & to part from ones native Land, but I presently heard a Voice within me of ye. true Bishop & Shepherd of Souls saying, That if thou goest I will go along with thee. . . ." So Ellis, emboldened by her sense of God's immediate speaking to her soul, immigrated to Pennsylvania.[74]

The Quaker-founded colony was uniquely appreciative of the spiritual capacities of females. Not only did the Friends' community value the "divine leadings" of women, but in early eighteenth-century Pennsylvania, those who respected the "prophesying of the daughters" dominated the civil government and wielded economic power. When Jane Fenn, as a domestic servant, had displayed her ministerial "gift" in the Quaker meeting, she recalled that this "gave me favour both with Friends and others, so that I might have had the best places either in Philadelphia or in the country." By her own account, Margaret Ellis, educated in the Welsh language, "could speak the English Language but brokenly" when she arrived in Pennsylvania as an unmarried woman. But as a gifted minister, Ellis was quickly noticed and befriended by leading Philadelphia Quakers, including Samuel Preston, a member of the Governor's Council and treasurer of the colony, and Hannah Hill, the widow of a former Speaker of the Provincial Assembly. Ellis wrote of these "Fathers & Mothers in Israel who were a great Comfort & Strength to me in a strange Land."[75]

Ann Roberts, another Welsh woman, was harshly rejected by her father for converting to Quakerism, having incurred his "heavy displeasure." But in her adopted land, Roberts's spiritual counsel was received by the Speaker of the Pennsylvania Assembly, John Kinsey, who also served as clerk of the Philadelphia Yearly Meeting. She encouraged him, in 1739, to "a coming up in faithfulness to what is made manifest & then there will be ye answer of peace in ye end. . . ."[76] Eighteenth-century women who conflicted with their Anglican families about their spiritual experiences (visions, internal voices of guidance), and "birthright" Quakers who described similar occurrences, were embraced by the Quaker community. Friends viewed such phenomena as the "divinely inspired gifts" of a ministry selected by God.

LITERACY

Jane Fenn, Catharine Payton, Abigail Craven, and other transatlantic travellers are significantly linked in that their biographies can be reconstructed largely from their own written records. The availability of sources such as the journals of Jane Fenn and Catharine Payton (printed by Philadelphia Yearly Meeting and London Yearly Meeting, respectively), as well as the publications and manuscripts of other female preachers, reveals both the careful preservation of Quaker women's writings and the literacy of those who crossed the Atlantic to preach.

Although the ability to write was not a stated requirement for Quaker ministers, the writings of nearly all of the female transatlantic travellers have survived in the form of signatures on wills, letters, journals, and religious tracts. Evidence regarding two of the ministers revealed some lack of education. A monthly meeting testimony noted that Alice Alderson, a convert to Quakerism, "had not much human Learning, yet in the course of her Ministry, she was frequently furnished with very copious expressions well adapted to the matter she had to deliver . . . being clearly led into the state of Meetings & enabled to speak feelingly to the Conditions of individuals." Mary Ellerton, a regular author of meeting epistles, had acquired the skill of writing but averred in a letter, "I have done my best at writing, I wish it can be pick'd out, for I was never learned to write."[77] But in a period when many women were obligated to affix marks on legal documents in lieu of signatures, the eighteenth-century transatlantic women ministers appear, in general, to have been better educated than their female contemporaries. Even eighteenth-century Quaker women preachers who did not travel across the Atlantic tended to be literate. Ministers such as Rachel Trafford (Catharine Payton's headmistress) and Mary Dudley (Payton's occasional travel companion) were schoolteachers. Others such as May Drummond, Benjamina Padley, and Abiah Darby published epistles, exhortations, and children's catechisms.

While the ministers' literacy reflects, in some cases, an affluent upbringing, the writings of female preachers from known moderate to poor backgrounds also have survived. Their literacy may have been a consequence of their Quaker affiliation. Friends took the initiative in providing schooling for their children, hiring schoolmasters and schoolmistresses to guard them from the "world's ways." Quaker schools were often attached to meeting-houses. Texts acquired increased importance as devotional aids in Quakerism, a religion devoid of ritual and a resident ministry. A rival Anglican missionary (of the Society for the Propagation of the Gospel in Foreign Parts) complained that "there were Variety of Books sent and placed in almost every Quaker Family, especially Barclay's Apology, to fortify the People in their Errors . . . whereas in the Houses of the Church People, few or no Books were to be seen." Many preachers born into Quaker families had, like Elizabeth Hudson, devoted much time when very young "to the reading of the Scriptures & ffr[ien]ds Books. . . ." Hudson recalled, "The reading whereof, often melted me into Tears of Joy Especially when I meet w[i]th passages that Su[i]ted my then Seeking State."[78]

All Quaker ministers were expected to be able to read the Bible. In 1702, London Yearly Meeting cautioned those who preached in meetings about misquoting the Bible, "for prevention whereof, its desired all those concerned be conversant in Reading the Scriptures."[79] The Society of Friends, in lieu of a highly educated ecclesiastical order, depended on the widespread participation of a literate laity. Quaker meetings documented all important decisions in writing. Lydia Lancaster, Elizabeth Ashbridge, and Sarah Morris were among the transatlantic ministers whose writing skills were also utilized in their duties as clerks for the women's business meetings. The Society of Friends' unique roles for women—their inclusion in the ministry and church business meetings—may have led to a higher rate of literacy for Quaker women than for women in the society at large.

The Quaker ministerial role may have drawn women with well-developed reading and writing skills as well. The importance of reading is apparent in many converts' accounts of their spiritual development. At sixteen, Elizabeth Webb came across a little Quaker book "which as the doctrine it contained agreed with the doctrine of the apostles, I was confirmed in my judgment, that their profession agreed with the truth." Elizabeth Ashbridge was convinced of Quaker principles when she "perceived a book lying upon the table, and being fond of reading, took it up; my aunt observed me, and said, 'Cousin, that is a Quaker's book.' She saw that I was not a Quaker, and supposed I would not like it. . . . But before I had read two pages, my heart burned within me . . . O, happy people, thus beloved of God!"[80]

Many of the transatlantic female preachers were remembered as having "excellent natural understandings," or superior intelligence, as well as ministerial "gifts." Hannah (Dent) Cooper, for example, was described as "a Woman of strong talents, which, being in subjection to the cross of Christ, fitted her for eminent usefulness in the world." Some women clearly had intellectual leanings which they felt obligated to struggle against for fear of being distracted from their more important religious "calling." Elizabeth Hudson (later Morris), the granddaughter and heiress of William Hudson, a former Philadelphia mayor and wealthy landowner, was raised among the city's Quaker elite. As a result of her youthful friendship with the granddaughter of Isaac Norris I, one of the wealthiest merchants of Philadelphia, Hudson had spent most of her time at the Norris's "Country Seat," Fairhill, later admired by John Adams in 1774 for its "fine Gardens, and a very grand Library." In Fairhill's outstanding library, where Norris had amassed a vast collection of books, including more than one hundred scientific titles from Galileo to Newton, Elizabeth Hudson had to wrestle with distractions from a religious "calling" (to live "for a far more noble end, to wit, to serve the Lord"). The luxurious selection of books was so "Ingrossing both of Our time & thoughts" that Hudson found she had to deny herself of them in order to receive the inward, spiritual "Visits of My Wonderfull Counsellor."[81]

Literacy could be an important avenue into both Quakerism and preaching. For Quakers, however, reading could just as easily lead one away from "Truth." Scholarly attainments and a cultivated style of language were dangerous temptations for ministering Friends, encouraging pride in one's own abilities, rather than reliance on the Holy Spirit.

But most of the women ministers were prolific writers as well as extemporaneous speakers in meetings. Epistles to Quaker meetings, published exhortations, and biblical commentary (such as Elizabeth Webb's interpretation of the Book of Revelation) were extensions of oral sermons. During her religious visit to the American colonies, Sophia Hume (a resident of London) had the assistance of the Philadelphia Yearly Meeting in publishing her book *An Exhortation to the Inhabitants of the Province of South-Carolina* (1748). After the printing, Israel Pemberton Sr. sent the book to London Quakers: "It is looked upon to be a well wrote book & in a Christian Spirit and so far as I Can find its Exceeding well Liked by Most or all that have had the oppertunity of Peruseing of it." Poetry, oftentimes, was viewed as another expression of religious inspiration. Ann Moore observed: "This verse pass often through my mind that I thought it was

> " *The* MEMORY *of the* JUST *is* BLESSED."
> On the morning of the 24th ult. departed this life,
> in the feventy-fecond year of her age, in certain hope of
> a joyful refurrection, SARAH MORRIS, an eminent
> Minifter among the people called Quakers.
> Her life and converfation were uniformly confiftent
> with her chriftian profeffion, adorning the doctrine fhe
> preached: Chearful without gaiety, ferious without aufte-
> rity, and pious without affectation, fhe was an ornament
> to fociety, and the delight of her friends and acquaintance,
> whofe affliction for their lofs could only be alleviated by
> an affurance, that it is her great gain. A long and pain-
> ful illnefs fhe bore with a fortitude and refignation becom-
> ing a chriftian, whofe expectations of enduring happinefs
> were fixed on that foundation, which ftandeth fure.

Obituary of the Philadelphia preacher Sarah Morris (1703–75), which
appeared in the *Pennsylvania Gazette,* November 1, 1775. As "Public
Friends," Quaker women were memorialized in monthly meeting
testimonies and newspaper obituaries. The Philadelphia Monthly
Meeting testimony regarding Sarah Morris noted: "She was endued
with mental qualifications and understanding superior to many. . . ."
Courtesy the Historical Society of Pennsylvania

not prefented for me only so I sat down and wrote it that others might read
and consider the weight thereof."[82] Nearly all of the preachers kept journals to note providential occurrences and provide spiritual guidance for
others.

Despite Quaker distrust of scholarship as an aid to ministry, Catharine
Payton (later Phillips) and Sophia Hume were able to utilize their extensive reading in theology, natural history, and other subjects to promote
Friends' principles in a range of publications, such as Hume's *Remarks on
the Practice of Inoculation for the Small Pox* and Phillips's *Considerations
on the Causes of the High Price of Grain.* Ministerial authorship had
broadened for eighteenth-century Quaker women to include not only the
"passive" expression of received religious revelation, but more reasoned
discussions of a variety of topics. Ironically, the Quaker ministry, which
sought a total reliance on God, with no credit due to the human "instrument," allowed these eighteenth-century women "of strong talents"
greater scope in literary expression than most of their non-Quaker female
contemporaries.

Entrance into the Public Sphere: Separate Identities

In every part of the eighteenth-century Quaker transatlantic community, women were consistently acknowledged to be among the "rightfully called" to preach. A spectrum of women were recognized as ministers by Quaker meetings. Female preachers who crossed the Atlantic on religious visits during the eighteenth century ranged from a seventeen-year-old maidservant of northern Ireland to a sixty-nine-year-old Philadelphia heiress, from a woman with "not much human Learning" to the author of treatises on economics and agriculture, and from an Anglican convert to a fourth-generation Friend. As "charismatic leaders," Quaker ministers were able to transcend such external differences by their display of special, inward "gifts": "inspired" preaching, prophetic visions, and telepathic sensitivity to others' spiritual states. Access to the Quaker ministry was largely "democratic" in that people's talents (evidence of an authentic "calling") were more determinative in their recognition as preachers than wealth (servants could become well-known "Public Friends"), family background (converts to Quakerism participated), or educational level (the unlearned could still minister effectively through "divine revelation").

Quaker women ministers differed markedly in personality, and were from varied social classes and geographical regions, but they were remarkably similar in their inward assurance, their preaching (and its outgrowth into authorship), and their authority in the Quaker community. Quaker theology gave women a conceptual framework for their spiritual experiences. Women's belief that they were assisted by a power greater than themselves often emboldened them to alter their life circumstances. Their reliance on inward promptings of the Spirit habituated them to a "functional autonomy" (viewed as a submission to God's will). Friends' recognition of female ministerial "gifts" gave these women prominence in the Quaker culture.[83]

Other eighteenth-century females, whose influence was largely confined to their households, were often unnamed in the records, subsumed in the memorializations of men. In writings, such as monthly meeting testimonies, the Quaker women ministers were remembered for their own qualities and achievements (through "divine grace"). No comparable body of literature exists for such an extensive number of non-Quaker women of this era.[84] In their public role as preachers, Quaker women achieved social identities distinct from their families. When Joseph Hatton was testified against by the Quaker meeting for his "weak Simple management" in the wake of his bankruptcy, his wife, Susanna, continued to be a well-respected minister: "Not one in those large meetings rose up with that Divine authority and dignity that she did."[85] The Quaker ministerial role was a unique one for eighteenth-century women, traditionally seen as adjuncts to their husbands or fathers, because they were recognized as religious leaders ("chosen instruments") by the Society of Friends on the basis of their own "gifts of the Spirit."

Three

"LOVE YT [THAT] MANY WATERS CANNOT QUENCH": WOMEN MINISTERS TRAVELLING

W H E N a storm descended on the ship *Syzargh* during its Atlantic crossing in December 1728, the waves became frighteningly large, driving the vessel onto the rocks off the southern coast of Ireland. As those who remained alive clung to the upper side of the ship, washed by "the devouring waves" (twelve people had perished from the cold or by drowning), the "divine leadings" of the Quaker female preacher on board seemed to promise security in the midst of the mercilessness of nature. One survivor remembered: "This extraordinary woman had a sense given her, that they would not be safe on that side of the vessel much longer. . . ." Despite the hazardousness of changing positions, Susanna Morris, an American minister bound for Bristol, England, "in the service of Truth," convinced the other voyagers to attempt this, "believing it would be the means of their preservation." Soon after the travellers fastened to the lower side of the ship, according to a witness's account, a great swell of the ocean threw the vessel flat on the opposite side so that if they had not moved, all would have died.[1]

But the dangers of the voyage from Philadelphia were not yet over. The forty-six-year-old Morris and the other shipwrecked travellers were forced to hold on to the partly submerged vessel "in that wet condition about nine hours, in a cold time of frost and snow" before being rescued. The distressed survivors saw, awaiting them on shore, the grim specter of "those savage people, the native Irish" who had come "to the seaside in great numbers" in order to plunder valuable cargo from the ship. As one voyager recalled, they were "intending no doubt to make a wreck of the vessel, which, it is said they do not, according to their barbarous custom, until all those in the ship are destroyed." The passengers were preserved by a Roman Catholic priest who, upon being informed there were some alive in the wreck, "charged those people upon the penalty of eternal damnation, not to hurt them in the least, but use all means in their power to save their lives."[2]

Although the catastrophe at sea had swept Susanna Morris's ship off course, the American preacher remained indefatigable in her religious mission. When Irish Quakers finally arrived with supplies and horses to retrieve the survivors (including the Quaker ship captain, Nathan Cowman, of Philadelphia, and Joseph Taylor, an English Quaker preacher returning from his American tour), Morris was accommodated at the Waterford residence of Elizabeth Jacob (the Irish minister who had previously journeyed with Abigail Craven). Prior to Morris's arrival, this Irish hostess, apparently "providentially-guided," had requested a certificate to travel to England on a similar ministerial "concern." Susanna Morris was thereby provided with a travel companion, transport, and provisions, the shipwreck only a brief interruption to her progress. The two women set forth on horseback, riding between the coastal trading cities of Waterford, Cork, and Dublin, the market towns and farming areas in Ireland, visiting Quaker meetings, as well as preaching where no Friends were settled. In January 1729, the County Tipperary Friends' meeting listed an expenditure of two shillings for stabling the horses of Susanna Morris and Elizabeth Jacob. In February 1729, the women visited Friends' families in Cork. On March 25, 1729, the Dublin Monthly Meeting, in a certificate directed to Friends in Great Britain, attested to Morris's "good and acceptable service amongst us" and the loss of her travel certificate in the disaster. An affidavit signed by several shipmates who had seen Morris's original certificate was attached to the Dubliners' document, to confirm American Friends' approval of her religious visit.[3]

In the spring of 1729, the two female preachers sailed across the Irish Sea to England. As a consequence of the women's extensive journeying, an English Quaker had to be reimbursed for a horse furnished to Morris that had fallen lame. Then, in June 1729, the Meeting for Sufferings in London granted Susanna Morris and Elizabeth Jacob any sum not to exceed thirty pounds for a proposed trip to Quakers in Holland.[4] Despite Susanna Morris's recent misadventure at sea, she braved more excursions by water: crossing the North Sea to Rotterdam (where a Dutch interpreter was relied upon), then back to England, a second visit to Holland (where their ship grounded on a sandbank), then a passage from Whitehaven, England, to Belfast, Ireland (where Morris completed a northern Irish circuit). After sailing from Dublin back to England, Morris finally made the return Atlantic voyage from London to Philadelphia in June 1731. During a tedious, eleven-week passage to the colonies, Morris endured another dangerous storm, which broke the ship's bowsprit, before she arrived safely in Pennsylvania. Undaunted by the difficulties of eighteenth-century travel, the colonial American woman had been away from her residence, on religious service, for nearly three years.

Increased Numbers of Women Travelling

The emergence of Quakerism, with its changed understanding of a legitimate ministry, had resulted in an increase in the number of women travelling in the English-speaking world. In the eighteenth century, Quaker women preachers regularly crisscrossed the British Isles and the American colonies (less frequently visiting continental Europe). Susanna Morris, for example, was only one of a stream of Quaker female ministerial visitors who passed through northern Ireland en route to other regions. On a list of members' turns to accompany visiting preachers (of either sex) to their next destination, kept by the Lurgan (Ireland) Men's Meeting, women were prominent among the visitors from diverse parts of the British empire. In March 1719, Margaret Barrow was escorted by Lurgan friends to Dublin; in April 1719, Mary Hayward was accompanied to Dublin; in May 1719, Mary Dover and Mary Harris were guided to Antrim; and in June 1719, three members travelled with Mary Hoskins and Elizabeth Stamper to Edenderry; while others attended Mary Ellerton and Mary Nixon to Dublin. In addition to Susanna Morris, who was guided to Coothill (after her Holland visit), other colonial American women visited Lurgan in the 1720s: Elizabeth Whartnaby of Philadelphia was escorted to Dublin, and Jane Fenn of Chester, Pennsylvania, to Coothill.[5]

Quaker meeting records reveal the customariness of the women's travel activity: from the County Tipperary payment, in 1718, for an express (a fast messenger on horseback) to go to Waterford to notify "abt. ye women friends haveing Meetings in ye County of Wexford," to expenditures for mending travelling female preachers' saddles, stabling their horses, and sending their correspondence. In a few extracts from the County Tipperary accounts: a man was paid for mending travelling preacher Ann Erwin's saddle in 1720; in 1725, a man was paid for "the two women friends horses yt. lodg'd at his house"; and in 1728, expenses included "women frds horses mending their Saddle & paying for Severall letters for them." Expenditures for women's ship passages also appear in accounts, such as the Yorkshire, England, Quarterly Meeting's payments for Mary Ellerton's voyages to America in 1702, to Holland in 1710, and to Ireland in 1712.[6]

The visibility of Quaker female ministers journeying to Friends' meetings in the eighteenth century was so great that a Quaker observer referred to it as "a day of women." As this Friend described the English scene in 1737: "Mary Slater [of Settle Monthly Meeting, England] is travelling in Lancashire with Molly Pace [known later as Mary Weston] of London, & Mary Cooper [of Yorkshire] is not returned from Scotland, Eliphal Harper [a Quaker female preacher from Massachusetts] & E[lizabeth]: Kendall [of Essex, England] are also in the North as are several other women & some men-friends also; but it seems much a day of women."[7] The women preachers' presence as travellers was also noted by people beyond the Friends' community, who encountered them on ships or at public lodgings. When Thomas Gent, a non-Quaker printer from York, England, sailed from Liverpool to Ireland in 1725, he observed that "the passengers, beside me, were two women, one of them a Quaker. . . ." A violent storm gathered during his voyage, and the ship's captain warned the passengers of imminent death. Tragedy was averted, however, when the voyagers were rescued by another ship. Thomas Gent recorded that he then "drank a cheeruping glass . . . rallied the captain for his timidity, and patiently heard the good Quaker woman deliver such a sermon as made us conclude she was filled with inspiration."[8]

The influx of female travellers was the effect of women ministers circulating from different monthly meetings: in Ireland, Scotland, Wales, England, and the American colonies. A number of Irish Quaker female preachers, such as Elizabeth Wilson of Moate Monthly Meeting, Elizabeth

Barcroft of Carlow Monthly Meeting, Elizabeth Balfour of Waterford Monthly Meeting, Elizabeth Hutchinson of Mountmellick Monthly Meeting, Jane Gee of Dublin Monthly Meeting, and Elizabeth Pease of Limerick Monthly Meeting, travelled repeatedly to other parts of Ireland, Scotland, Wales, and England. There were also many English women ministers who were zealous travellers, including Mary Wyatt of Essex Quarterly Meeting ("travailed 4 times into Ireland, & twice into Holland & Germany upon Truth's Account . . ."), Rachel Proud of Thirsk Monthly Meeting ("travelled widely, visiting most of the Meetings in England, . . . once in Ireland . . ."), Tabitha Hornor of Brighouse Monthly Meeting ("Once into Ireland, Once into Scotland, Twice in Wales, & several times thro' most parts of this Nation . . ."), and Mary Ransome of Hitchin Monthly Meeting ("into the North of England & Scotland, also into the West, & eastern parts of this Nation . . . often to the City of London . . .").[9]

In the American colonies, eighteenth-century Quaker women travelled diligently "in the service of Truth," as well. New England ministers, such as Rose Tibbets of Dover Monthly Meeting (New Hampshire), Hannah Hoag of Hampton Monthly Meeting (New Hampshire), Mary Wing of Sandwich Monthly Meeting (Massachusetts), Mary Hall of East Greenwich Monthly Meeting (Rhode Island), and Johanna Mott of Rhode Island Monthly Meeting, journeyed to destinations that included Barbados, Long Island, Nantucket, Pennsylvania, and, less frequently, Virginia and North Carolina. From New York, preachers such as Abigail Clemens of Flushing Monthly Meeting, Phebe Titus of Westbury Monthly Meeting, and Keziah Baker of Westchester Monthly Meeting travelled, among other places, to Rhode Island, Pennsylvania, and Virginia. In the southern colonies, Abigail Pike from Cane Creek Monthly Meeting (North Carolina), Elizabeth Norton of New Garden Monthly Meeting (North Carolina), and Sarah Janney of Fairfax Monthly Meeting (Virginia) ventured northward to Pennsylvania, New Jersey, and Long Island.

The Philadelphia Monthly Meeting was a thriving center of Quaker ministerial activity, with twenty women members journeying on religious service between 1704 and 1756. Many of these colonial American women had emigrated from England, Ireland, or Wales, where they had previously been active in the Quaker ministry. Philadelphia women such as Elizabeth Whartnaby (formerly Elizabeth Duckworth of London) and Margaret Preston (formerly Margaret Langdale of Yorkshire) had been travelling preachers in the British Isles; after immigrating, they continued their pattern of religious service in the colonies. Extracts from ten years of the Philadelphia meeting minutes illustrate the regularity of these women's religious travel; in 1720, Elizabeth Teague travelled to Maryland and Virginia. In 1721, Esther Clare voyaged to Great Britain, while Elizabeth Teague visited Long Island and Rhode Island. In 1724, Elizabeth Whartnaby returned to Long Island; later that year, Margaret Preston and Elizabeth Teague visited Long Island. In 1725, Esther Clare travelled to Maryland, Virginia, and North Carolina, and Elizabeth Whartnaby visited Maryland. In the same year, Elizabeth Teague journeyed to Maryland, Virginia, and North Carolina. In 1726, Margaret Preston went to Long Island, Rhode Island, and as far north as New Hampshire, while Elizabeth Whartnaby visited New Jersey and Long Island. In 1727, Whartnaby sailed to Barbados and Ireland. Esther Clare went to Maryland and Virginia. In 1728, Margaret Preston visited Maryland, Virginia, and North Carolina. In 1729, Mary Nicholls and Margaret Preston went to New Jersey and Long Island. Later that year, Margaret Preston and Sarah Knowles travelled to Maryland.[10]

The Quaker theological understanding that women, as well as men, could be "instruments" utilized by the Holy Spirit generated female ministerial travel in every region where eighteenth-century Friends' meetings existed. In every American monthly meeting sampled (nine out of the existing sixty-eight American monthly meetings), Quaker women were engaged in intercolonial travel. Hampton (New Hampshire) Monthly Meeting recorded ten female ministers among its membership travelling between 1705 and 1780. Haddonfield (New Jersey) Monthly Meeting listed nine women travelling between 1701 and 1769. Goshen (Pennsylvania) Monthly Meeting noted ten female ministers journeying on religious service between 1725 and 1772. Concord (Pennsylvania) Monthly Meeting had eleven women ministers who travelled between 1710 and 1781. Eleven female travelling preachers appear in the Abington (Pennsylvania) Monthly Meeting minutes between 1698 and 1754. Chester (Pennsylvania) Monthly Meeting had five women who journeyed between 1722 and 1757. Between 1721 and 1774, Gwynedd (Pennsylvania) Monthly Meeting listed eight women ministers presenting "concerns" to travel. Middletown (Pennsylvania) Monthly Meeting recorded six female travellers between 1689 and 1775.[11]

The seeds that had been planted in the seventeenth century, encouraging travel in the "service of Truth," had blossomed into a routine activity for many eighteenth-century women in the Society of Friends. The normality of travel for Quaker women, however, contrasted strikingly with the opportunities of their female contemporaries. According to non-Quaker conduct books, men were to "travel, seek a living . . . deal with many men . . . dispatch all things outdoor" while their wives "keep the house . . . oversee and give order within." In general, eighteenth-century women were infrequent travellers (except for occasional visits to relatives or for health cures). Since traditionally, women's primary function was reproductive, their sphere of activity was domestic and private (not mingling "promiscuously" with strangers). Concerns about propriety and safety, as well as the belief that a female's sole "calling" centered in the household, confined a large number of eighteenth-century women to their immediate environs. Geographical exploration of the world was assumed to be the prerogative of men. In colonial Massachusetts, Abigail Adams, a Congregationalist, wrote longingly of both her "great inclination to visit the Mother Country as tis call'd," and the restrictions on her desire to travel: "had nature formed me of the other Sex, I should certainly have been a rover."[12]

Yet the importance of Quaker women's spiritual role had overridden these traditional constraints on females. Quaker belief in another "calling" for women (as "chosen instruments" of spiritual wisdom) had greatly altered the female sphere of activity, not as a goal, but as an effect. The women's service in spreading the message of "Truth" was considered invaluable by Friends, and they were supported to leave their households. In 1751, a Quaker ship captain described a female preacher who had been recently transported across the Atlantic: "I hope her Labour will be attended w[i]th. Success. for my own part the very Sight of her made my H[e]art Rejoyse."[13]

The "Concern" to Travel

When recalling what impelled her to undertake the transatlantic voyage, Susanna Morris wrote: "At times I had a weighty concern of mind for several years to cross the great ocean in Truth's service; where the Lord might be pleased to lead me." For the American minister who nearly lost her life in a shipwreck, "giving up" to the "concern" to travel had been a struggle against her own will, fears, and reasonings. Attempts to ignore the inward "leading," however, had resulted in a loss of divine inspiration to preach. Morris remembered, "But I was so full of the reasoner, that I believe I did displease my God, and was so far in debt to him, that he was pleased to put me in prison a long year, and I never had in that time to open my mouth by way of testimony." Morris's eventual surrender to the "concern" to travel, by proceeding on faith across the Atlantic, reinvigorated her ministry: "But after I had strength given me to make those promises as aforesaid, my mouth was opened, and my tongue was loosed, and I was sent to go over the seas."[14]

Travelling on religious service, like preaching in the Quaker ministry, was to be initiated only on the basis of inward direction from God. "We understand . . . great desire in People to hear Truth declared and that a friend from England would visit you," the London Yearly Meeting responded to a group of Danzig Quakers requesting a preacher's visit to the European continent: "Now when the Almighty shall please . . . to move upon ye heart and Spirit of any one or more of his Servants & Ministers . . . to visit you we shall rejoyce—But yt time and Season is in ye Fathers hand. . . ." When ministers felt a "concern" to travel it was as if "cords of love [for God and for humankind were] drawing upon them." The impulse to travel was described as "drawings on the mind [or spirit]" to a particular destination. Distinguishing between one's own desires and "divine instruction" was sometimes agonizingly difficult; but the ultimate test was within. Before her voyage to America, Mary Peisley initially "was favoured with great tranquillity of soul, which made me look on the difficulties and dangers of the journey, with such eyes, that I began to fear that I had a will to go. . . ." Worried that her plans to travel were motivated by a personal desire, the Quaker preacher waited to know God's will about the trip, "and set my face against it, till I had a further manifestation of its being right. And here nature began to please itself with many pleasing prospects in my stay. . . ." Unable to ascertain which impulse was self-directed, whether to abandon the journey or not, Peisley decided to trust her original intuition, "I am now again, by the mercy of God, and by that faith which is his gift, fully resigned without any further manifestation; than in looking that way wherein I see a little light, peace and comfort to my poor soul; and in turning any other, fear, pain, and darkness, meet me."[15]

A prospective companion independently experiencing a similar "lead-ing" often was cited as confirmation of the legitimacy of one's own "con-cern" to travel. Elizabeth Hudson concluded that she was directed to travel to England with Jane (Fenn) Hoskins as she was standing in a meet-ing about to preach: "on my feet all hid from me And in an Awfull Silence England was presented [in my mind], as an Incumbent duty lain on me to Visit in Company with J Hoskins." Hudson discovered that Jane Hoskins, who was accompanying her, at that time, on travel in America, "had it like-wise on her mind but had never in all Our Journey proposed my going wth. her or had I ever mentioned my haveing any thoughts of Such an Undertaking."[16]

Although ministers were to wait for an inward "exercise," the London Yearly Meeting urged the preachers who were clustered in Pennsylvania in 1703 to travel, instead of relying on visitors from England: "There are many dark Corners in your parts [the American colonies] that hath not been, or very little visited, and knowing that many faithfull labourers have settled among you . . . we hope ye Lord will concern some of them to visit these uncultivated Places, and not too much depend upon old England for yt you lye upon ye Continent and can accomplish it with less difficulty." Eighteenth-century Quaker religious travel continued to be a way to seek out the "unconvinced," but it also increasingly functioned as a method of distributing the spiritually "gifted" across the Quaker community. With the reduction of persecution after the Toleration Act, London Yearly Meet-ing expressed hope that those "Gifted with a Publick Testimony . . . will in this Day of Liberty be diligent to Visit . . . Meetings; and more espe-cially those least frequented."[17]

Gatherings of Friends were not to rely on such "chosen instruments" or Quaker preachers ("y[ou]r. Eye need not be So unto man as to be under discouragements: when you have not instruments from . . . elsewhere"), and were admonished to not "Neglect their Dilligent Inward waiting upon God to hear his Life Giveing Voice for themselves." But, in practice, meet-ings were difficult to maintain without the occasional presence of a minis-ter to revitalize the faith. During the early years of Quakerism in Virginia, a Friend reported that meetings were well attended when travelling preach-ers were present but "few will com[e] & sett & waight [wait] with us when they are gon[e]."[18]

Ministerial travel ranged from a day's journey of a few miles to visit a neighboring meeting to an eight-thousand-mile trip on another continent lasting several years. Domestic travel (shorter trips within the minister's homeland) was the most typical form of itinerancy for both male and female "Public Friends." Part of the regularity of ministerial travel was due to the preachers' attendance of yearly meetings throughout the British Isles and the American colonies. Ministers routinely journeyed from other regions to attend these annual gatherings of Quakers and interested onlookers. At the New England Yearly Meeting held in Newport, Rhode Island, for example, several thousand New England Friends gathered, some from as far away as the Piscataqua region of New Hampshire and present-day Maine. In 1763, the female preachers in attendance who had come from beyond the compass of the Yearly Meeting included Ann Newlin from Concord, Pennsylvania, accompanying Alice Hall from Cumberland, England; Joyce Benezet and Sarah Morris from Philadelphia, Pennsylvania; and Elizabeth Smith from Burlington, New Jersey. The less demanding nature of regional travel allowed a preacher to take such trips more frequently than journeys overseas. Prior to presenting her "concern" to travel to England in 1709, Ann Chapman of Bucks County, Pennsylvania, had visited Long Island in 1701, Rhode Island in 1705, Maryland in 1707, as well as New Jersey and Long Island in 1708. Before travelling to America in 1718, Lydia Lancaster, of England, travelled to Yorkshire and Cumberland in 1709, to Durham, Yorkshire, and Northumberland in 1711, to Ireland in 1712, and to southwestern England and Wales in 1714.

Travel across the Atlantic was a major undertaking, and ministers usually described weighing the "concern" for several years, as Susanna Morris did, before presenting their proposal. A preacher also might need to wait many years in order to gain the meeting's approbation. Phebe Willets (later Dodge), a twenty-nine-year-old Long Island preacher, first presented a "concern" to travel with Susanna Morris to Great Britain in 1728. The meeting deferred consideration to see if her mother consented. Apparently Phebe's parent did not consent, because the proposed trip was not undertaken by the Long Island minister. Not until she was fifty-three years of age did Phebe Dodge renew her presentation to the meeting. After finally receiving a certificate from the meeting, Dodge journeyed in 1752 with the seventy-year-old Susanna Morris to the British Isles (Morris's third transatlantic visit). Gaining approval for religious travel was similar to achieving recognition as a minister. The preacher initiated the travel by presenting a "concern" before the monthly meeting. Again, the legitimacy of the "concern" was tested by its effect on the fellowship of Friends. After

Travel certificate for the preacher Sarah Morris, from the Philadelphia Monthly Meeting, July 26, 1771, and signed on behalf of the Philadelphia Quarterly Meeting, August 5, 1771. This certificate, expressing Friends' unity with Sarah Morris's religious "concern" to visit Great Britain, contains the signatures of many women ministers, including Elizabeth (Hudson) Morris, Mary Emlen, Joyce Benezet, Susanna Brown, and Rebecca Jones. Reproduced in Robert C. Moon, *The Morris Family of Philadelphia: Descendants of Anthony Morris, 1654–1721* (Philadelphia, 1898). *Courtesy the Historical Society of Pennsylvania*

Notice in the "Pennsylvania Journal," January 1772, of the ship *Pennsylvania Packet*, Peter Osborne, Commander. Sarah Morris embarked on this ship in March 1772 to pay her religious visit to the British Isles. The Philadelphia Quaker firm of Joshua Fisher and Sons organized one of the first transatlantic packet lines (with regularly scheduled sailings between Philadelphia and London). Many travelling Quaker preachers sailed on this ship over the years. *Courtesy the Historical Society of Pennsylvania*

For LONDON,
The SHIP
Pennsylvania Packet,
PETER OSBORNE,
COMMANDER;

HAVING part of her cargo engaged is expected to sail in the second month next. For freight or passage apply to JOSHUA FISHER and SONS, or said commander, on board the ship at their wharf, or at the London Coffee-house.

To be sold by JOSHUA FISHER and SONS, allum, brimstone, copperas, London porter, Warrington and Liverpool ale, pipes in kegs, and a few table sets of very elegant plain and copper-plate Queen's Ware. First Month 2.

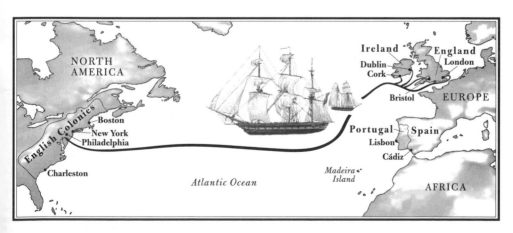

Primary Atlantic passages of eighteenth-century Quaker ministers (abstracted)

consideration, the meeting either advised a minister to wait in order to see whether the "exercise" increased, disapproved of it, or drew up a certificate of unity with the "concern." The meeting ordinarily inquired into the minister's "conversation" (the way of conducting oneself in the world), settlement of worldly affairs (family and business responsibilities), and the reception of the minister's testimony by the Quaker community before granting the certificate.

The Atlantic Voyage: Ocean Crossing

"My mind was gathered into perfect stillness for some time, and my spirit was as if it had been carried away into America; and after it returned, my heart was as if it had been dissolved with the love of God, which flowed over the great ocean, and I was constrained to kneel down and pray for the seed of God in America," wrote Elizabeth Webb, recalling the experience she had while seated in the Gloucester Quaker meeting-house in England, in 1697, that prompted her later visit to the American colonies. "The concern never went out of my mind day nor night, until I went to travel there in the love of God, which is so universal that it reaches over sea and land," Webb wrote. "But when I looked at my concern with an eye of human reason, it seemed to be very strange and hard to me; for I knew not the country, nor any that dwelt therein." Webb wrestled with doubts about her ability to undertake the journey but "death and darkness" attended her when she "let in such reasonings." Remembering that, according to the Bible, "the fearful and unbelieving shall have their portion . . . in the lake that burns with fire and brimstone," Webb resigned herself to obedience to the Lord, gaining peace.[19]

The intensity of Webb's "travels" of the spirit made physical obstacles, like the Atlantic Ocean, seem easily overcome. But eighteenth-century Quaker women preachers' mystical visions were given practical support by the Quaker organization and the rational capitalism of Quaker merchants. The travel certificate, expressing Friends' conviction of the authenticity of a "concern," placed an itinerant minister, like Elizabeth Webb or Susanna Morris, on terms of instant acquaintance with Quakers in different regions—allowing access to their hospitality, companionship, and funding. In the early "heroic" years of seventeenth-century Quaker missionary zeal, those spurred by a powerful inward "calling" had sometimes walked miles to spread the message of "Truth," or built their own small ships to cross the ocean. Missionaries had corresponded with George Fox and Margaret Fell, receiving some assistance from the Kendal Fund; but individual enterprise marked most early itinerant activity. By the eighteenth century, Quakers had developed a system to assist travelling ministers. The maturation of the Society of Friends had brought new corporate supervision of the ministry, but also new logistical support.

In pragmatic terms, crossing the Atlantic was a weighty enterprise in the eighteenth century, requiring not only a berth on a ship, but enough provisions for a five- to eleven-week passage (voyages from British North America to England were approximately half as long as the passage from England to the colonies). All Quaker meetings had a "stock" (or treasury) from which they could disburse assistance to poor Friends (including those "called" on religious service but not able to cover the expenses). Domestic travellers were assisted on a small scale by the Society of Friends. Hampton (New Hampshire) Monthly Meeting, for example, hired a horse for its member Lydia Norton to make a religious visit to Rhode Island. But the expense of "going beyond the Seas" was distributed across the membership, as each constituent meeting contributed proportionally to the yearly meeting's national stock: with the communal goal of seeing "Truth" flourish. London Yearly Meeting routinely funded the transatlantic westward voyages of eighteenth-century ministers (both the British going abroad and Americans returning home). In 1700, when Ann Dillworth, an American Friend returning to Pennsylvania after a religious visit to England, embarked from the port of Bristol, the Bristol (England) Men's Meeting disbursed almost eleven pounds to pay for her passage. The Bristol meeting then appointed representatives to the London Yearly Meeting to request reimbursement from the national stock.[20]

London and Philadelphia were the linchpins of the eighteenth-century transatlantic community of Friends. Both destinations were large seaports, hubs of trade activity, and served as points of transit to the provinces. Most Quaker preachers received certificates of unity with their undertaking from the important meetings of ministers and elders at these ports, before crossing the Atlantic. London, the seat of the imperial government, also served as the headquarters for the transatlantic Quaker organization, including the London Yearly Meeting, the most influential annual meeting in the

Society of Friends, and the Morning Meeting, or Meeting of Ministers and Elders. The concentration of Friends in the territory covered by the Philadelphia Yearly Meeting made it the most influential Quaker meeting in the American colonies: encompassing Pennsylvania, Delaware (known as the "Three Lower Counties"), New Jersey, and, eventually, parts of Maryland. The Quaker vision of a geographically dispersed community bound in God's Spirit, "that pure Love and unity in which his dear Children are bound up together I Can Say it is Love yt [that] many waters Cannot quench nor time and Distance ware away . . . ," encouraged Friends to strongly develop their transatlantic communications and shipping.[21]

Many of the eighteenth-century Quaker men active in the religious organization were simultaneously active in long-distance commercial ventures. Men such as John Hunt, a Quaker merchant in London, and Israel Pemberton Jr., a Philadelphia Quaker merchant, formed a transatlantic network of Friends linked by business and religious beliefs that provided support to the eighteenth-century Quaker itinerant ministry. Merchant members, like Hunt, of the Meeting for Sufferings in London assisted in arranging the ship passages for ministers departing from the British Isles. Depending upon market conditions, Hunt shipped to Pennsylvania cargoes of manufactured goods, tea, or other items likely to bring a profit. Like the Pembertons of Philadelphia, who specialized in importing English cloth, John Hunt kept informed of ship sailings, accommodating eighteenth-century Quaker ministers who were transported across the Atlantic along with the trade. Hunt, also a Quaker preacher, wrote to his business correspondent, James Pemberton of Philadelphia, in 1750: "Our ship Speedwell will have quantity of manufactures . . . if Capt. Stephenson needs cash or provisions please supply him and charge to our account . . . Mary Weston [a travelling minister] went on this boat."[22]

Numerous Quaker-owned ships commanded by Quaker ship captains carried the travelling preachers across the Atlantic in the eighteenth century. The Philadelphia Quaker firm of Joshua Fisher and Sons organized one of the first transatlantic packet lines (with regularly scheduled sailings between Philadelphia and London, whether fully loaded with cargo or not). Jane Crosfield sailed from England in the Fisher-owned *Pennsylvania Packet* (Captain Budden) in 1760 to pay a religious visit to the colonies. Rachel Wilson crossed the Atlantic on the *Pennsylvania Packet* (Captain Falconer) in 1768, with one of the ship's owners, Samuel Rowland Fisher, who greatly assisted her, "his Cheif Study to make every thing as easy as in his power."[23] Sarah Morris also voyaged in the *Pennsylvania Packet* (Captain Osborne) in 1772 on her visit to the British Isles. Frequently, several Quaker preachers would sail together on the same ship. Jane Crosfield of Westmorland, England, shared her passage to America in 1760 with George Mason from Yorkshire and Susanna Hatton from Ireland, each bound on a similar errand.

Increased sailings across the Atlantic provided more opportunities for eighteenth-century Quaker preachers to voyage: the overall number of transatlantic voyages had doubled between 1675 and 1740 as commerce grew between the British Isles and the colonies; intercolonial shipping tripled during this period.[24] The settlement of Quakers at major ports along trade routes ensured the compatibility of merchants' and itinerant preachers' destinations. In turn, Quaker merchants, who needed trustworthy agents in distant ports and expanding markets, were beneficiaries of the ministers' efforts to sustain, as well as enlarge, the Quaker community. In addition to London and Philadelphia, Bristol, England, and Dublin, Ireland, were popular ports for both Quaker transatlantic shipping and ministerial travel. Religious visitors to the colonies might also first port at Charleston (Charles Town), South Carolina, as the shipping traffic increased between the southern colonies and Britain, with the region's strong rice export trade.

Yet eighteenth-century Quakers had to balance their commercial pragmatism with the mysticism of their ministers' "inward leadings." The Meeting for Sufferings in London might arrange a ship for an itinerant preacher to sail in, but the final determination was made by the "Public Friend" on the basis of a spiritual sense. Rachel Wilson sailed to the colonies in 1768 on the Quaker-owned *Pennsylvania Packet,* but before embarking for America, Wilson waited for a spiritual confirmation "of that being the ship I ought to go in." Although the eighteenth-century ministers' ports of embarkation were largely determined by trade routes, the system to support the work of those "in the service of Truth" had to be flexible enough to accommodate the shifting "divine inspirations" of the preachers. Mary Peisley recalled, "Before my leaving Ireland, I had a sight of Charleston, South Carolina, being the port for me to land at, this continued until I returned to London, when I lost sight of it, which made me willingly conclude I might go with some Friends . . . for Philadelphia." Peisley went on board several vessels bound for Philadelphia "but could not see my way in any of them. On more deeply centring to the Root of life, in humble resignation to the Divine will, I found it my duty to continue some weeks at London. . . ." Peisley ultimately decided to sail for Charleston as she had originally seen in her vision. The Meeting for Sufferings adjusted accordingly. In July 1753, when the ministers William Brown, Catharine Payton, and Mary Peisley had been about to embark for America, the meeting had suggested that their expenses not exceed sixteen pounds each. But in September 1753, the actual bill for Peisley and Payton to South Carolina was brought in—a total of nearly forty pounds for only two of them—after they had changed plans. "There not being time to inform the meeting before their departure," the Meeting for Sufferings agreed to pay the higher bill.[25]

The travelling preachers had berths in the ship's cabin, sharply contrasting with the sailors' quarters in steerage. By the 1760s, on a packet ship (the first merchant vessels to stress the comfort of the passengers), Rachel Wilson found "ye Cabin & State Ro[o]me Rather Elegant" on the *Pennsylvania Packet*. But voyagers still had to supply their own seagoing provisions, which, in the case of ministerial travellers, were contributed by the Quaker community and often shared with the crew and other passengers. The "necessaries" taken on board ship had to sustain the voyagers for an indeterminate time at sea (perhaps nearly three months), since eighteenth-century transport was dependent on favorable winds (Wilson described the frustrating delays, when the captain weighed anchor, then dropped anchor, repeatedly, for several days as contrary winds prevented their departure from Gravesend, near London). For her voyage from England to America, Rachel Wilson was provided with: "30 Fowles, 12 Ducks, 4 hams, 2 doz. Madeira wine, 2 bottles Jamaica Spirit, Keg W.I. Rum, 4 bottles of brandy, 2 do. Vinegar, 6 lbs. Rusks, 2 lbs. Maple biscuits, 3 do. Ginger bread, 8 do. Raisins, ½ lb. Single Tea, 2 lbs. ground coffee, 2 do. Chocolate, 1 Loaf D refined sugar, 14 lbs. Musco sugar, 1 Pack cranberries, 2 qts. Oatmeal, 6 lbs. rice, 5 bushlls. Indian corn, 100 Eggs." Such "necessaries" might be supplemented on board ship with freshly caught fare, novelties for the normally landbound travellers. When recovered from the seasickness that plagued most passengers, Rachel Wilson, from the sheep-rearing country of northwestern England, described dining on two dolphins caught at sea: "as I had never seen anye Before it was Very agreable to Me & I Eat it with a pret[t]y good gust & found no Bad Efects from it."[26]

Hazards at Sea

Trusting "in the will of him at whos[e] com[m]and the Winds & Seas obey," the Quaker female preachers set sail for unknown lands. Improvements in navigational instruments, maps, and charts, as well as the construction of lighthouses, had helped reduce risks on the Atlantic, but eighteenth-century sea voyages were filled with potential dangers. Travellers made their wills before sailing, uncertain they would survive to return. Rachel Wilson prayed on board her ship bound for America "that we might not murmur or repine at what might be permitted to attend us now, when upon the unstable Ocean, for our refinement and the trials of our faith."[27]

At times, the Quaker women ministers were forced to cope without female companionship in their adventurous circumstances. Rachel Wilson parted from her husband in order to board the ship to Pennsylvania with three male Quaker passengers. She wrote, "We were now left Wm. Coleman, Saml. Fisher, James Brick, and myself, no other female on board which looked a little hard," but through the kindness of the Quaker men, "it was made abundantly easier than I could expect." Thomas Chalkley, a Quaker minister, felt compelled to write a letter of encouragement to two unmarried women, Jane Fenn and Elizabeth Levis, concerned about dangerous storms and rough sailors, voyaging to Barbados on religious service in 1724: "And, tender friends, though it may seem hard for you . . . to give up to go to sea, and also to divers[e] who love you . . . the Lord is stronger than the noise of many waters, and than the mighty waves of the sea. . . . And dear maidens, as your cross is great, you being two innocent young women, in giving up your names to cross the sea, which I know is a great trial, the seamen, too, generally being rude, dissolute people; so your crown will be great also."[28]

Isolated at sea, unable to obtain additional assistance to sail the ship, passengers were at the mercy of a sometimes unreliable, ill-mannered crew: "Our Vessel was heavy Laden and but few hands on Board, and if they had fallen out and Distroyed one another what would have becom[e] of us," worried Margaret Ellis en route from Pennsylvania to the British Isles in 1752. The Welsh-born American preacher and her female ministerial companion, Margaret Lewis, had to contend with a potential mutiny on board.

Ellis heard a quarrel between two crew members, "upon which I desired the Mate (in my own Language he being a Welch Man) not to Strike but Yet to keep his Authority." After the mate went below deck, Ellis discovered the mutinous stirrings, "an Evil Contrivance," among the sailors. After praying for guidance, Ellis discerned that "they must be treated kindly, upon which I went down to the Cabbin, and got some Cakes, Cheese, and Liquor, and distributed among them, Setting forth the Danger we were in, And how well it would be to think upon God, and our latter End. . . ." According to Ellis, the men's countenance altered, their spirits were quieted, and their voyage was unusually speedy. When the absence of seasickness made it feasible, Ellis regularly held religious meetings on board ship (as did most Quaker preachers): pointing out to the profane sailors the dangers of swearing, and persuading other passengers of "the great advantage that attended an humble waiting upon God." Margaret Ellis reported the impact of her presence upon the crew: "And they forbear Swearing when they saw me, or if I caught them Unawares they would confess they had forgot. . . ."[29]

Storms and shipwrecks were an ever-present danger, as few travellers crossed the ocean without encountering some turbulent weather. Rachel Wilson had hoped to have the companionship, on her transatlantic voyage, of a Philadelphia woman who had been shipwrecked and reduced to great extremity while sailing to London to transact business. The sudden sight of an unknown ship on the open sea held ominous significance for the eighteenth-century traveller as well: a mast and sails could be a chilling sight on the horizon. Unscrupulous men, like Edward Teach (known as "Blackbeard"), who plagued the eastern coast of America, preyed on vessels in this "golden age" of piracy. Jane Fenn wrote, on her 1727 crossing, "Saw a Sail to the Windward which Bore Down hard on us, but . . . Night coming on, we Lost Sight of her, the Captn and Men thought her to be a Pirate."[30]

Frequent wars between European powers during the eighteenth century made the crossing even more perilous for Atlantic voyagers. When Elizabeth Hudson sailed from Philadelphia to Ireland in 1748, a ship was seen in the distance but "Our Company apprehended no danger . . . they Said Suppos'd her an honest fellow going to the West they bearing that Course And the Reverse to Ours." Hudson and her ministerial companion, Jane (Fenn) Hoskins, had a "spiritual sense" that the strange vessel was the enemy, "it being the time of ye Spainsh and French war. . . ." On deck,

Hudson realized the ship, rather than moving on its way, had drawn nearer to them. She informed the captain, "who wth. his Glass Examin'd her more Closely and perceived her bearing down wth. all her Sails out, upon us having held us in play untill she had got to the windward of us." This discovery greatly alarmed the crew who believed it to be impossible to either resist or run, since the other ship, by stealth, had now gotten "such great advantage of us." After praying, Hudson recorded that a "thick fogg like Smoak" appeared between them and the vessel. In a "providential delivery," a fire had broken out on the enemy ship and the vessel soon fell far behind.[31]

Jane Crosfield travelled slowly across the Atlantic in 1760, protected in a "Fleet of 36 sail of vessels under convoy" during the Seven Years War. For the Maryland preacher Ann Moore, however, a sailor's cry of, "Yonder, I see a ship!" a few days before her vessel was to arrive at Great Britain in 1761, signalled the dreaded fate of capture by the enemy. Ann Moore wrote of a premonitory dream (as Susanna Morris had written, regarding her shipwreck) which enabled her to remain calm when the French fired a cannon at their vessel "and soon after came on board our Ship with drawn swords in their Hands, as tho' they meant to kill all before them. . . ."[32] After realizing their predicament, those on board, with the exception of Moore, had immediately begun donning their best clothes and concealing their gold in the hope of saving some valuables. The ship's captain cast the mail they had carried overboard to prevent information from falling into the hands of the enemy.

Although the French herded the captain and crew onto their ship, they released five people (including Ann Moore), setting them ashore in Catholic Spain. Moore had already endured several ordeals before the attack: six weeks of seasickness, a storm so great "that it seemed as though we should unavoidably be swallowed up in the waves but it pleased the great and gracious hand to preserve us," and "a trying time" of the ship lying becalmed for nine days. Having been seasick for so long, Moore was very weak and a mule had to be hired to carry her in Spain. She and her shipmates were forced to stay in Spain for several months until shipping was available to England. Not knowing the language and worried about depleting the small supply of money that the French had allowed them to take ashore, Moore still managed to write a religious epistle to English residents in Bilbao, warning them to cease doing evil in order to save their souls. She also debated the meaning of the New Testament with a Roman

Catholic priest at her lodging (discovering that, unlike herself, able to read the Bible in her own language, the priest could not read his own Scriptures, which were in Latin).

The colonial American woman wrestled with the "idolatry" she observed in the Spanish Catholic celebration at the conclusion of Lent. When Ann Moore, as a radical Protestant, witnessed the parade through the streets of saints' images, she "trembled as one in a strong ague." "A cry" ran through her heart: "O Lord, let them see as my poor soul see[s] that Christ *within* is the hope. . . ." Moore felt compelled to proclaim this in the streets but anticipated that she would be immediately imprisoned. She worried that she was not strong enough to fulfill this task and so would "mar the cause." But if she did not voice "the Truth," Moore feared that she would lose favor with the Lord. Finally, she felt herself resigned to do the will of God, but then felt that "the will [had been] accepted for the deed," and so departed from Spain in peace.[33] With the financial aid of Friends in Great Britain, Moore fulfilled her original religious mission.

Other Quaker ministers were captured on the open seas (including the male preachers John Griffith, carried into Bayonne in 1747, and Mordecai Yarnall, imprisoned by the French in 1757), but, as nonparticipants in the wars, they were eventually released and completed their religious journeys. War eventually proved to be the most formidable obstacle to the preachers' transatlantic voyages, however, when conflict erupted within the British empire, and England was at war with the colonies. Quaker transatlantic ministerial visits completely stopped from 1776 to 1781 (beginning again after 1781).

On Land: Itineraries

When Elizabeth Webb "gave up" to journey "in Truth's service," drawn "by the Spirit of love, to travel," she recalled that "the Spirit which led me forth, was to me like a needle of a compass, touched with a loadstone; for so it pointed where I ought to go, and when I came to the far end of the journey."[34] Quaker ministers tried to adhere to inward guidance by the Holy Spirit to determine itineraries. Certificates to travel in another country were worded in a more general manner than those directed to a specific region ("A Concern . . . hath been upon her Spirit for a long time to visit Divers parts of America"). Meetings recognized the problem of maintaining order without hindering a minister from following the changing senses of "divine direction."

A certificate of the meeting's unity with the religious journey protected Quakers from having their hospitality imposed upon by vagabonds and swindlers, and preserved the Society's reputation as well. But the approved trip could also be expanded when circumstances, like shipwreck, changed the destination, or the "concern" shifted. When Ann Moore set out from Maryland on an intercolonial trip to visit Pennsylvania and New Jersey, she felt strongly drawn to continue north, but she had received a certificate from her meeting that did not include this destination. Moore was torn between "fear I should offend the Lord and a fear of offending my dear and tender brethren because my certificate extended not so far as my concern, I being insensibly led along beyond my expectation." She remembered that "an awful fear" had struck her, after her certificate was signed, that she might go farther than she had been apprized of by her first "divine leading." Some of the elders had desired her not to "come home uneasy" because of one or two words left out of the certificate. Her travel companions encouraged her to continue forward and she did so, without negative repercussions.[35] Additional oversight of the ministry was provided by certificates preachers obtained from meetings they had visited on their travels, attesting to satisfactory religious service.

The ministers' travel routes were a combination of their "leadings" and knowledge of the locations of Quaker gatherings. A list, for example, showing the six colonial Quaker yearly meetings and their constituent quarterly meetings, as well as the number of the meetings for worship under their jurisdiction, was prepared to assist Rachel Wilson on her tour of the American colonies. But much of Wilson's decision making regarding the trip was spontaneous and improvisational because she sought to follow an "inner guide." Wilson's journal descriptions illustrate the degree to which other Quakers tried to adhere to a minister's "inward promptings." While on board a sloop bound for the island of Nantucket, Rachel Wilson noted that the Quaker captain was "cautious of acting without knowing my mind in passing by Martha's Vineyard in which only one fr[ien]ds family lived." Although there were twenty passengers on board and potential difficulty with the wind the next morning if the sloop anchored at the island for the night, Wilson felt "led" to stop at Martha's Vineyard to hold a meeting with the few Friends. The captain followed her directions.[36]

Transatlantic ministers attempted to visit most settled Quaker meetings, in addition to holding meetings for non-Quakers. Their itineraries were determined, in part, by where Quakers lived. In 1700, Quakers composed one-third of the population in New Hampshire and (present-day) Maine. Substantial Quaker meetings existed in Hampton, Newbury, Salem, and Lynn. Friends were in the majority in the southern Massachusetts communities of Sandwich, Falmouth, and Dartmouth, and on the island of Nantucket. Quakers in Boston, who had built their first meetinghouse in 1694, had expanded into a second building fifteen years later. Large numbers of Friends resided in the tolerant colony of Rhode Island. In New York, Quakers clustered on Long Island. An estimated six thousand Friends resided in New Jersey in 1700, and twenty thousand in Pennsylvania. Maryland possessed about three thousand Quaker inhabitants. Virginia had approximately five thousand Quakers, and the Carolinas included about five thousand. By the mid-eighteenth century, an influential Quaker community had developed in New York City. Overcrowding in Nantucket and throughout New England impelled many Quakers to move to the Nine Partners area above Poughkeepsie. Eventually, a chain of New York Friends' meetings stretched northward from what is now Westchester County, between the Hudson River and the Connecticut border. The Virginia Quaker population was enlarged, as well, over the eighteenth century by the migrations of Friends from the northern colonies who moved west within Virginia. During those years, Quakers from Pennsylvania, Maryland, Virginia, and the island of Nantucket also settled meetings farther south in the coastal region and in the backcountry of the Carolinas (especially in the Piedmont area of North Carolina). In 1760, approximately fifty thousand to sixty thousand Friends resided in colonial America.[37]

For most eighteenth-century Quaker religious travellers to the colonies, Philadelphia served as their American headquarters: "our senter [center] or our american home," as Elizabeth Webb noted.[38] Preachers visiting America typically made a circuit of the mainland colonies, completing loops of the southern or northern colonies for several months at a time, returning to their base in Pennsylvania before the next stage of their journeying. The sequence of these tours varied. Catharine Payton and Mary Peisley began in the south and travelled north, since they had arrived in Charleston, rather than Philadelphia.

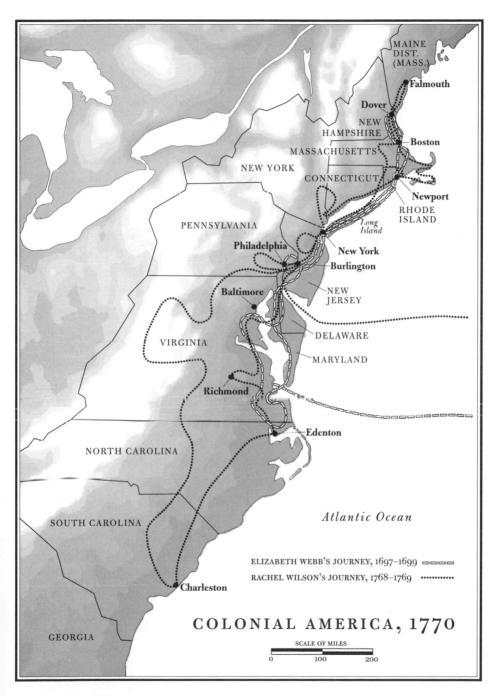

MAINE
DIST.
(MASS.)

●Falmouth

Dover●

NEW
HAMPSHIRE

●─Boston

MASSACHUSETTS

NEW YORK

CONNECTICUT

●Newport

RHODE
ISLAND

*Long
Island*

PENNSYLVANIA

Philadelphia●

●─New York

●─Burlington

Baltimore●

NEW
JERSEY

VIRGINIA

─DELAWARE

─MARYLAND

Richmond●

●─Edenton

NORTH CAROLINA

Atlantic Ocean

SOUTH CAROLINA

ELIZABETH WEBB'S JOURNEY, 1697–1699 □□□□
RACHEL WILSON'S JOURNEY, 1768–1769 ●●●●●●●●●

●Charleston

GEORGIA

COLONIAL AMERICA, 1770

SCALE OF MILES

0   100   200

The routes taken by two Quaker women ministers visiting British North America

As new Quaker settlements developed, the geographical range of the travel expanded for the eighteenth-century preachers. Elizabeth Webb, travelling in the colonies between 1697 and 1699, went as far south as the Albemarle Sound area of North Carolina, an early haven for dissenters, and as far north as Dover, New Hampshire. In 1750, when Mary Weston toured America, she visited the few Friends in Charleston, South Carolina, went along the coast to North Carolina, through Virginia, Maryland, Delaware, New Jersey, Pennsylvania, the New York mainland and Long Island, Connecticut, Rhode Island, Massachusetts, New Hampshire, and as far north as Casco Bay, in present-day Maine. (Although Mary Weston held several meetings in Connecticut, many ministers rode quickly through this colony, which proved to be the least permeable to Friends' influence.) Mary Weston wrote to Abigail Watson (formerly Boles) of her progress: "From two hundred miles to the Eastward of Boston to within forty miles of Georgia taking many meetings, where never any friend had been on that service before . . . rode about eight thousand miles, visiting almost every meeting in the several provinces . . . the number of which is greatly increased since my dear friend [Abigail] was in those parts. . . ."[39] When Rachel Wilson visited the colonies in 1768–69, she rode significantly farther inland than Weston had in the Carolinas and Virginia, as well as completing the circuit to Casco Bay.

Locating Friends could be haphazard in areas where the Quaker organizational structure was minimal. Connections formed in the minister's homeland were sometimes the only source of information about the unknown country. Mary Peisley had been acquainted with a Friend in Ireland who was among the recent Quaker immigrants to the Wateree River area of South Carolina. After writing to him, she eventually met the immigrant in South Carolina, and, with her English ministerial companion, Catharine Payton, visited every Friend's family in the area. In another South Carolina episode, Payton and Peisley set forward through wilderness on horseback, accompanied by two Quaker men, toward the Pedee River where they had heard there was a settlement of Friends. While staying at the residence of a Presbyterian planter, they encountered a young man who directed them twenty miles up the river to their destination. Payton and Peisley found newly convinced Friends who had not yet even established a meeting. The ministers believed they had been "divinely guided" to these isolated Quakers.

Although eighteenth-century religious travellers usually began in areas thickly clustered with Quakers, they also ventured into unfamiliar territories, relying only on their "inward leadings." Ann Moore, riding north of Newark, New Jersey, "having no knowledge of any friends living that way," arrived at a point of decision between a ferry and a road northward. Her companions asked her, "Well, which way?" Moore followed "the way the truth my guide turned," and chose the road. Moore and her escorts eventually encountered a traveller who informed them that, indeed, there were some Quakers who lived a few miles off the road they had selected. Moore's assessment, that the Lord was pleased "to send his pastors to his tender lambs in the wilderness to feed them that they may grow in grace and . . . be saved," was a theme in itinerants' journals.[40] The travelling minister was supposedly "providentially cast"—able to unerringly single out each remote enclave of Friends or seekers after true religion.

Many Quaker preachers visited the Caribbean islands, sometimes voyaging to the islands en route to or from Great Britain. In the West Indies, groups of Friends resided on Jamaica, Tortola, Antigua, and Barbados (which had five Quaker meeting-houses at its peak population of Friends during the eighteenth century). Ministerial visitors to the British Isles usually toured England, Wales, and Ireland (Presbyterian Scotland, with a smaller Quaker population, was less receptive to Quakerism and less frequently visited). London functioned as a base for travellers from the American colonies. In the eighteenth century, approximately fifty thousand Friends resided in counties throughout England and Wales, with a few Quaker groups in Scotland. English Quakerism's fertile ground, the northern counties of Westmorland, Cumberland, Lancashire, and Yorkshire, continued to have a concentration of Friends. Quakerism had also attracted followers in the north Midlands, parts of East Anglia, and the southwestern shires. Bristol, the second largest English port, was another Quaker stronghold. Friends clustered in the southeastern counties of England as well, particularly in the capital, London, which by 1678 had about ten thousand Quaker inhabitants. In Ireland, the small Quaker population of approximately five thousand was distributed among the cities of Dublin, Cork, and Waterford, the market towns of Wicklow and Carlow, and the agricultural areas of Leinster and Munster. Friends also lived in Ulster but, in the eighteenth century, meetings repeatedly complained of being "Weaken[e]d and thin[n]ed" by the immigration of many members to America.[41]

Travel Hazards on Land

The eighteenth-century women ministers seem to have been little deterred by the physical hazards of travel. Many female preachers braved the backcountry, off the well-travelled routes, as Mary Peisley wrote, "drawn in the love of God, to visit many of the back inhabitants, where I suppose, no Europeans had ever been on the like errand." During her 1750–52 American tour, Mary Weston asserted, in a letter to her husband in England, that she and her female companion had "traveled harder than any man has been known to do, rid about 1800 miles and took above a hundred meetgs in 4 months . . . finding my Concern to Lead me to back Settlements, where no English ffr[ien]d has Ever been before . . . in New England." Catharine Payton observed that she and Mary Peisley "were the first from Europe" to visit a recently settled Quaker community at New Garden, North Carolina. In 1753, Payton and Peisley crossed "through a wilderness country, wherein it was dangerous for women to travel, by reason of the swamps and deep creeks." Mary Peisley described travelling in the Carolina backwoods:

> in a very thinly inhabited country, through unbeaten paths in the woods, dangerous creeks and swamps, with wild and venomous creatures around us . . . We came hither from Charleston, taking no meetings in the way except in the families where we lodged, the distance being 150 miles, through woods & swamps, where our lives seemed in jeopardy every hour . . . I have sat down by a brook in the woods, ate my Indian corn bread, and drank water out of a calabash [the dried shell of a gourd-like fruit]. . . .[42]

Friends' theological understanding was particularly suited for the daunting difficulties of eighteenth-century travel. The minister Thomas Chalkley wrote, "But what are our lives to the life of the only begotten Son of God? And truly, we must give them up often, if we have the cause of souls at heart. . . ." The act of journeying was a religious testimony of faith, as Chalkley observed: "We had great inward joy in the Holy Ghost in our outward jeopardy and travels."[43] The Quakers, in general, were not very concerned about the physical limitations of the "weaker sex"—for God was able to do anything: if one was weak, He was strong.

Distances were long between residences in sparsely settled areas, and the women rode, at times, fifty or sixty miles a day. Horseback riding was physically challenging, and even more so when negotiating mountainous passages, stony roads, and muddy sloughs. The preachers often wrote of injurious falls from horses. When she travelled through Virginia in the wintertime, Rachel Wilson rode through snow, "the trees so Laden [with snow], & many Broken down that the Road was almost stopt up in Placis [places] my hors[e] Being ful[l] of spirit brush'd through . . . a Larg[e] tree, Under which thair was not Roome for Me & him, took me quite off." Her leg was so crushed by the fall, she feared she could not bear to ride. But Wilson rode fifteen miles to an inn, where notice was given to the neighbors and she held a meeting.

Even more daunting for the preachers were the frequent water crossings required to traverse the colonies. Numerous, swiftly moving rivers had to be ridden through. When heavy rains made a river dangerous to cross, Rachel Wilson noted that their horses swam and "we went over on a Log tho[ugh] not without fear[,] our Sadles & Bags Being first Born over. . . ." Writing to her husband in England, Mary Weston was forthright about her discomfort in crossing on ferries (which might be rafts or canoes lashed together) or sailing on a sloop to Rhode Island:

> indeed am Tyred [tired] have rode 15 Miles ToDay and crossed Two Ferrys . . . wch seems a very Disagreeable thing to me and here is abundance of ym[them] in America and I am informed its 100 Miles by water to Rooad[Rhode] Island wch I Dread. . . .[44]

In the "well-watered land" of the American South, where most farms were located near rivers for easy transport of crops to market, the women's religious visits might be undertaken in canoes. To arrive at a meeting in Pasquotank, North Carolina, Esther Palmer had to travel "8 Miles by Water . . . after Meeting we had a very rough Sea, as if we should have been buried in it, but thro' ye Lord's Mercys we were all well preserved." A large number of Quakers resided near the Chesapeake Bay, which stretched nearly two hundred miles in length. Maryland Friends had "a shallop [small boat] for Friends' service" to travel to the meetings along the Chesapeake shores. When Esther Palmer and Mary Lawson first attempted to sail across the bay, fierce winds drove them back ("when we were about half way over"), so they went to West River meeting instead. The following day, the women crossed safely; but boats sometimes overset, drowning the passengers.[45]

Travelling in the colonies, Quaker ministers also had to contend with the threat of hostile Native Americans, as during Queen Anne's War (1702–13), when "the Indians were very barbarous in the destruction of the English inhabitants, scalping some, and knocking out the brains of others, men, women, and children, by which the country was greatly alarmed both night and day" in the Piscataqua region of New Hampshire.[46] But in spite of the danger, especially in the northern regions of New England, the female preachers rode unarmed, demonstrating their reliance on God to protect them.

Although journeying in colonial America presented a host of distinctive challenges, travel conditions were difficult on the other side of the Atlantic as well. Elizabeth Hudson, an American visitor, complained of the horrendous roads in Scotland and the Edinburgh residents' habit of flinging filth out of their windows. In England, robberies were common. When Elizabeth Hudson was travelling across a Yorkshire moor on a bright, moonlit night in 1750, a man jumped out from behind a bush, seized her horse by the bridle, "& held him fast looking Ste[a]dily upon me." The servant accompanying Hudson was some distance ahead of her. The Quaker preacher concluded that the stranger was a thief and put her hand on her purse, but did not pull it out, waiting instead for the highwayman to demand it. Hudson "look'd full in his face Some time untill he let the bridle go Saying I was not the person he wanted. . . ." Hudson, relieved to be rid of the man "on such easy terms," rode off as fast as she could, "not a little frighten'd."[47]

But sufferings of the body could train the spirit. Mary Peisley wrote, "I can welcome tribulations and rejoice in such adversities, as have the least tendency to draw my mind nearer unto God, which I know must be by being weaned . . . from earthly satisfactions." Quaker ministers strove to achieve the state described by Peisley, "that to live or die, to be in health or sickness, in prosperity or adversity, in Europe or America . . . in the will of God, seemed just the same to me." Several of the female ministers did succumb to the physical strain of their travels, and died on their trips (as did some male ministers). Mary Rogers, for instance, contracted a "malignant fever" while visiting the West Indies on her return to England. A testimony from the yearly meeting in Dublin described Elizabeth Ashbridge's 1753 visit to Ireland, "wherein she endured so much bodily hardship in travelling and underwent so much spiritual exercise, that she fell dangerously ill" and died at age forty-two. Her travel companion and fellow Pennsylvanian, the elderly minister Sarah Worrell, had died in Cork, Ireland, only a short time before Ashbridge's death.[48]

Guides and Transport on Land

By the eighteenth century, monthly meetings on both sides of the Atlantic appointed members to provide "Horses for Publick Friends, who come from abroad to visit Friends in this Nation." Many Quaker meetings also had an official arrangement for providing guides to visiting ministers. Philadelphia Quarterly Meeting proposed, in 1703, "that traveling ffriends may be accomodated with guides or Companions from one Meeting to another, at least untill they Come to the other Meetings in the neighbouring Countys."[49]

In America, travel conditions greatly improved between 1700 and 1775: settlements burgeoned, and connecting routes were increasingly travelled. But paths, designed for local use, were often unmarked, and travellers frequently lost their way. Voluntary assistance provided by individual Quakers to "Public Friends" who were journeying on "a labour of love" was a significant part of the preachers' ability to travel. Catharine Payton and Mary Peisley, on a religious visit to the American colonies from England and Ireland in 1753, found that their appointed guide did not receive their letters in time to meet them. They were about 120 miles from Charleston, South Carolina, where their guide was supposed to rendezvous with the preachers, and escort them to the Wateree Friends' settlement. The British women waited at the home of a kindly, non-Quaker planter. A poor Quaker, who lived between the planter and the Wateree area, fortuitously stopped by the planter's residence on his way to Charleston with goods for market. When he heard their plight, he left his load in the planter's warehouse, turned around and guided them to the settlement himself.

Even with guides, the visitors sometimes went astray. In 1705, when Esther Palmer and Mary Lawson attempted to cross the Potomac River into Virginia, they became lost: "It being dark night, & after Sunsett, we were Exposed to danger, & loosing o[u]r way we got to land, but neither ye Boatman nor Christopher Mather nor George Harris (who were ye friends yt Accompanied us out of Maryland) Knew where we were." Without any knowledge of their location, the women were forced to camp outside overnight: "We gott through Mercy to Shore & made a Comfortable Fire being very Easy in our minds, we were fain [content] to Continue theer till Morning it raining Sometimes upon us: Blessed be ye Lord he delivered us that night from Eminent [imminent] danger." Occasionally no Friends would be available as guides and a "stranger" would be hired. While visiting Virginia, in 1698, Elizabeth Webb noted, "Eliza. Loyd and Ii hired a man and 2 horses and went to Edward tomas his hous[e]." Unpredictable circumstances forced the women to be enterprising, even travelling, at times, without a guide. In 1723, Susanna Morris and her companion, Ann Roberts, were shipwrecked on a sandbar while crossing the Chesapeake Bay on a religious visit to Maryland, Virginia, and North Carolina. After retrieving their horses who were bruised in the storm (Morris's horse died after they arrived in North Carolina), the two Pennsylvania women rode "between sixty and one hundred miles" to Friends' settlements, with "no guide for us but the Holy One."[50]

Travelling Companions

Except in areas where few Friends lived, the extended Quaker community assisted the female preachers in overcoming such traditional limitations of gender as physical vulnerability, and accusations of licentiousness because of the women's public activity. A number of Quakers might accompany the travelling ministers for stages of a journey. When Elizabeth Hudson was escorted by Friends in New Jersey, the size of their group created difficulty in getting lodging, "their being no publick Houses [inns] on this Road And our Number too large for a private one."[51]

Mary Weston rode through the New England woods in the 1750s with "13 [Quakers] in Company." At that time, "the Canada Indians were very busy in these Eastern parts wounding and taking Captives all they could lay their Hands on, so that most people were gone into Garrison . . . and none dare to walk or ride without Arms," except for the intrepid Quaker travellers. The soberly dressed figures, passing through the countryside unarmed, were an amazing sight to inhabitants who wondered at their foolishness or courage. The New England colonists concluded that "we were very bold to go through the Woods at that time," expecting that "every Soul of us [would] be cut off." Weston noted that there "was plenty of Wolves and Bears, which made a hidious Noise," and affirmed that her party had been preserved by kind Providence.[52]

Ministers were escorted through hazardous country, at times, by means of a fluctuating human chain composed of both men and women going some distance away from their residences, with small groups detaching themselves and returning home to be replaced by new companions for the next stage. When Moses Brown, a convert to Quakerism in Providence, Rhode Island, was asked to escort Mary Leaver, an English visitor, through New England in 1774, Brown agreed, because "when Friends come 3000 miles on religious visits alone, and are infirm and weakly they need every assistance and incouragement to make their journeying comfortable, as deep and trying times often attend them."[53]

Sometimes the voluntaristic system of the Quakers broke down, especially if worldly affairs took precedence over religious service. Ann Moore described a lapse when she crossed the Susquehanna River in Pennsylvania "but no friends with us. I seemed to think the Friends, so-called, where we lodged at the ferry were too rich in the things of this world to have any time to go with us." But, typically, there was a remarkable level of participation by both sexes. Although Mary Weston had arrived from England with no ministerial companion, she never travelled alone in the American colonies. Quaker companions were collected en route before Weston entered the New England woods. After Weston parted "with our kind Frds E Dean and Daughter, who attended us all the way from Salem," she went to "Berwick 11 Miles calling at Joseph Verney's whose Wife Abigail rode with us to John Morrell's, who with his Wife joined the rest of our Company next day to conduct us through the Woods to Biddeford."[54]

British travellers to the American colonies confronted a greater variety of circumstances than their American counterparts who toured Great Britain, but American visitors found that they were similarly escorted by local Quakers. Deborah Morris, travelling in England in 1772 with her aunt, Sarah Morris, a Philadelphia preacher (who had accompanied

Rachel Wilson on her 1768–69 American tour), wrote: "Our kind friend J. Dickeson, went with us as far as Market-Weighton, 10 miles, where we dined and he left us to the other kind Friends who see us safely to York, where William [Tuke] and his kind wife received us like parents . . . [at Otley] we found R[achel] Wilson [the English preacher], son John and daughter Rachel, who came on purpose to accompany us to Settle, and then to Kendal, Our good friend T[homas] Corbyn was also in company, and Thomas Hull, of Uxbridge."[55]

The female itinerant minister was a constant, visible reminder that being a member of the "weaker sex" was not a release from public service or travel. The example of women travellers from abroad inspired other Quaker women, even those who were not preachers, to new travel activity. When Susanna Morris was temporarily without a companion to visit Ireland in 1730 from Whitehaven, England, she saw a Quaker woman in a meeting who, "although not a minister . . . mourned for the abomination of the times." The Englishwoman, agreeing to accompany Morris, had "kept a school for children, but had put it by the week before, but knew not why until I came, and had no companion to go with me across the sea." Mary Pemberton, the wife of Israel Pemberton Jr. of Philadelphia, miles away from her accustomed surroundings as a result of escorting Mary Weston, wrote to her brother-in-law from New York ("Perhaps thou may think it Strange that I who have never been so far from home before this time, Should date a Letter from this Place, But being here on Account of Accompanying our ffrd Mary Weston so far on her Journey to New England . . .").[56]

Although many Quakers might escort a preacher for a few miles, only one person of the same gender would be recognized as an official companion. This Friend, chosen carefully by the preacher on the basis of a spiritual affinity, would travel with the minister for a substantial section of the trip. The role existed not so much for purposes of safety (male ministers travelled in pairs as well) but for spiritual assistance: usually so the burden of religious service did not rest entirely on one preacher in the course of a journey. Susanna Hatton was advised: "Be not hasty to embrace the offer of any companion in service try their spirits and feel the liberty of truth in it." The companion, in most cases, was another "Public Friend." Rachel Wilson did not have a female companion when she left England for America: "I was very Low Vewing My own Weakness in the Lon[e]ly Sittation

Deprived of all outward helps to Bear a part in the work by Publick testimony."[57] Ministers often tested the authenticity of their "leadings" with each other: if another spiritually gifted person felt a similar "opening," it could be a confirmation of the message's divine origin.

The companion shared a "concern" to visit the same areas. When their "concerns" led in different directions, they parted company amiably. The arrival of a visiting minister frequently sparked a local minister's "drawings" to travel. When Rachel Wilson reached Fairfax, Virginia, on her tour of the American colonies she found "at this place our fr[ien]d Sarah Janney Lived who had bin under an ingagement for sometime to pay a Religious Visit to the Southern parts that when she heard of my Coming it Revived the Concern and as my Dear fr[ien]d Sarah Morris [the Philadelphia preacher] did not find Strength to go forward it ap[p]e[a]red to Me Providential to have a Companion so agre[e]able provided under the same ingagement with whom fr[ien]ds was so well Satisfied that she had a Certificate." "Giving up" to accompany another minister on a trip could entail great sacrifice. In North Carolina, Catharine Payton temporarily parted with Mary Peisley, and a local minister, Rebecca Tombs, volunteered to ride with Payton. The extremely cold weather affected Tombs so severely that she died before they could return to her family.[58]

Various stages of a transatlantic visitor's circuit of a nation might be accomplished with successive companions, who were regional preachers on "concerns." Rachel Wilson was joined by Esther Fisher and Sarah Morris from Philadelphia in the Middle Colonies; Sarah Janney of Fairfax, Virginia, travelled with her through the South; Sarah Hopkins of New Jersey accompanied Wilson on a tour of New England. This activity created an interregional network of women ministers. Sometimes an accompanying preacher would return with the visiting Quaker to her country of origin to pay a reciprocal ministerial visit, as did Jane Fenn of Chester, Pennsylvania, following a trip through the colonies with the Irish preacher Abigail Boles.

Often, deep bonds were formed when women journeyed together "in gospel labour." Mary Weston wrote of her Irish ministerial companion, Mary Peisley, when they toured England: "shou'd think it a blessing to have her continualy with me; we travelled above 1500 Miles together, & the longer I was with her the harder it was to part. . . ." Friendships also were formed with male preachers who travelled with the women on ships or attended the same meetings. Regardless of gender, Quaker preachers watched over each other's growth in religion. When Lydia Lancaster gave religious advice to Samuel Fothergill, she wrote: "Thou willt bear with me as an old friend . . . my love to thee runs parallel with that of my own Soul . . . farewell my friend & Brother in the nearest Kindred."[59]

Travel Accommodations

On Elizabeth Wilkinson's trip to America in 1761, she recalled that "when we came to anchor [in Philadelphia] many Friends came on board to invite us to lodge with them. . . ." "Weighty Friends," those people very active in the Quaker organization, such as elders and ministers, were particularly attuned to aiding the travellers. When Jane Fenn landed in Bristol, England, in 1727, she was "kindly Receiv'd by Friends there, and Lodged at Richard Champions [widower of the American minister, Esther Palmer Champion]." When Ann Moore arrived in London, England, John Hunt, the merchant and member of the Meeting for Sufferings, "kindly invited me home with him and to make his house my home when in the city; which kind offer I accepted and went with him to their morning meeting."[60] Men like Henry Gouldney of London, Richard Champion of Bristol, Israel Pemberton Jr. of Philadelphia, and Joseph Pike of Cork, who were simultaneously leaders in the Society of Friends and prominent traders well positioned in the ports, frequently hosted visiting ministers.

Preachers met with vastly different conditions while travelling and they were "to be Content & thankfull for Such Entertainment as they meet withall among friends." Since eighteenth-century Friends included politically powerful Newport merchants in Rhode Island as well as struggling farmers in the Carolina backcountry, Quaker accommodations could range from Governor Stephen Hopkins's country seat in Rhode Island to a poor Friend's cabin. The women ministers' socioeconomic status might be opposite to that of their hosts, but travelling preachers were honored guests as "the Lord's servants"; therefore, they were introduced to new circumstances, whether of poverty or wealth. In cities such as London and Philadelphia, where there were large numbers of Quakers, ministers often were invited to stay with prosperous Friends in the district. David Barclay, a wealthy linen draper and merchant, hosted many ministers, at "one of the finest houses in Cheapside opposite the Church of St Mary Le Bow" in London. Israel Pemberton Jr.'s formal Italianate garden was considered to be a showplace of Philadelphia "with a number of evergreens, carefully clipped into pyramidal and conical forms."[61]

The luxurious hospitality offered by rich Pennsylvania Quaker merchants sometimes disturbed the religious travellers. Elizabeth Wilkinson, a reformist minister from the simpler surroundings of rural northern England, cautioned Anthony Morris and his family in 1763 against competing socially with "the Grandeur of their Houses, Tables, Entertainment, &ca." When Elizabeth Wilkinson fell ill with a fever in Burlington, New Jersey, she lodged for several days at John Smith's elaborate estate, acknowledging that Smith was "a great Man being One of the Governors Council yet a good Friend, where no Care or Endeavours for my recovery . . . was awanting." The preachers' status as spiritual counsellors allowed them to form liaisons that transcended such social differences. After returning to her more modest residence in the English countryside, Elizabeth Wilkinson continued to correspond with John Smith's daughter, offering religious advice, although Wilkinson acknowledged that "our Stations in Life is so widely different."[62]

Much of Quaker hospitality was reciprocal. While Mary Weston was hosted at the Philadelphia residence of Israel Pemberton Jr. on her visit to the colonies in 1750, John Pemberton, her landlord's brother and the younger son of the Pemberton family, was travelling on religious service in England. Weston wrote to her husband remaining behind in England, "pray my Dearest take Notice of their son John now w[i]th you. . . ." Catharine Payton and Mary Peisley lodged at John Churchman's house in Pennsylvania. Churchman "was not yet returned from a [ministerial] visit to Friends in England; but his wife and son gladly received us," noted the British female visitors. Itinerant ministers sought out the homes of Friends who earlier had made religious visits to their areas, reversing their host/ guest roles. On her tour of America in 1768–69, Rachel Wilson stayed at the residence of William Shipley in Wilmington, renewing her acquaintance with his wife Elizabeth (Levis) Shipley (who had journeyed in the ministry to England in 1744). Rachel Wilson also lodged with the minister Susanna Lightfoot, who previously had travelled in England. Wilson noted, "As I had not seen her for 14 years it was truly pleasant to Meet in the Love which first united in Gospel Labour." Abiah Darby, a travelling minister and the wife of Abraham Darby II, owner of the Coalbrookdale Iron Works in England, frequently hosted preachers at her home. In a sample of a few months in 1748, the Darbys entertained the Quaker ministers Benjamin Holme, Ebenezer Large of New Jersey, John Millard, John Burton of Yorkshire, Alice Alderson of Westmorland, Sarah Routh, and Catharine Payton of Worcestershire.[63]

Hosting the travellers was an act of religious devotion for Quakers, and ministers often had to choose between competing invitations. The Society of Friends encouraged voluntary hospitality: "We doubt not y[ou]r tender reception of them therein & y[ou]r Christian care towards them in any thing yt may be necessary or convenient for their furtherance in their Travells as you find cause." A scriptural model cited was 2 Kings 4:9–10, in which a chamber is made for a frequent passerby who is a holy man of God. The Quaker sojourners were viewed not only as unpaid fellow laity, but as messengers sent by God. The possibility of receiving spiritual consolation was an additional incentive for providing accommodations, as preachers usually had a "setting" in the evening with their host's family. There was a continuity of surnames of Quakers in particular areas who hosted visiting ministers year after year. Elizabeth Webb, on a trip in 1698, had lodged with Jane Pleasants, widow of John, in Curles, Virginia. In 1732, Alice Alderson and Margaret Copeland stayed with Thomas Pleasants at Curles while visiting the southern colonies. When Mary Weston made a trip to Goochland, Virginia, in 1751, she visited another Pleasants brother who had recently moved to "that new settled place . . . many of us lay in his little Loghouse."[64]

Jane Fenn, like most itinerant Quaker ministers, rode extra miles when no Quakers lived in the towns where she was preaching in Great Britain, in order to lodge at a Friend's house. But Quaker ministers following "inward leadings" could not always be hosted by Friends. At times, women preachers travelling in the American wilderness had to be satisfied with "lodging in the woods in cold frosty weather, on damp ground." Mary Peisley described camping in the Carolina backwoods: "At night have slept contentedly in my riding clothes, on a bed hard enough to make my bones ache." Peisley wrote of "a rheumatic pain" in her "jaws and head" that had resulted from sleeping on wet ground with insufficient warmth. The preachers, like other travellers, also stayed in the homes of hospitable non-Quakers, or stopped at inns. In North Carolina, Mary Peisley wrote, "We were often kindly entertained, according to their ability, at the houses of those not of our Society. . . ." In the southern colonies, the women sometimes lodged at the residence of the local justice or sheriff, who "treated us very Kindley." Such accommodations could prove to be evangelical opportunities, as the preachers engaged in religious discussions with their hosts. In Kent County (Delaware), Esther Palmer and her companion stayed with the Robsons, who escorted the preachers to their meeting at the courthouse the next day. The couple, deeply affected by the travellers' testimonies, were "Much brocken [broken] and very tender & pres[s]ed us to visit them again."[65]

For the traveller in "the service of Truth," eighteenth-century public lodgings were often inadequate as well as costly. When a minister had a "concern" to preach where no Quakers lived, as Ann Moore did in "that wicked city of Albany," New York, in 1758, she found that her money ran out quickly. Although Moore felt directed by God to stay longer, "it was so expensive that we could not if we intended to get home." An unexpected encounter with a Quaker acquaintance produced the necessary funds. On another trip to the British forts, Moore returned to the haven of the nearest Quaker settlement to garner spiritual and material support before starting out again on her perceived duty. The New York Friends "provided several things for us to subsist on by the way. Everything in that part of the country being so very unreasonable dear. . . ." Inns were not reliable; they often had squalid conditions. While visiting America in 1750, Mary Weston arrived at "a nasty dirty house call'd an Ordinary, where was obliged to lodge but got little Sleep for Fleas and Bugs and scarce anything we could eat." Weston was relieved when she came within Quaker "territory" again. "However, the next Day got as far as Lancaster . . . and were joyfully received by our Friends Peter Worrell and Wife, having comfortable Lodging."[66]

Communication During Travel

Eighteenth-century Quaker religious travellers benefitted from the systems developed for business—not only shipping routes, but also lines of credit and channels of communication. Members of the Fisher family (the Philadelphia Quakers who owned the ship that had transported Rachel Wilson to America) accompanied Wilson on sections of her journey and arranged accommodations en route through their mercantile contacts.

When Rachel Wilson neared Charleston, South Carolina, she noted, "a Merchant over took us who having heard of us by our kind frd Joseph Fisher & son tould us his partner John Coran Expected us to lodg[e] with him."[67]

The merchant, Israel Pemberton Jr., facilitated communications for the travelling preachers he hosted. During Mary Weston's American visit, Pemberton maintained a regular correspondence with her husband in London. Daniel Weston wrote to Pemberton, "I observe thy kind offer to forward letters that may come in her Absence as also to Advise me therein when Opp[ortunit]y. Offer. . . ." As a trader with a network of correspondents, Pemberton was able to keep Daniel Weston informed of his wife's health and movements. As Mary Weston's Philadelphia landlord, Pemberton had her mail directed to him, forwarding it to her during her travels around the colonies. The travelling preacher wrote to Pemberton frequently, advising him of her next destination. When Pemberton received news from his London correspondents about the health of Mary Weston's family, he relayed this to her as well. Mary Weston also relied on her Philadelphia host to send extra articles of clothing for changing weather conditions: "Should be glad of a pair of Cloth shoes if Could be Conveniently conveyed . . . I am oblidged to ye My good ffrd for sending my other Garment . . . like shall want it soon for ye weather grows Cold in these parts."[68]

In addition to acting as postmasters, merchants sometimes functioned as bankers for the ministers. Daniel Weston requested of James Pemberton, during his wife's sojourn in America, "If by any Accident or otherwise She Shou[l]d want any Cash more than She'l be furnished with from the Sale of her little Venture, I request thy further Aid therein, for which thyne or her Draft Shall be duly paid here." Transatlantic ministers, like Mary Weston, sometimes had a small "adventure" (or Venture)—the sale of which would help finance their travels. (It was profitable for transatlantic voyagers to travel with a few saleable goods since, as passengers, their articles were freight-free.) John Sinclair, a Charleston, South Carolina, mercantile correspondent of James Pemberton, alerted to Mary Weston's intended visit, left an invitation for her to lodge at his house. Later, in a business letter to James Pemberton, John Sinclair showed the effects of Daniel Weston's instructions. Sinclair noted to Pemberton that Mary Weston "wants 20 Ster[ling] w[hi]ch I shall pay her & draw on you for. . . ."[69]

The Society of Friends effectively used communications, as well, to maximize the impact of a preacher's visit, while contending with the shifting directions of inwardly guided ministers' itineraries. Yorkshire (England) Quarterly Meeting advised Friends, in 1714, that when any travelling minister came to the area to send "Notice to other Meetings with Speed . . . And that upon such notice friends in every Meeting doe as generally as they Can Come up to such meetings as maybe appoynted by such travelling Friends . . . that travelling Friends Labour and Service may not be Slighted." Quaker meetings paid for express riders to notify Friends of itinerant preachers' sudden appointments of meetings for worship: "pd. ye Express yt went to Killconner to give notice of Betty Beal & Betty Taylor haveing a Meeting there."[70]

Travel Schedule

The ministers pushed themselves physically on their journeys with a near-daily pattern of travel. Convinced that they were on a mission from a Master to whom they would eventually have to give an accounting, the Quaker preachers were spurred on by a kind of urgency, wanting no undone task on their consciences. God had sent them as messengers "over Sea & Land to call to the Inhabitants of the World to come to Repentance & amendment of Life: & whether they would hear or forbear he would get him honour through his Servants & Messengers & would be clear of the Blood of all."[71] Rather than travelling from a central place of accommodation, the ministers tended to move each day, lodging at different locations almost every night. The longest period that Jane Crosfield remained in one place (besides Philadelphia which was her headquarters when not out on the road) was a week at Governor Stephen Hopkins's "Country house" in Rhode Island.

August 11, 1750, was an ordinary day on Mary Weston's journey, and one that could be taken as representative of most Quaker itinerants' schedules (although in sparsely settled areas a preacher rode farther in a day). On that day, Weston rode eight miles to Bethpage on Long Island for a meeting. Weston preached for about an hour, despite the hot weather. She noted that "the extreme heat of the Season overcame many—I could scarce keep from Fainting divers times in the Meeting, yet it was my Lot to stand near an Hour, being supported far beyond my Expectation with Divine Strength."[72] After dining at a Friend's home, Weston rode five miles to Jerusalem, where she stopped briefly at another Quaker residence. Then Weston continued eight more miles to her lodgings at Westbury.

The length of stay in a community was determined, in part, by the minister's health. Elizabeth Hudson spent some weeks in Bristol, England, "recruiting—hav[in]g tired her horse & almost worn herself out by pushing too hard." Weather conditions also affected the trip timetable. Mary Weston wrote to her husband about her journey from Philadelphia, "We are hastening to ye furdest part of New England as fast as we Can, ye Season being so Extream hott here and a sickly time. . . ." But travel often seemed to be in spite of seasonal cycles, rather than adapted to them. Jane Crosfield passed through Massachusetts in midwinter and through the southern colonies in midsummer. Ann Moore journeyed to Schenectady, New York, in January and early February of 1758 through deep snow. Her non-Quaker landlady said to her, "I wonder how you could bear to travel in such weather. It must be for some extraordinary thing." "Yes," Moore responded, "it is for the Lord's sake."[73]

The primary external factor that shaped the ministers' trip schedule was the chronology of established meetings. A five-day sample of Jane Fenn's activities during her journey in the British Isles illustrates what was typical for a travelling Quaker preacher:

> First Day, went to Clonmell, was at their two Meetings for Worship, Lodged at Daniel Wyly's this was 9 Miles   Second Day, at their Meetings for Worship & Discipline   Third Day, went to Killcommon, had a Meeting in Joshua Fennell's House, which was to Good Satisfaction, this Night went to John Boles [residence of Irish preacher, Abigail Boles] wch. was 15 Miles. Fourth Day, no Meeting, wrote Letters to Pennsylvania &c Fifth Day, went to Cashel, was at the Burial of an Ancient Friend. . . .[74]

No timetable was enforced upon the ministers. But Quakers were well aware of the potential dangers of itinerancy: the travelling ministry was not to be confused with vagabondage. Catharine Payton had to fend off charges that she travelled "to gratify a roving or curious disposition." After almost three years in the colonies, Payton's stay in America "was considerably longer than usual for Friends who visit it from Europe . . . but quite in the unity of the sensible body of Friends, who saw that we were industriously engaged in the service . . . to accomplish the duties assigned me, in as short time as I could."[75] Most transatlantic visitors spent from one to four years on their journeys.

Another reason for a fairly constant pace of movement was to avoid imposing upon Friends' hospitality. Ministers were warned to "be carefull not to Make Their Visit burthensome, nor the Gospel Chargeable To any friends." An indication of what was considered an excessive stay is found in a complaint about a minister who visited Cork, Ireland, in 1743. The journey of Elizabeth Smith (an English preacher from Norfolk) had been problematic from the beginning. Smith had been bound for the Isle of Man when her ship was blown off course from the destination listed on her travel certificate. Arriving in Ireland, Smith received permission from Irish Friends to visit meetings in their country. Smith already had been away from home two years and spent two more years travelling in Ireland. Irish Quakers complained that "her stay being so long & tedious in places, (in some one, in some two, & in others 3 months in each place) made Frds uneasy—tho' she is a weakly young Woman, yet does not seem so much Naturally, as by too Indulgent Methods used."[76]

But ministers also were cautioned against hurrying too quickly through their visits in their haste to return to their families. They were advised to wait for "divine guidance." After Esther Palmer had finished a tour of the southern colonies with Mary Lawson, she still did not find herself "clear" of Maryland and Virginia. Believing that she had further religious service to perform there, Palmer returned south with another companion, Mary Bannister, receiving the meeting's approval. The Irish preacher Mary Peisley exemplified the extreme quietist stance, not wanting to mix any human will with the "divine inspiration" to minister. "My stay being prolonged in this country, has been altogether unexpected to myself," Peisley wrote to her relatives in Ireland, "and I have been held in such uncertainty for some months past, as not to be able to give my friends any information respecting future movements. I have stood as a soldier waiting for the word of command, to march whithersoever my holy leader may be pleased to direct. . . ." Only an inner sense dictated whether one had completed one's service; in Peisley's words, "hoping from the looseness which I then felt from all parts of the [North American] continent, that I might be permitted to return home."[77]

Travel Changed the Women Ministers

In an era when most women did not journey beyond their immediate environs, Quaker female preachers were introduced to new peoples and considerations through their travels. When the women arrived on a foreign continent, they confronted experiences far beyond their domestic circle of cares, shaping new concerns. Journeying in the American colonies, many British ministers saw slaves for the first time. Elizabeth Webb, arriving in Virginia in 1697, saw "great numbers of black people that were in slavery." Never having seen Africans before, "they were a strange people" to Webb and she "wanted to know whether the visitation of God was to their souls or not." Later Webb had a dream that satisfied her that "the call of the Lord was unto the black people as well as the white" and she realized that they were among the people to whom she was to preach. For overseas visitors especially, "the poor Indians the Natives of America" were a focus of interest. While visiting Philadelphia from England, in 1761, Elizabeth Wilkinson, for example, was informed about some Christianized Indians and immediately wanted to confer with them: "Understanding there are many of the Friendly Indians come to Town I had a desire this day to speak with them."[78]

As the itinerant ministers escaped women's customary domestic insularity, their knowledge increased with exposure to the range of conditions in the colonies and in Europe. Ann Moore of Maryland, put ashore unexpectedly in Spain, discovered that the Spanish workingmen's wages were far below American standards, "For we learned by traveling in that country that men had but a shilling a day. . . ." Interested in the different flora and fauna on the American continent, Elizabeth Wilkinson arranged to have rattlesnake skins sent back to England. American travellers to the British Isles, like Elizabeth Hudson, were impressed by historic antiquities they saw, but particularly the sites they had read about which were associated with early Quaker martyrdom and missionary activity. Deborah Morris, not a preacher, but a companion on Sarah Morris's religious visit to England, was affected by seeing Pardshaw Crag, Cumberland, where "the first rise of Friends in these parts" met under a great rock cleft on top of a very high hill. "This place I had often heard of, but never expected to see it."[79]

There were lasting effects from these women's travel experiences. After Abigail Boles returned to Ireland from her visit to America in 1725, she ordered books, including *A History of the Indians,* presumably to deepen her understanding of the Native Americans she had first encountered on her tour abroad. The observations made by Catharine (Payton) Phillips, while riding across England, spurred her to write *Considerations on the Causes of the High Price of Grain,* a treatise advocating agricultural reform. "An attentive observer," she wrote, "in travelling over this nation, must see, that the improvement of waste land, and making the best of commons in their uninclosed state, is very condemnably neglected."[80] When the women returned to their own places of residence, as seasoned travellers, they carried the authority of firsthand experience of other regions, as well as the friendships they had formed with companions, hosts, and others along the way.

Journeying with Friends from diverse locales created interregional acquaintances for women who, when not travelling on religious service, might be separated by the duties of independent households. Following a trip in the ministry with Tabitha Hornor of Leeds, England, Abigail Boles of Ireland maintained a correspondence with her for over twenty years. Hornor called Boles "my dear mother; & Sister in true fellowship & labour of the Gospel," referring to their love as "passing the love of Women, purely seraphic, & will I hope reach beyond the grave, into that center of holy Joy, which is indivisible." The lifelong importance of these bonds of friendship formed by women's "gospel labours" was also evident in the will of Sarah Morris, an unmarried Philadelphia preacher. The bulk of Morris's estate went to her brother, but she bequeathed sums to eight women ministers from different regions, listed as "esteemed friends." Among the preachers remembered in the Pennsylvania woman's will were Ann Moore of Maryland, Elizabeth Smith of New Jersey, and Martha Petell of Massachusetts. If Sarah's brother predeceased her, Sarah Morris's estate was to descend to her unmarried niece, Deborah Morris, who had served as a companion on her religious visit overseas.[81]

Hundreds of Quaker women were regularly traversing the colonies and/or the British Isles in the eighteenth century. The Quaker community's faith in the potential access of all humans to the Inward Light enabled them to approve travel initiated by women's "inward leadings." Eighteenth-century Friends provided remarkable logistical assistance for female, as well as male, ministers' journeys. The mystical vision of a transatlantic community, unified in the Spirit, was given practical support by the Quaker organization and the enterprise of Quaker merchants. Ministers could sail in Quaker-owned ships, lodge in Quaker homes, and ride in the company of other Friends. Quaker women's sphere of activity was altered by their efforts "in the service of Truth," creating repercussions that extended well beyond their participation in religious meetings.

Four

"DUTIFUL WIVES, TENDER MOTHERS": THE FAMILY ROLES OF THE WOMEN MINISTERS

I SUPPOSE your Welch [Welsh] Warriors have Enter[e]d the feild [field] again," Mary Weston wrote to Israel Pemberton Jr., in March 1753. Weston was referring to a female preacher who had recently given birth, Margaret Lewis (of Welsh ancestry), and her travel companion, the Welsh-born Margaret Ellis. In June 1752, the two American Quaker women ministers had sailed from the colonies, preparing to journey on "Truth's account" through England and Wales. Margaret Lewis had been "sickly most part of the time" during the five-week Atlantic crossing. After departing Philadelphia, Lewis had discovered belatedly that she was two months' pregnant. Mary Weston (herself recently returned from a religious visit to America) hosted the American visitors when they arrived in London. Weston observed that Lewis (a mother of nine children) "seem'd much discouraged at first about it but is now rather Easier. . . ."[1]

In spite of being "4 months gone w[i]th. Child, a tiresome unpleasant Condition to Travel in in that Mountainous Country [of Wales]," Lewis and Margaret Ellis had set off as planned from London, in August 1752. Accompanied by Quaker parliamentary lobbyist Richard Partridge, they preached in the English Midlands and then moved into the rugged mountains of Wales. Passing through Denbighshire, Merionethshire (Ellis's birthplace), Montgomeryshire, and Radnorshire, the preachers held meetings in town halls, inns, and Friends' houses. In spite of Margaret Lewis's pregnancy, her ministry was "well receiv'd both here and else where. . . ." The expectant mother maintained a strenuous schedule, comparable to that of any itinerant minister, until two months prior to delivery. Then the female preachers settled into Quaker lodgings at Bristol, England, to await the baby's arrival, while Richard Partridge returned to London. In January 1753, Lewis gave birth to "a brave Boy," as certified by a midwife and six other women (the attendants present at an eighteenth-century childbirth).[2]

From London, Mary Weston relayed news of the women's movements to Quakers in colonial America. She noted that Margaret Lewis had been "hinder'd very little* [written in margin: "*from traveling"] by her Circumstance." Indeed, the "Welsh Warriors" began journeying again two months after Lewis's lying-in. Certificates of unity with Lewis's "Testimony for the Truth" reveal that she attended the Welsh annual meeting, as well as London gatherings, after the delivery of her baby. Not until Margaret Lewis's ministerial "Labour of Love" was completed did mother and child make the long Atlantic voyage home. The child, Peter Lewis, was almost two years old at the end of 1754 when he first met his father, Nathan Lewis, a prosperous, devout Quaker farmer of Chester County, Pennsylvania.[3]

A spiritually "gifted" woman in the Society of Friends could pursue her ministerial "calling" without renouncing marriage or motherhood. In contrast to a Catholic nun, the Quaker woman who dedicated herself to obeying God's will was not expected to withdraw from the world and remain celibate. Reforming Protestants had rejected Catholic religious celibacy, arguing that: when God created Adam and Eve, He had "Solemnized the First Marriage that ever was."[4] As radical Protestants, Quakers did not require such extreme asceticism to rise above "inferior" nature. Female, as well as male, Quaker preachers overcame their carnal selves, not by denying their gendered identities or procreative capacities, but by speaking from the Inward Light. Since Quaker female preachers were accepted as both biological creatures and spiritual vessels, their activities as divinely chosen "instruments" brought about redefinitions of familial roles.

Marriage Patterns

While nearly all of the female transatlantic ministers married, these eighteenth-century Quaker women, as a result of heeding their "inward guide," displayed a striking independence in their decisions regarding marriage. "I had several offers of marriage, some appeared likely, but I did not see it my way for some years, & thought one great concern was enough to bear . . . ," wrote Abigail Craven, the Irish preacher, who married at age thirty-five. Catharine Payton, who married at forty-five, observed, "My mind had been, and was under strong restrictions in regard to entering into the marriage state, should I be solicited thereto; for as it appeared that for a series of years I should be much engaged in travelling for the service of Truth, I feared to indulge thoughts of forming a connection, which, from its incumbrances, might tend to frustrate the intention of Divine wisdom respecting me." Mary Peisley proceeded with utmost caution toward the opposite sex, because she worried that "my own affections and the affections of others, would . . . have stolen me out of His hands, who has an absolute right to dispose of my body and spirit, which are His," not marrying until she was thirty-nine years old. Quaker parental permission was required for marriage but, reversing the relatively progressive Puritan procedure in which children were allowed a veto over marriage arranged by their parents, Quaker parents retained a veto only over marriages initiated by their children. Friends' belief in the individual's guidance by the Holy Spirit encouraged Quakers to respect "divine leadings" in terms of marital choice as well.[5]

A clear pattern emerged across regions, distinguishing these "chosen instruments" from their Quaker counterparts without "gifts" in the ministry. Whether in the British Isles or the American colonies, a majority of the transatlantic travellers who had begun to preach as young adults deferred marriage, marrying often ten years later than average for Quaker women. (Those who experienced a "calling" to the ministry later in life, with few exceptions, had married at ages typical of the general Quaker population.) Historians have found that the average age of first marriage for colonial American Quaker women was 22.8 years; the average age for Irish Quaker women was 24.07 years; and the average age for English Quaker women was 26.95 years.[6]

Mary Peisley had vowed "by the blessed assistance of Israel's God, not to bury that talent which He had given me. . . ."[7] As Peisley's biblical allusion (Matt. 25:14–30) indicated, the female preachers were concerned for their own salvation, as well as for the salvation of the world, and were determined to avoid being "unprofitable servants." The women's belief that they had received invaluable "gifts" in the ministry prompted them to make the exercise of these "gifts" a central purpose in their lives. The overwhelming nature of the "calling" (the spiritual, physical, and emotional reserves required to fulfill divine directives) contributed to the delay of many women in marrying. Fearing that emotional entanglements would distract from their religious service, weakening their capacity to lay down their lives for His sake, and, in particular, that romantic love would distract from love of the Creator, many women ministers deferred involvements.

In addition, eighteenth-century Quaker women ministers were more fearful, perhaps, about their ability to heed an inward "calling" after marriage because of their legally required obedience to spouses. There was also concern that the attendant responsibilities of marriage, such as household tasks and childbearing, would interfere with ministerial travel. Although all Quakers were obligated to find marriage partners of the same faith to avoid being "unequally yoked," for the female preachers, shared membership in the Society was not necessarily enough to risk marriage. Catharine Payton hesitated to marry a man, in spite of his Quaker affiliation, because she "doubted his having advanced in religion, so as to render a nearer union with him safe." Among Payton's considerations in choosing a marriage partner was "his sympathy with my religious engagements."[8]

A woman might legitimately remain single or defer marriage, within the Society of Friends, because of Quaker recognition that another "calling" for women existed beyond their function in the family. The women's service in spreading the message of "Truth" was as valuable as their familial duties, and preachers were encouraged to place a priority on their spiritual vocation. Although itinerant ministers met many Quakers on their journeys, John Alderson, a preacher himself, advised them "not to think of marriage till their errand was finished, lest they mar their service." John Alderson's own mother, Alice, had crossed the Atlantic on religious service, not marrying until age thirty-nine. When Mary Fyfield, an English preacher, had received a certificate for a "concern" to travel but then placed marriage ahead of her service to God, she met with Friends' disapproval. "I have understood that previous to uniting in marriage with Owen she [Mary

Fyfield] had obtained a certificate in order to visit our American churches, but which that event [her marriage] prevented the accomplishment. . . . She therefore sunk in the esteem of those who thought they saw in an abatement of fervour a dimunition of her gift in the ministry," wrote James Jenkins, an eighteenth-century Quaker observer.[9]

The Ministers' Spouses

Yet the same God who could guide women into the ministry could also indicate, through "inward promptings" of the Spirit, those men to whom they would be "rightly joined in marriage." As Susanna Lightfoot lay dying, the elderly preacher told her husband, "I desire thou may give me up cheerfully as thou can into the hands of him whom we have reason to believe brought us together." In their choice of marriage partners, as in every decision, the women ministers sought to know God's will. Catharine Payton worried about "the injurious consequences which might ensue . . . should our affections be engaged contrary to the Divine will." She concluded that it was safest to relinquish the correspondence she had maintained with a male friend, "hoping, that if Divine wisdom designed a nearer union betwixt us, he would prepare my friend to be a suitable helpmate for me." In an extreme example of reluctance to act without the conviction that the marriage was divinely sanctioned, Payton waited twenty-three years after her first acquaintance with William Phillips until her "way opened clearly" to the accomplishment of the marriage.[10]

The Quaker marriage procedure (requiring presentation of the couple's intention to marry at two monthly meetings, an investigation into their clearness from other engagements, and parental consent) encouraged unhurried contemplation of the marital decision. At every step, ministers of either gender carefully focussed inward, evaluating the spiritual correctness of the possible connection. The preacher Samuel Neale had "long had a prospect of an union with my beloved friend and sister in the faith of the Lord Jesus, Mary Peisley," but to verify that "my dependence was not on my own judgment in this weighty undertaking," Neale first mentioned his intentions to some relatives and Quaker elders. Their unity with Neale's proposal strengthened his belief "that the God of my life was pleased therewith, and that it was in his counsel, who had often united our spirits. . . ." Yet Neale continued to test the merit of this potential union.

After a visit to Peisley, Neale "concluded to return home in obedience to an impulse or draft of spirit which I felt secretly to draw me, and not to urge my dear friend to appear at the next monthly meeting [to present our marriage]." After being "thoughtful and down in spirit by intervals," Neale gradually felt "conscious of having followed the dictates of what I thought my safest guide." Neale and Peisley then appeared before two monthly meetings: "a solemn enjoyment of divine peace and love attended our spirits, which centred them in calmness and serenity."[11]

George Fox had set a precedent for Quakers by justifying his marriage to fifty-five-year-old Margaret Fell as a spiritual union, not one whose aim was simply procreation. Age (and childbearing) was less important when wives were religious assets who could assist men on their journey to spiritual salvation. As spiritually talented individuals, the women ministers were considered valuable helpmeets for those seeking to lead religious lives. Samuel Fothergill, for example, had been struggling with his religious development when, at twenty-three, he married Susanna Croudson, a thirty-eight-year-old Quaker preacher. After his marriage, Fothergill's brother attributed "his quick and steady progress" to the ministerial wife's "watchful, affectionate concern for him." Samuel Neale had been another wayward Quaker who reformed into a pious minister, marrying at age twenty-eight to a woman twelve years his senior. When his wife, the preacher Mary Peisley, died suddenly, Neale wrote, "My loss is great: I have lost a sweet companion, a true friend, a steady counsellor, a virtuous example, a valuable instrumental pilot, and a deep and sincere sympathizer in afflictions and trials."[12]

The denial of the carnal self required in order to be spiritually obedient to God did not signify a complete absence of romantic affection in the ministers' spousal choices. "My sweetheart as well as myself desire (if it may suit thy convenience and freedom), that thou wilt favour us with thy company at our marriage," wrote Aaron Ashbridge, a wealthy Quaker farmer in Chester County, Pennsylvania, of his upcoming marriage to Elizabeth Sullivan, the thirty-three-year-old preacher. When Catharine Payton did wed after a long deferral, she emphasized that her selection of a partner "was attended with such singular circumstance, as marked its being superior to nature," but admitted that "nature had its share in it." The blend of human attraction and spiritual motives in spouse selection was recognized by Quaker ministers, as well as the need for material security. Eighteenth-century Friends did not find economic considerations irreconcilable with the desire to do God's will. When Abigail Boles proposed a match for her friend (another female preacher), she described the man as "first an Honest Religious man well Quallified for Service in the Church & well Esteemed of both by friends and Others" but also "in good [financial] Circumstances in the world."[13] Quakers tried to bridge the practical needs of daily existence with the eternal demands of the spirit.

Quaker discipline (marrying a non-Quaker could result in disownment) limited the prospective marriage partners available in a region, often forcing Friends to seek spouses in another district. "I really think there is several very valuable Young Women here," William Redwood, a Quaker merchant of Newport, Rhode Island, wrote to John Pemberton of Philadelphia in 1749, "and I wish we had young men Suitable for them, but we have not, and I believe must borrow a few Young men from your parts." Women ministers who travelled were exposed to a wider circle of marriageable Quaker men than those women who remained at home. Catharine Payton felt obligated to suggest "some caution necessary to be observed by young women in a single state, who travel in the service of the ministry, towards those of the other sex, who are also unmarried," including the evaluation of men's "motives for accompanying them." Payton warned that "when we are singularly made instruments of good, in the hands of Providence, to any soul, there is a natural aptitude to lean a little to the instrument, and to prefer it above others." A female minister who excited admiration and gratitude in those inspired by her preaching had to steer safely between dangerous extremes, to "preserve the unity of the Spirit, [while remaining] free from mixture of natural affection."[14]

Yet some women *did* marry men whom they had first encountered in their ministerial travels. Thomas Lightfoot, of Pennsylvania, served as a guide to Susanna Hatton during part of her ministerial tour of the American colonies. After the religious visit was completed, Lightfoot journeyed to Hatton's residence in Ireland, proposing marriage. Lightfoot then brought Susanna back across the Atlantic to permanently reside on his farm in the colonies. Esther Palmer, of Long Island, who wed the prominent English Friend, Richard Champion, never returned to America after journeying in the ministry, settling in Bristol. The mobility of Quaker women preachers further accentuated their independence in spousal selection, since parents, in some cases, might never meet their son-in-law. Quaker parents depended on the Quaker meeting's testimony of the prospective mate's character, but trusted mostly the internal discipline of their children adhering to the Inward Light. Joseph Cooper Jr., a Quaker elder of New Jersey, "felt his mind drawn towards" Hannah Dent, a preacher from Yorkshire, England, while she was travelling on religious service through the American colonies. Cooper proposed marriage, which Dent apparently found acceptable, sending the proposition to her parents in England and requesting her home meeting's certificate indicating her "clearness" from any other engagements. But Dent continued her ministerial travel for over eight months after the marriage proposal, not wedding Joseph Cooper Jr. until she had faithfully fulfilled "the work she had been liberated to perform," then settling in New Jersey.[15]

Quaker communities, as well as Quaker men in search of a treasured spouse, welcomed the settlement of a woman minister in their midst. When Susanna Hatton had contemplated a move from Ireland to America earlier, "divers Friends were so affected with the thoughts of her leaving them, that they contributed their cares and endeavours to get her resettled amongst them." When she eventually relocated to southern Ireland with her first husband, Joseph Hatton, her departure from Ulster was "much regretted by the religious part of Friends in that province, amongst whom she had been a bright and excellent instrument." Such "gifted vessels" often were able to marry outstanding men in the Quaker community, even if they themselves were from poor or obscure backgrounds. Susanna Hatton was an impoverished widow when Thomas Lightfoot, an affluent Quaker farmer, pursued her to Ireland in the wake of her American tour. Jane Fenn, who began her life in the colonies as an indentured servant and rose to eminence as a Quaker minister, married a prosperous Chester County Friend, Joseph Hoskins. Over half the transatlantic female preachers married men of comfortable means. Other women ministers came from well-established families, however, and simply married their socioeconomic peers. Two of the wealthiest Philadelphia families were linked when Elizabeth Hudson (who had inherited considerable estate from her grandfather) married Anthony Morris, wealthy brewer and property-holder. Morris Morris, husband of Susanna, was one of the most extensive landholders of Richland Township, Pennsylvania. Samuel Watson, second husband of Abigail Boles, was a gentleman of Killconner, Ireland, "his Circomstances . . . being very Considerable in ye world." Many preachers' spouses held leadership positions in their communities (seven husbands were assemblymen in the Middle Colonies). But meetings provided financial assistance to the struggling families of some preachers, like Comfort Hoag of New Hampshire.[16]

Marriage certificate of the Philadelphia preacher Elizabeth Hudson and Anthony Morris in 1752. The couple stood in a Quaker meeting, promising to be faithful and loving spouses to each other, with the Lord's assistance. They and their guests, including Quaker ministers Esther White, Elizabeth Shipley, and Sarah Morris, then signed the certificate. Reproduced in Robert C. Moon, *The Morris Family of Philadelphia: Descendants of Anthony Morris, 1654–1721* (Philadelphia, 1898). *Courtesy the Historical Society of Pennsylvania*

More common than wealth among the preachers' husbands was their high level of activity in the Society of Friends (either as ministers themselves or in appointed offices). Ann Roberts "met with great difficulties in respect to her outward circumstances," but her husband, Rowland Roberts, was a valued "Public Friend" in spite of "his trials arising from pecuniary losses, and limited means. . . ."[17] The most important criteria in the ministers' spousal selection were shared spiritual values. Mary Peisley, for instance, reconciled the apparent conflict between her affections and utilizing her "divinely given" talent, by marrying a man who experienced a similar "calling," the preacher Samuel Neale. At least seventeen spouses were (or became, after their marriages) Quaker ministers: Rowland Roberts, Isaac Wilson, Thomas Lightfoot, Joseph Hatton, Ruben Ellerton, James Dillworth, Samuel Neale, Daniel Morgan, Thomas Atkinson, William Biles, Joseph Hoskins, John Leaver, John White, George Gibson, Richard Waln, John Stones, and Robert Turner. Many husbands were "weighty Friends" (or church leaders), even without "gifts" in the ministry. Morris Morris served as an elder, overseer, and representative to his quarterly meeting. Joseph Cooper Jr., the husband of Hannah, was the clerk for both his monthly and quarterly meetings, as well as a representative to Philadelphia Yearly Meeting. Richard Champion, the husband of Esther, frequently hosted travelling ministers in Bristol and was a representative to London Yearly Meeting. The office of clerk of the London Yearly Meeting, the leading position in the Quaker organization, was held by two transatlantic preachers' spouses. Prior to becoming Mary Weston's second husband in 1765, Jeremiah Waring was a respected elder and clerk of the yearly meeting. After Rachel Wilson's death, her husband, Isaac, a minister, also served as clerk of the national gathering in 1778.

But not all of the preachers' spouses were exemplary Quakers. Several husbands were disowned for excessive drinking, bankruptcy, or, in one case, adultery. Ann Moore of Pennsylvania, later of Maryland, was married to a Quaker schoolteacher who was disowned in 1753 for "drinking Strong liquor to Excess." Richard Waln, the second husband of Mary Lewis, was disowned by Philadelphia Monthly Meeting for alcohol abuse. Lydia Lancaster's husband was also disowned for drunkenness and indebtedness. The meeting noted that Lydia "had a large experience in affliction being deeply tried therewith in her nearest temporal conexion. . . ."[18]

Marital Obligations of the Ministers

The Quaker marriage ceremony itself exhibited a greater gender egalitarianism than such unions in other churches. Standing in a public meeting as they exchanged identical vows, the bride and groom were equally dependent upon God. At a New England Quaker meeting-house in 1728, Stephen Harper took the hand of Eliphal Perry, a female preacher, and said, "I desire you [the Friends in attendance] to take notice that In the fear of the Lord I take this my ffriend Eliphal Perry to be my Wedded Wife promising to be a faithfull & loveing husband unto her untill Death Shall Seperate us." Then Eliphal publicly declared, "I desire you to be my Witnesses that By divine Assistance I take this my ffriend Stephen Harper to be my Husband promising to be a faithfull & loveing Wife unto him untill Itt Shall please the Lord By death to Seperate us."[19] When Mary Peisley and Samuel Neale married, a Friend aptly preached on words from the prophet Isaiah, "Thy Maker is thy husband." The sermon reflected the ministerial couple's view of their marriage as legitimized by their superseding union with the Creator.

Eighteenth-century law required that wives be obedient to their husbands, but the correct Quaker hierarchy of human love placed the Divine Being at the pinnacle. Paradoxically, this more important submission to divine authority required of a Quaker woman modified her subordination to her husband. Since Friends believed in the individual's direct access to God, an "inspired" woman experienced increased autonomy vis-à-vis her husband: "But if the Spirit of the Lord Command or move a godly and spiritually Learned Woman to Speak, in that case she is the Lord's more than her Husband's, and she is to Speak, yea, though the Husband should forbid her." There were instances when the Quaker meeting clearly supported a minister's religious service over the demands of private relations. When Jane Biles laid her "concern" to travel to England before the Philadelphia Yearly Meeting of Ministering Friends in 1700, her husband objected. He said "yt: [that] he had well weighed ye Thing & Could not find it his business to give her up to go, or to part w[i]th. her." The meeting, however, supported the wife's "divine leadings," overriding her husband's objections: "having duly weighed her Exercise concerning her going, & her Husbands opposition left her to her liberty so far as related to ye Meetings Consent therein, not being Satisfyed w[i]th. ye opposition her husband made."[20]

Under English common law, the husband had a right to his wife's sexual and housekeeping services, and a faithful wife did not stray "too much from home."[21] But within Quakerism, the capacity of women to feel "drawings" to travel on religious service affected this traditional notion of conjugal obligations. Only a few months after Ann Roberts had sailed for England on a religious visit with Mary Pennell, in July 1732, her husband, also a preacher, presented his own "concern" to journey to the same country. The Quaker meeting, however, fearing that affection for his wife was prompting the visit, postponed Rowland Roberts's case for months until they were convinced of the spiritual authenticity of his undertaking.

In Quakerism, a woman's duties to her husband were delicately balanced with her service to God, since evidence of a legitimate "calling" to the ministry included the way in which one treated family members. Two Pennsylvania preachers, husband and wife, were chastised by their meeting for disunion. A committee of Friends advised them "to Live more Loving & Affectionate towards another for time to come" because "such an unbecoming Conduct was very Disreputable in frds makeing ye Appearance they do [as Public Friends]." It was apparent that travel in the ministry was not to be a means of shirking domestic responsibilities. In 1703, an English Quaker woman moved to London, borrowed money from the meeting to set herself up in trade, and preached in the meeting. When a letter arrived from her former meeting in Wiltshire accusing her of several gross charges including "her willful absenting herself from her husband and children without her husbands Consent," she was advised to refrain from appearing in the ministry and return home to her family.[22] The Quaker meeting, preparatory to granting a certificate for a trip, whether religious or business, always asked if a spouse (whether husband or wife) consented to the journey.

Yet Quaker meeting records are filled with references to women travelling, while their husbands remained at home. The Middletown Monthly Meeting in Pennsylvania reported: "John Cowgill acquaints this Meeting that the difference between him & Robert Heaton is not [ended] by reason of his wife being absent on Truths account but says that the first opportunity after she returns . . . he will endeavour to have it ended." The Quaker preacher's ideal spouse, in a striking inversion of traditional gender roles, was memorialized in the testimony to Rachel Wilson's husband: "His wife was much engaged from Home in the Cause of Truth, and though the separation was a close Trial to them, yet he was always willing to give her up to the Service, frequently accompanying to the neighbouring Meetings, and at all times strengthening and encouraging her to follow the pointings of Duty; being sensible that Obedience to Divine Requirings brings Peace."[23] Friends (whether husbands or wives) were expected to be supportive of spouses' legitimate spiritual "concerns."

Countless letters testify to the acceptance of Quaker women's absence from the household on ministerial service. Joseph Hatton, of Waterford, Ireland, wrote in 1755, "My Deare Spouse is not at home being gon[e] yesterday week . . . wheare She has mett with oure Dear friend Samuel Spavold [another preacher] the[y] are together visiting the mettings thereabouts . . . She hopes to be at home tomorra or next day." While travelling on a religious visit, Jane Crosfield wrote to her husband, a yeoman farmer in northern England, when she learned that he had fallen ill: "My greatest aflickishon at present is upon thy account to think when thou had so much need of me was so far frome thee. . . ." However, she concluded that she was only halfway through her ministerial trip: "I desire thee my Dear Dear love to take great care of thyself. . . ." In 1747, Isaac Hall, an English farmer in Cumberland, wrote somewhat plaintively to his long-awaited wife, Alice Hall, "My dear it is near 10 Weeks since thou left England . . . I hope thou will be at home when the o[a]ts is ripe. . . ."[24]

Husbands' willingness to endure their wives' journeys was made possible by their religious framework of meaning. Quakers strove to live in this world but remain focussed on the eternal, "weaned and redeemed from earth and earthly satisfactions." Family members were to be "loved as the work and gifts of the Creator" only. They were "possessed with due caution from this consideration, that they are allotted us but for an uncertain season; and that it is therefore our interest to be able to surrender them when called for, with as little pain or anxiety as is consistent with our state. . . ." The consequence of too much attachment to other human beings was "the immoderate descent of the affections" which "ties us down to the earth and earthly possessions, shackles us in sensual gratifications" and "effectively prevents the soul's ascending towards God." Catharine Payton had cautioned that "the object that is worthy of [love] . . . spending its force upon, or being united to without limitation, must not be dependent on time, for that death deprives it of; but durable as its own existence, and so perfect as fully to satisfy an everlasting desire of possession. This can be nothing else but the Eternal Excellency." Balancing the temporal and the eternal, Quakers created families and maintained human relationships, yet tried to preserve a primary devotion to God and an awareness of the spiritual dimension, practicing a "worldly asceticism." Catharine Payton wrote to another female preacher, "I am glad to find thou canst so readily obey the pointings of the Divine hand; and that thy husband so freely resigns thee to its disposing. No doubt nature will feel in these separations, but as your happiness does not consist in the gratification of earthly desires, but in doing and suffering the will of God, your union in that life which can never end, will be increased by absence."[25]

Even the courtship of eighteenth-century minister Elizabeth Hudson was overshadowed by her religious journeying. Her spouse-to-be, widower Anthony Morris, had escorted Hudson and a female companion on their religious visit to a nearby region, "in this Journey my Husband that now is first acquainted me with his Intentions of offering himself to me as a Suter [suitor] for Marriage wch. I was to take under Consideration . . . but we did not keep Company upon that Score for Some time after, wch affare I think I duely weighed, and . . . Concluded to Accomplish." Hudson continued, "But before that was done, between the monthly meetings in wch. we proposed our marriage I performed a Visit to friends Within the Virge of our Quarterly Meeting Eliza Morgan being my Companion."[26] Mary Lewis of Chester County, Pennsylvania, presented a "concern" to travel to New England on the same day that her intentions to marry were declared before the meeting. Less than a month after her marriage, Lewis left on a five-month religious visit with another female preacher.

The sacrifice of personal needs, when religious duty called the marital partner away, did not indicate that Quakers were completely insensitive to the spouse's feelings. Since an eighteenth-century wife's tasks typically included food preparation, textile production, and the maintenance of a clean, well-ordered household, additional people were often pressed into service to fill in for the female preachers who were occupied with more important spiritual labors. When Rachel Wilson departed England for a religious journey to America, she wrote to her husband in reference to servants, friends, or relatives: "I've now & then thought of Atty as I know things will Ly [lie] pret[t]y hevey upon her but I hope with costem [custom] Itl be Lighter to Bothe her & John I Reflect with pleasure & thankfulness of their Being Both Capbele [capable] & willing to do their part in contributing to thy ease now, in my absence." Ministers made concerted

Mary Weston (1712–66) wrote to her husband in a letter dated December 3, 1750 (Old Style), describing her travels through "Lonely Woods." Weston's religious "concern" led her to "back Settlements, where no English ffr[ien]d has Ever been before. . . . We have traveled harder than any man has been known to do, rid about 1800 miles and took above a hundred meetgs in 4 months. . . ." Weston spent two years on her religious tour of the American colonies, separated from her husband and young daughter, who remained in England. Correspondence became invaluable for the travelling preachers and their families during such separations. *Reproduced with permission of the Library Committee of the Religious Society of Friends in Britain* attempts to maintain a correspondence with their mates while travelling. Twenty-eight letters, written by Rachel Wilson to her husband, who remained in England during her tour of the American colonies in 1768–69, have survived. She wrote, "As I find thair is a Vessel from New York Liekly to go soon for Ingland—tho I only wrote from philadelphia ye 17th—am not willing to omitt this Convaence [conveyance]—as I know how agreeable it is to hear from Each other I wo[ul]d not Neglect doing what is in my power During our Seperation to Make it as Somewhat tolerable."[27]

The efforts of other Friends to keep a spouse informed of the minister's movements and health while travelling showed an awareness of the difficulty of these separations. Henry Gouldney wrote to Abigail Boles's husband during her religious visit to England: "I doubt not but thy love to her Service for ye Truth is such, that thou can contentedly give her up thereto and as thou so does a blessing will attend thy resignation." Gouldney forwarded John Boles's letter to the intended next destination of his wife, reiterating that her absence was "for ye good of Souls, so that if she should be instrumental in Saveing of one; her Labour w[oul]d be well bestowed."[28]

Catharine (Payton) Phillips wrote of her husband's "great affection [which] rendered it hard for him to be so frequently separated from me," but she also recounted instances of his near telepathic "sympathy" with her religious engagements. When she felt a "leading" to visit Plymouth, England, he independently found "his mind forcibly drawn to Plymouth."[29] Other husbands, too, sometimes escorted their ministerial wives on religious visits. William Biles, unable to convince the Quaker meeting of the legitimacy of his opposition to his wife's religious voyage, persuaded the meeting to allow him to accompany her to Great Britain. Husbands supported their wives' "calling" in other ways as well. Daniel Weston, a wealthy merchant, paid his wife's transatlantic passage (usually supplied by the meeting treasury) when she travelled alone to preach in the American colonies.

When spouses parted in order to travel there was a distinct possibility that death would take one of them before the trip's completion. Thirty-three out of the fifty-seven transatlantic women ministers were married at the time of their lengthy religious voyage across the Atlantic. Ann Dillworth had been given liberty by the meeting to visit Great Britain in the ministry, but a similar "concern" to travel abroad presented by her husband, James, also a Quaker preacher, had been rejected by Philadelphia

Yearly Meeting of Ministering Friends. During Ann Dillworth's absence on religious service, a yellow fever epidemic swept through Philadelphia leaving her husband, James Dillworth, dead. Mary Lewis was preaching abroad, in Ireland, when she received word of her husband's death in 1735 ("which Exercise was heavy on her, yet the Lord supported her") and was "willing to return home as soon as Could. . . ." Four of the female preachers died during their religious visit overseas. When Elizabeth Ashbridge died at the age of forty-two in Ireland, her husband, Aaron, referring back to the Quaker faith, which ultimately recognized the priority of the eternal over the temporal, wrote: "Sufficently convinced that her Lord and Master called for her services abroad, my heart was willing to give up the darling object of its love. Though it has pleased the Divine Will to remove her without indulging my longing desire to see her again, yet fully satisfied that she is called from the troubles of time to a happy eternity, I am resigned and enjoy a grateful composure of mind."[30]

Women Ministers' Increased Authority Within the Family

A Quaker woman minister's spiritual authority, acknowledged by the Quaker community, elevated her authority within the family as well. Since Friends sought to live in accordance with God's will, decision making in private life could also be strongly influenced by a ministerial spouse's "providential direction." Elizabeth Shipley's religious vision prompted her husband, William, to relocate their residence and establish new enterprises. Elizabeth Shipley believed that she had been shown by Providence in a dream the place where her family was to live as "instruments of great benefit to the place and people." She was promised by God that "the blessing of heaven should descend upon them and their labours." On a ministerial journey from Pennsylvania to Maryland, Elizabeth recognized the location shown in her dream. Her husband then purchased a lot there, trusting in his wife's "divine leading." William Shipley became the virtual founder of Wilmington, Delaware, building its first vessel for foreign trade, introducing various industries, and catalyzing the rapid growth of the village, which led to a town charter in 1739.[31]

Belief in the guidance of the Holy Spirit experienced by women could heighten their discretionary power over familial property as well. George Fox had supported separate treasuries managed by women's meetings, promoting the concept that couples jointly owned their possessions: "No believing husband, will hinder his believing wife, to administer some of their temporal things to them that are in necessity," in spite of the fact that a "feme covert," or married woman, subsumed in her husband's legal identity, could not own property.[32] Some Quaker wills suggest that the community recognition of the highly developed spirituality of a "Public Friend" affected the trust reposited in a ministerial wife by a husband (and, even, an adult daughter with a "gift" in the ministry by her father). Two wills by the fathers of female preachers reveal a possible link between religious behavior and authority over property. In Ireland, John Boles, a wealthy Quaker landowner, chose his unmarried daughter, Ann Boles, and her brother-in-law as coexecutors of his will. Boles had several adult sons and daughters, all married, except for his third child, Ann, a minister. John Boles bypassed his eldest son (and his son's heirs) to bequeath his dwelling house and 170 plantation acres to his daughter Ann. His eldest son, George, was given one English crown and one pound sterling per annum, and his grandson, John Boles, the eldest son of George, was given one English shilling and no more (perhaps in response to the poor character this grandson had already exhibited). After the will was proved, John, this son of George Boles, was testified against by the Quaker meeting because he had been "Endeavouring Contrary to truth & Justice to bribe Ann Boleses Serv[an]t. to make way for him to gett into ye possession of her house to wch. He have noe Just right. . . ." The patriarch, John Boles, had entrusted his executors (Ann and her brother-in-law) with substantial discretionary power. In the event that any of his grandchildren married without the consent of the executors, the misbehaver's share of inheritance was to be divided among the other grandchildren. The choice of a minister, a spiritual counsellor and a guardian of morality, as an executor who could link material bequests to correct religious behavior appeared to be a plausible decision for this Irish Quaker.[33]

Daughters were less likely to be named as executors of their fathers' estates in the eighteenth century, particularly if there were adult sons in the family. But in spite of his married daughter's status under law as a "feme covert," Samuel Levis, a prosperous Pennsylvania Quaker, chose Elizabeth (Levis) Shipley as a coexecutor of his will, along with her brother-in-law and mother. Elizabeth Shipley's responsibility was puzzling in view of her gender, marital status, and order of birth. She was the fifth child and third daughter of Samuel Levis, whose two eldest sons were alive at the time of his death. Samuel Levis's will was primarily concerned with provisions for his widow. Elizabeth and her brother-in-law were named trustees of property directed for the use of Levis's widow, and after death, for the use of his eldest son. The designation of Elizabeth, a "feme covert," as trustee of the land eventually to pass to her older brother, may indicate a special trust in her capacity to administer the estate. She was the only recognized minister among Levis's children. These ministerial daughters, Ann Boles and Elizabeth (Levis) Shipley, were also significant beneficiaries of their fathers' wills (Elizabeth was to be the beneficiary, after her mother's death, of a trust her father had set up of his plantation's profits; Ann received her father's plantation), and this may have contributed to their selection as executors.

A number of factors affected a man's choice of executor of his estate, but the wills of various ministers' husbands, at the very least, illustrate trust in their wives' wisdom as well. In spite of Ann Dillworth's absence on religious service when her husband, James, contracted yellow fever, he appointed her "whole & Sole Executrixe . . . if itt please God that shee arive safe here again." The will was to be administered by James Dillworth's brother-in-law and a male friend only "if shee should be Removed by death before herr Arivall." Ann Dillworth's second husband, Christopher Sibthorp of Philadelphia County, also made Ann his sole executor, giving her both his real and personal estate in fee simple "to be used & distributed unto her Children as She shall think fitt & convenient." Ann was not only to execute his bequests, but to decide the inheritances herself, as was Elizabeth, the wife of Abraham Rawlinson of Lancashire, England. Abraham Rawlinson gave to his minister wife, Elizabeth, all his "bonds bills mortgages goods chattels rights creditts and personal Estate" in trust during her widowhood to use the interest for the maintenance of herself and a daughter "as in her discretion she may think fitt and if necessity require she shall have power to take a part of the whole stock for her own reliefe and comfort." With the exception of a certain portion reserved for his daughter after his wife's death, Rawlinson directed that the remainder of his personal estate be left "in the power of my Wife to dispose of to such of my Children or grandchildren as she shall think fitt."[34] Eighteenth-century men usually gave their property to adult children and grandchildren, charging the eldest son with the maintenance of his mother. But Ann Dillworth Sibthorp and Elizabeth Rawlinson were given significant discretionary power over their husbands' estates despite the existence of adult children.

Ordinarily, the wills of married women (because of their "feme covert" status) in the eighteenth century had no legal authority. But Friend John Leaver honored his ministerial wife's directives. Mary Leaver, an esteemed, well-travelled preacher of Nottingham, England, had predeceased her husband by five years. In John Leaver's will, he mentioned that "my late Dearly beloved wife Mary Leaver made a Will without Legal Authority so to do part of which I have complied with and performed and am minded to perform and fulfill the remainder. . . ."[35]

The will of Quaker transatlantic preacher Mary (Hayes) (Lewis) Waln of Pennsylvania is an even rarer eighteenth-century document. Her will *was* legally authoritative in spite of the fact that her death preceded her husband's. Waln, a prosperous widow, apparently entered into a prenuptial agreement before her second marriage which enabled her to reserve her property in a separate estate. Her will begins: "Be it Remembered that I Mary Waln the Wife of Richard Waln . . . by Force & Virtue of certain Powers and Authorities to me given and granted by my said Husband do make this my Last Will & Testament. . . ." Through equity procedures, a separate estate could be created for an eighteenth-century married woman, thereby removing her property from her spouse's control. In colonial Pennsylvania, a separate estate was enforceable only if it existed in the form of a trust for a woman. Depending on the nature of the settlement, the trustee or third party who supervised the estate in the name of the woman either followed the woman's instructions (if the settlement terms gave her an active use, a married woman could act as a "feme sole"—able to contract, sell, mortgage, or devise her property as if she had never been married) or acted as her business manager (settlements written to preserve the family estate from a husband's creditors often gave the woman no power of control over the principal but guaranteed her an income).

Mary Waln designed a settlement that gave her active control over her property. She then used her "feme sole" powers to create separate estates for her two married daughters—giving them active control over their property as well. She directed her executors to sell "all my Houses Lots of Ground Land Tenements Rents and Hereditaments and all my Estate" for "the best Price." One-third of the proceeds of the sale and one-third "Part of all Moneys due or belonging to me by Bond or otherwise" were placed in special trust with her friend James Bartram so that he would "put the same Moneys out at Interest on the best Security that can be gotten for the Sole and Intire Use" of "my said Daughter Hannah Pennell, the Wife of

Joshua Pennell, during her Coverture, And not for the Use or Benefit of her Husband, Or otherwise to dispose of or Apply the same Moneys as she my said Daughter Hannah shall direct or appoint, without the Consent Controll or direction or Appointment of the said Joshua Pennell notwithstanding her Coverture, Whose Receipt, alone without her Husband, shall be a Sufficient Discharge for the same. . . ." The wording is worth quoting in full as it seems to express a strong protest against the practice of "coverture" (the legal status of a married woman under the authority, or protection, of her husband). Waln directed another one-third of property sales and bonds to be placed in an identical trust for her other married daughter. The final third of her sale proceeds and bonds were given directly to her son. Prior to marriage with Richard Waln, Mary Lewis had served as coexecutor with her adult sons of her first husband's will. As Mary Lewis, she had been given the east end of the dwelling house to reside in and privileges for maintenance by her eldest son (a more typical arrangement for eighteenth-century widows), in addition to three hundred pounds in a form that she was to choose (whether in bonds or mortgages). In her second marriage, Lewis made certain that she preserved financial control over her property.[36]

Another will, atypical of the colonial period, was left by Job Harvey of Chester County, Pennsylvania, the second husband of Rebecca (Owen) Minshall, a transatlantic preacher. By law, a wife's personal effects automatically became her husband's property upon marriage. Rebecca Minshall, an affluent widow, apparently had negotiated a prenuptial agreement as well. Jointure agreements were a form of marriage settlement usually designed to serve as an alternative to dower and to compensate for the loss of property that a woman suffered at marriage. The will of Job Harvey confirmed to Rebecca "all those gifts Donations Grants Priviledges Comprised & Mentioned in Certain Deeds or writings of Jointure made to her before our Intermarriage," including an annuity of eighteen pounds. But in a further unusual bequest, Harvey gave to his wife, Rebecca: "the Sole Use of all those goods which She brought with her and were hers before our Intermarriage during the time She shall Remain my Widdow." Attached to an inventory of Job Harvey's personal estate was a separate inventory of the "Goods which were his wives before their intermarriage and by his last will are bequested to her during her Widdowhood."[37]

The Waln and Harvey wills may simply reflect the self-interest of wealthy widows who had learned the value of economic independence

"The Residence of David Twining, 1787,"
painted by Edward Hicks (1780–1849).
Hicks, a nineteenth-century Quaker minister,
painted this recollected scene from his childhood. Hicks was adopted by Twining, a
devout Quaker, and raised on his farm. This
painting expresses Quaker virtues of domestic life: orderliness and peacefulness. *Courtesy Abby Aldrich Rockefeller Folk Art Center,
Williamsburg, Virginia*

before they remarried. Or, the wills may reveal an itinerant woman minister's increased sense of an identity separate from her husband (as well as discomfort with the contrast that "coverture" presented with her authority in other realms). Quakers did not alter the law to increase women's legal autonomy or property rights, yet the ministerial role modified the law in practice. The Quaker emphasis on individual spiritual vocation challenged the patriarchal family structure that framed the legal status of eighteenth-century women. The Quaker community's acceptance of single, adult women who had a "calling" beyond marriage and motherhood was its greatest modification of the legal subordination of women to men. As a "feme sole," a woman possessed independent legal privileges. Friends' religious duties also modified married women's status under law, as meetings supported women's adherence to "inward leadings" even against their husbands' objections. Quaker women's religious authority augmented their familial authority, at times, apparently enabling them to exert greater control over property than was usual for eighteenth-century females.

Women Ministers' Motherhood: Family Size

"Dear and loveing Wife these comes with my dear love to thee . . . ," wrote Isaac Hall, a Quaker farmer in Cumberland, England, who remained at his residence during his spouse's religious visit to Ireland in 1747. Having received news of his travelling wife from a friend, Isaac continued in his letter, "they gave him an account that thou was very well & thy horse performed very well so fare, which I was very glad to hear for it is a great Satisfaction to me to heare of thy wellfaire [welfare]. . . ." The Quaker husband was particularly concerned about his ministerial spouse's health because of her pregnant state, "for I am very often thoughtful about thee considering they [thy] condition," but he strove to be supportive of Alice's spiritual purpose: "But I Bel've the Lord will be a Strength & Suport unto thee . . . and I hope thou will have the Returns of Peace in thy Bosom at Last."[38]

Among the eighteenth-century transatlantic preachers, a majority of the fifty-two married women gave birth to children. Quakers did not advocate an extreme ascetic view regarding sexual relations within a minister's marriage. In 1660, when husband-and-wife Quaker missionaries from Cumberland, England, were imprisoned in Boston, three New England Quaker prisoners refused to worship with them because of the wife's pregnancy, but this was an isolated case.[39] The most obvious repercussion of the women's ministerial role on childbearing came from the women's deferral of marriage. This postponement, in some cases, resulted in no children (there were twelve childless marriages in the group of transatlantic women preachers) or fewer children. An important duty of the eighteenth-century wife was to reproduce (among other reasons, children provided necessary labor), but in the Quakers' more spiritualized, companionate form of marriage, childbearing may have been less crucial for "gifted vessels" whose religious guidance and community status made them desirable helpmates.

Since the ministry was considered to be a lifetime vocation if one remained faithful to one's "gift," many women who had been ministers prior to marriage simply continued their pattern of travel during their childbearing years. A seventeenth-century epistle from the women of London's Box Meeting had advised young female preachers not to travel when pregnant, but the religious "calling" was apparently too strong for some eighteenth-century ministers to ignore. Jane Crosfield was away from her Westmorland home during the first six months of her pregnancy. When Crosfield learned that her husband had fallen ill during her absence, she wrote an impassioned letter arguing that it would have been more difficult to remain at home: "If I had been at home should not abeen easey from thee day nor night which might abeen too hard and caused me to amiscaried [have a miscarriage]and that would ad[d]ed both to thy aflickishon [affliction] and mine." She anticipated criticism from others for her decision, but did not plan to shorten her religious journey, "the [though] many both friends and others [both Quakers and non-Quakers]may be redey [ready] to think and say I should not have gone, but have cause to belife [believe] this day and in thee way of my duty . . . I desire thee my Dear Dear love to take great care of thyself if not for thy own sake for mine and thy poor babie one yet unborn . . . If I visit what meetings have thought of, visits will take me new [near] 9 weeks yet."[40]

Eighteenth-century medical wisdom indicated no strict regimen for prenatal care. Women tended to continue their normal activities until shortly before delivery, avoiding violent exercise in the first or last months of pregnancy. Alice Hall had been an indefatigable traveller before marriage at the age of thirty-four, having already visited Ireland twice and most parts of England, Wales, and Scotland. She continued this pattern throughout the creation of her family. About four years after her marriage, when Alice Hall was four months' pregnant, she presented her "concern" to travel in the ministry to Ireland. At that time, in 1747, she had two children, three-year-old John and sixteen-month-old Sarah. The meeting, after inquiry, found that "nothing appears to hinder her liberty," and granted her a travel certificate.[41] The female preacher travelled on religious service at least until the sixth month of her pregnancy.

An eighteenth-century woman, colonial American or English, could expect to have a child an average of every twenty-four to thirty months (with shorter or longer intervals depending on whether one was nursing).[42] Jane Crosfield had married at the age of thirty-four, after religious visits to Ireland, Wales, and other parts of England. She gave birth to her first child fourteen months after marriage. There was an interval of twenty-six months before her second child was born (during which she went on a two-month religious visit to nearby counties). Her third child was born twenty-three months after the second child (she was on a visit to southern England during six months of this pregnancy). A twenty-two-month interval separated the third and fourth births. Her last child was born twenty-four months after the previous one. Her final conception was at age forty-three. In spite of the fact that she had taken two religious journeys in the midst of childbearing, Crosfield's rate of conception was not noticeably different from that of a woman who remained in the household.

Rachel Wilson of Westmorland, who eventually became a mother of ten, married at age twenty, although she was already a recognized preacher. Her first birth occurred about eleven months after the marriage. During this first pregnancy, she travelled in the ministry for two months in northern Britain. Twenty-five months separated the births of her first and second children; thirty months separated the births of her second and third children (during this interval, Wilson was away for seven months visiting the south, west, and east of England "in the service of Truth"); twenty-three months separated her third and fourth children; twenty-eight months separated her fourth and fifth children (during this time, Wilson travelled for two months on religious service to nearby counties). On another trip, during four months of her pregnancy with the fifth child, she visited Wales and southern England. Thirty-two months separated her fifth and sixth children; twenty-nine months separated her sixth and seventh children (during this interval Wilson travelled for four months to Ireland); twenty-seven months separated her seventh and eighth children; only eighteen months separated her eighth and ninth children (the eighth child died at four months); her last child was born twenty months after the previous one. Wilson conceived her tenth child at the age of thirty-eight, having journeyed on religious service during two pregnancies. Since the women ministers tended to travel away from the household for only a few months at a time every couple of years (except for transatlantic trips, which entailed an absence of several years and often were taken after the women had borne most of their children or when they were unmarried), their religious travel did not greatly interfere with their childbearing.

There may have been regional differences, however, in attitudes toward ministerial travel before a woman's reproductive career was completed. In contrast to these English women from Lancashire, Westmorland, Cumberland, and Yorkshire (areas that provided the earliest Quaker missionaries), Susanna Morris of Pennsylvania wrote: "Yet willing as I was to do the will of God, I went not much abroad from my Family Untill I had born all our thirteen Children, but one." Only eight married women (all of whom were Americans) who were preachers at a young age had a long interval in their travels that may have indicated a desire to complete their families before journeying on religious service. Several women began travelling at about age thirty-nine. Margaret Lewis of Chester County, already the mother of nine children, probably had hoped that she had reached the end of her childbearing when she set sail for England at the age of forty. The London Quaker community reacted to Lewis's unexpected pregnancy as a "Circumstance yt [that] gives some of us no Small Concern. . . ." John Pemberton, an American preacher himself travelling in England, wrote to his parents, Israel and Rachel, about the apparent novelty of the situation—a minister giving birth while on a religious journey, observing in February 1753: "I hear M. Lewis is Lately delivered (of a Child. (a Strange thing)."[43]

Women Ministers' Child Care

There is no official statement in the Quaker meeting records regarding the care of children during a ministerial mother's absence, but typically Quakers did not travel with their children on religious service. George Fox explained, in 1685, how Quakers had contended with the problem in the early years of the movement, "when ffriends went out of the north in the service of the Lord . . . ffriends that stayed and kept up their meetings at home did look after ffriends business, and assist their ffamilys." Fox's message, to not allow family cares or business to distract from spiritual "callings," continued to be a strong tenet of eighteenth-century Quakerism: "Therefore take heed, lett not the outward care of this world . . . insnare or tye you from labouring in the Lords worke. . . ."[44] The absence of a standardized procedure in the Quaker discipline suggests that solutions were created on an ad hoc basis.

When Margaret Lewis gave birth during a ministerial journey, circumstances may have forced her to rely on someone else's nursing services. The meeting certificate brought back from Bristol by Lewis stated that her son had been "more Particular under the Care of a Friend within the Compas[s] of this monthly Meeting." According to the meeting, "the Friend Under whose Care her Child hath been hath Signified to Us that She is Well Satisfied with what She hath done for the Child or its Mother For the Time the Child hath been with her." Abiah Darby, an English preacher, "although a nurse" or breast-feeding, did leave her eight-month-old daughter in the care of a neighbor for a few days while she and her husband attended the Wales Yearly Meeting.[45] No other direct evidence of a female travelling minister placing her infant out to a wet nurse has been found.

There was strong ideological support among Quakers for mothers to breast-feed their own infants. Most objections to breast-feeding (that it would ruin a woman's figure or interrupt sexual relations) were viewed by Friends as prideful and fleshly concerns. The Dublin Monthly Meeting in Ireland felt it necessary to comment on the subject in 1707, suggesting that some Quaker women were using wet nurses: "it haveing been proposed to this meetinge whether it bee not ye duty of all Mothers of Children to give them suck or nurs[e] them. . . ." The meeting appointed men to visit the next women's meeting "& let them know how the members of this meeting are unanimously of yt. mind, yt women who are of ability doe nurs[e] their children." The Quaker minister Sophia Hume wrote a scathing attack on the practice of wet-nursing in 1751. She called it "unnatural Conduct" on the mother's part and "inhuman Treatment of our tender little Ones." She suggested that "the Death of many an Infant . . . may be chargeable on their Parents, on this Score" for a stranger would not take the same tender care as a parent would.[46]

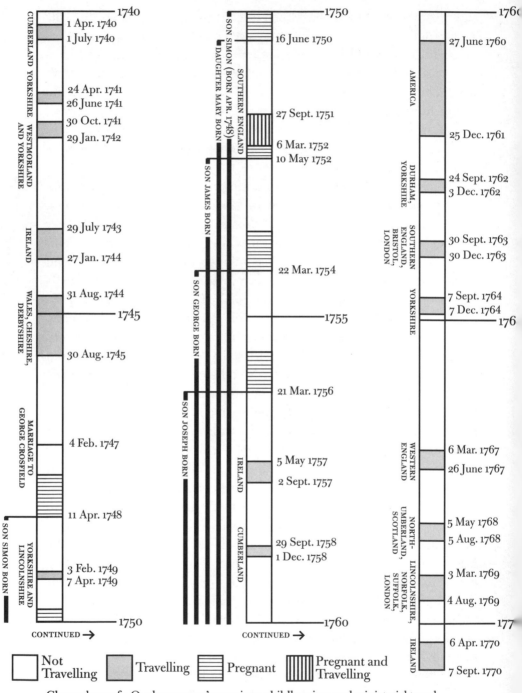

Chronology of a Quaker woman's marriage, childbearing, and ministerial travel.
Jane (Rowlandson) Crosfield (born November 5, 1712; died February 2, 1784).

Yet, Alice Hall requested a certificate to travel to nearby counties in England when her fourth child, Hannah, was less than five months old. The youngest child of Rebecca Turner, of Yorkshire, England, was only three months old when her concern to visit Lancashire and Cheshire was approved. James Dillworth (also a minister) presented his intention to travel with his preacher wife from Pennsylvania to New England shortly after she had given birth to their daughter. The tender age of these infants could mean that their mothers relied on some type of hand-feeding or a nurse. Many women travelled on religious visits regardless of whether they had young children at home. Seventeen of the forty transatlantic preacher-mothers journeyed when they had children at home aged two or younger.

Female ministers were considered "nursing mothers" to the general Quaker community for providing spiritual sustenance to humanity (Quaker male preachers were known as "nursing fathers"), giving "divine food, this sincere milk of the word . . . by which the babes in Christ have been nourished." They were often weaning their own children, however, in order to travel to spiritually "nurse" others. Ann Moore, a minister from Maryland, wrote (in the journal of her trip across several colonies in 1758) of her companion's "dear fatherless children one being weaned from her breast when she set out with me."[47] Eighteenth-century women had no set age to wean children but examples range from seven and a half months to thirteen months. The timing of Jane Crosfield's presentation of "concerns" to travel reveals a probable pattern of weaning children: in 1748 when her son was ten months old, in 1751 when her daughter was fifteen months, and in 1757 when another son was fourteen months.

Husbands who remained at home during their wives' travels were relied upon for aid in child care. The letters from Isaac Hall to his wife, Alice, indicate that he was supervising their three-year-old son and sixteen-month-old daughter in her absence while continuing his farming tasks: "My dear it is near 10 Weeks since thou left England . . . thy Son John is grown a great lad & he is very hearty and he goise [goes] to ye hay field & works till he Sweat he is fresh couler'd he is Exceeding active he is very strong [.] thy douther [daughter] Sarah is hearty and fresh Couler'd. . . ." Isaac Hall also mentioned that his own mother "helps us all she can." Daughter Sarah, although she "has not got all her teeth yet," Isaac explained, could now walk hand-in-hand with her brother John "unto her Grand Mothers."[48]

Grandmothers were a common alternative to maternal care. Jane Crosfield's mother-in-law lived with her and cared for the children while she travelled in the ministry. Elizabeth Webb noted, in the account of her eighteen-month visit to America, that when she returned to Gloucester, England, she "found my mother and [c]hildren in good h[eal]th my husband being gon[e to] [Lond]on to ye yearly m[ee]ting."[49]

Older children, servants, and, in some cases, slaves (American yearly meetings did not disown members for slave-holding until the eve of the American Revolution) were undoubtedly also depended upon to complete domestic tasks during the mother's absence. Since the span of childbearing for most eighteenth-century women was approximately twenty years, those female preachers who did not marry at a late age often had adult children at home as well as toddlers. When Margaret Lewis set off for Great Britain, unknowingly pregnant, she left a two-year-old at home. Her eldest child, however, was twenty, and with the seven other children was probably able to perform the household chores and supervise younger siblings. Rachel Wilson had two married daughters when she departed England for a journey to America, although her youngest child was eight. The wealth of spouses released some women ministers from their household duties (although several women's families were in "low circumstances," receiving financial aid from the meeting). Sarah Baker of Dublin, Ireland, was married to a man "Endowed with Worldly Substance," allowing her to employ several household servants. She travelled while her children were very young. Ann and James Dillworth, who travelled several times together in the ministry, immigrated to Pennsylvania with one indentured servant. In New York, Phebe Dodge's husband bequeathed "the negro girl, Rachel" to her when he died, but Phebe later manumitted the slave.[50]

Ultimately, the willingness of Friends to share responsibilities in the common goal of promoting "Truth" made possible their unremunerated laypersons' ministry. Quaker preachers' capacity to place the inward "calling" before "outward things" required a reliance on the Friends' community as an extended family. The first converts to Quakerism often had broken from their families of origin in order to join this new "household of faith" based on spiritual kinship. Friends became "as one family and household in certain respects, [so] do each of them watch over, teach, and instruct, and care for one another." In the eighteenth century, Rachel Wilson, her mother, and her husband each journeyed, at times alternating familial duties with religious service. In addition, Ruth Seaman, a young female minister who occasionally travelled as well, moved into the Wilson household (a family of ten children), "where she was of great service during their frequent absences in the ministry."[51]

As part of one "Family of God," the Quaker meeting had a sacred obligation to assist in the rearing of Quaker children. If the immediate family was in financial need, the Quaker meeting might make loans, give money, or place the children out as apprentices so that the family could survive. If both parents died, the meeting served as a parental substitute: arranging for child care and protecting the orphans' rights.[52] The case of Susanna Hatton, a widowed mother of six, demonstrates how the "outward cares" of an eighteenth-century ministerial parent were handled by the Quaker meeting—freeing her to "labour in the Lords worke." Hatton, an Irish minister, had already travelled extensively in Great Britain and America, when she presented a "concern" before the Waterford Six Weeks Meeting on January 20, 1760, to revisit America. Susanna Hatton's children ranged in age from sixteen to seven. The Meeting for Sufferings in London financed Susanna Hatton's passage to the colonies. She did not return home to Ireland until December 1762, having been "abroad on Truth's Service" for almost three years.

In the interim, the Waterford Six Weeks Meeting acted as a surrogate parent for the travelling minister's family. Hatton's seven-year-old daughter was "taken under the care" of a rich Friend. Her sons were placed in apprenticeships. Following Hatton's departure from Ireland, the Waterford meeting recorded: "As no suitable place in the Province has offered to put Robt. Hatton Apprentice to, And his Mother having proposed that in that case he shou'd be placed with Tho. Williams to the shoemaking trade, Henry Martin & John Hutchinson are desired without delay to get him accordingly bound on the terms said Williams proposed viz. to Advance a fee of five Pounds & Friends to keep the boy in Clothing during his Apprenticeship Shoes Excepted." During Susanna Hatton's absence, the Waterford Men's Meeting received information that another Hatton son, who had been bound as an apprentice, had misbehaved. The Waterford meeting disciplined this son and placed him out again—this time to a Friend in Dublin. The willingness of the Quaker meeting to take on parental duties diminished the burden on this impoverished widow of being the sole child-care provider, permitting her to fulfill her ministerial "calling."[53]

Quaker Attitudes Toward Motherhood and Child Rearing

"And when she came to be in a Married State, her love to Truth was such, that when she found her Mind engaged in the service thereof, she at several Times wean'd the Child from her Breast and left those enjoyments that was near and comfortable in their places, as Husband and Children, whom she dearly loved, and esteem'd, which the Lord had given for a season yet in the midst of her enjoyments, she left all for the service of Truth"; so reads a Quaker meeting's memorial concerning the preacher Mary Greenhow of Cumberland, England. The sketch described Greenhow's travel to Ireland, Wales, and most parts of England, and concluded that "it is very hard to part with one who hath been so loving and dutiful a wife to her Husband, and so careful and tender a Mother over her Children."[54]

The notion of exemplary motherhood found in memorials of deceased eighteenth-century Quaker female ministers differs sharply from the nineteenth-century ideology of domesticity (in which a woman devoted herself to family and home) so influential in English and American culture. Service to God first (which in Quaker belief might demand public speaking, as well as travel), then husband and children, was the correct hierarchy for a woman; altering the traditional domestic ideal. Nor was the Quaker ethos like the monastic withdrawal from the world for a life of religious devotion to God. Quakers sought a balance, without renunciation of the world, seeking to keep their focus on the Creator. Mary Greenhow's submission to the perceived will of God, her self-denial in parting with "those enjoyments that was near and comfortable," her maintenance of a proper perspective toward the affective attachments in her life "which the Lord had given for a season," and her continued zeal (in spite of marriage and childbirth) for the cause of Truth, made her an ideal maternal figure for the Society of Friends. Greenhow was admired because "she at several Times wean'd the Child from her Breast" and endured extended absences from the household to promote the Quaker tenets. A Quaker female minister's concern for the general good signified that she was truly a "nursing mother" to a spiritually hungry population. Since Friends' parental goal was to transmit to their children the Quaker principle of obedience to the Inward Light, there was no inherent contradiction in their characterization of a woman who was physically absent from the household for extended periods on the Lord's service, as "so careful and tender a Mother over her Children."

An epistle written by Mary Leaver to her daughters reveals a preacher's view of the duties of motherhood. Leaver's central concern was that her children "experimentally" know God, for once their "hearts have been melted into tenderness by the visitation of divine love," they would not be "strangers to an inward principle" which would instruct them in the Truth. The travelling minister-mother taught by example the importance of belief in God. Many of the women's travel journals were addressed to their children. Recorded with an instructive intent, their experiences were presented to offspring as illustrations of providential care and the consequences of faithfulness. Susanna Morris expressed her primary desire for her own many children: "that it may be with you as it is with me at Certain times to do the Lord's will may be more to you than Your Meet [Meat] & Drink they will surely pass away: but to obey Your Everlasting happiness bring true peace on Earth. . . ."[55] The impact the eighteenth-century travelling preachers had on their families is suggested by the number of their children who also became ministers. Among the women preachers' children who journeyed extensively in the ministry themselves as adults were Rachel Wilson's daughter, Alice Hall's son, and Susanna Hatton's son.

The distinctive Quaker conception of the maternal role must be placed, as well, in the context of general eighteenth-century beliefs regarding child rearing. As mistress of the household or farm (and, possibly, assistant in her husband's business), an eighteenth-century wife could not absorb herself in child care; nor was she expected to. A woman's primary responsibilities were childbearing and maintaining the household (including food preparation and textile production). Her duty was "extensive" mothering (the bearing of many children), instead of "intensive" mothering (the nurturing of a few). Not only was there a general lack of sentiment regarding child rearing, but it was also not a clearly feminized task. During the eighteenth century, the supervision and training of children was often shared with wet nurses, servants, older children, fathers, grandparents, and masters (to whom children might be apprenticed as early as age seven). Advice literature on family life was primarily directed toward the father, whose role as governor of the family was clearly encoded in law and social custom.[56]

After the mid-eighteenth century, a shift from the Calvinistic view of babies (corrupted with Adam's sin) to a Romantic belief in infant innocence ("trailing clouds of glory do we come / From God, who is our home") resulted in a new sentimentalization of childhood.[57] Children acquired new importance as individuals when family size limitation enabled mothers to focus more on each child's development. Economic changes in the late eighteenth and early nineteenth centuries, the development of a market economy and industrial manufacturing, relieved women of some household tasks. The growing segregation of the father's workplace from the home increased maternal responsibility for child rearing. Mothers now spent a substantial portion of family life involved with child rearing. This redefinition of family functions, in an altered socioeconomic context, placed new emphasis on the emotional bonds between mother and child. Motherhood was elevated to a sacred, specialized calling. By the early nineteenth century, didactic literature on family life was largely directed to mothers.

Eighteenth-century Quakers were influenced by general attitudes of their time, but their religious beliefs and sectarian status resulted in a distinctive focus on child rearing. In the earliest years of the movement, Friends' millennial expectations were reflected in the absence of emphasis on domestic life in their writings. After their apocalyptic hopes were defeated, however, the Quakers needed to reconsider the family and succeeding generations. As a result of their failure to evoke worldwide conversion, they increasingly saw themselves as forming an isolated "family" of believers within the larger, corrupt culture. The correct rearing of their own children became a central Quaker preoccupation by the eighteenth century. Friends not only rejected predestination, but believed that children could not rely on familial religious heritage for salvation. Their children needed to have an experiential "convincement" of Friends' principles. The Quakers, therefore, introduced a new doctrine of Christian nurture to promote this spiritual experience.[58]

Eighteenth-century Friends agreed with Calvinist parents that children shared the tendency toward sin (imparted to all humans by Adam), but differed in not assigning sinfulness to children until they had reached the age of reason and had the ability to distinguish right from wrong. Robert Barclay wrote: "Sin is imparted to none, where is no Law. / But to Infants there is no Law: / Therefore Sin is not imputed to them."[59] The Calvinist view of the total depravity of humans was modified further by Friends' belief in an Inward Light, or divine guide, that could flourish in each human if the sinful aspects of one's nature were weeded out. Since Quakers believed that children were malleable beings highly susceptible to external influences, Quaker child rearing emphasized seclusion from the "world's evils." The "tender minds" of children were easily corrupted: their natural inclination to evil might predominate and obscure the Inward Light. Early parental impressions were then important in shaping their children's future religious life and chance for salvation. Quaker parents were to maintain a godly atmosphere within the household. Both mother and father were to set examples of piety, plainness, and self-denial. Sarah Baker, a travelling minister, was commended for "having a godly care upon her heart for the good of her Children & Servants that they might be Educated and Nurtured up in the fear of God and out of light and frothy discourse & behaviour that tended to vanity." The Friends' plain style of life (in clothing, furnishings, and language) discouraged pride and other distractions from the Truth. If children were indulged, they would lack the self-restraint necessary to adhere to the Inward Light and would succumb to evil temptations. According to the Quaker meeting, "The habit of obedience . . . will prepare the infant mind for a more ready reception of the necessary restraints of the cross, it may be considered, in part, as preparing the way of the Lord: whilst those who neglect to bend the tender minds of their children to parental authority, and connive at their early tendencies to hurtful gratifications, are, more or less, making way for the enemy and destroyer."[60]

Quaker parents were to impress upon their children an awe of the Divine Being and to acquaint them with the Scriptures. The ministerial role, which had elevated Quaker women's spiritual authority not only in the community but within the family, meant that a woman shared equal authority with her husband as "household priest" in Quakerism—providing religious instruction to their children. Unlike other early modern Protestant patriarchs, the Quaker father did not supersede his wife as biblical interpreter for the family. Mary Leaver acted as an advisor (regarding her children's conduct), as well as an exemplar. She warned her daughters to be mindful of the company they kept and the books they read, guarding against conformity to "the foolish fashions of a vain and unstable world."[61]

The concern with which the Quaker community approached child rearing, however, did not mean that they shared later cultural values attached to familial relations. The early Quaker family was not "child-centered" in the sense of the term's later associations: a sentimental view of childhood. The careful nurturance of a child's religious growth, instilling obedience, self-discipline, and humility, was congruent with an exemplary mother's absences from the household "in the service of Truth."

Most eighteenth-century transatlantic female preachers came from families accustomed to enduring hardships for the maintenance of religious
principles. As members of a severely persecuted group in seventeenth-
century England, many of their Quaker relatives had been separated from
their families for "Truth's Sake," during periods of imprisonment. Since
religious service required the widespread participation of laypeople (with
Friends' rejection of a professional clergy), Quaker children commonly
experienced the temporary absences of parents (who were serving as representatives to church business meetings or as itinerant preachers). Both
parents of Ann Parsons, one of the eighteenth-century transatlantic
preachers, used to attend the Philadelphia Yearly Meeting "leaving their
large family of young children at home" for several days. Their Pennsylvania residence "in one of the settlements the farthest in the wilderness,
and most distant from the bulk of the English inhabitants" was watched
over by amicable Indians. Mary Dow, a Quaker woman minister living on
the New Hampshire frontier, reminded her children "how you staid at
home alone, when we went to meetings, and how the Lord preserved
you. . . ."[62]

In Quaker ministerial families, the long periods of physical separation
did not represent a lack of emotional attachment but rather the denial of
self "in the service of Truth." Catharine Payton wrote of the preacher's
struggle "betwixt affection and the pursuit of the service before me . . . but
I was enabled to pursue my duty [leave on a religious journey], and to com-
mit . . . [my family] to the care of gracious Providence." The affection for
family members is evident in the letters that the women preachers wrote
while abroad. In 1750, Mary Weston ended a letter to her husband and
seven-year-old daughter from America with "ye most Endeared Salluta-
tions of Love thou Can Conceive Shall Conclud[e] in w[hi]ch our precious Girl has a Large Share who I talk and think of Every day & offt
Dream I am w[i]th her and in thy Armes but oh as thou says must have a
Deal of Patience before yt [that] Comes to Pass." In another letter, Weston
asked her husband to "write by Every Ship, bound to any port on ye Continent but Especially to Philadelphia or Eastward for Really my Dear I am
almost impatient to hear from ye and my Dear Child haveing no Account
since our moveing Parting." Correspondence became exceedingly valuable
to the Quaker itinerant ministers, who lived with uncertainty about their
families' welfare for months at a time. Rachel Wilson noted that friends

"brought me several Letters from my Dear Husband and Children, which gave me great [Releve] relief."[63]

Quaker travelling preachers attempted to discipline their personal wills in order to submit to the sovereign will of God. In letters written to her family during her American trip, Rachel Wilson tried to convey both her love of her family and unswerving trust in the divine will. Wilson wrote to her husband, "Every Litle intelegence is pleasing—tho[ugh] I was preserved very quiet & still when Deprived of hearing from anye hand for Many Months through one Disappointment or another." When, during her religious journey, Rachel Wilson received word of her long-sickly child's death, she restricted her emotional reaction—which might have implied that she was not completely resigned to the providential order. She wrote: "Tho[ugh] Long Expected & in agood Degree prepared ["for ye shock" is crossed out] yet it was Efecting [affecting]—at this Distance—tho[ugh] I am fare from Murmuring or ye Least Repining at ye acct of providence but Rather thankful with thee he went of[f] so quiet at Last . . . thairs Som[e]thing in me yt [that] wo[ul]d haved Lieked to have bin [been] present . . . yt I have no Caus[e] to Dought [doubt]—of Being in my place. . . ." The true believer met each act of Providence, death or life, with equanimity, "Depending from day to day upon yt Arm of power yt is altogether Sufficient in Every Imergence [emergency] & qualifies for Every Servis he Calls too."[64]

The women ministers' overwhelming perception of the Creator's precedence lessened their sense that their own lives, and even their family connections, were their possessions. Believing in the necessity of such "Truth's service," Alice Hall, of Cumberland, England, visited America in 1761, recommending her children (ages seventeen, fifteen, and twelve), as well as her husband, "to the protection of that hand which is ever sufficient." After travelling through the southern colonies and New England, Hall "found herself very full of pain yet kept on visiting the Meetings. . . ."[65] Alice's husband, Isaac Hall, who had patiently endured all of his wife's previous absences on religious visits, when the children were toddlers, received the news that his wife had died at age fifty-four in Philadelphia, far from her family. Another itinerant minister, Ann Moore, captured by the French, and later released, on her voyage across the Atlantic, wrote to her children: "For oh sweet Lord and Savior, He gave me power to resign my life and you, my dear children, at that time as though you were no more mine for I expected no other than that my life would be taken for thy testimony I should have to bear. Remember this, my dear children, and believe the word of the Lord who said, 'Whosoever will lose his life for my sake shall find it.' "[66]

Quaker Religious Beliefs Changed the Family System

Quaker belief in the capacities of both women and men to be directly guided by the Holy Spirit affected the Quaker family system. The primacy of a ministerial "gift" was reflected in the tendency of the Quaker women transatlantic preachers, regardless of region, to defer marriage for several years. As "spiritual vessels," these women were sought-after helpmates, valuable for their religious wisdom. Quaker marriage was a spiritual union, not merely procreative, as spouses assisted each other's religious growth. The inclusion of women in the ministry required Quaker husbands to fill a newly supportive role. Preachers not only tried to choose spouses who were sympathetic to their "religious engagements" but the Quaker meeting also, at times, clearly supported the precedence of the women's inner "calling" over the demands of private relations. As "dutiful wives," the Quaker female ministers believed that their religious activities were not a liberation from their obligations to their spouses, but the greater subjection of the self to God's will. Submission to the Lord, however, modified Quaker female preachers' legal subordination to their husbands, since their religious authority, validated by the Quaker community, translated into increased authority in the family.

A companionate marriage, based on shared religious values, was essential to create a godly household in which children could experience the Inward Light. Part of the instruction a "tender" Quaker preacher-mother provided to her children was her own example of submission to God's will: heeding the "concern" to travel in the ministry. Encouraging "gifted" women to place a priority on "labouring in the Lords worke," the Quaker community supported them in leaving their households by helping to manage their "outward affairs." Quakers served as an extended family or one "household of faith" assisting the children and spouses of absent Friends.

The normality of a Quaker ministerial mother's frequent absences from the household and her equal authority as a religious instructor to her children were evident in a letter written by Mary (Murfin) Smith, of New Jersey, to her son about to sail to the West Indies. Smith (not a transatlantic religious traveller) was journeying regionally in the ministry with Margaret Preston, through the southern colonies in 1728, "being zealous for the honour of God, and devoted to the good of her fellow-creatures." The preacher, and mother of nine children, wrote to her son: "My Dear Child,—It being somewhat uncertain whether I may get home before thou goest abroad; if it should happen that thou goest this fall of the year, I take this opportunity to salute thee with these few lines, desiring thy prosperity and welfare every way. My tender advice to thee is, that thou often think of thy Creator in the days of thy youth . . . In his own time he will more clearly make known to thee what is his will, and enable thee to come up in the true performance of thy duty to him . . . Experience hath brought me to speak of the goodness of God, and of his preserving hand . . . Thy tender and loving mother, Mary Smith."[67] In Quaker culture, the service of a woman as a divinely chosen "instrument" resulted not in the abdication of marital and maternal roles, but to a striking redefinition of them—allowing for the importance of an individual's spiritual vocation.

Five

"IN THE SERVICE OF TRUTH": IMPACT OF WOMEN MINISTERS' TRAVELS ON THE TRANSATLANTIC QUAKER COMMUNITY

A N N W H I T A L L (1716–97), a Quaker farmwife in New Jersey, wrote in her diary after hearing the travelling ministers Jane Crosfield and Susanna Hatton preach when they passed through her region: "O if it was posabal [possible] for us to be like har [her] & Susana Haddon [Susanna Hatton] who can exce[e]d them tu [two] weman [women] . . . O whot [what] a littel did I under go [undergo] to what our dear fri[e]nds Jan Crosly [Jane Crosfield] & Suseanna Hadden dus [does] in won [one] week a traveling about & the tears run[n]ing down thair faises [faces] for our sins. . . ." Whitall, the mother of six sons and three daughters, lived on a ninety-acre farm seven miles below Philadelphia, on the opposite side of the Delaware River, where her husband cultivated wheat, tended cattle, and planted an apple orchard. Ann Whitall contended with the hardships of colonial life, the epidemics and accidents, with self-made remedies (such as rattlesnake root boiled in hog's fat for burns) and the spiritual consolation provided by visiting Quaker preachers: "O I think if it wont [weren't] for the Comfort that I git [get] sometimes at Meeting to here [hear] some of such worthies of the same mind with my self I cud [could] not a stud [have stood] til now I must a sunk [have sunk] in sor[r]ow."[1]

Whitall heard the visitors from England and Ireland at several meetings, as Jane Crosfield and Susanna Hatton crisscrossed the American colonies. In September 1760, both preachers were at Haddonfield (New Jersey) Quarterly Meeting; in October 1760, Susanna Hatton visited Woodbury, Whitall's local meeting for worship; in December 1760, Jane Crosfield preached at nearby Haddonfield meeting; and in August 1761, Crosfield attended Woodbury meeting. The New Jersey farmwife transcribed what she remembered of their sermons, applying their advices to her life. Susanna Hatton encouraged her listeners not to fear "Man O mortal man . . . whose breath is in his norstrels [nostrils]" but to emulate the biblical David who did the Lord's will. Whitall noted of the Irish preacher: "O such a[u]thority as she spoak with who is like har [her]. . . ." Jane Crosfield, according to Whitall, "did speak well & with a grat [great] del [deal]of sorow, O what hart cud [could] be so hard as not to mourn & cri with har [her] this day so ful of troubel she wos for us & spok[e] much to the mourners & thay that has sorow & trobbel every way, it madc me glad to se[e] har [her], to halp [help] us a long. . . ." Crosfield advised them, "Be Children of the light & Children of the day," predicting that some there would not live long and ought to prepare for the last day: "Som[e] wor [were] ful of truobel as the Prophet wos of old, but the Lord did comfort him & so he will you: shc said. . . ." Long after the women ministers had departed from the community, Whitall referred to them in her diary: "O how did Susana Hadden [Hatton] & Jan Crosway [Jane Crosfield] cry among us . . . it very much evects [affects] me when I thinks of them tho[ugh] Jan[e] is gon[e] hom[e] & I may never se[e] har more but often thinks of har. . . ."[2]

Across the Atlantic, Richard Partridge (1681–1759), a Quaker political lobbyist and wealthy merchant in London, England, shared with Ann Whitall, whose life centered on the farm household, a similar respect for the messages of these "chosen instruments" of God. As the agent for the colonial governments of Rhode Island and Pennsylvania, Partridge was acquainted with the leading men of politics in eighteenth-century England and America. He kept the colonial governors and assemblies informed of intended parliamentary legislation and represented their interests, developing influence with the king and Parliament. Partridge was known for his "great Freedom of Access to the King's ministers, and all the Publick offices." Yet Richard Partridge, a political sophisticate, carefully recorded Margaret Ellis's "experience of the dealings of the Lord with me from my

Youth" (from the first call of God inwardly to her soul that she "was seeking ye Living amongst ye Dead," which convinced her to leave the religion of her upbringing, to her emergence as a Quaker, when she "heard as it were the sound of a Trumpet with a Call to all the ends of the Earth"). In 1752, Partridge transcribed the visiting American minister's spiritual autobiography as he accompanied Ellis to English and Welsh meetings during an interval in his parliamentary lobbying.[3]

Eighteenth-century Quakers from all walks of life valued the "divine leadings" of the travelling preachers, not distinguishing between the spiritual efficacy of male and female ministers. In Wales, where British Friends were laying the foundations for the Industrial Revolution, John Kelsall (1683–1743), first as a schoolmaster, then as a clerk at Charles Lloyd's Dolobran Forge and the Dolgyn Ironworks, kept a journal in which he recorded the religious counsel of visiting Quaker preachers. The technical work at the forges was not allowed to interfere with Quaker meetings for worship and discipline, which Kelsall often attended in the company of his Quaker employers, their partners, and his fellow workmen. In March 1711, at the Dolobran meeting, Kelsall heard Ann Chapman, a minister from Bucks County, Pennsylvania, who "appeared a plain and innocent woman truly concerned for the prosperity of truth everywhere." Chapman was en route to the Wales Yearly Meeting, which Kelsall also attended. He observed Chapman preach for a third time when she returned to his local meeting, in June 1711: "A. Chapman was very excellent and noble in the truth being heartily concerned that all might keep to the testimony thereof in all things and live in faithfulness thereto." In July 1711, at the Dolobran meeting, Kelsall listened to Elizabeth Webb, a preacher from Chester County, Pennsylvania, who was travelling to South Wales. Kelsall recorded that "Elizabeth was concerned . . . in shewing how that man's mind in Paradise before the Fall was exercised only on heavenly things, and the same exercise should all be found in who come to the regeneration by Jesus Christ . . . she had also a word of counsel to the poor, and rich," reminding them to keep their eye on the Lord, while in their labors or enjoyments. The Pennsylvania visitor, according to Kelsall, was "exceedingly notable in prayer."[4]

The eighteenth-century transatlantic community of Friends extended from furniture makers in Newport, Rhode Island, to wool merchants in Cork, Ireland, but Quakers were linked by their belief in immediate divine revelation, and a desire to live in accordance with God's will. They sought assistance from those "gifted" in the ministry who circulated throughout the English Atlantic world.

Visibility of Women Travelling Ministers in the Quaker Community

A very large number of Quakers encountered the preachers visiting from overseas because of the comprehensiveness of these travellers' tours. Catharine Payton in almost three years travelled more than 8,750 miles, mostly by horseback, on the North American continent. Before accompanying Catharine Payton to America, Mary Peisley paid a thorough visit to England lasting two years and nine months, riding 5,000 miles, and attending 525 meetings. Elizabeth Wilkinson, in the colonies about one and a half years, rode an estimated 4,327 miles. A few of these women made a transatlantic visit more than once: Elizabeth Webb, Jane Hoskins, Sophia Hume, and Susanna Hatton undertook this religious service twice; Susanna Morris went abroad three times. The almost continuous movement of these ministers, their daily combination of travel and meeting attendance, enabled them to cover a tremendous amount of territory. Overseas visitors usually tried to attend every Quaker meeting in a nation at least once. Sometimes they looped back for a second or third visit.

In addition, the appearances of transatlantic visitors were supplemented by preachers who were travelling regionally. A fairly constant stream of Quaker ministers came through Ann Whitall's region, which was well situated, not far from the port of Philadelphia. The New Jersey farmwife heard itinerant preachers at least monthly, including many from nearby colonies or neighboring meetings. Ann Whitall's diary reveals that she had heard most, if not all, of the transatlantic preachers visiting from the British Isles during her era. The frequent arrivals of such travellers were especially important to Whitall, since her meeting was temporarily bereft of preachers: "I many times thought what wo[ul]d be com[e] of us O if we had won [one] such a man a mong us as Willem Ricket or Samuel Notingham [other itinerant preachers] or Susana Hadden [Hatton] or Jan Crosway [Jane Crosfield] to help us along but we ant [ain't] worthy of such, or it wo[ul]d Plees [please] the Almyty [Almighty] won [one] to send such a won [one] to live among us. . . ."[5]

When notice was given that a travelling preacher was in the area, Friends also made special journeys to see the visitor, particularly if she or he were from overseas. Crowded meetings, with an atmosphere of heightened anticipation, were reported when such a "stranger" was present. A "Public Friend" who had travelled an extensive distance "in the service of Truth" was expected to be greatly "gifted" in the ministry and, perhaps, had a "concern" to deliver a particular message to the people of that locale. Mary Weston, visiting from London, England, noted at a meeting she attended in Boston, Massachusetts, "Many Friends were at it, expecting some great Things from a Londoner." Local preachers were encouraged to give precedence in a meeting to the visiting minister, who was perceived to have a special need to "clear" herself or himself by voicing the "concern" that had prompted the travel. An observer noted that, when Abigail Boles of Ireland visited London in 1722, "her Service was extraordinary . . . She came at a time we had few or no Strangers [visiting preachers], and our own publick ffriends gave way to her, so that at most of ye Meetings ye weight [of the ministry] lay on her."[6]

When several visiting ministers were in a city with a number of Quaker meeting-houses, such as Philadelphia or London, the travellers were distributed to different meetings on first day (Sunday) in order to avoid being constrained by "a tender regard" for the others' service. Since the eighteenth-century Quaker order of ministry was not determined by gender, women had a great capacity to be heard. Ministers deferred to those who appeared to be experiencing the strongest inward "motions" to preach. When Elizabeth Wilkinson unnecessarily abbreviated her sermon because she "was so afraid of being in the Way of others," Wilkinson was told by the other ministers who were present: her companion, Hannah Harris, and the male preacher, Robert Proud, "that I kept the [spiritual] Key, they could neither of them get up till I had done. . . ." A minister might feel divinely directed to perform a particular religious task as well: Elizabeth Wilkinson found at a meeting that "tho' there was Wm. Horn, Isaac Andrews, Sarah Morris & others [ministers present] they could not do my Task which was to caution parents to be more concerned for their Childrens good in a Religious respect, than to get great portions for them."[7]

Travellers also appointed one-time meetings in which they had the opportunity to "clear themselves," or impart their message, in addition to their attendance at regularly scheduled meetings. The American preacher Benjamin Ferris deferred to his ministerial wife, Phebe, and her female companion, when he encountered them while the spouses were travelling separately on religious service in 1756. He remained silent in the meeting because the women had appointed it out of their "concern" (presumably to fulfill a divinely enjoined mission). Benjamin Ferris noted: "The service of the meeting fell to the two Women as they had appointed It and I not feeling any Great Necessity laid on me at that time I Expected to be there After the Yearly Meeting Again so was Not Uneasy ab[ou]t the women Takeing Up the time in the meeting to Clear themselves In which I thought they was Right."[8]

Ministers timed their trips in order to arrive at many of the monthly, quarterly, and yearly meetings. Hundreds, at times, thousands, of Quakers from different areas gathered at the annual meetings (which lasted several days, including meetings for public worship, as well as for church business), where they often heard regional or transatlantic visitors. According to Mary Weston's journal, several thousand people attended the New England Yearly Meeting in Newport, where she preached, "I think the biggest I have seen in America, and the Lord was pleased to own us therein." The itinerant preachers also sought out Quakers who lived far from Friends' meetings, in more isolated circumstances. In Virginia, Rachel Wilson "with Defficulty" travelled to a remotely situated Quaker residence where she was received kindly, "Being glad to see us as thay had but a few Visits from thair friends, Lying at Such adistanc[e] from any that Bore our Name above 60 Miles from any Meet[in]g."[9]

In order to labor individually with Friends, preachers from far away frequently paid religious visits to every Quaker household in a community, as Susanna Morris did in Bristol, England. Religious service of this type could take several months or even years in a city with a sizable Quaker population, such as Philadelphia. Dining and lodging with Quakers extended a minister's influence, since preachers typically had religious opportunities with their hosts. Years after the visit of two American female preachers in England, Sarah Stephenson (later a Quaker preacher herself) recalled the profound impression made on her as a child in 1753, when "those worthy servants of the Lord, Elizabeth Ashbridge and Sarah Worrell, from America, came to my uncle's house, and . . . staid some days." Stephenson remembered, "One evening, during this time, Elizabeth, in a very weighty manner, addressed me, in the language of unspeakable love . . . Her words were piercing, and deeply affected my mind."[10]

A substantial proportion of the transatlantic Quaker community had firsthand experiences with women ministers from abroad and regional travellers: encountering them at meetings, hosting the visitors, or escorting them on their journeys. When the preachers were not physically present, they reached Quakers in other areas with their writings, especially their epistles (formal letters which were extensions of their oral sermons) read in Quaker meetings or published. The Philadelphia Monthly Meeting reported that "A paper from Susanna Freeborn [a Rhode Island minister] was Read at this meeting being Good advice to ye youth of this province which the meeting agrees shall be Read at our next youths meeting and then Sent into other parts of the Province that Soe it may have Its Service." A reprint of *An Epistle in true Love containing a farewell exhortation to Friends' families,* written by Elizabeth Jacob, the minister from Waterford, Ireland, for example, was the first Quaker work to be published in New England; copies of it were distributed to New England Friends' households.[11]

Women Ministers Elevated as Public Figures

Among the Quakers, the words of a woman "speaking in the Light" were of weighty import, since their advices were valued as revelations by the Holy Spirit. When Mary Ellerton visited Pennsylvania from England in 1704, her prophecies were preserved to be reflected upon by Friends. At Rowland Ellis's barn, the Yorkshire woman warned the increasingly prosperous colonists to not be tempted from their spiritual worship by materialism, "notwithstanding you are letting your Hearts into the Earth & plowing it up & building great Houses the Lord will shake the Earth under your Feet & it shall tremble[.] If you are not faithful God will try & visit this Wilderness Land the Storms shall beat & many Trees shall be rooted up. . . ." Ellerton delivered variations of this message at Haverford Meeting House, Radnor Meeting House, and Philadelphia Meeting House in the following days. The English visitor was considered by Friends to have "an excellent Searching Gift in the Ministry."[12]

Paradoxically, in attempting to allow the Holy Spirit to speak through them, such "gifted vessels" became elevated as public figures in the Quaker community. Many Friends' meetings, as well as individual Quakers, kept lists of the travelling preachers who visited their areas and the advices they had delivered over the years. A "Record of Friends Travelling in Ireland,

1656–1765," for example, noted that in 1733: "Mary Penill [Pennell] who landed here in the Seventh Month last year, with John Cadwalader and Ann Roberts from Pennsylvania, came now (accompany'd by Grace Skyrin from Westmorland) after she had been thro' several parts of England and Wales, they had good service amongst us . . . Mary said the Lord was about to Concern some that were young in years in that Meeting . . . She was largely open'd in the Mysteries of Gods Kingdom, being well qualified for the Work of the Ministry."[13]

"Public Friends," such as Mary Ellerton and Mary Pennell, were not to court popular applause and personal devotion (their obligation being to efface themselves and direct their audience to God), but individual preachers did acquire reputations for more or less exceptional "gifts" in the ministry. Mary Peisley of Ireland was described, by a London Quaker in 1749, as having "none to equal her of the rising Generation . . . She having the universal Esteem of the best of Friends wherever she comes, & greatly admir'd in the exercises of her Gift . . . it will be near Spring before she can reach our City, tho' our Frds. are almost impatient for her She having a great name amongst us."[14]

Poetry was written in honor of the travelling ministers by admiring Friends. When Mary Peisley journeyed across England visiting Quaker meetings, a poetic tribute was addressed to the Irish female preacher: "From town to town diffus'd the joyful sound, / Thy voice, persuasive, echoes wide around. / With joy attentive thousands hear thy tongue, / Descant on good and evil, right and wrong; / . . . ." The author, pseudonymously named "Philanthropos" (loving humankind), declared of the Quaker woman, "Thy softer form conceals an hero's mind." Other Quakers with literary inclinations, such as Hannah Griffitts (1727–1817) of Pennsylvania, viewed preachers of either gender as heroic figures in the cause of righteousness. Jane (Fenn) Hoskins, Sarah Morris, Susanna Lightfoot (formerly Hatton), Mary Leaver, and Elizabeth Robinson were the dramatic subjects of many Griffitts poems. In a verse commemorating Jane Hoskins, Griffitts characterized her as a "Messenger of Heaven": "How from her lips,—Did living language flow, / . . . Firm & unshaken, in her Master's Cause, / From Sin & death, recall her kindred race, / To Seize Salvation, & the day of Grace, / . . . ."[15]

Memoirs of preachers' lives, exemplary of faith, also were popular reading among Friends, particularly those of transatlantic travellers, known by a wider range of Quakers. The journal written by the transatlantic preacher

86 *The* GENTLEMAN's MAGAZINE Vol. XX.

An Epistle from a Curate *of a polite Village near London, to his Friend in the same Office at a greater Distance.*

WHEN you prevented *Tuesday's* sun,
And fought, with health-inspiring
For exercise and—food;   [gun,
If game engross'd not all your care,
You might observe a sweeter air
Perfume each field and wood.

You might (so true friends sympathize)
See *Phœbus,* with prophetic rise,
Describe a golden show'r:
Oh, be that day rever'd by me!
Few, very few, glad days there be
Fraught with such annual store.

The REPIQUE. *To Miss* A.M.P.

" ON *earthly* things set not thy heart "
(Advis'd a grave divine)
" When *Anna's* beauties aim the dart,
" Defensive arms be thine."
' No *earthly* thing my bosom warms,'
(The am'rous swain replies)
' For *Anna* boasts celestial charms,
' And heav'n is in her eyes.' RIDER.

To M.P. *a Native of Ireland, now in England, visiting the Meetings of her Friends, the* QUAKERS.

IN thee, bright maid! accomplish'd, we behold
What antient seers of future times foretold.
Now pour'd on all the gifts of grace divine,
Our sons and *daughters,* undistinguish'd, shine:
The sacred energy the *virgin* feels,
And heav'nly truths, with heav'nly force reveals.
Warm'd from the skies with love of human kind,
Thy softer form conceals an hero's mind.
Each private tye dissolv'd, thy native shore,
Nor father's wishes, can retain thee more.
In vain old ocean swells the mountain-wave,
And, loos'd in vain, the madding tempests rave;
Thy fearless virtue ploughs th' *Hibernian* deeps,
Thy zeal, unweary'd, constant vigils keeps:
Britannia's isle beholds, with wond'ring eyes,
Thy toils, that brave stern winter's frowning skies.
From town to town diffus'd the joyful sound,
Thy voice, persuasive, echoes wide around.
With joy attentive thousands hear thy tongue
Descant on good and evil, right and wrong;
From mystic phrases wholesome doctrines draw,
And moralize the rituals of the law.
From these, with evangelic skill display'd
The nobler plan that blest *Emanuel* laid;
'Tis thine to spread the gospel's brighter beam,
A Saviour's love is thy exhaustless theme!
A Saviour's death! a benefit to all!
Wide as the curse deriv'd from *Adam's* fall.
His guilt remov'd, our own is all our share,
Our own, aton'd by penitence and pray'r.
Whate'er the Bigot's fierce religion be,
'Tis but a name, if 'tis not Charity.
The true criterion of our faith is deeds,
One act of love outweighs ten thousand creeds.
While such the topics, thy discourses tend
To warm th' indiff'rent, and the stubborn bend;
To aid the weak, to startle the prophane,
To fix the wav'ring, mortify the vain;
Reduce the erring, the distress'd to chear,
And almost make the Hypocrite sincere.
The peace, that conscious goodness gives, be thine;
Long may'st thou feel an influence all-divine;
Long by thy hearers be thy words rever'd,
Long may they practise what from thee they heard.
Long scenes of bliss, on earth, thy toils requite,
And endless raptures in the realms of light.
Oxfordsh. Jan. 10.   PHILANTHROPOS.

[*We hear that the stature of this maiden is as remarkable as her accomplishments, being near* 6 *feet.*]

In 1750, *Gentleman's Magazine,* the leading English periodical, published a poem about Irish Quaker preacher Mary Peisley (1717–57), then on a religious tour of England. In the poem, entitled "To M.P. a Native of Ireland, now in England, visiting the Meetings of her Friends, the Quakers," Peisley was portrayed as the fulfillment of the biblical prophecy from Joel, "In thee, bright maid! accomplish'd, we behold / What antient seers of future times foretold, / Now pour'd on all the gifts of grace divine, / Our sons and daughters, undistinguish'd shine. . . ." When Mary Peisley visited Pennsylvania in 1755, she was an important figure in persuading American Quakers that payment of taxes, in support of the French and Indian War, violated religious principles. *Courtesy Department of Special Collections, Davidson Library, University of California, Santa Barbara*

Jane Hoskins was one of the first to be published (1771) by Philadelphia Yearly Meeting. An eighteenth-century Quaker, James Jenkins, observed that an edition of the *Journal* of life and travels of the English itinerant minister Catharine Payton "is in the hands of many Friends."[16]

As wisdom figures, the women ministers were sought out by Quakers who visited them for "heavenly conversation" or even resided in their households for a while. Quaker preachers, whether female or male, served as spiritual role models for both sexes. John Griffith (who later became an eminent Quaker preacher himself), as a young man in 1732, chose to reside for some time at the home of the minister Susanna Morris (who had travelled across the Atlantic in 1728) and her husband, Morris Morris: "induced thereto by an expectation of receiving help by her good company and example, in my religious progress; in which I was not disappointed. She was indeed a safe way-mark, as far as I could observe, in every point of view; and I thought as much refined from dross, as any I ever knew." The dependence of Quakers upon the spiritual leadership of such "gifted" Friends was evident in a letter written by Mary Peisley to Richard Shackleton, a devout Friend in Ireland, after the recent death of such a "Mother in Israel," Abigail Watson (formerly Boles): "Yet methought thou looked like a child that had lost a mother, or a young soldier who had had his leading officer taken away, and he left to consider how he should make the next step to preferment. Thou writes of expecting to be nursed at Kilconner [with the spiritual "food" of Abigail Watson, previously resident at Kilconner]." But Peisley, faithful to Quaker tenets, encouraged Shackleton to rely upon his own relationship with God: "Methinks it seems high time for thee to be weaned, and come up to more manly stature than that of a sucking child. Remember, dear friend, that many of our elders are taken away. . . . so that the affairs of the church are consequently likely to fall into the hands of a younger generation."[17]

The importance of the preachers to the effective functioning of the eighteenth-century Quaker community was revealed in the careful notice of their attendance at the yearly meetings. When Richard Partridge, the colonial agent in London, wrote to John Kinsey, the Speaker of the Pennsylvania Assembly, in 1745, he not only informed him about governmental matters ("the Affairs Relating to ys. Province remain at present quiet here . . . the King gone to Hannover & left ye Affairs of ye Kingdom to Lords of the Regency"), but also described the Quaker ministers, including four female preachers from the American colonies, who were attending

London Yearly Meeting. At this yearly meeting, Partridge observed "We had ye Company of our Friends Eb[eneze]r. Large, Eliza.[beth] Shipley, Susan[n]a. Morris, Hester White & [Elizabeth] Morgan."[18] As conduits of God's Spirit, the ministers could electrify a gathering with their inspired preaching, enabling those attending to experience the "presence and power of the Lord." Ministers' ability to preserve members in the right path, as well as "enlarge the borders of Zion" (by assisting in people's "convincement" of Quaker tenets), made them invaluable to the Society of Friends.

On both sides of the Atlantic, Quakers closely followed the movements of the ministers, their shared religious leaders, as they traversed the British empire. John Hunt (1712–78), the London merchant and member of the Meeting for Sufferings, not only informed his Philadelphia mercantile correspondent of his commercial activities, but announced the impending departure of two American Quaker ministers who had been on a religious visit in England: "Our Friends S. [Susanna] Morris [on her second transatlantic visit] & E. [Elizabeth] Morgan are now near taking ship on board the Mary. B: Martin who I suppose will sail next Week." Hunt also notified his associate Israel Pemberton Sr. of the planned journey of the English preacher Thomas Gawthrop, "who is now going to your parts on a Visit to Friends."[19] As was typical of eighteenth-century Friends, John Hunt did not segregate his temporal occupation from his religious beliefs in correspondence. The preaching of those "gifted" in the ministry provided the foundation for the well-ordered, capitalistic eighteenth-century Quaker culture, inspiring Friends with purpose, reinforcing ethical standards and spiritual principles, and connecting otherwise atomistic individuals. As public figures in the larger Quaker community, women ministers had the opportunity to exert influence well beyond their families.

How the Women's Ministry Influenced Quaker Lives

Ministers' expressions in meetings were widely varying, ranging from prophecy to scriptural explication to personal testimony. Susanna Morris wrote that when God sent her into His service among the flock it was "sometimes to tell others, what the Lord, the God of the living, had done for my soul; and at other times, to declare what he did require at their hands." Without an established priestly class, Quakers often strove to assist each other by revealing their own struggles and progress in spiritual growth. Mary Peisley counselled a Friend, "Thou art to trod the same dangerous steps that I had to stumble over, with the advantage, that she who has gone the road before thee, is made willing to lend thee her hand, and to point the snares and traps that lie in the way." Peisley's own "inward inquiry" had been encouraged by other preachers, "some of the Lord's messengers who spoke comfortably to her state and encouraged her in her perseverance and well-doing." Pressing listeners to heed their internal guide to "Truth," ministers generally cautioned people about the dangerous, deluding world with its hindrances and distractions from "Christ within." When Peisley described her own spiritual evolution, she noted how easily "the tumultuous noises, pleasures, and allurements of this world stifled the still small voice which would have directed me, saying, 'This is the way, walk in it'. . . ."[20]

"Public Friends," women as well as men, attempted to direct attention heavenward, reminding Quakers of the spiritual realm. Since "animal life must perish," it was important to not live in utter forgetfulness of God. One's eternal spirit must be developed in order to have hope of entering the kingdom of heaven. Friends were told that "the important business of life" was not spending strength in the gratification of sensual appetites but in pursuit of a good conscience toward God. Concerned for people's immortal souls, Quaker preachers warned worshippers to be ready for death's final change or face "the dismal consequence of being launched into eternity unprepared, shut out from eternal felicity and doomed to everlasting misery because of a few transitory pleasures."[21]

Female preachers had many evangelical-like successes "reaching" those people who, although raised as Quakers, had not experienced a personal "convincement," prompting them to embark upon more spiritual lives. In 1718, according to American Quaker records, "Friends and others had a remarkably awakening visitation, through the ministry of Lydia Lancaster and Elizabeth Rawlinson, from Great Britain . . . Their labours of love not only animated the faithful, but aroused the negligent, and tended to awaken some who were in the slumbers of spiritual death." Lydia Lancaster left "many seals of her ministry" in colonial America, contributing to the emergence of new Quaker preachers. In Nansemond County, Virginia, the labors of the two transatlantic visitors, especially those of Lydia, so deeply affected two Quaker brothers, Joseph and Robert Jordan, "that they were strengthened to yield themselves wholly into the Divine hand, and were thus enabled to come forth in the ministry of the Gospel."[22]

The young men developed into eminent ministers, and acknowledged the visiting British women as having been crucial "instruments of good" to them. Robert Jordan was also influenced by the renowned Irish preacher Abigail Boles, who had "extraordinary service" at the Choptank Yearly Meeting in Maryland. Jordan later wrote the acrostic verse to Boles (see page 54), using the image of a vital, life-giving apple tree to describe the fruitfulness of her ministry. Joshua Brown, another minister, remembered the preaching of Elizabeth Levis (later Shipley) at Nottingham Meeting in Pennsylvania when he was sixteen years old: "My mind was much reached, and greatly humbled through the power of truth attending her ministry. I was made sensible of the need I had of knowing a real change from the propensities of nature, and the work of the new birth." When Brown heard Levis at another meeting, "her labour there was as the clinching of the nail," confirming his new religious commitment.[23]

In their ministerial role, the women also strengthened the faith of the already "convinced," conveying their religious messages not only through sermons but in exchanges of letters with Friends long after they had visited an area. As "gifted vessels," the women preachers became acquainted with a wide range of Quakers, from the humblest farmers to the leading businessmen and politicians. Sampson Lloyd II of Birmingham, England, was patriarch of a Quaker family prominent in the iron and banking industries, and Margaret Ellis was a spinster who worked for her livelihood and boarded with a devout couple in Radnor, Pennsylvania; yet Ellis wrote to him, "Knowing thou art my Brother in Truth . . . I am not willing to drop our Correspondence whilst on this side the grave for thy kindness . . . I cannot forget." Margaret Ellis had lodged with the Sampson Lloyd family during her ministerial tour of England. After her travels, Ellis continued to offer spiritual counsel to her former host through correspondence. Like other Quaker ministers, Ellis gave spiritual consolation to those in distress, interpreting the ways of God to promote greater faith. When Ellis learned of the death of Lloyd's wife, she encouraged him, "The Lord knows what is best for us . . . I sincerely desire that the Spirit of truth may be with thee, and keep thee from Sinking too low, for it Seames to me thou has known A Pinching time Since we parted; for we have need of the Spirit of truth to help us day by day with dayly Bread, as for my part notwithstanding the

Lord has bin with me over Sea and Land and Speaks peace to my Soul, yeat [yet] I have as much need now as Ever, to have my Strength Renewed in him."[24]

The female preachers attempted, as well, "to Awaken & Stir up all unfaithfull & Hypocritical Professors of Truth—with much Labour of Love for the Restoration of Backsliders." Their extemporaneous deliveries were often efforts to reinforce Friends' adherence to the Quaker discipline, since these testimonies were an outward expression of faith. The itinerant ministers became shared points of reference for farflung Friends on opposite sides of the Atlantic, helping to forge a common Quaker culture with their preaching. George Keith, a rival Anglican missionary, agreed that it was these "travelling preachers that keep the Quakers so strong in countenance." Since attentiveness to the Inward Light required the disciplining of appetites, the ministers counselled, "Let moderation and the limits of Truth bound thee in all things, eating, drinking, sleeping, and apparel." Pride, vanity, and envy were other "sins of the flesh" luring people away from God. Plainness in speech and appearance was repeatedly advocated; the women's preaching sometimes had immediate impact on listeners.

On an early trip to England, Susanna Morris felt filled with God's Spirit "to warn the people against all pride . . . which had no small effect on some there, for I was told, after that meeting, one man went home, and burnt his wig; for when pride was spoken of, the wigs were also put with some offenses; being then very much in fashion." Mary Weston heard that her ministry in Newport, Rhode Island, had affected some of the Quaker youth to such an extent that they discarded their extravagant finery afterwards "to the joy of parents and other Friends." Sarah Stephenson recalled years later the words of Elizabeth Ashbridge to her when the minister had lodged at her uncle's house: "What a pity that child should have a ribbon on her head." Stephenson, a young girl at the time, impressed by Ashbridge's profound tone, did not sleep that night, and "in the morning, not daring to put on my ribbon, I came down without it."[25]

By hosting ministers visiting from elsewhere, Friends emphasized their participation in a community of Quakers beyond their immediate neighborhoods, strengthening them in the maintenance of their differences from those of other faiths. Since Quakers' lives were to maximally express spiritual truth, no aspect of their existence was beyond the oversight of the ministry. Wherever Friends resided, Quaker principles required renunciation of the "vain customs" of drinking healths, cursing, betting on horse races, playing at cards or with dice, and duelling. Unedifying diversions were cautioned against, including the theater, music, and dancing, since these activities often led to wanton behavior. The preachers rejected much of the popular entertainment of the day: bullbaiting, cockfighting, or any activities which excited "people to rudeness, cruelty, looseness, and irreligion. . . ." Reading "vain and hurtful books," such as novels, was considered to be morally dangerous and an unprofitable use of time, poisoning one's mind with irreligious notions. Hours not devoted to religious service or earning a livelihood were to be spent on "innocent Divertisements" like gardening, contemplating the divine creation in Nature.[26]

Friends' habits of being self-disciplined, frugal, industrious, and plain were directly related to the "divine messages" vocalized by the travelling ministers—female, as well as male—and to the individuals' adherence to their own "inner promptings." When Mary Weston travelled through some English counties in 1735, her companion, Elizabeth Hutchinson of Cork, Ireland, exhorted Friends to "a diligent Improvement of their Time . . . the Lord . . . [having] entrusted every one with a Gift to improve to his Honour." The emphasis on productive pursuits—"Improve thy time to the glory of Him who gave thee a being"—tended to produce diligent Quaker workers, enabling many Friends' businesses to flourish. Instead of viewing rational capitalism and religious mysticism as irreconcilable opposites, Friends believed that order and economy were evidence of adhering to the Inward Light, since "Truth" was neither confused nor excessive. A French visitor to Pennsylvania, Jean Pierre Brissot de Warville, noted "the order which the Quakers are accustomed from childhood to applying to the distribution of their tasks, their thoughts, and every moment of their lives." This "spirit of order" economized "time, activity, and money." Bankruptcy was considered to be a spiritual failure, as good management reflected spiritual health. Joseph Jordan, the Virginia Quaker preacher, was praised for being a "good economist," when he managed his father's estate after his parents' death, discharging the trust with "good judgment and moderation." After her non-Quaker alcoholic husband died, Elizabeth Ashbridge was saddled with his debts, although the creditors had no legal claim on her. Since some said they would not have trusted her husband but for Elizabeth's sake, Elizabeth "took the whole debt on herself, and beside supporting herself reputably, paid off nearly the whole debt during her widowhood, during which time she also frequently travelled in the ministry."[27]

Recognizing "no dividing-line between the religious and the mundane," Friends tried to infuse their temporal occupations with their spiritual values, providing a unique avenue of influence for spiritually authoritative Quaker women. Ministers encouraged Friends to set a new standard of honesty in commercial relations ("that soe they may be preachers of Righteousness unto ye world in their words and actions"). Since the Spirit of Truth, for Quakers, was divine, the maintenance of the integrity of one's word by faithfulness in promises was a sacred obligation. Friends in trade were advised "to keep to a word in their dealings as much as possible." Quaker merchants were to set a fair, fixed price on their goods. The "Children of Light" developed a reputation for honoring contracts and selling quality goods. Robert Jordan I, the parent of the ministerial brothers of Nansemond County, Virginia, typified many pious eighteenth-century Quakers, in entertaining "the Lord's messengers" (travelling preachers) at his home, being charitable to the poor (including providing free medical assistance to them, "the practice of physic"), and earning a livelihood as "a man of trade and commerce," having "obtained a good reputation in the world."[28]

The stripping away of superfluity and carnal indulgence, counselled by Quaker preachers, contributed to the elegant simplicity of design developed by Quaker cabinetmakers, clockmakers, and other artisans in Newport, Philadelphia, and London. Quaker shipbuilders, uneasy about vain images, omitted figureheads. Quaker traders were advised not to sell worldly fashions like "Striped or ffigured Stuffs." Since Quaker principles precluded the manufacture of cannons, gunshot, and other war supplies, Abraham Darby I of the Coalbrookdale Ironworks in England launched a new line of iron manufacture. He innovated by substituting iron for brass in the casting of domestic ware—pots and pans. His daughter-in-law, the travelling minister Abiah Darby, often preached at mealtimes or spoke a few words of advice to business visitors who came to the noted Ironworks (where the coke-smelting of iron was perfected). Working for God's glory and the benefit of humankind, Friends tended to be as hopeful about improving material life through a more efficient production of necessities as they were optimistic about perfecting the human spirit. Counselled against "idle diversions," Quakers concentrated on "serviceable" employments, including the patient experimentation necessary to achieve technical advances. In the British Isles, Quakers importantly contributed to the development of industries, pioneering in iron, brass, tin plate, and porcelain manufacture.[29]

Encouraged to reject tradition for their own direct experience of God, Friends found scientific pursuits congenial. From George Fox's justification for his religious beliefs ("this I knew experimentally") to Robert Barclay's defense of women's ministry on the basis of the resulting "convincements" of people ("this manifest experience puts it beyond all controversy"), Quakers were experimentalists. The emphasis on the study of Nature as part of the appreciation of divine creation led many Quakers into botany and medicine. Quakers were elected Fellows of the Royal Society of London for Improving Natural Knowledge in numbers disproportionately large to the percentage they formed of the general population: performing outstanding work in natural history, medicine, clockmaking and instrument making. The noted Quaker physician Dr. John Fothergill and the Quaker merchant Peter Collinson, members of the Royal Society, were part of a transatlantic science network linking colonial Americans with European scientific trends. The English Quakers sponsored John and William Bartram's botanical explorations of America. Collinson, who traded extensively to the American colonies, also launched Benjamin Franklin (not a member of the Society of Friends) on his series of "Philadelphia experiments," which gave rise to the single-fluid theory of electricity.[30]

When Quakers held political office in Pennsylvania, New Jersey, Rhode Island, and North Carolina, they looked to "chosen instruments" for wisdom or within for the guidance of the Holy Spirit. A number of colonial American governors were Quaker preachers themselves, including Samuel Jennings of West Jersey and John Easton, John Wanton, and Walter Clarke of Rhode Island. Wanton, of Newport, served as the Rhode Island governor from 1733 to 1742, "in all concerns listening to the still small voice of divine emanation, and being obedient thereto." Respecting "divine leadings," Friends in public office were receptive to religious advice from Quaker women ministers, like Ann Roberts of Pennsylvania, who felt "led by the Spirit," at times, to encourage them to be faithful in executing their duties, to adhere to Quaker testimonies, and to rely on God. Roberts wrote a letter in 1739 to John Kinsey, a Quaker who became Speaker of the Pennsylvania Assembly, warning him of "ye old serpent [Satan] that envied our first parents [Adam and Eve] still continues in ye same to us endeavouring to bring in unbeliefe & imposibilities raising mountains in ye way but . . . all power in heaven & in earth is given to the Son [Christ] & such as follows him faithfully & truly shall have ye victory."[31] During that same year, when war with Spain appeared imminent, John Kinsey led the opposition to the Pennsylvania governor's demand to the Assembly for funds for military defense, which would have subverted the Quaker pacifist testimony, and Friends' position prevailed. In Quaker culture, permeated by religious values, women's ministerial oversight could extend to every aspect of life.

Addressing Regional Dilemmas

Preachers promoted common religious principles in the transatlantic Quaker community, but Friends also lived in diverse regions with difficulties distinctive to their areas. Quakers believed that ministers were guided by the Holy Spirit to address the specific spiritual state of a person or a meeting. While travelling in 1748, Mary Peisley found in a meeting that "I was led in particular to some person, who was under a temptation to join in marriage with one of another society, and likewise to declare that I had no outward information. After meeting, an elderly Friend told me that I had hit the mark to an hair's breadth; for there was a young man, who he knew was under such a temptation, and had been advised against it." When Elizabeth Hudson was journeying in England, she was "led in a peticular maner to Speak to some one who had in there youth been visited [with divine grace] but through unfaithfulness had lost a good State and had commited great Abominations," when a man got up in the meeting, "shew'd great Uneasiness & seem'd as if he would have gone out of meeting but turn'd back sat down . . . as if greatly Effected."[32] Any accuracy in the ministers' statements in the meetings increased their already formidable authority, giving greater weight to their counsel.

Elizabeth Wilkinson's travel journal of 1761–63 revealed the spectrum of messages a preacher felt "concerned" to deliver in response to the varied conditions of Quakers in America. In the Carolinas, where colonists were struggling with sickness, Wilkinson prayed that the Lord "would be pleased to stay his hand & say it was enough & spare the people a little longer. For it was a time of great Mortality amongst Friends & others." To Quaker merchants and land speculators in New York, Wilkinson found it her duty "to Caution our Society that as they were spreading in the Land they might be careful to be as way Marks & not Stumbling blocks to any Enquirers & to be just in all their dealings & engagements." On the island

Letter dated August 13, 1739 (Old Style), written by the Pennsylvania preacher Ann Roberts to John Kinsey, clerk of the Philadelphia Yearly Meeting, who became Speaker of the Pennsylvania Assembly, urging him to "a coming up in faithfulnes[s] to what is made manifest." Quaker women in their ministerial role, desiring the "growth & prosperity of truth," felt "led," at times, to offer religious advice to government leaders. *Courtesy the Historical Society of Pennsylvania* of Nantucket, where seafaring and Quakerism were family traditions, Wilkinson warned "against depending on their being descended from an Ancient & honourable Family which would do nothing for them unless they were found walking in the footsteps of those Ancient Worthies." In nearby Rhode Island, where Newport's commercial expansion had been stimulated largely by its ambitious Quaker merchants and such "Quaker grandees" were an integral part of the colony's politics, the visiting preacher felt she had to warn against "deporting themselves in one way to their Friends & in another towards the great men of the Earth [government leaders] which was an abomination to the Lord." In Salem, Massachusetts, Wilkinson reminded the now tolerated Quakers of earlier times of persecution and "how easy a thing it was for them to come to Meeting now to what it was formerly & to desire they might not be carried away in this time of outward Ease but walk humbly."

In Pennsylvania, Delaware (known as the "Three Lower Counties"), and New Jersey, the English minister addressed the problems associated with material abundance. At Georges Creek meeting, she recalled that "a few Words arose in my Heart to leave among them . . . I feared those that the Lord had blessed many ways & increased the Labour of their hands were attributing it to their own Industry & neglecting to walk reverently before him." At Franklort meeting, she was afraid that "their Souls Enemy has Led too many into an inordinate pursuit of the World." At Chester, where Friends were embarked on accumulating estates, in part in order to preserve their children within the Quaker fold, Wilkinson "had a glimpse of something to say" soon after she entered the meeting-house, "which was to caution parents to be more concerned for their Childrens good in a Religious respect, then to get great portions for them." Finally, in a meeting at the Great House in Philadelphia, "Some Matter came so close & clear that it made me tremble: & I had no way to escape but thro' wilful disobedience: & it was a Subject I had never had to meddle with. . . ." Wilkinson felt compelled to preach to the urban Quakers, who were verging toward atheism, "that it was to be feared some present . . . were exalting themselves as if they were Independent Beings, whereas they could not make one Hair white or black, yet had gone such Lengths that they were ready to call all in Question even the Truths of the Gospel and then the Being of a God."[33] The belief that "inspired" preachers spoke from the same Holy Spirit enabled a minister from one region to be equally authoritative among Quakers in other regions.

The women ministers performed other functions on their travels, in addition to preaching sermons, to assist resident Quakers. While visiting Nantucket, Rachel Wilson, feeling "Deeply ingaged under the sence of the state of that Meet[in]g," told them that if she had judged "by the Sight of the Eye" she would have thought the message she had to deliver was scarcely proper for that meeting. But the English visitor expressed it anyway, "which was that Ex[h]ortation of our Dear Lords if thy Brother Haith any thing against thee go first Reconcile thy Self to thy Brother Before thou of[f]erest thy gift at the altar. . . ." Wilson afterwards discovered several long-standing disputes on the island, which were bringing discredit upon the Society of Friends. A quarterly meeting committee had been trying for many years to convince the concerned parties in one conflict to submit to arbitration. After Rachel Wilson and her companions intervened, "truth favoring our Labour," the parties finally agreed, and bonds were drawn and signed.[34]

Moses Brown (1738–1836), scion of a prominent Baptist mercantile family of Providence, Rhode Island, and eventually a Quaker convert, recalled Wilson's assistance in mediating the conflict: "To the credit of Rachel Wilson, and the influence of her Divine Master, this settlement was made, for it was through her wise and discreet management and influence, she prevailed on Stephen Hopkins [a Quaker merchant and, at times, governor of Rhode Island] and me to undertake to go and attend to the business. It was my lot to examine the record, and, in so doing, a worthy man, then a Minister, . . . was cleared of the charge made against him, which fully paid me for my trouble and care in the business at the time, which I mention to the memory of Rachel Wilson, as without her favoured influence as an instrument, the work would not have been effected. She was indeed a wise and favoured Minister, and an apostle of usefulness to me." The other furious dispute on the island regarded the signing of a certificate of unity with a visiting Friend's ministry (some Quakers had taken offense at what he had delivered, while others supported him). Noting that Satan seldom missed an opportunity to lay waste the work of God, Rachel Wilson endeavored to halt any further division. She successfully encouraged both parties to acknowledge that they had erred: "Missed it and Beg of the quarterly Meet[in]g to pass it by."[35]

Friends accepted the women ministers' arbitration efforts, believing that they were especially attuned to the Holy Spirit. The women waited in silence to discover God's will in the situation, or as Margaret Ellis did, relied on directives imparted to them in dreams. When Margaret Ellis was asked to help resolve a difference in a meeting, she prayed "to the Lord to this purpose, that he would be pleased to manifest to me how the matter really was & that I might have Wisdom given me to be instrumental in reconciling the said difference." That night, in a dream, an elderly man with white hair and clothing appeared to her. He explained the situation to Ellis and advised her to visit the families in order to settle the conflict. After Ellis awakened, she followed the instructions "received" in her dream.[36]

The travels of the women ministers contributed greatly toward maintaining unity in the Society of Friends, helping to prevent the descent into schisms. When Susanna Morris and Elizabeth Jacob visited Twisk, Holland, in 1729, the town's small population of Friends was meeting in two separate locations because of a disagreement. One local preacher had separated from the original meeting with a loyal contingent, while the remaining members met with another minister. A Quaker man asked Morris and Jacob for help, convinced that they could be instrumental in reconciling the parties divided for ten years. The women ministers met with them all in one place. With the assistance of an interpreter, the preachers left the Dutch Quakers in "peace and love with each other, and they seemed glad that we were sent amongst them."[37]

As religious leaders recognized throughout the Quaker community, female preachers shared in the widening gap between designated "Public Friends" and other eighteenth-century Quakers. One contemporary complained of the "vast deal of power exclusively exercised by a certain number . . . a hierarchical influence govern'd the Society: our Ministers, & Elders, were looked up to, as great folks indeed!" He had been taught "to believe that Ministers & Elders were members of *every meeting* into which they went." A preacher's "divine leading" could be powerfully authoritative. Since their "concerns" emerged from what was believed to be divine direction, these ministers were not constrained to address only female issues or only the women's meetings for church business. Rachel Wilson felt compelled to visit the Falls (Pennsylvania) Quarterly Men's Meeting for business "with a particular Request not to give place to a Rending, Dividing Spirit which I feared was s[e]cretly Lurking which if given way too was in danger of doing great harm." When Susanna Hatton requested to sit with the Waterford (Ireland) Six Weeks Meeting ("under a weighty Concern of Spirit to Advize Friends . . . & to Deliver the Counsel of the Lord faithfully"), Hatton's message "well deserving Our Observance" was transcribed into the men's minutes. The Quaker method of decision making provided an unusual opening for female participation, since the Society of Friends did not arrive at decisions through the will of the majority (nor, theoretically, on the basis of political or economic power). Rather, those who most convincingly appeared to be speaking "in the power of the Lord" wielded the most influence.[38]

Innovative Stances

Elizabeth Wilkinson, like the other travelling preachers, sometimes found it her duty to mention a topic among Quakers in a meeting "which was really very hard to do." But under a "Sence & persuasion of its being his [God's] requiring," she was "helped above the Fear of men." Centering inward to know a "stay to our minds beyond all Visibles," she risked incurring the wrath of those she exhorted. Elizabeth Hudson compared the ministry to a fountain of living water and the ministers to pipes. Each pipe had a part to play in conveying water to diverse parts of the city. If each pipe did not perform its service, it frustrated God's grand design. The preachers, by vocalizing what they experienced as God's will, functioned as the "conscience" of the Quaker transatlantic community, clarifying the spiritual ideals. They strove to "encourage the growth of truth and righteousness . . . labouring to turn people from darkness to light, and from the power of satan, unto God."[39] But because Quakers believed in ongoing divine revelation, this was an evolving conscience. Visiting female preachers not only upheld Quaker standards but helped to shape new positions taken by the Society on various issues.

The women engaged in constant self-scrutiny to evaluate whether they had delivered the "divine message" faithfully. Mary Peisley, for example, after a meeting, found some weight upon her spirit but could not tell the cause: "I examined myself, and brought things to the closest scrutiny, to know whether I had done or omitted anything contrary to Truth, but could find no condemnation. At dinner I felt the spirit of supplication [prayer], which I gave way to, and found my mind free and easy." In the "service of Truth," Quaker preachers remained sensitive to every change in their own spiritual states. All described alternating cycles of discouragement and inspiration: times when they were "poor in spirit and low in mind," with no connection to God, followed by "Divine openings," when "the Lord's eternal power broke in upon us, to the comfort and refreshment of our souls."[40]

At times, it was difficult to maintain their fellowship with the body of Quakers while having fidelity to what they believed was God's "leading." Mary Peisley wrote that "the Lord has often made use of me in his hand, as a sharp threshing instrument, and put such words in my mouth for them, as they could hardly bear; so that on all sides, the poor creature [Peisley] is greatly despised and rejected," as she encountered Quakers who disagreed, or felt offended by her statements. The ministers did attempt to receive constructive criticism from those watchful of their spiritual growth, especially from other preachers and elders, but, ultimately, they relied upon their inward sense of divine authority. "And though the manner in which Truth led me was often misconstrued, and wrongfully censured, . . . my God knew it was in obedience to Him," Peisley asserted.[41]

For the Quaker church leadership, as well, supervision of the "inspired" ministry, preventing the spread of delusions that would mislead the "flock," had to be skillfully managed so as not to result in censorship of genuine "Divine openings." Often, the ministers were at the forefront of change, their "leadings of Truth" conflicting with the Quaker consensus. They struggled with social pressure as well as their own self-doubts as to whether, indeed, they were obeying divine will. In 1752, Susanna Morris, for example, felt "led" to speak "against the use of spirituous liquors" and "against the too frequent use of tobacco, in all its shapes, as an evil also." During this period, a prominent London Quaker merchant and member of the Meeting for Sufferings, John Hanbury, controlled the tobacco trade with the colony of Maryland, and conducted a large part of that trade with Virginia. In addition, Pennsylvania Quaker merchants frequently traded in West Indies rum. Not only might Susanna Morris's "Divine opening" hurt Quaker commercial interests, but it was an innovation beyond the established Quaker discipline. Tobacco was not recognized as harmful. Rum was widely used by eighteenth-century Friends, routinely given to laborers to strengthen them for intense work during harvest. The Society had prohibited drunkenness, or the abuse of liquor, but not alcohol itself.[42]

Israel Pemberton Jr., clerk of the Philadelphia Yearly Meeting (the most important position in American Quaker church government), apparently chastised Susanna Morris for the stance she had taken. Morris sent a penitent, self-examining letter to him, questioning her "leading of Truth." "Worthy Friend Israel Pemberton," Morris wrote, "I send these few lines to let thee or Any other of my Good Friends know that I never was Concerned to Speak against All the Use of Tobacco; but the too frequent use of that & all other Strong things that Steals away the Heart from the Truth—And if by any Shortness of mine, I have said any thing disagreeable to Truth, and not to ye Edification of my Frds. or Trespassed against any of you there or Elsewhere, I Can truly say I am Sorry for it, And then I hope my Frds. will freely forgive me & at times Pray for me that the Lord our God may help me in all places to Divide ye word aright as it may best please him the Most High, and while I am in the Body I hope I Shall be preserved with you my Dear Frds. in the Gospell Fellowship & Unity of the Brethren which I Greatly Vallue and desire in all my Undertakings. . . ." Morris concluded her letter with the hope that Friends would support her in her "concern" to visit Great Britain for the third time, "giving up to the Lord's requirings" at seventy years of age, "to go over ye Seas to do Some Small Service for him yet, & atho' Stri[c]ken in Years, yet I can heartily trust my great Master that he is Able & Willing to go Along with me & to bring me Safe Home." The woman minister signed her letter to Pemberton "these from me who Am a Friend & hope So to remain to all the Lovers of Truth."[43]

The Pennsylvania Friends did approve Morris's third visit overseas. Susanna Morris crossed the ocean with the Long Island preacher Phebe Dodge and with Mary Weston (returning to her London residence after her American religious visit). But although Friends had granted Morris a certificate of unity with her efforts "in the service of Truth," Israel Pemberton Jr. apparently was still worried that Susanna Morris would advocate a misguided position regarding rum and tobacco, and that her preaching would have serious effects. Mary Weston, who had lodged at Israel Pemberton Jr.'s residence in Philadelphia, reported to him by letter, keeping him informed about the subjects of Morris's testimonies in the English meetings. Weston noted that on their ocean passage she and Dodge had been seasick most of the voyage, "but ye good old Hero [Susanna Morris, the survivor of several shipwrecks] much ye same as on Shore." According to Weston, Morris's "Service Among us been very Acceptable both in ye publick meetings at this our Annell [annual] Assembly and others before yt [that] Came on, nothing perticuler respecting Tobacca. . . ." Again, in August 1752, Weston reassured Pemberton about Susanna Morris: "This good Woman never Shone so much in our parts as in this Visit her Ingagements in ye Gospel Labour I believe was to general Satisfaction, very Seldome if at any time touch[e]d on ye Subjects of rum and tobacca."[44]

Susanna Morris's own convictions appeared to strengthen, however, and her desire to obey the inward promptings of "Truth" was stronger than her fear of being censured by the Friends' community. She wrote of her preaching (presumably out of Weston's hearing) in the British Isles regarding the use of spiritous liquors and the too frequent use of tobacco: "I am fully of the mind, that these things are a great obstruction to that glorious work . . . and I think I have the mind of Truth therein. Sure I am, that I was constrained so to testify to many, in this my journey, yea, in public meetings." And, as part of the growing reform movement within Quakerism, other inwardly seeking preachers began noticing the dangers of such accepted customs. New Jersey Quaker preacher John Woolman, in 1756, observed that even "those whose lives are for the most part regular, and whose examples have a strong influence on the minds of others, adhere to some customs which powerfully draw to the use of more strong liquor than pure wisdom allows." Woolman noted in his journal, "By great labor, and often by much sweating, there is even among such as are not drunkards a craving of liquors to revive the spirits; that partly by the luxurious drinking of some, and partly by the drinking of others (led to it through immoderate labor), very great quantities of rum are every year expended in our colonies; the greater part of which we should have no need of, did we steadily attend to pure wisdom." Elizabeth (Reed) Levis, a Pennsylvania minister, penned an epistle, *Some Friendly Advice and Cautions,* in 1761, because her spirit was burdened by the misbehavior resulting from the free use of spiritous liquor, especially at harvest time. In 1769, John Woolman pointed out the link between rum and the slave trade: to consume the former was to patronize the latter. Prompted by the preachings of such conscience-stricken Friends, the entire Society of Friends gradually shifted attitudes toward alcohol, moving toward a policy of encouraging abstinence. After 1762, Friends were dissuaded from keeping public houses (or taverns). By 1777, the Philadelphia Yearly Meeting ordered that Quakers were not to enter into the manufacturing or selling of liquors and those involved were to desist. A gradual agreement by a number of ministers on a specific "divine revelation" could move the Society of Friends to a new position on an issue.[45]

The Need for Reform

Mary Weston pointed to the need for reform in the 1750s, describing the "Weight of [spiritual] Exercise [for a minister] that attends travelling in this Day of Liberty and Ease . . . a kind of Lethargy is so evidently seen in the [Quaker] Churches in many Places." The ministers noted that toleration had actually weakened the religiosity of many Quakers. Unwilling to offend their non-Quaker neighbors, members often avoided challenging stances that might bring renewed persecution upon them. To identify oneself as a Quaker in the eighteenth century, one no longer had to endure the kind of sufferings encountered by an earlier generation. As a consequence, many Friends had become conservative and complacent. In the British Isles, Friends' skillful political negotiation to maintain their tolerated status had allowed members to achieve material prosperity. The "Richest Trading men in London" now worshipped at the eighteenth-century Gracechurch Street Friends Meeting.[46]

Quaker entrepreneurial spirit had been assisted by a strong sectarian network, as they traded with their coreligionists throughout the English Atlantic world. Quaker concern for the education of the young, including helping to establish them in business, had resulted in a steady growth of trade among Friends. The penalties under which British Quakers still labored also had prompted them to pioneer in new areas of the economy. The intermarriage of Quaker families, such as the Lloyds and the Barclays, consolidated firms, further contributing to their success in industries such as banking, brewing, iron making, and mining.

A community that had grown rich, successful, and powerful, in part by following the principles preached by the ministers: diligence in the productive use of one's talents, with little dissipation of fortune or time spent gratifying appetites, now faced problems arising from the effectiveness of those principles. Absorption in business and the acquisition of wealth made it more difficult to remember spiritual values. Mary Peisley warned her brother, "Thou mayst frequently find it very hard to have thy mind composed and staid on the Truth, when coming out of a hurry and multiplicity of business." Joseph White, an American preacher, observed that eighteenth-century London Friends were so involved "in almost every branch of trade, and in commerce and conversation that there [was] scarcely time for the busy and active part . . . to reflect" on their religious condition. In addition, as the Society of Friends matured, Quaker religion was becoming "national": "descending like a patrimony." More and more, new members were "birthright" Quakers, the children of Friends who automatically had been given membership; yet, many had not had their own experiential "convincement" of Quaker tenets. For a number of eighteenth-century Quakers, their religious affiliation had become a formality: familial, not spiritual.[47]

In the American colonies during the first half of the eighteenth century, Quakers enjoyed their greatest secular power. Friends were political leaders in some colonies and achieved great commercial success in ports such as Newport, Philadelphia, and New York. Those who had acquired substantial acreage at low prices during the initial settlement of regions accumulated large estates. Quaker men active in politics and commerce had dealings with those of other faiths, encouraging gradual worldly accommodation. Increasingly, affluent Quakers living in such cities as Newport and Philadelphia (as well as in the British Isles, in London and Bristol) participated in a common culture of the wealthy elite, drifting away from distinctive Quaker "testimonies," in conformity to the "vain customs and fashions" of the world.

Mary Ellerton's earlier prophecies regarding Quakers in Pennsylvania, her warnings about materialism, seemingly were being fulfilled. Fifty years after Mary Ellerton had cautioned the Quaker colonists against "letting your Hearts into the Earth & plowing it up & building great Houses," Samuel Fothergill, another English preacher visiting Pennsylvania, commented on the apparent spiritual decline. In 1754, Fothergill summarized how he believed American Quakers had changed: "Their fathers came into the country in its infancy, & bought large tracts of land for a trifle; their sons found large estates come into their possession & a profession of religion which was partly national, which descended like the patrimony from their fathers, & cost as little." Fothergill continued, regarding the Pennsylvania Friends: "They settled in ease & affluence, & whilst they made the barren wilderness as a fruitful field, suffered the plantation of God to be as a field uncultivated, & as a desert. Thus, decay of discipline & other weakening things prevailed, to the eclipsing of Zion's beauty . . . A people . . . bent of their spirits to this world, could not instruct their offspring in those statutes they had themselves forgotten."[48]

By the mid-eighteenth century, it was clear that the discipline was not being strictly or uniformly enforced by meetings throughout the transatlantic Quaker community. Worldly Friends were no longer upholding the agreed upon "testimonies." Quakers failed to reprimand delinquency because they thought: "It is my child, or friend, that I am loath to offend lest I should suffer in my interest or gain his ill-will." Pennsylvania Quaker meeting records confirm the ministers' impressions that succeeding generations were increasingly violating Friends' discipline, and that there was a laxity in enforcement of principles. Meeting records reveal little misbehavior between 1682 and 1715 among the first Quaker immigrants to Pennsylvania. By 1745, there were eight times as many offenses as for any year before 1716. Marrying contrary to Quaker discipline had been rare before 1715, but later (among the Quaker immigrants' children born in the colonies), it was the most typical offense. Yet disownments were uncommon.[49]

The growing worldliness of Quakers also affected the spiritual health of their ministry. In 1748, Mary Peisley wrote to a Quaker male preacher, J. T., who was apparently neglecting his ministry because of distractions in this "lukewarm, backsliding, degenerate age": "Consider what thou art doing with these excellent talents, which the great Lord has committed to thy trust. If thou should cease to use them to the honour of His name. . . . Do not again become a slave to the world." As Quaker men were developing industries, opening markets, and serving in governmental assemblies, the lure of such worldly affairs could outweigh the call of religious service.[50]

Dr. John Rutty, a Quaker elder of Dublin, Ireland, offered an explanation, in 1751, of an observed rise in the number of female religious travellers: "Ministers have allowed the cares of the world to interpose: this is a temptation more incident to the men than to those of the female sex, whose superior diligence in their travels on this account we have of late years been witnesses of." Women's exclusion from many of the political and commercial activities of their time may have assisted them in the maintenance of Quaker principles during the Society's prosperity and increasing cultural assimilation. When two female ministers from Pennsylvania, Elizabeth Ashbridge and Sarah Worrell, fell deathly ill during their religious visit to Ireland in 1755, overcome by their gospel labors, one of them said that "it looked as if two poor, weak Women were sent to lay down their lives as a Sacrifice, whilst strong Men cou'[l]d stay home and be at ease."[51]

A crisis in Pennsylvania, generated by the British and French imperial struggle for the North American continent, highlighted the decline of Quaker standards. William Penn had believed that Quakers could balance political government and church leadership in his "holy experiment" of Pennsylvania. Friends could be "in the world" to improve it, but not "of it," maintaining a focus on the eternal. But that balance of temporal and spiritual "callings" had begun to fail. The crisis revealed a growing Quaker division between conservatives, whose priority of retaining political power and economic interests left them open to worldly accommodation, and reformers, whose priority of remaining faithful to religious principles enabled them to renounce secular power and critique the "world's" culture.

The Society of Friends historically had argued that human life could not be meaningfully separated into various spheres: practice must be consistent with principle. Spirituality, if genuine, infused all of one's life. This traditional Quaker confrontation of the "world's ways," the integration of religion with all endeavors, had been especially significant for women.[52] Women's ministerial leadership had allowed them to speak out on almost any subject concerning Friends, even though they were excluded from such public leadership in secular culture. Quaker pragmatism had always remained open to mysticism through a willingness to receive divine revelation. Many of the mid-eighteenth-century transatlantic visits were prompted by ministers' perception that the current generation had slipped from these traditional Quaker religious values. The evil attacked most vehemently by the reformers was an attempt by some Friends to compartmentalize religion from other activities, such as politics. Reform-oriented ministers, women as well as men, sought a return to the religious zeal and discipline of the first generation of Quakers. These preachers opposed materialism, lifeless formalism of worship, and worldly compromises that undermined Quaker ideals.

Leaders of Reform

A small group of like-minded reformist ministers from Ireland, England, and America, concerned about spiritual declension in the Society of Friends, increasingly began working toward the same kinds of reforms. Among these were Mary Peisley, John Churchman, Mary Weston (Peisley's travel companion during part of her English journey), Hannah Harris, Elizabeth Wilkinson, John Griffith (who had resided with Susanna Morris), William Brown (brother-in-law of John Churchman), John Pemberton, Catharine Payton, John Woolman, and Samuel Fothergill. These travelling ministers' efforts would dramatically alter the direction of Quakerism, as they shifted attitudes about public officeholding, slavery, pacifism, and asceticism, among other issues, and transformed the Society by expanding the meeting structure, expelling indifferent participants, and strengthening members' commitment to Quaker tenets. Although Quaker male preachers, such as John Churchman, John Woolman, and Samuel Fothergill, spearheaded major reforms, their contributions will be discussed only briefly as this section focusses on the contributions of the women ministers' travels to reform.

The inception of the Quaker reform movement is associated with John Churchman's journey through the British Isles, and his proposal of a concrete method to reform the Society through the establishment of additional meetings of discipline to allow closer supervision of members. Churchman, a Pennsylvanian, had had a "divine revelation" that his primary task in travelling abroad was not evangelical, but reforming. He was to cleanse the corruption within his own church: "The greatest enemies of the Truth were the professors of it who did not observe the instructions of the grace of God." About the same time that Churchman in Pennsylvania was experiencing "drawings on his spirit" to visit the British Isles, the Irish Quaker minister Mary Peisley was already travelling in England and feeling "led" to promote a similar reformation. On her English journey, Peisley wrote in April 1749, "Often is my mind brought very low under the sight and sense of the few in this day, who are made rightly willing to bow their necks to the yoke of Christ." Peisley believed that the Quaker elders had become "dry withered fruitless trees, twice dead, plucked up by the roots, being rich in words and expressions of former experience, but out of the power of Truth." As a confrontation of their empty words, and a demonstration of a true spiritual ministry, Peisley sat in silence in many meetings, "for I believe it is the will of our God to have his people drawn from sounds to Him the living substance." Her silence shocked Friends who had grown accustomed to hearing preaching from a minister who had come a great distance on a "concern."[53]

Mary Peisley's origin in Ireland, where Quakers had always practiced a stricter discipline than elsewhere, undoubtedly influenced her reforming fervor. But the Society was suffering from some of the same problems that Friends had noticed in other faiths: religion, for some, had become formalistic, hollow, and pharisaical. The Irish minister, who strictly adhered to waiting for "divine openings" of Truth before preaching, discovered that some Quakers had become a greater hindrance than non-Quakers to her ministry. These nominal Friends feared the criticism of those of other faiths if Peisley sat silent in meetings. Peisley wrote: "At another place [on the English religious journey] where I had a meeting, the professors of Truth [Quakers] had heard of my being silent at several meetings, and were afraid of the cross and reproach of men, so took me a back way to the meeting, for fear (as I apprehended) their neighbours who were not of our Society should see us, and come there; yet Providence so ordered it, that a large number came to the afternoon meeting, to whom Truth was declared [Peisley felt "inspired" to preach] . . . after which I had to speak closely to the professors." She bewailed these "false brethren" of her own religion: those "who have lost the spirit and power of godliness, but retain the form; being clothed with a pharisaical righteousness . . . O! the great loss we that are young have, for want of steady elders to go before us." Mary Weston, who had accompanied Peisley for twenty-three weeks, wrote in November 1749 of the "Degenerate State of ye Churches" in many parts of England, where "Elders and leading men in meetgs of Discipline" were indulging transgressions of Quaker testimonies, "poor blind leaders of ye blind. . . ." They compared unfavorably with the "Zeal Godly Fear and wise Circumspection" of the earliest Quakers.[54]

When John Churchman arrived in England in July 1750 with his brother-in-law William Brown and John Pemberton (Pemberton had sailed for his health, but while accompanying Churchman on his travels, he appeared in the ministry), the Pennsylvania minister also felt "led" to sit in silence in many meetings, receiving censure from London Friends. Churchman challenged those who loved "to have the itching ear pleased," without truly receiving and practicing ministers' messages (to "be found doers thereof"). The visiting American male preachers were offended, like Peisley and Weston, by the spiritual dullness of the generality of English Quakers: their payment of tithes, extravagance, vanity, drunkenness, disorderly marriages, and deism. But the Pennsylvanian visitors were favorably impressed by some Quakers in the British Isles. Their occasional companions on religious service included the young Irish minister Samuel Neale (later Mary Peisley's husband). Neale, a "birthright" Quaker, had led a "career of vanity and dissipation," until he had been "reached" through the ministry of Catharine Payton during her visit to Ireland. Neale recalled the dramatic awakening: "My state was so opened to that highly favoured instrument in the Lord's hand, Catharine Payton . . . that all I had done seemed to have been unfolded to her in a wonderful manner. I was as one smitten to the ground, dissolved in tears . . . so wrought upon by the power and Spirit of the holy Jesus, that like Saul, I was ready to cry out; 'Lord, what wouldest thou have me to do?' "[55]

John Pemberton and John Churchman also stayed with "Our very D[ea]r. Landlady [the preacher] Hannah Harris, in Cumberland, where we quartered near 7 Weeks she may be truly called a skil[l]ful mother in Israel," where the American reformers received sympathetic encouragement in their labors. Harris, who was even then experiencing her own religious "concern" to visit America, accompanied them to meetings. When Pemberton and Churchman landed in Ireland, they encountered the preacher Susanna Hatton, as well, characterizing her as "a Choice ffriend of the Primitive Order"—one who embodied the principles of the earliest Friends.[56] Peisley, Payton, Harris, and Hatton were among those ministers in the following years who would promote reformation in the American colonies.

Mary Weston (who had earlier travelled in England with the Irish preacher Mary Peisley) arrived in Pennsylvania in July 1750 almost exactly when Churchman and his companions landed in England to begin their four-year reforming visit. On her American journey, Weston also preached by example, sitting in silence at times when she felt that the meeting attenders were too dependent on "words" instead of their own, inward spiritual experience. In Portsmouth, Rhode Island, Weston remained silent in a meeting, convinced that the worshippers' expectations were "too much outward," until the women separated from the men in order to hold their church business meetings. The visiting Londoner had such an elevated reputation as a minister, however, that when she suddenly felt inspired to preach in the women's business meeting, it was "to the no small Mortification of the Men Friends." Many of the men left their own meeting "and hovered about the Door and Windows, very thick" in order to hear her.[57]

Weston tried to confront some of the spiritually dull American elders as well, whom she felt were leading the young ones astray. She wrote to Abigail Watson (formerly Boles), who had visited the colonies almost three decades earlier, that the number of Quaker meetings had greatly increased but also "pride, idleness & fullness of bread . . . tho' perhaps in their flourishing cities Philadelphia, N: York, Boston, Newport, &c. idleness not so much, as a worldly spirit, or eager pursuit after riches which hath wounded many poor souls . . . and given wings to their offspring who are . . . flying from the pure lowly appearance of truth in the heart." At a ministers' meeting in Salem, Massachusetts, Weston gave advice on the method of Quaker preaching to her New England coreligionists. Weston instructed the "weighty Friends" at several places, in spite of it being "difficult to admonish those who have been elders & fathers of the church." But, as she boldly said (inspired by the biblical words of Elihu) to some elders of Middletown Meeting in Pennsylvania: "Great Men are not always wise, neither do the Aged understand Judgment, when destitute of Divine Wisdom which inspires with true Knowledge." One of Mary Weston's important contributions was to assist in persuading Israel Pemberton Jr., the powerful layman and leader in American Quaker church government, to join the reformist cause. Israel Pemberton Jr.'s gradual conversion to the reformers' belief that the Society needed a dramatic spiritual cleansing profoundly affected the evolution of Quakerism in Pennsylvania. The wealthy Philadelphia merchant and assemblyman eventually lent respectability to ascetic visionaries such as preachers John Churchman and John Woolman.[58]

During the 1740s, Israel Pemberton Jr., with aspirations to become Speaker of the Assembly, had not seemed a likely candidate for supporting an effort to revive religious zeal in the Society. Like most members of the so-called Quaker party, Pemberton had been preoccupied with his political opposition (including the Anglican proprietors: sons of William Penn; the governors; and some jealous, non-Quaker Pennsylvanians), suspicious that they might attempt to eliminate civil and religious liberties in Pennsylvania. Historically, the two offices of Speaker of the Assembly (the preeminent post for Pennsylvanians) and clerk of the Philadelphia Yearly Meeting (the preeminent office in American Quakerism) had been held simultaneously by one man. But, in 1750, upon the death of John Kinsey, who was Speaker of the Assembly and clerk of the yearly meeting, the two offices were divided between two men. Isaac Norris II became the Speaker of the Assembly, and Israel Pemberton Jr. was appointed clerk of the yearly meeting (prior to his conversion to reform ideals).

Soon after Israel Pemberton Jr.'s yearly meeting appointment, Mary Weston warned the assemblyman to place the more important work of the spiritual kingdom before political ambition. Weston stayed at Israel Pemberton Jr.'s Philadelphia residence during part of her American religious visit, and had been escorted by Pemberton's wife, Mary, on her travels. Weston wrote, "Thou art qualified I grant to be serviceable both in church and state, but oh let the lesser always give place to the greater."[59] The church was in disarray, and urgently needed reform, Weston told Israel Pemberton Jr. She urged Pemberton to help restore its spiritual vitality. Pemberton's brother John was even then accompanying John Churchman on his mission to reestablish church discipline in England. Between 1750 and 1755, Israel Pemberton Jr. increasingly adopted such counsel, and his reforming stance distinguished him from his yearly meeting clerk predecessors. Since the Philadelphia Yearly Meeting leadership had great influence, Pemberton's embrace of the reformist cause helped to move the Society of Friends in a new direction.

After Mary Weston returned to England in 1752, Mary Peisley of Ireland and Catharine Payton of England travelled on religious service to the American colonies in 1753. Although the Quaker reformation in America is associated with the English preacher Samuel Fothergill's visit in 1754, the two women "stayed longer, traveled at least as much, and promoted the same reformation as he did—but sometimes more pugnaciously." Mary Peisley was known, and, at times, praised by Friends, for seeking not "to please man, but the Lord. . . . and zealously appearing against what she thought wrong in any, without respect to person; being neither moved by the smiles or frowns of mortals, from performing what she apprehended to be her duty." Another Irish Quaker preacher, James Gough, wrote of Peisley's adherence to "inward leadings": "I am ready to conclude, that none in our day . . . adhered with more steadiness to His guidance through a variety of probations."[60]

When Mary Peisley and Catharine Payton arrived in America, they landed at the port of Charleston, South Carolina, where they found a tiny, not very flourishing community of Quakers. The Charleston Society of Friends had dwindled in membership; for several years, they did not even hold meetings. These Quakers lived in the midst of a pleasure-loving culture whose leading citizens largely belonged to the established Church of England. Peisley noted that a major reformation was required among Charleston Friends in 1753. There was not just an individual "backslider" who needed cautioning; disorders were everywhere. "The discipline was quite let fall," wrote Peisley, "and I found it my duty to endeavour to revive it. Herein I met with open opposition and evil treatment, especially from one of my own countrymen [an Irishman], who was of a libertine spirit, and had been under the censure of Friends in his native land." It seemed to the British visitors that Charleston was functioning "like a city of refuge for the disjointed members of our Society, where they may walk in the sight of their own eyes, and the imagination of their own hearts, without being accountable to any for their conduct, and yet be called by the name of Quaker, to take away their reproach. We did not meet with one in that place that kept to the plain language [using "thee" and "thou," instead of "you"], except one young man."[61]

The women lodged at the residence of John Sinclair, a Quaker merchant who previously had hosted Mary Weston. But their host had broken a fundamental rule of Quaker discipline by marrying a non-Quaker, and his flagrant violation disturbed the reformers. They found some peace in hoping for the conversion of Sinclair's wife: "We lodged at the house of one that had married out of the Society, which we went to with fear and reluctance, having first tried all means to avoid it. Here we were greatly straitened; but I think we were providentially cast there for his wife's sake, who is under convincement, a tender-hearted, good-natured woman . . . and he well esteemed for a fair reputable trader." Peisley recalled, "He received us with much civility and hospitality, which yet did not blind our eyes, or prevent our telling him the truth." In spite of enjoying his hospitality, the preachers were determined to reinforce the Quaker principles. Peisley asserted, "I have gone so far as to acquaint him, that I was ashamed to walk the streets with one under our name, who deviated so much from our principles as he did; which he always took well, and would acknowledge his faults."

The women preachers paid a religious visit to every Quaker family in Charleston. They encountered opposition from some Friends who perceived them to be interfering outsiders advocating a standard more stringent than local habits. Peisley and Payton attempted to revive the Quaker testimonies, such as adherence to "plain language": "by this and such like labour, I understand we have driven several from the meeting, who could not bear sound doctrine, though ever so private." Peisley was convinced, however, that this attrition would ultimately strengthen the Society. Certain that she was doing God's work in upholding the standards, Mary Peisley did not mind if her actions led to a decreased number of members: "Amen, to these leaving the profession, whose lives and conduct are a scandal to it, and I wish to be made more and more instrumental, in the hand of my God, for division in the Society, between the precious and the vile . . . for of a truth it was His Spirit, if ever I knew it, and not my own, that led me to this close work." The women's confrontations stirred up a great deal of anger: "One appeared in open opposition, at a meeting appointed for conference, in order to take steps for reviving the discipline amongst them; he attacked me in particular," recalled Mary Peisley, "but I had then little to say to him, and what I did say, was in great mildness; he arose in a violent passion and left the room; since which we have seen no more of him at meeting or elsewhere."

Discipline, as the ministers understood it, was not just a form for form's sake, but served an active purpose as "a wall of defence against the encroachments of many dangerous enemies . . . a hedge to shelter from the various baneful blasts, destructive to young and tender plants." It protected people, with their weak and frail natures, from coping with many dangerous and confusing temptations. This "wall of defence" was to shield children particularly, who were vulnerable to corrupt influences as they tried to develop spiritually. Peisley and Payton believed that the first way of restoring this "hedge" was to reassert the barrier between the Society and the disbelieving world by having "all unsanctified spirits, both of your own and other societies, excluded the privilege of sitting in your meetings for business; otherwise we believe it will be building with the rubbish." The presence of non-Quakers, who attended out of curiosity, had become common at the Quaker meetings for church business. Wherever Peisley and Payton travelled in the colonies, they requested select meetings of Quakers during discipline decisions, since the attendance of members of other religions "rendered it difficult for us to discharge our duties." In North Carolina, Peisley recalled, "The weighty part of Friends joined us, and seemed to conclude they would strive for an amendment." The Irish female preacher effected another change: "I also proposed their holding a meeting for the elders to confer in, before the ministers joined them, in order to their hearing a more full and perfect account of the state of the ministry in each meeting, and to have them both held before the quarterly meeting. This was agreed to."

Peisley was so concerned about "the exceedingly low state of the ministry and discipline in most, if not all, the monthly meetings" in Virginia that she wrote an epistle to the yearly meeting held at Curles, in June 1754. She noted that while some seemed to glory in the apparent increase of Friends' membership by marriage to non-Quakers or by birthright, "we fear many come in amongst you with unsanctified spirits, to make a profession of the Truth, which is now easy, without a possession or sure inheritance in it . . . they have but increased ungodliness in the Church, by adding chaff instead of the solid, weighty wheat." The female visitors were especially troubled by the avarice of those who had been "called" to the ministry "and through a desire of some kind or other of filthy lucre . . . are become formal, blind, and unfaithful . . . whose candles are already put out by the baneful breath of the spirit of this world."

Occasionally in their confrontational preaching, the travellers addressed topics that were secret and painful, with apparently great accuracy. In Maryland, "we were falsely accused of speaking from outward information,—when in truth it was from the opening of the word of life," Mary Peisley recorded. "This we were frequently suspected of, and charged with, by unbelievers, who knew not the intelligence of the Spirit, though they made professions of it." At other times, the women angered attenders by sitting in silence, disappointing "these wrong spirits, by closing our mouths in silence one meeting after another; which greatly displeased the people, and drew upon us great reproach, lies and slander."

In spite of criticism and conflict, the women gave advice that was recorded by meetings. At the New England Yearly Meeting in Rhode Island, where they also found the discipline "sadly out of order; in particular, that unwise practice of having meetings for discipline mixed with the world's people, and such as were proper subjects to have it exercised upon," the female preachers' labor led to a minute being made against this disorderly practice and sent to the quarterly and monthly meetings. The travellers hoped that their efforts would lead to a stronger Society of the "right-hearted." Reviving the Quaker discipline would separate people with genuine religious commitment ("those who served the Lord") from nominal "professors," "winnowing" the members so that Quakerism would shine again in "its ancient beauty."[62]

The women ministers worked very closely with the male reformers. Mary Peisley wrote that Samuel Fothergill and Joshua Dixon, another visiting English preacher, "have been great helps and comforts to us in their work and service, and are nearly united in spirit, particularly the former."[63] Samuel Fothergill had sailed with the American ministers John Churchman and John Pemberton when they returned home in 1754, in order to pay his religious visit to the colonies. Unlike those reformers who often preferred silence to preaching, Fothergill spoke eloquently to crowds on his travels from 1754 to 1756, detailing the spiritual declension of American Friends with tremendous impact.

At the Philadelphia Yearly Meeting of September 1755, the reformers' effect upon Quaker life became truly apparent. The movement that had begun with only a few concerned Quakers travelling in the ministry, pressing the need for a reformation, was eventually supported by hundreds of Friends attending the yearly meeting. The clerk of the yearly meeting, Israel Pemberton Jr., now convinced that the Society was in spiritual jeopardy, was willing to more fully implement what the visitors had prescribed. In the fall of 1755, Philadelphia Yearly Meeting began an internal reformation, while most Pennsylvanians were preoccupied with the threat of French and Indian attacks. A committee of men Friends, including Samuel Fothergill, John Churchman, and John Woolman, revised the disciplinary code, not substantially changing the regulations, but placing new emphasis on the need for elders and overseers to enforce them. To regularly examine the state of the Society, every meeting was to read queries about members' behavior and provide answers to these queries at the next higher level of meeting. Greater supervision of ministers and elders was ensured as well: select meetings of these "shepherds of the flock" were to be established in every monthly meeting and were to report on their members' behavior to the quarterly meetings of ministers and elders. Mary Peisley, John Churchman, Samuel Fothergill, and other reformers had been suggesting many of these innovations on their travels, and now their advices were codified by the Philadelphia Yearly Meeting.[64]

The minutes of the Philadelphia Yearly Meeting of women Friends in 1755 showed unprecedented activity as well. For the first time, a joint yearly meeting committee was formed, in which women and men together prepared an epistle to constituent meetings, exhorting them to adhere more closely to the discipline. The 1755 Philadelphia Yearly Meeting of men Friends also proposed that "some solid women Friends" should accompany Quaker men in visiting the quarterly and monthly meetings to examine how thoroughly the discipline was enforced. Mary Peisley wrote of her own and Catharine Payton's diligence during that fall and winter in Philadelphia: "I have been in 160 families [more than 35 percent of city Friends], and attended six meetings every week whilst in town, as health permits; besides visiting the sick and afflicted, and taking some excursions to the country. . . . we now go together, having tired most of our companions, besides a couple of men Friends, who go to show us the doors, and be witness to our labours; there are nearly as many yet to visit, as I have been with." The visitors offered religious counsel and labored with individuals to renounce their misbehavior, such as immoderate drinking or ostentatious dressing. As a result of her family visits, Peisley noted that she had

Old Haverford Meeting, Delaware County,
Pennsylvania. Photograph by Gilbert Cope,
taken in 1908. At this Quaker meeting-house
(built by Welsh Quakers in 1697), the visiting
English preacher Mary Ellerton prophesied
in 1704, and Jane Fenn, the Pennsylvania
minister, first encountered David and Grace
Lloyd. Friends met in plain meeting-houses,
without the ornamentation of steeples.
Seventy-three American Quaker meeting-
houses built in the colonial period were still
standing in the latter half of the twentieth
century. *Courtesy Chester County Historical
Society, West Chester, Pennsylvania*

"been made instrumental to help back some of the before-mentioned lambs to the fold."[65]

Quakers believed that they had been "called" as a people to be like Israel of old, a holy nation, to show forth the praise of God in the world, and not to act like "worldly" others who were living in spiritual death. Honoring His precepts brought forth God's providential care of them. Travelling preachers had warned Friends that without reform and amendment of lives, God would withdraw His favor from Quakers and punish them by sending war, pestilence, or other disasters. Both the changes in procedure and the inspections proposed by the 1755 Philadelphia Yearly Meeting generated dramatic results among Pennsylvania Quakers. Sixty-four percent more violations were discovered than in the year before as a result of Friends more thoroughly enforcing the discipline. The visitors' success in Pennsylvania in 1755 demonstrated the importance of having reform-minded local Quakers, especially one in the pivotal office of clerk of the yearly meeting. Ministers travelling in other parts of America, in New York and New England, had not immediately succeeded in reviving the discipline. But by the 1770s, the reformation affected Quakers throughout the colonies: the number of disciplinary cases increased, and disownments outnumbered pardons.[66]

Reform and Pacifism

The 1750s crisis in Pennsylvania, precipitated by the imperial struggle between France and England for North America, also prompted reactions that, in some respects, furthered the progress of the reformation. Never had an international war so threatened Pennsylvania, and Quakers dominated the provincial government. This juxtaposition of events and circumstances forced difficult choices upon the Society of Friends. The Quaker female preachers visiting from England and Ireland helped to shape the Pennsylvania Friends' responses to the increasingly distressing events occurring in the American colony. Mary Peisley understood that it was "a difficult time for Friends in these parts, who are concerned to keep up their Christian testimony against wars and bloodshed: and especially to such as are concerned in state affairs."[67]

Quaker pacifism prohibited Quaker legislators from enacting laws that raised and equipped armies. No Quaker-controlled Assembly in Pennsylvania had ever done this, because Friends were not to violate Christ's peaceable testimony. Quakers had interpreted Christ's statement "Render therefore unto Caesar the things that are Caesar's," to mean that Christians should pay taxes to their sovereign (who might use it to prosecute wars), as long as they did not specify how the money was to be used. But in February 1754, His Majesty's secretary of state ordered that the province had to prepare for the possibility of a French invasion, and the Assembly had to supply the armed forces. In July 1754, the French drove George Washington and his soldiers out of western Pennsylvania. By early 1755, the Pennsylvania Assembly had begun transgressing Quaker ethics, authorizing seven of its members, including Speaker Isaac Norris II and James Pemberton, the politically ambitious brother of Israel Pemberton Jr., to spend money directly on provisioning the king's troops.

In March 1755, the English preacher Catharine Payton felt a religious "concern" to speak with the Quaker members of the Pennsylvania Assembly. Payton requested that "weighty" Friends arrange an interview between her and the Quaker politicians. In this conference, Payton urged the assemblymen to remain faithful to the Society's pacifist principles. The female minister pointed out the difficulty of remaining in governmental office on the eve of war and preserving Quaker ethics. She seemed to be suggesting that Quakers withdraw from the Assembly rather than compromise their pacifism. The Englishwoman affirmed that her actions were not improper interference in government affairs, but were the obligations of her ministerial role "and my commission to that country, which was to preach Truth and righteousness, and strengthen the hands of my brethren, against their opposers."[68]

By the end of the month, the ministers of Philadelphia Yearly Meeting added their warning to Payton's in a letter addressed to all Friends, not just to the Quaker assemblymen: "Cease from those national contests productive of misery & bloodshed."[69] Pennsylvania Quaker church leaders, such as Israel Pemberton Jr., and Quaker officeholders, such as Isaac Norris II (who was allowing his political decisions to override his religious concerns), were now divided. The distance from political power of women preachers, like Catharine Payton and Mary Weston (who had counselled Israel Pemberton Jr.), may have contributed to their ability to see the pitfalls of governmental office, as they stressed reliance on God instead.

The decisions made by the Assembly against the background of the approaching war with France confirmed reformers' suspicions that the holding of political office often jeopardized Quaker testimonies. Quaker legislators were now unethically prosecuting a war, and all Quakers had become accomplices to their misuse of revenue. Although, traditionally, Friends had paid taxes required by the civil government, the situation in Pennsylvania was novel, and the reformation, which had begun as a conservative movement to uphold established Quaker principles, evolved into a progressive movement. The reformist ministers' attempts to purify Quakerism, to listen more carefully to the Holy Spirit, resulted in an evolution of Quaker conscience. While visiting Pennsylvania, the Irish preacher Mary Peisley innovated beyond the Quaker discipline by actively urging Friends not to pay the tax that supported war. When a Quaker man requested her ministerial advice, Peisley responded in a letter, "In regard to the matter proposed by thee, I shall answer briefly, without entering into the debates on either side, and say, that I am of the judgment, that if thou stand single and upright in thy mind from all the false biasses of nature and interest, stopping thy ears to the artifices and pretexts of self-love, with all the fallacious reasonings of flesh and blood, and the subtle whisperings of an unwearied enemy, thou wilt find it more safe to suffer with the people of God, than to enter on, or undertake doubtful things, especially when thou considers the use which has been, or may be made of that tax [for waging a war]." Peisley asserted that she did not intend "to lessen parental authority or filial obedience" in advocating this radical, ethical stance. She believed that God had designed "that His people in future ages should make an improvement on their labours, and carry on the reformation even further" and that "some of this generation, in these parts of the world, [would be carried] higher and further in righteousness than their forefathers were carried, even such as were honourable in their day, and are fallen asleep in Christ."

The Irish minister encouraged her correspondent to share her advice with any of his acquaintances who "may be in like situation with thyself, that is, undetermined: not however that I want to expose this [letter], with any other view than to strengthen the minds of the weak and wavering" (modestly suggesting that her name be concealed if her counsel would have the same effect on readers). Peisley expected that the Society of Friends would be divided by these attempts at reformation within, warning that those who labored for reform, "in this degenerate age, must differ in their trials from [earlier Friends] . . . and will find them to be of a more severe and piercing kind:—theirs were from the world, and such as they might justly expect therefrom . . . ours will chiefly arise from [other Quakers] those under the same profession, clothed with the disguised spirit of the world, and that amongst some of the foremost rank (so called) in Society."[70]

At the Philadelphia Yearly Meeting in September 1755, a number of reformist Friends discussed the ethics of paying taxes that financed war, reporting they were uneasy about such payment. The Quaker Assembly's recent actions had troubled some Friends' consciences so much that they had refused to vote in the next election. Samuel Fothergill worried "lest a Breach incurable be made by the Assembly's enacting what many tender minds cannot comply with." But members of the Assembly, perceiving they were in danger of being labeled unpatriotic by the general public, drafted a larger bill to raise money for war by taxing the citizens. Twenty protesting Quakers, including Samuel Fothergill, Israel Pemberton Jr., and John Woolman, publicly addressed the entire House, but Speaker Norris defended the legislation. The same yearly meeting committee that had been created to promote reformation in the church by visiting meetings then drafted a message, "An Epistle of Tender love & Caution to Friends in Pennsylvania," expressing their apprehension about the tax.[71]

"The Assembly have sold their testimony as Friends to the people's fears, and not gone far enough to satisfy them," Fothergill observed. The defeat of General Edward Braddock's army in July 1755, and the Indian attacks on the frontier through the fall and winter of 1755, terrified Pennsylvanians, many of whom were demanding that the Assembly take more action. In response, the Pennsylvania Assembly passed an act for a volunteer militia—the first such act in the history of the peaceful province. Quaker assemblymen who voted for it and any Friends who volunteered to serve as soldiers again violated Quaker ethics. When Catharine Payton and Mary Peisley attended the general meeting of ministers and elders in Philadelphia in the spring of 1756, in the company of Samuel Fothergill and John Churchman, they witnessed a grim spectacle. Several bodies of massacred frontier inhabitants were being carted through the streets to incense the citizens against the Indians and stimulate the war effort. People followed the corpses, cursing at the Indians and blaming the Quakers for not providing defense for the colony.[72]

In April 1756, several assemblymen, heeding public demand, asked the governor to declare war on the Delaware Indians and offer bounties for their scalps. Other Friends pleaded with the Quaker members of the Assembly, "by the Profession You make of being the Disciples . . . of our

Lord Jesus Christ, the Prince of Peace," to stop the proclamation of war and scalp bounties. But the Assembly did not change course. Devout Quakers were shocked: the original peace between William Penn and the Delaware Indians had been a fundamental aspect of their identity as a people in the province. In addition, such violence opposed long-held Quaker testimonies. Quaker travelling preachers had repeatedly counselled Quaker colonists living on the frontier, where they were in danger of Indian attacks, to avoid using guns for defense or even hiding in garrisons. Friends were to depend on God, not on weapons of war or fortified places to protect them. Mary Weston had preached this not only in words, but by example, riding unarmed through the New England woods where "none dared to walk or ride without Arms" because of Indian warfare in the early 1750s. She had noted that the frightened colonists "appear'd mightily encouraged & strengthen'd by our Visit."[73]

In Pennsylvania, reformers repeatedly urged all Quakers to withdraw from the Assembly so that they would not collude with its aggressive policy by their presence. Other Friends, however, although distressed by the Assembly's actions, were worried about the consequences of discarding their political power. They had hoped to guarantee the protection of their religious liberties and political rights by remaining in government. Finally, unable to reconcile their consciences with the Assembly's legislation, six Friends (including James Pemberton, the brother of the yearly meeting clerk) resigned from the House on June 4, 1756, beginning the movement that would finally end with the complete exodus of Quakers from government twenty years later.[74]

When Mary Peisley completed her American tour, the Irish minister characterized it as "the most dangerous painful journey that ever I undertook . . . to both body and mind." Peisley and her companion Catharine Payton had found that the "ancient worthies," or early Friends, and their testimonies for Truth almost had been forgotten by Quakers of the current age. The female preachers, exhibiting no fear of worldly authority or even of fellow Quakers' animosity, had not placated listeners. Neither had they compromised with political and economic interests. They had continually tried to maintain the highest ethical standards in their counsel, even advocating defiance of parental authority, if need be, for the cause of righteousness. Samuel Fothergill, who had joined Peisley and Payton in their labors to revive the church, departed from America with them, sailing back to the British Isles on the same ship in the summer of 1756. An American Quaker woman wrote to Fothergill's wife about "those precious ministers, Mary Peisley, and C. Payton, whose Services were great in these parts of the world."[75]

The women ministers' influence lingered long after their departure from the continent. Some thirty years later, Anne (Emlen) Mifflin noted that she had been influenced by Mary Peisley and Catharine Payton when they were travelling in America in the 1750s. Anne Mifflin left her parents' home during the American Revolution because they approved of the use of Continental currency and disapproved of Anne's conscientious boycott of it. Mifflin wrote that she was "thus led forth by the hand of an heavenly Parent, from an earthly Parents house for the advancement of his own testimonies." Mifflin's defiance of her parents in order to strictly adhere to Quaker principles had been inspired by these ardent reformers of the 1750s. They had placed renewed emphasis on seeking not "to please man, but the Lord," reviving the religious zeal of the seventeenth-century Quakers, but in the context of reform, rather than of conversion.[76] Peisley had warned that the chief obstacle for eighteenth-century Friends would be the spiritual dullness of their fellow Quakers more tied to worldly interests.

When the reformers returned to the British Isles in 1756, many London Quakers were outraged by the American stance against taxes, offended by what appeared to be the arrogance of the Americans (and what seemed to be an implicit critique of their own ethics in paying taxes). The situations of Quakers in England and Pennsylvania, however, were very different. English Friends were experts at political compromise and the exchange of interests, but they had to negotiate a tolerated existence, not bear the responsibility of governing society. The reason for the reformers' tax protest in America "was not altogether the payment of the tax but that the tax should be raised, directed, & the use allowed by an assembly the major part whereof were of our profession [Quakers]. . . ."[77]

Vocal critics of the reformers' actions in the colonies tended to be those British Quakers whose political and economic interests were jeopardized by the ethical stances. Since 1751, a few members of the Meeting for Sufferings in London had been collaborating with the Pennsylvania proprietor Thomas Penn and the British government to protect the Ohio River Valley. English Quaker merchant John Hanbury was among the land speculators, mostly Virginians, who had organized the Ohio Company, obtaining a grant from the king for thousands of acres west of the Allegheny Mountains in Pennsylvania, Maryland, and Virginia, on both sides of the Ohio River.

By 1754, the French were unmistakably threatening the Ohio Company's interest, and the land speculators, disregarding religious principles, desired a military defense of the area.

The American tax protest also deeply embarrassed British Friends at a time when they were the most politically vulnerable. A growing number of the Society of Friends' adversaries—including the Presbyterians, the Anglican rector William Smith, and the Anglican proprietor Thomas Penn—were searching for a pretext to oust the Quakers from political power in Pennsylvania. Smith had published anonymous pamphlets which unfairly laid all the blame for the troubles in Pennsylvania on inflexible Quaker pacifism and Quaker greed, although the Assembly had allotted money for weapons, forts, and scalps. The American Quaker protest against a war tax was circulated by Smith in London, where it gave "great disgust at Court," as it seemingly validated Smith's assertion of Friends' selfish sectarianism. Misinformed or partisan government leaders reviled Friends: "You owe the people protection & yet withhold them from protecting themselves. Will not all the blood that is spilt lye at your door?"[78]

In early 1756, a petition was presented by Friends' adversaries, falsely depicting the province as utterly defenseless because of Philadelphia Yearly Meeting machinations. The petitioners' goal was to remove all Quaker legislators from the Pennsylvania Assembly and to make oath taking a requirement for serving in the colonial government (in violation of the provincial charter), which would prevent Friends from ever holding political office. In response, the Meeting for Sufferings vigorously lobbied their English governmental contacts, accepting a compromise that Friends would voluntarily resign their Assembly seats for the duration of the war, to ensure that American Quakers would be able to serve in the future.

London Yearly Meeting sent two English Friends to America—John Hunt and Christopher Wilson, both ministers and members of the Meeting for Sufferings. Their mission was to persuade the Pennsylvania Quakers to withdraw from the House and to pay their taxes. Ironically, the efforts of reform-oriented ministers such as Catharine Payton had already helped to achieve the conservatives' first goal, but for an opposite reason: in order to preserve religious principles, rather than as a political compromise to preserve worldly power. All the Friends who would withdraw from the Assembly during the war did so before the arrival of Hunt and Wilson in Pennsylvania—five days after the October 1756 election. For the first time in the history of the province, the Assembly did not have a Quaker majority. The two English messengers themselves began to doubt the ethics of their other instruction—to persuade protestors to pay their war taxes.

There was growing support for reform among the body of Friends in the British Isles and America. Catharine Payton had pointed to the incompatibility of wartime service in government with Friends' tenets, and the enlarging pacifist conscience of Friends would make it increasingly difficult for Quakers to hold public office. The Pennsylvania tax protest in 1755–56 had been based on the unique conjunction of a Quaker-controlled Assembly raising and spending sums to wage a war. But instead of ending the tax protest after Friends no longer formed a majority of the House, reformers broadened their concern. When a new tax was enacted in 1757, Israel Pemberton Jr. wrote: "We think something more than a testimony against our apostating brethren is required & do not find ourselves at liberty to pay." Now reformist Friends were not merely troubled by Quaker complicity in war, they were troubled by war itself, and refused to pay a tax "for the king's use" to support it, even if levied by non-Quakers.[79]

Although serving in the Assembly was temporarily inexpedient, office-holding per se was still considered perfectly ethical by the Society of Friends. The Quaker tax protest was a private act, not officially sanctioned by the Society. But even though the tax protest was a personal decision, Philadelphia Yearly Meeting leaders became disturbed by the notion of Quaker magistrates having to prosecute citizens for not paying taxes (subverting the religious freedom guaranteed by the Pennsylvania charter). Forcing people to go against their religious beliefs was "Essentially repugnant to that Liberty of Conscience for which our Ancestors deeply suffered."[80] Unhappy with this discrepancy, Philadelphia Yearly Meeting finally issued an order in 1758 that Friends had to resign from any public office (as constables, justices of the peace, and county commissioners) that obliged them to enforce payment of taxes that financed the French and Indian War. Quaker magistrates who ignored this yearly meeting order were not disowned, but they were denied admission to the Quaker meetings for church business.

"Our Connections with the Powers of the Earth are reduc'd to small Bounds," the Meeting for Sufferings (Philadelphia Yearly Meeting) confessed, after the Quakers were no longer a majority in the Assembly. Yet pious Friends fervently desired that this circumstance "may have the proper Effect to establish the Church in Righteousness, & fix our Trust in the Lord alone for Protection & Deliverance." Reformers were advising that Friends forgo "expedient, worldly schemes to save themselves," rely less on politics and more on God. But some Quakers found themselves unwilling to relinquish such worldly power. Repeatedly elected as trusted representatives by Pennsylvania citizens, these Friends justified remaining in the Assembly by claiming that they were protecting people's constitutional rights against the proprietor's actions, ignoring their own violation of religious principles. The conflict between Quaker values and those of the "world's" culture became insurmountable with the onset of the Revolutionary War. Radical Whigs' abolishment of the provincial charter prompted Philadelphia Yearly Meeting in 1776 to insist that all members holding public office resign or be disowned. When Quaker men withdrew from political power after the reformation, they rejected an area of activity from which women had been formally excluded, and focussed on the concerns they had always shared with Quaker women: morality, the education of the young, and philanthropy.[81]

Reform and Abolitionism

When the British preachers Mary Peisley and Catharine Payton travelled through the American colonies in 1754, they observed, "One thing which Friends here [in Virginia], as well as in North Carolina, Maryland, and some other parts of America, were in the practice of, gave us considerable pain, and we apprehended was in part the cause of Truth's not prospering amongst them, as otherwise it would, that is, buying and keeping of slaves; which we could not reconcile with the golden rule of doing unto all men as we would they should do unto us."[82] Although Peisley and Payton were primarily focussed on the strict enforcement of Quaker discipline and strengthening Friends' meetings, they perceived the negative effects of slavery upon Quakers, and were disturbed by this practice, which violated Christ's precepts.

Quaker attitudes toward wealth and slave-holding, like those toward pacifism and officeholding, altered over time. Some uneasiness about slavery had always existed among Friends. George Fox had advised seventeenth-century Quaker slaveowners in Barbados to Christianize slaves, and treat them like white bondsmen, releasing them after their terms of service, but Fox's advice to free the slaves was not taken. Most early Friends, reflecting the attitudes of their time, had viewed slavery as a potential evil, but unobjectionable if used properly. A number of wealthy Quakers in early Pennsylvania had emigrated from Barbados and Jamaica where they had owned slaves. Isaac Norris I, clerk of the Philadelphia Yearly Meeting in the early eighteenth century, was one of the principal importers of slaves in Pennsylvania. Quaker leadership in Pennsylvania from 1710 to 1750, therefore, had not been receptive to the idea of abolition, considering it a threat to their private property. Mid-eighteenth-century reformers, however, scrutinized with new intensity the effects of wealth and slave-holding on spiritual values.

Among reformer Friends, John Woolman was the first to record his opposition to slavery. In 1742, Woolman's conscience was troubled after writing a slave's bill of sale. Following a fact-finding journey to the South, the New Jersey minister wrote his famous pamphlet, *Some Considerations on the Keeping of Negroes*. After Israel Pemberton Jr. became the reform-minded clerk of the Philadelphia Yearly Meeting, excerpts from Woolman's pamphlet appeared in the 1754 yearly meeting's annual epistle to its members. In 1755, the Philadelphia Yearly Meeting, attended by Peisley, Payton, Fothergill, and others, expressed disapproval of the slave trade among Friends, although no sanctions were applied. But afterwards, monthly meetings did inform slave purchasers that the Society disapproved. The disasters of Indian attacks, earthquakes, and war that struck Pennsylvania in the years following 1754 were thought by many Quakers to be God's chastisement for the inhabitants' irreligious behavior. John Churchman, like some others, connected these calamities with slave-holding: "As it were in a moment, mine eyes turned to the case of the poor enslaved negroes." With the new reformist leadership of Philadelphia Yearly Meeting in the 1750s, and the disciplining or disownment of many religiously indifferent members, previously rejected reforms, such as the abolition of slavery, could be seriously considered. As the Society of Friends moved away from the political center of Pennsylvania life, after 1756, idealistic reforms also became more viable. With renewed vigor, eighteenth-century Quakerism was defining itself by its spiritual integrity, rather than by its worldly power, or the size of its membership. In 1758, the yearly meeting declared that Friends who purchased or sold slaves could not participate in the meetings for church business unless they showed repentance.[83]

Slave-holding still was not contrary to Quaker discipline, but female reformist ministers, concerned about the family as a conduit of Quaker values, were increasingly troubled by the impact of slavery on the household. The domination of master over slave was not a good model for "tender" Quaker children learning humility, moderation, and self-discipline. Elizabeth Wilkinson, travelling in 1761–62, asked that the slaves belonging to a Friend address the Quaker's children by their actual names instead of the deferential titles of "master" and "miss." While John Woolman and Anthony Benezet were among the primary leaders of abolition within the Society, the travelling female preachers supported the effort. Rachel Wilson, preaching in the southern colonies in 1769, felt "called" to "request of [th]Em to keep thair hands Clear from purchasing Negros as believing it never was intended for us to trafick with any part of the Human Species & if thair was no Buyer thair wo[ul]d be no Sell[e]rs."[84]

By 1776, Philadelphia Yearly Meeting finally resolved to disown Quakers who refused to free their slaves. As an outgrowth of their internal reformation, Quakers had become the first people to abolish slavery among themselves and to champion abolition everywhere. Their elevation of conscience would eventually have tremendous repercussions for American culture, as Friends' testimony against slavery sent ever-widening ripples outward.

Reform and Indian Rights

The war of the 1750s also had drawn Quakers' attention to the plight of the Indians. In 1671, when George Fox had visited the American colonies, he had asserted the access of every human being to the Inward Light. Fox had demonstrated this principle by asking an Indian if something within himself reproved him when he lied. The original peace established by William Penn with the Delaware Indians, and their subsequent amiable relations, had been evidence of the "Truth" of Quaker beliefs. Consequently, when troubles with the Delawares later erupted, Friends told the Pennsylvania Assembly that since Indians were not devoid of understanding or a sense of justice, it behooved the assemblymen to inquire whether the Indians had been mistreated. Quakers' failure to restore peace with the Delawares through public office, following the government's declaration of war and scalp bounties, had prompted Israel Pemberton Jr. to work privately and philanthropically.

Pemberton organized the Friendly Association for Regaining and Preserving Peace with the Indians by Pacific Measures to investigate Indian grievances and address any legitimate complaints. The Friendly Association's attempt to act as an intermediary between the government and the Indians raised a political uproar. Aiding the Indians seemed like treason to many Pennsylvanians and aroused great animosity against the Quakers. Ironically, the discontents which had provoked the Indians to attack were largely land frauds by the Pennsylvania government. The reformers learned that a few Quaker leaders of the preceding generation had colluded with the proprietors in wrongful actions toward the Indians. There had been greed and fraud both in the fur trade and in land speculation. From 1757 through 1762, the Friendly Association asserted that the Delawares had been defrauded of land in the Walking Purchase of 1737, assigning much of the blame for the war to that corrupt transaction and to the proprietors, the Anglican sons of William Penn.[85]

In their ministerial role, Quaker women were involved in Friends' negotiations for peace with the Indians. During Catharine Payton's visit to Pennsylvania, she attended a Quaker peace-making attempt: "An Indian chief, with other Indians in friendship with Pennsylvania, being occasionally in Philadelphia, Friends obtained leave of the governor to have a conference with them; in order to endeavour, through their interference to bring about an accommodation with the Indians now at war with the British colonies. As we were admitted to attend this conference, I mention it. It evinces the veneration the Indians retained for the memory of William Penn, and for his pacifist principles; and their great regard to Friends, whom they stiled his children." Payton was fascinated by the Indian women who sat in on this conference, like dignified "Roman matrons," perhaps seeing a similarity to the position of Quaker women ministers: "I was informed that they admit their most respected women into their counsels." In 1761, the Irish minister Susanna Hatton preached at Easton where the governor, the Council, and a number of Quakers were gathered for a treaty conference with the Indians. Many of the Indians wept as Hatton acknowledged them "as our Bretheren & Sisters . . . by Creation & trusted some of them would be so by regeneration, incouraging them to trust in God."[86]

The Quakers' increased awareness of the mistreatment of Indians had spread to Friends in the British Isles, and visiting preachers counselled colonists to treat the Indians with justice and fairness. When Elizabeth Wilkinson arrived in America in 1761, she had a recurring "concern": "My mind is at this time nearly drawn to the poor Indians whose place this was as well as the whole continent." In Pennsylvania, the English minister preached at an Indian settlement and "went to Pennsbury to see the mansion House of that great, good man William Penn whose name is honoured to this day by the Indians & others. The thoughts of the degeneracy of his descendants . . . made me feel sorry." Wilkinson's "concern" that Quakers make proper remuneration to the Native Americans for their lands ("to do as they would be done by"), in Virginia, was so overwhelming that she "could not be easy without Laying before the Friends there the concern I was under to write to Friends in the back settlements on that Account and having their Concurrence I writ what was on my mind. . . ." In the Carolinas she further cautioned "Friends against settling on Lands not agreed for with the Indians."[87]

Reform and the Marriage Discipline

The women ministers were strong leaders of reforms to preserve the Quaker family and to ensure the religious education of children. During the early years of Quakerism, the problem of transmitting Quaker values to children was not a leading concern, because the Society was primarily expanding through converts. But as the Society matured and "birthright" Friends swelled the membership, Quakers became more aware of the need to strengthen the religious commitment of succeeding generations. Although the reform-oriented Philadelphia Yearly Meetings of 1755 (which enforced discipline and oversight) and 1758 (which imposed sanctions against slaveowners and officeholders) had had important effects, spiritual declension was still evident in the Society. When Elizabeth Wilkinson toured the colonies, she noted of Quakers in America, "for in many places it may with Sorrow be said that on that very Account of Mixed Marriages Our Society appears as a Motled Generation." "Marrying out" (to non-Quakers) was the most violated Quaker testimony after 1755 in spite of biblical warnings against marrying the people "of other nations of the heathens or of other religions."[88]

Quaker meetings apparently had been overlooking these irregular marriages, hoping they would be a means of recruitment; but Friends were recruiting indifferent members into an increasingly formless church. Growing confusion about identifying members of the Society of Friends had been part of the initial impetus for the reformation. When Mary Peisley and Catharine Payton, for example, had attempted to deliver advice only to Quakers in some American meetings, they had discovered that no one knew who to exclude "because of their being so connected in marriage, &c., and the discipline being so sadly let fall, that they knew not who were or who were not proper members."[89] Instead of enlarging the membership of the religiously committed, the practice of allowing "mixed marriages" had brought people into the Friends' community lacking any conviction of Quaker tenets.

When people of different religious persuasions married, reformist preachers believed that the union, not grounded on shared religious values, likely had been based on worldly values. Indeed, it was clear that the motive for many such matrimonial matches had been the enlargement of an estate. Elizabeth Wilkinson asserted that "too much coldness & remissness appears in Parents therein," who overlooked the "marrying out" of their children if there were financial gain in the match. Quaker ministers warned Friends against the subtle delusion that by amassing wealth they were fulfilling a religious obligation to their offspring. Ann Whitall, the New Jersey farmwife, listened to the visiting English reformers Hannah Harris, Alice Hall, and Elizabeth Wilkinson and agreed with their assessment of the Society's problems: "I was much concarned about about [sic] the folen [fallen] state we ar[e] now in the Chorch is in a ginaral [general] man[n]er." Whitall herself observed "so many Mixt Mariges & runing away," and the pardoned, but impenitent offenders in her own meeting: including a woman who brazenly slept during worship, "the boldest & most impident that ever I sow" who "semes proude of whot she has dun."[90]

Reformers assumed that two believing parents were needed in order to create a godly atmosphere for raising children, so that the next generation could have an experiential conviction of Quaker beliefs. The Society had been automatically admitting the offspring of such "mixed marriages" to full membership, treating these children as equal to those whose parents were both Quaker. But the preachers had seen that this liberal admission of poorly instructed children had produced a "motled Generation" of Quakers. Elizabeth Wilkinson had a dream during her American travels in which she saw a row of young, green trees unprotected by a hedge. One young tree was growing out of line, inclining toward the highway, and it was being damaged by the shadow of a large, withered old tree. In the dream, the English minister then enclosed all the young trees with a hedge. The meaning of the "night vision" was clear: Quaker elders had shirked their duty to the Quaker youth, and the visiting minister wanted to rebuild the discipline as a "hedge" of protection for the development of the next generation.

In 1762, Wilkinson and Hannah Harris (the hostess of John Churchman and John Pemberton during their 1750s tour of England) brought the subject of "mix'd & clandestine" marriages to the attention of the select yearly meeting of ministers and elders at Philadelphia. The meeting, especially the Pennsylvania minister Joseph White, strongly concurred with the women's "concern," so they brought the matter before the yearly meeting of men Friends. At the Pine Street Meeting House, where the Quaker men held their annual meeting for business, Hannah Harris spoke, then Elizabeth Wilkinson, and then the visiting Irish preacher Susanna Hatton, expressing their sense of the spiritual danger of the toleration of irregular marriages. The substance of the women's "concern" was then minuted "to be handed down as advice to the Quarterly & monthly meetings."[91]

Largely because of these women ministers' "divine leadings," the Philadelphia Yearly Meeting recommended that Friends ought no longer to either solicit or wait for confessions from those who "married out," but speedily disown them. If the misbehavers volunteered acknowledgments of their transgressions, the meetings were to pardon them only if they were well assured of the offenders' sincere repentance. For no other violation of the discipline than irregular marriage did the Society discard its usual, patient policy of waiting months, or even years, for the acknowledgment and reform of offenders. The Philadelphia Yearly Meeting of 1762 also changed its treatment of the offspring of such mixed marriages, no longer automatically admitting them to membership, but examining if the child had had a religious education. As in 1755, the new directives from the yearly meeting had immediate, dramatic effects. After the yearly meeting appointed committees to inspect all the quarterly and monthly meetings for any mismanagement of this discipline, there was a large increase in disownments for marriage offenses.[92]

The travelling female preachers counselled Quakers throughout the colonies on these issues. When Elizabeth Wilkinson journeyed through the American South, for example, she was approached by a Maryland

Yearly Meeting committee on discipline. According to Wilkinson, they came "to our Lodgings & desired our Company: & after a time of Silence several of us spoke what was on our minds . . . [with the] unanimous Result that all Such as marry Contrary to the approved way of Friends should be publickly denied." This change in the enforcement of Quaker discipline sharpened boundaries, further separating Friends from the larger "world's" culture, creating a smaller, more unified sect.[93]

Reform Increases the Number of Women's Meetings

In their ministerial role, women had significant impact within the Quaker organization: bringing forward "concerns," having them recorded, and, at times, incorporated into the yearly meeting's directives to its constituent meetings. Yet women's business meetings had not developed an equal importance in Quaker church government. Women's ability to make policy and enforce discipline within their business meetings was quite limited, and, in some places, such meetings had never been established. For reformist women ministers, used to spiritual authority in their ministerial role, and raised with the Quaker ideal of gender egalitarianism in religious service, this disparity in the Society of Friends between principle and practice had become distressingly evident. When the English preacher Mary Weston attended the women's monthly meeting at London Grove, Pennsylvania, in 1751, she wrote pointedly: "I thought it a favour & high priviledge I had to sit amongst them for I was sensible the God of heaven eminently owned the Females in that Service; tho' so much despised & slighted as their Help in church Government is by the great & wise Men of the Age, even in our Society."[94] As a result of her travels, Weston had become highly conscious of the differences that had evolved between the English and American Quaker organizational structures, regarding the importance of women's business meetings. A Philadelphia Yearly Meeting of women Friends had been created at the same time that a men's yearly meeting had been settled in Pennsylvania. Pennsylvania women's meetings sometimes played a crucial role in the disciplining of members—within Bucks Quarterly Meeting the women had power over the disownments of female members. London Yearly Meeting, however, had never created a women's meeting for business as a counterpart to the men's meeting at the highest level of Quaker organization; and in parts of England, women's meetings at the quarterly and monthly levels either had never been settled or had been neglected.

Quaker reformers, both female and male, saw the value of encouraging women's service to strengthen the Society. They wanted to create additional women's meetings for church business to assist in oversight of the membership and the maintenance of discipline. When the American preachers John Churchman, John Pemberton, and William Brown visited England from 1750 to 1754, among the many disorders they had seen in English Quakerism were the gaps in the English meeting system that prevented a full utilization of its female members. John Churchman thought that English Quakers "were entirely dropt as to the true Service and use of them."[95]

London Yearly and Quarterly Meetings, dominated by the merchant, banker, and professional Friends of the city, were among the most conservative of the Society, and the most resistant to the reformers' "innovations." When Sophia Hume, the eminent minister whose writings had been published by the Society, attempted to establish a separate women's meeting for London Friends, she was unsuccessful. John Pemberton described her efforts in 1750:

> She w[i]th: Several other Wo[men]. have lately Petitioned the Men to Grant them a Meetg: for Business, but to no purpose, they Condescended thus farr, that if they would they might come & set with them but would not allow them a separate meeting. Our ffriends also have taken Som[e] pains with them on that acco[un]t. But without Success at present.[96]

Other reformers labored in the British Isles to expand the number of women's meetings. John Griffith (the American minister who had learned from Susanna Morris's spiritual example) was living in England in 1753. He noted that in his county of Essex, "we have lately settled womens qr.[quarterly] meeting and also—Endeavourd to promote the Establishment of womens mo.[monthly] meetgs where they were not, but things are very low amongst us Respecting discipline &c, tho[ugh] there seems of late to be Stirings up and down in divers[e] minds for a better Regulation."[97]

Travelling in the ministry had linked American reformers with British reformers; such journeying had also connected women with other women.

A delegation of female preachers from England, Ireland, and America, with the support of John Pemberton and William Brown, in June 1753 requested at the London Yearly Meeting the establishment of a women's yearly meeting on the same foundation as the men's—with the annual attendance of representatives from constituent meetings. Susanna Morris, the visiting Pennsylvania minister, advanced the proposal with Sophia Hume, Mary Weston, Mary Peisley, and Catharine Payton. Morris "had seen that such a system in America worked well . . . whereby they might become acquainted with the condition of their sisters throughout the land and administer advice." When American Quaker women had sent epistles from their yearly meeting to England, they had thought they were "addressing the Society of our sex at large," but then discovered that these were not copied or circulated. Samuel Neale, the Irish reformist minister sympathetic to the women's cause, heard Susanna Morris's "living" testimony at the men's yearly meeting. The proposition, Neale concluded, "I had no doubt, was from the motion of Truth." But this joint effort of British and American female preachers failed because some of the men "were too strongly wedded to their ancient practice." London Yearly Meeting leaders told the women that "there could not be two heads to one body."[98]

The "generality" of Quakers had favored the reformers' proposals in 1753 for a women's yearly meeting and for a national meeting of ministers and elders, but "stiff and self willed" London Friends had resisted them. For the sake of harmony, the reformers relinquished the proposals for that year. The following year, when three principal opponents were "providentially" prevented by illness or business from attending the London Yearly Meeting of 1754, the proposal of a national meeting for ministers and elders was adopted, but the proposed women's yearly meeting was rejected. Conservatives also tried, but failed, to exclude female preachers from the select meeting of ministers and elders.[99]

The Londoners "think themselves so whole, happy and well they need not a reformation," Mary Weston complained in a letter, in August 1755, to John Churchman (after he had returned to America to assist in the reformation there). The reform-oriented Philadelphia Yearly Meeting of September 1755 continued to exert pressure on London Friends:

> Experience convinces us the Concurrent labours of our Women Friends contribute much to the promotion of the comely order of the Discipline we have thought it at this time

necessary to enforce the Authority of their Meetings and sincerely desire they may be settled and maintained in all places where they have not yet been established. . . .[100]

London Quarterly Meeting and London Yearly Meeting still refused to create counterpart women's meetings for discipline, but the yearly meeting did encourage its constituent monthly meetings to settle separate women's meetings where there were none.

Success was not achieved until 1784 when four American women ministers (Rebecca Wright, Patience Brayton, Mehetabel Jenkins, and Rebecca Jones) visiting from New England and Pennsylvania supported their British "sisters" in a deputation to the London men's meeting to once more request a women's yearly meeting. In response to the sentiment that it would be preposterous to have a body with two heads, Rebecca Jones, a Philadelphia preacher, reminded the Friends of their mutual dependence on God: "There was but one head to the body which is the Church, and that in Christ Jesus male and female are one." The women finally won their point. However, the London Yearly Meeting warned that the newly established women's meeting was not to be "so far considered a meeting of discipline as to make rules, nor yet alter the present Queries, without the concurrence of this meeting."[101]

Impact of Women Preachers on Eighteenth-Century Quakerism

The eighteenth-century Quaker ministry allowed a significant number of women to have visibility and impact in their community. Their "divinely inspired" messages were listened to and, often, carefully transcribed. They served as spiritual exemplars for Quakers of either gender, including government officials, merchants, and farmwives. Since Friends believed that such "chosen instruments" were guided by the Holy Spirit, a preacher from one region could be equally authoritative among Quakers in another part of the world. Consequently, the travelling ministers had a tremendous capacity to shape Quakerism in areas far from their residences. No comprehensive account of eighteenth-century Quakerism in Pennsylvania can omit Mary Peisley, Catharine Payton, Elizabeth Wilkinson, and other Friends who visited the colony from the British Isles. American visitors abroad, such as Susanna Morris, Elizabeth Ashbridge, and Margaret Ellis, also importantly affected British Quakerism. The women who crossed the sea on religious service were truly transatlantic public figures: religious leaders known and emulated by Quakers on both sides of the ocean. Their visits unified the transatlantic Quaker community, as a spectrum of Friends heard the ministers' messages, as well as read their epistles and journals.

Since Quakers believed that religion was sovereign and should infuse every aspect of life, women in their ministerial role exercised a legitimate leadership overseeing the range of Quaker men's and women's behavior. A Quaker man could solicit a woman preacher's opinion on paying government taxes. Catharine Payton could deliver advice to Quaker members of the Pennsylvania Assembly to remain true to their pacifist principles by withdrawing from political office. When Quaker activities in government and other "outward affairs" contradicted Friends' religious principles, women ministers participated in reform efforts to resist the segregation of spheres. Mid-eighteenth-century reformers also reversed any tendency to diminish the opportunity for female service in Quaker church government, advocating the establishment of additional women's meetings at all levels of the Society.

Ministers' efforts to revive religious zeal in mid-eighteenth-century Quakerism transformed the Society. Quakers ceased tolerating indifferent or misbehaving members. The Society disciplined those not committed to Friends' principles of integrity, humility, simplicity, orderly marriage, and religious child rearing. In this smaller, more united group of Quakers, preachers who wanted to "perfect" their faith by adhering more closely to God's will moved the Society to even higher ethical standards. Quaker withdrawal from governmental office had the effect of placing eighteenth-century Quaker men and women in more comparable positions. Friends' "now clearer loss of mastery over public affairs" enhanced the authority of the Quaker ministers and their teaching that "Friends must depend finally upon Providence and not upon worldly prospects."[102]

Six

FROM "WITCHES" TO "CELEBRATED PREACHERS": THE NON-QUAKER RESPONSE TO THE WOMEN MINISTERS

I N July 1656, two English Quaker female missionaries were seized by the authorities upon entering the port of Boston. After being carefully searched for marks that might identify them as witches, Anne Austin and Mary Fisher were imprisoned in the Boston jail for five weeks. Hundreds of Quaker pamphlets in the women's possession were confiscated. The local inhabitants were forbidden to make contact with the women, out of fear that the heretical and seditious contagion carried by the travellers would spread. The Massachusetts magistrates, forewarned about the activities of these "Ranters" (described as "railing much at the ministry and refusing to show any reverence to magistrates" in England), had dreaded their visit like the arrival of cholera.[1] When Austin and Fisher were released from confinement, they were unceremoniously deported from the Massachusetts Bay Colony. Thereafter, ship captains who transported Quakers to the colony, and residents who entertained such dangerous visitors, were fined. In 1658, colony officials passed legislation banishing Quakers from the province upon pain of death. Four Quaker missionaries, three men and one woman, were executed under this law.

One hundred thirteen years later, in July 1769, the *Boston-Gazette, or Country Journal* recorded the arrival of another English Quaker female evangelist: "Wednesday morning came to town from Philadelphia, last from Rhode-Island and Nantucket, Mrs. Rachel Wilson, an eminent preacher among the friends. At Noon she preached to a large audience, and gained applause. Her discourse was nervous, pertinent and solemn; in which, as in the whole of her deportment, she clearly displayed the most lively imagination, a singular penetration, and most of that general benevolence, which is the distinguishing characteristic of the true christian." A dramatically contrasting reception was accorded these Quaker women from two different centuries: instead of being suspected of witchcraft, the eighteenth-century female preacher was welcomed as a "true christian."[2] Far from attempting to prevent the spread of Quaker influence, the Massachusetts press brought the Friend's visit to the attention of the populace. Rather than persecuted by colonial magistrates, the Englishwoman spoke to an approving crowd and was treated with respect as an acknowledged preacher of a recognized religious society.

Rachel Wilson's travel journal corroborates the *Boston-Gazette*'s account. The English preacher described the Quaker meeting she held in Boston, the traditional center of American Puritanism, "to which many of the [non-Quaker] inhabitants came and a open time we had amongst [th]Em many of [th]Em Expressing thair satisfaction and thankfulness for the opertunes [opportunity]." When Wilson returned to Boston about two weeks later, from a trip northward, she ministered twice more at the Quaker meeting-house. These additional gatherings, however, did not satisfy the popular demand for Wilson's preaching. City leaders urged the Quaker female minister to arrange a meeting in a larger hall, in order to accommodate the numbers of people, beyond the Quaker membership, who wanted to attend: "Heads of the town was pres[s]ing for the meeting to be held in the hall aLong Comedeus [a long commodious] Room as the [Quaker] Meetg hous was quite too smal[l]." Although Wilson had planned to depart Boston the following day, "in the night such a weight Came over my mind that I could but Sleep Li[t]tle and it planly apered [plainly appeared] thear was a furder [further] servis for me in Boston."

After visiting Friends' families the next morning, Wilson decided to accept the hall reserved for her gathering by the Boston public officials: a sizable space on the second floor of Faneuil Hall, used for town meetings. This Faneuil Hall site was to figure increasingly as a place where colonists met to challenge Parliament's authority, since Rachel Wilson's tour of the colonies was made on the eve of American resistance to British colonial

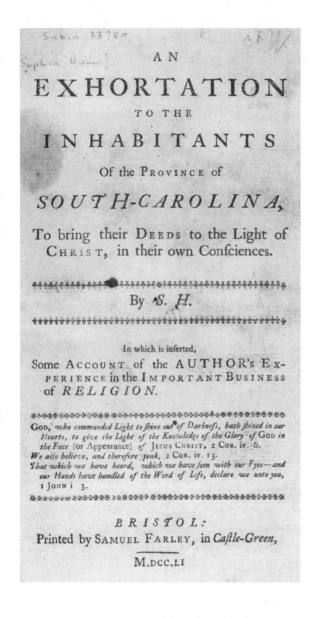

Sophia Hume, "celebrated writer and preacher" (*Virginia Gazette,* August 6, 1767), returned to Charleston, South Carolina, the scene of her earlier years as an Anglican "lady of fashion," to warn the pleasure-loving populace of the danger in forgetfulness of God. Hume authored several tracts, including this *Exhortation* (first published in Philadelphia, 1748) and *An Epistle to the Inhabitants of South-Carolina* (London, 1754), in which she explicated Scriptures to appeal for a spiritual reformation. Israel Pemberton Sr., the Quaker merchant, noted in 1748 that Hume's *Exhortation* (reprinted in five later editions in England and America) was well liked by those who had the opportunity to read it, "not only of our Societ[y] but likewise of others." *Courtesy William Andrews Clark Memorial Library, University of California, Los Angeles*

This article in the *Boston-Gazette, or Country Journal* (no. 744, July 10, 1769), described Rachel Wilson's Boston sermon in complimentary terms—strikingly different from the reception given Quakers in the previous century. Many newspapers detailed the Quaker female preacher's religious tour through the American colonies. The *South-Carolina Gazette* of February 9, 1769, for example, reported that "Mrs. Rachel Wilson, a celebrated preacher among the people called Quakers arrived here by land from Philadelphia. On friday, sunday, and tuesday, she preached to very crouded [crowded] audiences, of different persuasions. . . ." *Courtesy Houghton Library, Harvard University* policy. In the wake of protests against the Townshend duties, Boston was under military rule in 1769, with nearly four thousand redcoats stationed at the port, and growing antagonism between the soldiers and the towns-people. But on this summer evening, above the first-floor market, in Faneuil's "handsome large brick building," Rachel Wilson held a meeting "very Large and hott." She observed that most of the leading citizens of Boston were present: "There was Most all the pepol [people] of Note thairs [there] . . . [who] behaved with great civilety some Reached to and acknowlidged to the truth." The English Quaker minister concluded, "Thear [there] Seems a Seeking pepol [people] in Boston. . . ." Wilson, reared on accounts of the sufferings of early Quaker martyrs in New England, realized that a remarkable shift had taken place in the Bostonians' response to visiting Quaker preachers. Her Quaker host in Boston, Benjamin Bagnall, told her that "since he Lived thair they scearcly [scarcely] wod [would] speack to a frd [Friend] and now no place more open to Receve fr[ien]ds which seemd a comfort to the [h]onest old man to see such a change in his time."[3]

Elsewhere in the American colonies, an alteration in attitudes was also evident. In New Haven, Connecticut, where, in 1699, even a male Quaker preacher from England, Thomas Story, had been prevented from holding a meeting, "the magistrate not favouring it," Rachel Wilson, in 1769, was readily granted the courthouse for her use. Historically known for "laws and magistrates . . . very strict and severe against Friends" (who were labeled "Hereticks"), Connecticut was almost devoid of Quakers.[4] Yet a large crowd attended the meeting Wilson had appointed. The inhabitants, mostly Congregationalist, packed the upper room of the courthouse to such an extent that there was not enough air, forcing the gathering to be moved to a more spacious, lower room.

In Charles Town (Charleston), South Carolina, where few Quakers lived under a Church of England establishment, Rachel Wilson and her travelling companion from Fairfax, Virginia, Sarah Janney, were obligated to hold "two meetings in the old Baptist Meeting House (our own meeting-house being too small for the congregation)," preaching to "Crowded Audiences of all Denominations."[5] The *South-Carolina Gazette* of February 9, 1769, reported: "Last thursday Mrs. Rachel Wilson, a celebrated preacher among the people called Quakers arrived here by land from Philadelphia. On friday, sunday, and tuesday, she preached to very crouded [crowded] audiences, of different persuasions. And yesterday morning she set out upon her return, by way of Camden." In Williamsburg, Virginia, the *Virginia Gazette* announced on March 23, 1769, "Last night, Mrs. Rachel Wilson, an eminent preacher among the people called Quakers, whom lately arrived from England, came to this city from South Carolina; and this day she preached to several of her own persuasion, as well as a number of other people. She is on her way to the Northward." Newspapers described Rachel Wilson's tour of 1768–69, from South Carolina to Casco Bay (Maine), in terms similar to those used to characterize the earlier ministerial expeditions of "the great itinerant," George Whitefield. The open-air preaching and emotional delivery of Whitefield (ordained in the Church of England) had drawn large audiences of diverse religious affiliations.

The response that the eighteenth-century Quaker female preacher received was overwhelmingly ecumenical as well. Members of other religious denominations invited the famed English visitor to preach to them in their meeting-houses. She observed: "I had several other Requests from Diferent quarters to have meetgs with [th]Em thair meet[ing]hous doors was opene for me."[6] In Bordentown, New Jersey, when the Quaker meeting-house was found to be too small to contain all the people, the Baptists offered their meeting-house as more convenient, and Wilson accepted. The Presbyterians suggested their meeting-house as a site for Wilson's meeting when the courthouse proved to be too small for the public in Elizabethtown, New Jersey.

Wilson generally attracted crowds wherever she ministered. Her audiences, composed of the uneducated masses and society's elite, extended beyond the Quaker community. The governor of New Jersey, William Franklin (the son of Benjamin Franklin), and his wife were among the notable residents attending Wilson's meeting in Burlington, New Jersey. After the meeting, Rachel Wilson had a private religious conference at the governor's residence. She noted in her journal: "We also Visited the Governer & his wife who whear Both at Meetg with meny of the principle hinnabitants. We had a Solem Season in the Governers house with which thay Expresed thair Satisfaction." Students from Princeton (the College of New Jersey), the training ground for the Middle Colonies' next generation of leaders, wrote to Rachel Wilson on May 20, 1769: "Madam, We, whose names are subscribed, Students of the College of New Jersey, would regard it as a Singular obligation if you would favour us with a Sermon on Monday next" in response to a religious "concern" Wilson had expressed to have a meeting with them. The document was signed by fifty-one students, including Philip Freneau (later Revolutionary War poet), Frederick Frelinghuysen (later U.S. senator), and Samuel Stanhope Smith (later professor of moral philosophy and college president). Wilson recorded in her diary: "Finding My Self not quite clear apointd a meeting at Prince town [Princeton] at half Past four which was held in the College to pret[t]y good Satisfaction tho[ugh] so Crowded that a good part stoud [stood]. the Students Behaved well and several of [th]Em Came & speack to Me after." In Newport, Rhode Island, Reverend Ezra Stiles, a Congregationalist minister and, later, president of Yale College, joined with the crowds attending the Quaker yearly meeting on June 9, 1769. Stiles recorded in his diary that he had "heard Mrs Wilson, an eminent Quaker Preacher lately come from Westmoreland in England. She spoke above an hour. She is a pious sensible woman." Rachel Wilson also received a request from an assemblyman to preach to the Rhode Island Assembly, then in session. But the celebrated English preacher refused, replying that she had no commission from God to do this nor could she go at man's bidding.[7]

The dramatic alteration in the reception of Quakers, noticeable in eighteenth-century America, had included a change in response toward Quaker women in their ministerial role. Rachel Wilson achieved public prominence as a female Quaker leader, and was recognized as a skillful preacher by many in the larger culture. Wilson was given a hospitable welcome by even non-Quaker governmental leaders who listened to her religious advice. While in Virginia, Rachel Wilson had visited Assemblyman Patrick Henry at his residence, who "rec[eive]d us with great civility & we had an open time [a religious session] in the famley." Upon arrival in Williamsburg, Wilson also had called on the royal governor, Norborne Berkeley (Baron de Botetourt), who only recently had moved from England to the colony, in October 1768, to assume office. Although Wilson was politically constrained as an eighteenth-century woman, as an acclaimed spiritual figure, she counselled the governor to faithfully perform the duties of his office. Wilson recalled that he "Rec[eive]d us kindly & seemed well Satisfied with the Conversation and told me it was his Desire to fill up his plaice properly to do what he ought to do & not to be bias[e]d by party." The Quaker female preacher responded to the governor that if this was his determination, "to fill up his place properly," she was certain that "he wod [would] be a Blessing to the pepol [people] he took his Leve [leave] very affectionatly & wished my Jornay [journey] might be prosperous."[8]

Letter, dated May 20, 1769, from the students of the College of New Jersey (later Princeton University), containing a request for the visiting English Quaker preacher Rachel Wilson to deliver a sermon. Among the signers were Philip Freneau (1752–1832), later a Revolutionary War poet, and other men who would have illustrious careers in the early American Republic (nine signatures are not reproduced). *Reproduced with permission of the Library Committee of the Religious Society of Friends in Britain*

Quaker Women Preachers as Public Figures in the Non-Quaker Culture

Rachel Wilson, described by a contemporary as having a "fine figure, and striking presence, . . . gifted with a clear, distinct voice, and all the pathos of pure, unstudied eloquence," was clearly an extraordinarily talented speaker, but Wilson was part of a larger trend as well. A number of eighteenth-century Quaker women ministers not only acquired eminence within their own religious society but also became public figures beyond the Quaker community. In Great Britain, May Drummond, a Quaker convert (in 1731) from the Scottish gentry, attracted a following among Friends and non-Friends alike. Drummond, characterized as having a "ready wit . . . her expressions particularly fine & unaffected," never visited the American colonies, but held great public meetings in the west and south of England in 1735 and 1736. The English press detailed her movements: "Mrs. Drummond, the famous Quaker preacher, came to town on Thursday night, having been the admiration of the countries, where she made her progress." Thomas Story, another Quaker minister whose preaching had garnered newspaper notice, wrote of May Drummond in 1735 that she was "followed everywhere & admired by all ranks & professions, priests and people, more than any of our profession ever was." The *London Daily Post* reported on Drummond's sermon at the Bull and Mouth Quaker Meeting House in August 1735 and, later, her travels in northern England and Scotland: "Edinburgh, Jan. 23. Celebrated Mrs. Drummond returned from her travels and held forth to the Fraternity of Quakers, yesterday" (Jan.30, 1738/9 edition) and "Sunday Se'nnight Mrs Drummond preached to a polite auditory at Rippon at a Public Inn in that Town" (June 23, 1739 edition). The Quaker female preacher's fame increased when she had an interview with Queen Caroline, the consort of King George II of England.[9]

Mary Peisley, visiting Penrith, England, in 1748, found that "some of the town's-folks being at the forenoon meeting, and the town pretty large, the report spread, and the people came until the house could hold no more with convenience." When Peisley had a "concern" to preach in a nearby town where no Friends had held a meeting before, the female preacher was told, "If the folks of Penrith heard of the meeting, the streets, much less the house would not hold them. . . ." The sites of the itinerant women ministers' meetings were often too small for the general public who wanted to attend, and "many who could not get in were at the windows."

While travelling in Ireland, in 1748, the American preacher Elizabeth Hudson, like numerous Quaker women ministers, preached to crowds of non-Quakers: "Our minds being drawn Out towards the people of the Town, publick notice was given and very large meetings we had." In Nenagh, Ireland, Hudson "had a large meeting in the Town Hall of the Towns people mostly who having had notice of Our Comeing were gather'd about the house in great numbers." Two companies of soldiers stationed in the town, fearing that the old hall would give way under the weight of the mob, kept the crowds in order until the female preachers were ready to begin the meeting, "And two of there principle Officers lent us their hands to help us up the Steps."

At a great outdoor assembly of Friends and others held at Evesham, England, in 1771, a Quaker man noted that the women ministers were particularly successful at drawing the attention of the masses: "Catharine Payton, Rachel Wilson, Isaac Sharples, & Geo. Boon were the principal ministers, but the ministry of the two first mentioned were best calculated for claiming, & gratifying the attention of the multitudes who frequented the meeting." Catharine Payton "stood for nearly two hours and with great clearness and ability explained the peculiar tenets of our Society, and a crowded audience paid a silent and so far respectful attention." As part of their evangelical outreach, individual travelling ministers not only appointed meetings for the public but the Society also held annual "circular meetings" (so-called because the gatherings rotated between different locations), which "were commonly very large, and held in an open place, to which some thousands of the neighbouring people used to resort."[10]

Curious onlookers, including notable figures of eighteenth-century British society, visited the regular Quaker meetings for worship to hear the women preach. When Deborah Morris, for example, accompanied her aunt, Sarah Morris, a Philadelphia preacher, to England on a religious visit in 1772, she noticed at Gracechurch Street Friends Meeting "many straingers [non-Quakers] & among ye others Cathern McCally [Catharine Macaulay] A famos Historyon [historian]." In the audience, along with the other non-Quaker visitors, was Catharine Macaulay (1731–91), admired by John Adams and many political radicals as "one of the brightest ornaments not only of her Sex but of her Age and Country," famed as the female author of a scholarly, multivolume history of England.[11]

Eighteenth-century Quaker women travelling in the American colonies found those of other persuasions in their audiences as well. In Maryland, Virginia, and North Carolina, in 1744, Jane (Fenn) Hoskins remarked, "It appeared to me to be a time of gathering, and great openness among people of various ranks. They followed us from meeting to meeting, treating us with respect, and the marks of real love and affection. . . ." In New Jersey, in 1745, Elizabeth Hudson "had a nights meeting held in the friends house But it was much too small for to Contain the number of people who Came so that many stood out of doors this meeting was mostly of Prisbeterians." Mary Peisley, whose spiritual service "principally bended towards Friends" in 1753, found that the American Quaker meetings she visited were "pretty much mixed with people of other societies." In 1756, when Jane Hoskins visited Boston, Massachusetts, she observed that "Friends of the place was exceedingly kind, and . . . people of other societies were also, insomuch that I was made to admire . . . When I got out to meetings they were crowded, the people continuing to carry with much respect towards us; and when we left that town, several accompanied us on the way, and some, not of our community, went to Rhode Island, and were at all the meetings with us, which were large and crowded." Sophia Hume, raised in Anglican high society in South Carolina, had earlier visited Charleston, in 1747, from London, England, where she had converted to Quakerism, to preach to the pleasure-loving populace of her former homeland. On her return visit to America, the *Virginia Gazette,* on July 6, 1767, noted that in Charleston, South Carolina, "Yesterday Mrs. Hume (the celebrated writer and preacher lately arrived from England) delivered an exhortation to a numerous body of people, of all professions [religious denominations], at the Quakers meeting house."[12]

Many kinds of people came to hear the women ministers. Margaret Ellis felt "called" to preach, in 1739, to a crowd of blacks in Philadelphia preparing for a funeral. In spite of being told that none frequented these burials but other blacks, Ellis attended the event and preached that the Lord "was no Respector of Persons, for both Rich and Poor Black and White Bound and Free, he would have mercy on, provided they would think on his Name." More blacks came from the streets and houses while she was speaking: "Some reported there was hardly A dry Eye Among them . . . they Amounted to full Three Hundred." The Quaker female preachers also addressed Native Americans, attending many of the treaty-making conferences held with the Friendly Association. When Susanna

Hatton preached to the Native Americans during the treaty negotiations at Easton, Pennsylvania, in 1761, a Native American interpreted for her as "she recommended them to the inward Monitor, setting forth what an excellent priviledge it was to be favoured with it and that it was freely offered to people of all Nations Colours and denominations." At several of her meetings, there were "a Large Number of Indians" who "satt very Solid. . . ." Concern about the impact of the female ministers on the struggle between the anti-Quaker proprietary group and Pennsylvania Quakers for control of Indian affairs testified to the Quaker women's visibility. The Anglican proprietor of Pennsylvania, Thomas Penn, wrote to his provincial secretary, Richard Peters, in 1761: "I am sorry to hear the Quakers are sending up their Female Preachers to the Indians, as it is calculated to draw those poor People to a dependance upon them, else a conviction of their peacable Principles would be very useful."[13]

Those outside of the Friends' community not only listened to the women preach, but read some of their messages as well. Sermons of some popular Quaker ministers, such as Rachel Wilson, were printed by non-Quaker publishers to capitalize on the market of avid auditors (see, for example, *A Discourse Delivered on Saturday, the 10th Day of August, 1769, At the Friends Meeting-House, in Beekman's Precinct, Dutches County, In the Province of New-York. By the Celebrated Rachel Wilson, (One of the People called Quakers.) To a numerous Audience of different Persuasions, Taken in Short Hand, from the Mouth of the Speaker . . .* [New York, 1769]). Sophia Hume, of London, primarily addressed her works, *An Exhortation to the Inhabitants of the Province of South-Carolina* (1748) and *An Epistle to the Inhabitants of South Carolina* (1754), to the non-Quaker inhabitants of her native land. According to Israel Pemberton Sr., Hume's *Exhortation* was well liked by those who had the opportunity to read it, "Not only of our Societ[y] but likewise of others." On June 9, 1767, the South Carolina newspapers acknowledged Hume's authorial efforts in their announcement of the arrival from London of "several Passengers, particularly Mrs. Sophia Hume, well known for her Writings in Favour of the Quakers." Although Hume's works were published under the auspices of the Quaker Yearly Meeting, eighteenth-century Quaker women ministers' pronouncements also appeared in the general press. The leading eighteenth-century English periodical, the *Gentleman's Magazine,* printed Frances (Henshaw) Dodshon's epistle to King George III, written "in such language as Divine

Wisdom shall see meet [suitable] to inspire," in June 1775. The Quaker female preacher urged the king to be lenient to his rebellious American subjects and "prevent the effusion of blood, the rending of a potent empire."[14]

Influential journals published others' writings about the eighteenth-century women ministers, also, their public activity making them the subject of laudatory poetry. In 1735, the *Gentleman's Magazine* printed a poem, "On the noted and celebrated Quaker Mrs. Drummond." The lines written "by a young Lady" lauded May Drummond's piety: "No more, O *Spain!* thy saint *Teresa* boast; / Here's one outshines her on the *British* coast, . . ." "Verses on several of the Quaker teachers," which appeared in the *London Magazine* for 1736, disparaged some Quaker ministers, but praised Drummond: "But see where gentle Drummond next appears, / With sense and judgment far above her years," described Susanna Padley as warning "the sinner of impending woe," and likened Mary Wyatt to "the Cumaean Sybil in her cave." In 1750, the *Gentleman's Magazine* published the tribute to the Irish Quaker female preacher Mary Peisley entitled "To M.P. a Native of Ireland, now in England, visiting the Meetings of her Friends, the Quakers," likely written by a Quaker ("Philanthropos"). The panegyric began, "In thee, bright maid! accomplish'd, we behold / What antient seers of future times foretold. / Now pour'd on all the gifts of grace divine, / Our sons and *daughters*, undistinguish'd, shine . . . ," and was followed by the non-Quaker editor's note in brackets: "We hear that the stature of this maiden is as remarkable as her accomplishments, being near 6 foot [tall]."[15]

The general public was made further aware of the Quaker women in news items, such as the visit, in June 1753, of a Quaker minister (Ann Mercy Bell, of Yorkshire, who preached repentance in the streets of London that summer) to Parliament. *Gentleman's Magazine* recorded of Bell's activity: "A female quaker who was in the house, to see the king on the throne, began to hold forth as soon as his majesty was gone, against the vanity of dress, and preached for half an hour." Notice of Frances Paxton's second marriage (at which she preached) appeared in the *Gentleman's Magazine* of 1755: "Wm. Dodsham [Dodshon] of Durham,—to Frances Paxton; being of the people called Quakers, the lady made a learned discourse upon the occasion." Frances Henshaw, later Paxton, a Quaker convert (in 1736) from an affluent English family, was a well-known minister in northern England. Her obituary, identifying her as "Mrs. Frances

The English Quaker preacher Rachel Wilson (1720–75) attracted crowds on her tour of the American colonies from 1768 to 1769. She was compared in eloquence to George Whitefield, the charismatic revivalist preacher. This *Discourse* was taken down in shorthand and published by a non-Quaker to capitalize on the market of avid auditors. *Courtesy Houghton Library, Harvard University*

A

DISCOURSE,

DELIVERED

On *Saturday*, the 10th Day of *August*, 1769,

AT THE

FRIENDS *Meeting-House,*

IN

BEEKMAN's PRECINCT, *Dutches County,*

In the Province of

NEW-YORK.

BY THE CELEBRATED

RACHEL WILSON,

(One of the People called *Quakers.*)

To a numerous Audience of different Perfuafions,

Taken in short Hand, from the Mouth of the Speaker, by one of the Audience.

NEW-YORK: Printed.

NEWPORT, Rhode Island: Re printed, and Sold, by SOLOMON SOUTHWICK, in *Marlborough Street,* 1769.

Dodshon, a principal speaker among the people called Quakers," was printed in the *Gentleman's Magazine* of 1782. The *Virginia Gazette* of 1772 reprinted the notice of an English woman minister's death at age ninety-two: "that faithful and distinguished Labourer in the Gospel, amongst the People called Quakers in this city [Bristol, England], Lydia Pocock, Commissioned from on high, she was indefatigable in sounding an Alarm to the Supine."[16]

The female preachers also came to the attention of eighteenth-century readers in political satire, travelogues, and writings of an apocalyptic or controversial nature. In *The Great Crisis* (1725), Richard Roach cited "the appearance of the she-preachers among the Quakers," as well as Jane Lead, the foremost female visionary of the Philadelphian Society, and the French quietists Antoinette Bourignon and Madame Guion as evidence of the approaching Millennium. Roach, an Oxford scholar and member of the Philadelphian Society for the Advancement of Piety and Philosophy (a community of intellectuals and mystics influenced by Jacob Boehme), envisioned the female ministers as harbingers of a new age for humanity in which women were beginning to draw men up to heaven. Another author, however, viewed the practice of women preaching not as an apocalyptic sign but as a grievous error. In the pamphlet *A Dissertation Upon The Liberty of Preaching granted to Women by the People call'd Quakers* (1738), which was written in the form of a letter to May Drummond, the critic asserted that "in all my Travels I have seen a great many wonderful Things; yet to see a Woman acting, as you do, . . . 'tis a Wonder I never before met with in any other part of the World." Although the critic reluctantly acknowledged that Drummond had acted "so admirably well the Part of a Preacher," a Quaker rebuttal to this work which had "depretiated the Female Sex below the Standard of Holy Scripture and sound Reason" quickly followed—Bernardus Utopiensis [John Rutty], *A Second Dissertation on the Liberty of Preaching Granted to Women by the People called Quakers: In Answer to a late Dissertation on that Subject* (Dublin, 1739).[17]

The power wielded by Quaker women ministers was critiqued for political ends in a satire by William Smith, an Anglican priest, in his effort to dislodge Friends from the government of Pennsylvania: "Each Saint in Petticoats foretells our Fate, And fain wou'd guide the giddy Helm of State." Smith, the presumed author of *A Letter from a Gentleman in London to his Friend in Pennsylvania, with a Satire Containing Some Characteristical Strokes Upon the Manners and Principles of the Quakers* (1756), was charac-

A poem by a young lady, "On the noted and celebrated Quaker Mrs Drummond," appeared in *Gentleman's Magazine* (September 1735). This ode to the Quaker preacher May Drummond portrayed her as a symbol of woman's capacity. The verses were a reworking of a poem addressed to pioneer feminist Mary Astell, entitled "To Almystrea, on her Divine Works" (1722), by the English poet Elizabeth Thomas (1675–1731). *Courtesy Department of Special Collections, Davidson Library, University of California, Santa Barbara* terized by Benjamin Franklin as a "common Scribbler of Libels and false abusive papers . . . against Publick Bodies and private Persons, and thereby keeping up Party Heats in the Province." Travellers' accounts, like those of the Frenchman de Crèvecoeur and the Swede Peter Kalm, further publicized activities in Quaker meetings, when they observed the religious society as part of their tours of the American colonies or of the British Isles.[18]

By the latter half of the eighteenth century, the Quaker female preacher had acquired enough widespread visibility to become a cultural stereotype, meriting usage as a character in a novel. In H. H. Brackenridge's picaresque novel of early America, *Modern Chivalry: Containing the Adventures of Captain John Farrago, And Teague O'Regan, His Servant* (Philadelphia, 1792), the hero turns for assistance to a public figure, the Quaker woman minister, no longer a witchlike "enthusiast," but now the embodiment of benevolent wisdom, when he contemplates how to assist another woman's recovery from an unfortunate situation: "Thought he, I am in a city where there are a great body of the people called Quakers. This society, above all others, is remarkable for humanity, and charitable actions. There is a female preacher, of whom I have heard; a Lydia Wilson: I will inform this good woman of the circumstance; and, if she gives me leave, I will bring this stray sheep to her; she may have it in her power to introduce her to some place, where, by needlework, and industry, she might live, until it may be in my power . . . to restore her to her family." Brackenridge had attended the College of New Jersey in 1768, and may personally have heard the celebrated preacher Rachel Wilson deliver her Princeton sermon. His memory of the travelling minister likely provided the inspiration for his character Lydia Wilson, the admirable Quaker, "[a] pious woman [who] readily undertook every office in her power."[19]

Historical Reasons Contributing to Increased Acceptance of Quakers: In England

To understand the remarkable change in the reception of Quaker women preachers from the seventeenth to the eighteenth centuries, the shift in attitudes toward the Society of Friends must be examined. In England, the religious strife of the Civil War years had left a legacy of disillusionment with fanaticism and a reaction against "enthusiasm." By 1700,

Latitudinarianism, which stressed reason rather than revelation, was a prominent trend among Anglican ecclesiastics. Doctrinal differences became secondary to a shared morality, as an undogmatic outlook diminished the importance of earlier religious controversies. The Toleration Act of 1689 had permitted Protestant dissenters from the Anglican church to designate their own preachers. Moderation and toleration became prominent virtues as the Church of England, although reestablished as the national church, was obliged to share its spiritual leadership with a number of dissenting sects. In a profound redefinition of religion, one's mode of worship had become an issue of private moral judgment, no longer to be determined by the state (a principle legally recognized by the Toleration Act). This new notion of religion, as a matter of individual conscience, permitted what previously had been deemed heretical—diversity of religious opinion (although this freedom was still limited to Christians). England was famous and distinctive in this period for its religious toleration: allowing each man to worship in his own fashion. In 1733, Voltaire, the French philosopher, marveled: "England is properly the country of sectarists. . . . An *Englishman,* as one to whom liberty is natural, may go to heaven his own way."[20]

Recent discoveries by Isaac Newton and other scientists stimulated British intellectual skepticism, encouraging the movement away from narrow, intolerant sectarianism. In this latitudinarian atmosphere, men like Dr. John Byrom and James Boswell visited various places of worship with a scientific attitude of inquiry. Interested in learning the opinions and practices of different sects, Byrom maintained "the absurdity of persecuting one another for differences of opinion." Diaries of eighteenth-century British inhabitants verify that they occasionally attended the worship services of other religious groups. While on a journey from his London residence, Dr. John Byrom, an Anglican, stopped in the town of Henley, England, to "hear a piece of a Quaker woman's sermon" in 1731. James Boswell, Samuel Johnson's biographer, told Dr. Johnson on Sunday, July 31, 1763, that he had heard a woman preach at the Quaker meeting he had attended that morning in London. Queen Caroline (1683-1737), the wife of George II, who met with the Quaker preacher May Drummond, enjoyed the discussion of religious and philosophical topics, especially when these inclined toward the unorthodox. She rebuked the Anglican bishops for their opposition to the Quakers' Tithe Bill in 1736. The queen's chief study was divinity; she was "speculative and latitudinarian" and "extended her patronage to the dissenting sects." Other intellectuals, as well, like Catharine Macaulay, a member of the Church of England, with many Dissenter friends, attended Quaker meetings, having "a mind too enlightened for bigotry." Increasingly, reflective thinkers admired certain Quaker principles such as their testimony against war and, eventually, their abolition of slavery. Hannah More, another "bluestocking," or learned woman, wrote to Horace Walpole in 1790: "If it were not that I should be obliged to wear such frightful clothes, and preserve such a mournful silence in worship, I have some thoughts of turning Quaker myself; they seem to be almost the only people who exhibit anything of Christianity in their *actions;* ours is but talk. And I am almost inclined to think people who upon principle can neither go to war or go to law must be in the right." Horace Walpole himself wrote in a letter in 1780, "I am a settled Whig; for if one thinks, one must before my age have fixed one's creed by the lamp of one's own reason: but I have much Quakerism in my composition, and prefer peace to doctrines."[21]

For foreign visitors, especially from France and Russia, religious toleration was a novelty, and the Quakers were the most intriguing example of England's religious diversity. Czar Peter the Great of Russia "was fascinated by the Quakers." During his visit to England in 1696, he met William Penn, and received Quaker literature. The czar attended Gracechurch Street Meeting and several Quaker meetings in Deptford, where he was studying the art of shipbuilding. In 1712, while in the North German province of Holstein, Czar Peter again sought out a Quaker meeting, attending with his Russian entourage. He commended what he heard at the meeting, declaring to his followers that "whosoever could live according to that doctrine would be happy." European travellers to eighteenth-century England were often effusive in their admiration of the Society of Friends because of its contrast with oppressive, authoritarian institutions in their native lands. After dining with a Quaker physician, a foreign visitor, Faujas de St. Fond, wrote, "During the remainder of the night I meditated how I should become a Quaker, for if happiness exists anywhere on earth it certainly dwells among these worthy people. . . . I love the Quakers, they inspire me with involuntary veneration." The symbolic importance of the Quakers to the French Enlightenment intellectuals dramatically elevated the public image of Friends.[22]

Voltaire, the French Enlightenment *philosophe,* brought the Quakers to the attention of the world in his *Letters Concerning the English Nation* (1733), transforming the "heretics" of the seventeenth century into exemplars of the Age of Reason, now associated with virtue and moderation. During Voltaire's stay in England, from 1726 to 1729, he researched the Society, attending Quaker meetings and acquainting himself with Friends' tenets. Voltaire, like other Enlightenment thinkers, sought to improve the human condition. He perceived that authoritarian institutions, such as a state-supported church, were often corrupt, and interfered with virtuous, individual development. Believing that conscience, a "moral sense" present in a human since birth, was a trustworthy inner guide along with reason, Voltaire asserted that independence could be achieved from dominating, external authorities. For Voltaire, "the good Quaker" was an example of the constructive individual who did not require the outward disciplines of an autocratic state or a coercive church. Voltaire admiringly described the moderation and benevolence of a Quaker businessman he visited in England: "a hale ruddy complexion'd old man, who had never been afflicted with sickness, because he had always been insensible to passions, and a perfect stranger to intemperance. I never in my life saw a more noble or a more engaging aspect than his."

Voltaire's *Letters* sensationally presented Pennsylvania as a utopia of equality and religious freedom, indelibly etching the image of Quakers as "peaceable," "mild," and "gentle." William Penn's seventeenth-century pamphlets to recruit settlers for his province of Pennsylvania had already circulated widely throughout western Europe, promoting an idealistic depiction of life in the Quaker colony. In addition, Penn's friend and chief land agent, Benjamin Furley, who had hosted political refugees such as John Locke and Lord Shaftesbury in Rotterdam, had publicized the colony in correspondence with intellectuals and liberal politicians across Europe. But Voltaire ventured even further, concluding: "William Pen[n] might glory in having brought down upon earth the so much boasted golden age, which in all probability never existed but in Pensilvania." According to Voltaire, William Penn had "enacted very wise and prudent laws," using reason that would "injure no person upon a religious account, and . . . consider as brethren all those who believe in one God" (particularly important in a rational age which newly valued liberty of conscience).

The French thinker found impressive and liberating that, in this American province, even the least important of the subjects was not obligated to take his hat off in the sovereign's presence; the government was without one priest in it; and the people were without "arms, either offensive or defensive." Championing the "enlightened" Quaker model, Voltaire implicitly critiqued his own society's institutions. Penn was cited as the greatest law-giver since classical antiquity in Montesquieu's entry in the *Encyclopédie* (1751–80). Other eighteenth-century French works, such as Raynal's *A Philosophical and Political History of the Settlements and Trade of the Europeans in the East and West Indies* (1784), and Brissot de Warville's *New Travels in the United States of America 1788* (1791), also presented the Society of Friends in largely praiseworthy fashion. But in spite of a similar opinion concerning religious freedom, Quakers differed from the Enlightenment thinkers by placing their primary reliance on the immediate inspiration of the Holy Spirit. Quakers called Satan "the Reasoner," able to deceive one into disregarding "divine leadings." For Friends, constructive behavior, "walking in the Light," was the effect of adhering to inward religious experience, since rationalizations could be delusive. Voltaire, however, had not been impressed by the preaching method of the Quakers, finding their mode of worship incoherent and irrational.[23]

England's rapidly expanding economy after 1689 suggested that toleration of religious dissent had financial benefits as well, since Friends pioneered in various industries and developed trade networks. Quakers increased their influence, often gaining royal patronage, through success in different occupations as merchants, industrialists, craftsmen, and physicians. Daniel Quare, for example, a Quaker watchmaker, skillfully constructed timepieces for English monarchs, his inventions famed in the courts of Europe. European diplomats and courtiers honored him with a large attendance at the wedding of his daughter with Sylvanus Bevan, a respected London Quaker apothecary. Quare had access to the king, through his outstanding work, gaining the monarch's support of the Affirmation Act of 1696 (which gave Quakers an alternative to swearing oaths). John Hanbury, a wealthy Quaker tobacco merchant, had great "personal weight and interest with the Ministry." Since Hanbury traded extensively with Virginia planters, he was consulted by Parliament for his expertise on commercial topics. David Barclay, the son of Robert, author of the *Apology*, was a London linen merchant, and a major transatlantic exporter. His colonial American contacts made him valuable to the imperial government as well. The Quaker physician John Fothergill of London "was at the top of his profession, and among the patients in his large and lucrative practice were [Benjamin] Franklin and Lord Dartmouth." The earl of Dartmouth served as the British government's secretary of state for the colonies. Fothergill's close relations with Lord Dartmouth permitted him to give political as well as medical advice. The master of the Friends' school in Ballitore, Ireland, Abraham Shackleton, "an able and very serious Quaker," made a "strong and lasting impression" upon Edmund Burke (1729–97), the powerful orator, author of *Origin of Our Ideas of the Sublime and Beautiful* (1756), and influential Whig member of the British Parliament from 1765 until his death. Burke, who advocated that colonists should be allowed to enjoy all the rights of Englishmen, and opposed the slave trade, had received part of his education at the Quaker school. The Anglican's later political activity on behalf of Dissenters stemmed in part from this experience. For many years, Edmund Burke's closest friend was Richard Shackleton (1726–92), the devout son of the Quaker schoolmaster. Burke and Shackleton formed a debating club with other friends in the 1740s, meeting in Dublin to discuss morality, history, politics, and philosophy. Richard Shackleton was also in a group of young Irish Quaker friends, which included the preachers Mary Peisley, Samuel Neale, and Elizabeth Pike, who met regularly to encourage each other's spiritual development.[24]

By the 1720s, the English government had come to respect the Quakers' political organization, especially at the polls. Sir Robert Walpole, the most influential politician in England during the first half of the eighteenth century as the prime minister (although the title was not official at the time), recognized the power of the Dissenters' vote, including that of the Quakers, who voted in a bloc. When confronted by possible defeat in the Norwich elections, Walpole had called upon the Quakers for support, in particular his friend John Gurney, from a family prominent in the woollen industry. The duke of Newcastle, like an increasing number of government leaders, actively courted Quaker votes as well, in his district of Sussex. Eighteenth-century Quakers were a powerful lobby. John Pemberton, the American Quaker preacher, asserted to Ezra Stiles, the Congregationalist minister, in the 1770s that "Friends were well respected at [the English] Court & had great Influence there . . . and that the Quakers in London had used their Influence in favor of America with success at Court—particularly that they had wrote them that had it not been for their Interposition, greater Severity had been used in the Bo[ston]. Port-Bill, that they had much moderated the late Acts." In December 1774, David Barclay and Dr. John Fothergill, pillars of the Quaker community in London, in liaison with some highly placed members of government at Whitehall, even engaged in secret negotiations with Benjamin Franklin in an attempt to avert the British government's war with the colonies.[25]

Typically, Friends' connections with people of rank were used to further the Quaker struggle for religious freedom. In spite of the Toleration Act of 1689, and despite theological latitudinarianism, English Friends were still penalized in significant ways. They continued to be disqualified from being members of Parliament and attending English universities, and were still forced to contribute to the maintenance of the national church "which in the first forty years of the eighteenth century cost the Quakers more than £167,000." In 1715, for example, Quaker lobbying began when the act allowing an affirmation instead of an oath (a political compromise negotiated by some Quakers) was nearing expiration, and Friends at London Yearly Meeting were divided over whether the form of affirmation was consistent with Christ's doctrine against oaths. In order to urge a reframing of the affirmation to make it acceptable to all Friends, Thomas Story, a leading Quaker minister, who had attended school with the third earl of Carlisle, visited the nobleman to confer on the subject. The earl's son, Lord Morpeth, a member of the House of Commons, was asked "to solicit the favour of the House of Commons for further redress." In 1736, this type of Quaker persuasion permitted the Quakers' Tithe Bill, for further ease concerning tithes, to pass the House of Commons by a very great majority. But the bill ultimately failed, not passing the House of Lords, because the Anglican bishops had thrown their influence against it, by 54 votes to 35.[26]

Well-known converts to Quakerism, like Thomas Story, who was acquainted with many of the nobility and gentry in eighteenth-century England, advanced Friends' respectability. As the Quaker brother of a leading Anglican ecclesiastic, George Story, the dean of Limerick in Ireland, Thomas Story sometimes drew crowds curious to hear "the Dean's brother." Born into a prominent Anglican family in Cumberland, England, Thomas Story was a lawyer known for his skill at debate and his willingness to discuss religious issues. Those "of high station found Story to have an acceptable way." The Quaker preacher knew Sir Thomas Liddel of Ravensworth Castle, regularly visited Sir John Rodes, a Quaker convert, at Barlbrough Hall, and was hosted, in 1732, by the earl of Carlisle at Castle Howard, Yorkshire, who acknowledged "how great an esteem he had for Friends as an honest religious people." Story, who also sold rare trees to owners of large estates, dined with people of rank, and engaged in theological conversations. Apparently worldlier than most Quaker preachers (he was rebuked by Joseph Pike, a Quaker merchant of Cork, Ireland, in 1723 for dressing too fashionably: "thou goest a little too fine and modish and particularly as to thy hat and long hair, etc."), Story related well to those outside the Quaker community.

Quaker ministers, such as Catharine Payton, Tabitha Hornor of Leeds, and Thomas Story, also preached occasionally to the crowds, including many people "of quality," that gathered at fashionable spas like Bath and Scarborough for their health in the eighteenth century. Thomas Story wrote, at Bath in 1719, "the opportunities were exceptional. Large companies of the nobility and gentry attended the various Meetings so that the Meeting House could not hold them . . . more than one meeting lasted for two or three hours." When the *London Daily Advertiser* printed Thomas Story's obituary in 1742, it emphasized that Story was loved not only by the Society of Friends but by many others "not of the meanest rank who had the pleasure of his acquaintance."[27]

Other prominent converts who became Quaker preachers, like May Drummond and Frances Henshaw, attracted further publicity to the Society of Friends. May Drummond was from "a considerable family" in North Britain. She was "convinced" at the Edinburgh Yearly Meeting after hearing Thomas Story speak. At that time, Drummond's brother was lord provost of Edinburgh. Another brother, Alexander Drummond, served later as British consul at Aleppo, 1754–56, and authored *Travels through the different Countries of Germany, Italy, Greece, and parts of Asia, as far as the Euphrates, with an Account of what is remarkable in their present state and their Monuments of Antiquity* (1754). When May Drummond attended the Quaker yearly meeting in 1731, with about thirty of her acquaintances, Thomas Story had preached on subjects pertinent to them. The visitors suspected he had had a prepared sermon in his pocket, but Story insisted he had been guided by the Holy Spirit. Thereafter, the young Scottish woman frequently attended Friends' meetings "to the great surprize of her acquaintances, who are generally of the greater and more polite sorts of both sexes, and to the grief and trouble of her relations, who are all against her, save only a younger brother." May Drummond's public appearance in the ministry renewed her family's pain, but she had "a turn of expression, on any subject she is upon, very taking to most hearers, especially the more polite sort of both sexes." In addition to Drummond's "having good utterance and matter," her character and circumstances drew many to meetings wherever she travelled. Drummond's testimony appealed to people of all ranks but "especially the greater sort; by whom she is more followed and admired at present than any one amongst us, the notion of her being a lady of quality (which yet is a mistake of her degree) raising a curiosity to hear her, which occasions crowds not always to her satisfaction."[28]

The Quaker minister Thomas Chalkley told of Drummond in London having the "opportunity of declaring her convincement to our noble Queen Caroline, our great King George's royal consort. The kind treatment and good reception she had with the Queen spread so in the city and country that many thousands flocked to hear her and more of the gentry and nobility than ever was known before to our Meetings." In 1735, at the movable yearly meeting, at Chester, held for the northern counties of Cheshire, Lancashire, Westmorland, and Cumberland, there was "a public Meeting for Worship which was exceedingly large, consisting of some thousands; for the Quarter Sessions of the Peace happening at the same time, all or most of the bench of Justices came to the Meeting, and many of the women, under the distinction (among them) of Ladies, and a very great crowd." May Drummond, Joshua Toft, and Thomas Story were the main preachers and the response was so favorable that, "in the close of this Meeting several of the great ones asked if there would be any more [meetings]. . . ."

Initially, Frances Henshaw (b. 1714), who resided near Leek, England, was reluctant to join others in flocking to May Drummond's meeting when the Quaker preacher was in her locality. But this decision troubled the young heiress's conscience. After much spiritual exploration, including correspondence with the non-Quaker theologian William Law and the encouragement of Quaker ministers John and Joshua Toft, who lived in her neighborhood, Henshaw converted to Quakerism. Friends gave material and spiritual assistance to Frances Henshaw when her conversion displeased her prominent family. Although the twenty-three-year-old's decision distressed her relatives, Henshaw drew acclaim from "the great people" with her preaching, and her fame increased in the district.[29]

In the eighteenth century, Quakers appealed both to "enlightened" society, the elite culture valuing order and tolerance, and perhaps, flirting with unorthodox beliefs such as "deism" (rejecting Christianity in favor of a natural religion based on reason) and to the lower classes in awe of the supernatural but increasingly alienated from formal religious observances. The

M.ᵣ MAY DRUMMOND.

Portrait of the Quaker preacher May Drummond (c. 1710–72), a convert from a prominent Scottish Presbyterian family. Thomas Story, the Quaker minister, wrote of Drummond in 1735 that she was "followed everywhere & admired by all ranks & professions, priests and people, more than any of our profession ever was." May Drummond was known for her eloquence, characterized as having "a ready wit . . . her expressions particularly fine & unaffected." Her fame increased after an interview with Queen Caroline, the consort of George II of England. Painting attributed to Jonathan Richardson (1665–1745). *Reproduced with permission of the Library Committee of the Religious Society of Friends in Britain* traditional parish system in England did not meet the needs of many people, especially in the new industrial districts. The vitality of an itinerant ministry in the eighteenth century became even more evident when the evangelical preaching of the travelling ministers George Whitefield and John Wesley (ordained in the Church of England but emphasizing the need for a "New Birth" through God's grace) eventually reawakened a sense of personal religion in thousands of men and women. In 1739, when Thomas Story dined with Lord Lonsdale of Lowther-hall, they conversed about the Methodists who had recently emerged in England. Story perceived a similarity to Quakerism in their professing to preach by qualification of the Holy Spirit, and their insistence on the need for regeneration, not just ordination, in the ministry. Story was sympathetic to the Methodists' trials, reminiscent of earlier Quaker struggles, as he recognized that some national priests who were threatened by their challenging principles had begun to persecute them.[30]

For the Society of Friends, however, a major change had occurred in the British reception of Quaker travelling preachers by the third decade of the eighteenth century. At the yearly meeting for Wales, held in Ludlow, Thomas Story marveled at the huge contrast: magistrates who had persecuted Friends in earlier times were now arranging halls for the Friends' meetings and appointing constables to protect the Quaker services from any disturbance. Already at meetings in Scotland in 1728, Thomas Story "perceived the state of that people was much altered for the better since I first knew that place, and the old prejudices much worn away in many of them." At the Chester Yearly Meeting in England, where the Quakers were regularly drawing audiences of several thousand, Story found that, in 1731, "many of the more reputable sort" spoke well of the testimony delivered "for which many Friends were thankful to the Lord our God, who hath wrought so great a change in the minds of the people, not only in this place, but also in most places at this day throughout all Britain, and the British Dominions every where." In Kendal, in 1733, Story actually received "a thousand thanks from one of the Justices for my good instructions. . . . However it was much better than being sent into a dungeon for it, which was often the portion of those who made way in times past, by their sufferings for this liberty." The increased tolerance of Quakerism corresponded with the decline of sectarian fervor. When Thomas Story visited London, he observed: "At this time Deism was much advanced in the City and Nation, and the former zeal of all sects near expired; yet our Meetings were much crowded on First days." But Story concluded that few were ready to actually convert and live according to the Quakers' high standards in 1734, although crowds approvingly attended Quaker meetings: "For the people throughout this nation at this time are generally willing to give us a fair and peaceable hearing, and with good acceptance as to the truth of our doctrine; but the Cross of Christ being yet too heavy for them, as they weakly think, and finding ease and a false rest in death under their priests who sooth them in their sins, they yet rest short of the Kingdom. Nevertheless the spirit and power of persecution is greatly lessened in this nation since the blessed Truth shineth forth therein, in and among our first Friends."[31]

Historical Reasons Contributing to Increased Acceptance of Quakers: In America

Religious toleration evolved differently in American circumstances. An important distinction between the situations of Friends in England and in America was the governmental power held by American Quakers in several colonies. The autonomy of governments granted by charter, as well as the diversity of religious groups in early America, caused Quakers to initially suffer harsher treatment (for example, in the Puritan-governed Massachusetts Bay Colony) than they had endured in England. Eventually, however, in the American environment (the very preponderance of dissenters from the Church of England, the lack of preexisting ecclesiastical institutions, as well as the ones weakened by remote conditions, and, again, the independence of proprietary governments), Quakers were able to win greater religious toleration than they were able to achieve in England. There was complete freedom of worship in Rhode Island, New Jersey, and Pennsylvania, and, without the need to swear oaths or pass other religious qualification tests, Quakers served in political office in these colonies.

In Rhode Island, an early Quaker refuge from persecution in the Massachusetts Bay Colony, the Reverend MacSparran, a Church of England priest in Newport, noted in 1753 that the Quakers were, "for the most part, the people in power." For most of the eighteenth century, Rhode Island inhabitants elected Quaker governors and numerous Quaker assemblymen (as a charter colony, governors were elected by the populace, in contrast to royally appointed governors in a crown colony). In colonies with Quaker-dominated governments, the travelling religious leaders of the Society of Friends were particularly notable visitors, and governmental leaders might attend their meetings. When the English preacher Mary Weston arrived at a Quaker meeting in Newport in August 1750, it was enlarged "on account of the Assembly sitting at that time, who on hearing of an English Friend being come to visit that Island, adjourned the House and came in a Body to Meeting headed by the Governor."[32]

A former governor of Rhode Island, Gideon Wanton, escorted Mary Weston on her New England religious visit, as did other leading citizens of the colony, wealthy Quaker merchants and their wives, such as the Newberrys and the Richardsons. The English minister Jane Crosfield lodged at Governor Hopkins's "Country house" for a week during her religious tour in 1760–61. Stephen Hopkins (a Quaker until his disownment by Smithfield Monthly Meeting in the 1770s for refusing to free a slave) served as governor of Rhode Island at various times between 1755 and 1768. Rachel Wilson recorded in her travel journal that "we went home with Stephen Hopkins that night to Providence," when the former governor accompanied Wilson from Smithfield to Providence on her American journey in 1769. Joseph Wanton, another Quaker, was governor during Wilson's visit, when she was invited to preach to the Rhode Island Assembly. Friends' prestige, as political, commercial, and social leaders in Rhode Island, encouraged the general population to flock to the Quaker yearly meetings in Newport. Reverend Ezra Stiles, the Congregationalist minister in Newport who heard Rachel Wilson's sermon, served as librarian at the Redwood Library, founded by the Quaker philanthropist-merchant Abraham Redwood.[33]

In the Quaker-founded colony of Pennsylvania, Friends were very influential, the ruling group rather than an embattled minority for the first half of the eighteenth century. Visiting English Quaker preacher Catharine Payton was able to have "a religious opportunity" with a number of politicians from the Pennsylvania Assembly, because Payton knew that "the major part of its members . . . [were] then under the profession of Truth [Quakers]." Even after they no longer formed a numerical majority of the colony's population, Quakers were consistently elected as representatives by Pennsylvania inhabitants of other religious affiliations. When many Friends withdrew from public office in response to the French and Indian War, the provincial secretary, Richard Peters, believed their resignations would not end Quaker influence in politics, claiming that the new members who replaced them would do "just such as the Quakers and Mr. Franklin please to recommend." Eighteenth-century Quakers were among the prominent citizens of Pennsylvania, as businessmen, landowners, and philanthropists. The funeral of Anthony Morris, a wealthy Quaker brewer and property-holder, for example, drew "a very great number of the most substantial Inhabitants as well as a vast number of Friends from different parts." When Ann Moore, the Maryland minister, preached at the funeral meeting in Philadelphia in 1763, "the Governor the Recorder many of the Councill Aldermen severall Ministers (of other persuasions) many Lawyers, & a great number of Merch[an]ts & Private Gentlemen &c." were in attendance.[34]

After the Quaker establishment of West Jersey, Friends served in government, as governors, councillors, and assemblymen, and many acquired considerable estates. A variety of denominations flourished, however, among the later immigrants to New Jersey, as it transformed into a royal colony. The colony's Quakers still were able to utilize their political influence in England, appealing to the Meeting for Sufferings in London to secure a favorable appointment of a royal official when they became disenchanted with Lewis Morris, an intolerant New Jersey governor favoring eastern, Anglican interests. John Hunt, the London Quaker merchant, in a letter to Israel Pemberton Sr. in 1746, wrote: "Governour Belchier [Belcher] is appointed Governour of the Jersey's which was owing to the application of Friends here in his favour and we hope he'll have a proper regard to our Society in his administration." The New Jersey Quaker initiative was led by the Smiths, the eminent merchant family of Burlington (daughter Elizabeth Smith was a travelling preacher). Richard Partridge, the London Quaker lobbyist, secured the appointment of his Congregationalist brother-in-law, Jonathan Belcher, drawing on the support of Quakers across Britain. Governor Belcher likely demonstrated the effects of Quaker political influence in his treatment of itinerant Quaker minister Samuel Fothergill in the mid-1750s. Fothergill recalled: "I had a meeting that day in the seat of government of the Jerseys, in the Presbyterian meeting-house; the governor, J. Belcher, procured it, and attended the meeting. I dined with him afterwards, and met with a kind, affectionate reception."[35]

In the early eighteenth century, Anglican priest John Blair reported that in North Carolina, Quakers are "the greatest number in the Assembly, and are unanimous, and stand truly to one another in whatsoever be their interest." Quaker politicians included John Archdale, who served as governor of the Carolinas from 1694 to 1696. For the first twenty-five years of settlement in North Carolina, Quakerism had been the only organized form of religion. Early Friends had fled persecution in Virginia and clustered in the Albemarle Sound area. Eventually, Anglican planters passed legislation demanding oaths of political officeholders (forcing Quakers' removal from the Assembly) and establishing the Church of England, but a substantial Quaker population remained in North Carolina. In South Carolina, there had been Quakers, as well, among the earliest settlers in 1675. Mary Fisher, the English missionary to Boston in 1656, had immigrated with her second husband, John Crosse, to the colony. As early as 1682 Friends had held a monthly meeting in Charles Town, but by 1719, the number of Quakers in South Carolina had dwindled, as many of their offspring became Anglican. The travelling Quaker preachers received kind treatment, however, from the descendants of early Quakers in South Carolina. Mary Weston stayed at Thomas Elliott Jr.'s residence at Stonoe, "where we were very lovingly received and respectfully treated by those descendants of Friends tho' they do not go under our Names & lodging there that Night." Weston observed on her visit in 1751 to Charleston, "Elliotts, people of Note [with Quaker forebears, who numbered South Carolina assemblymen among their family members] in that province, who constantly attended the [Quaker] mtgs. [while Weston was there]."[36]

Even in colonies where Quakers never held major positions in government, like Massachusetts, they wielded political influence through their network of coreligionists in England and the other provinces. Friends had established a regular meeting in Boston by 1677, after English Quakers had courted public opinion by printing accounts of the injustices Friends had suffered in the Massachusetts Bay Colony. Quakers' petitioning of the king and Parliament for toleration, claiming the privileges of English law, had prompted King Charles II to force the New England Puritans to overturn the legislation of 1661, which banished Quakers upon pain of death. Following the Glorious Revolution of 1688, Massachusetts lost the privileges provided by its original charter, and had to accept more intrusive royal authority. Sectarians were eligible to hold public office under the charter of 1692. By the 1710s, local officeholding by Quakers, in a Massachusetts town such as Lynn with a significant Quaker population, rose to levels proportional to their numbers. Persistent lobbying by "the well-organized joint efforts of the Yearly Meetings of Rhode Island and London," moved the

Massachusetts legislature to grudgingly exempt Quakers from tithes to the established Congregational church in 1728, but the standards for exemption were made so stringent that many could not qualify, and Friends were still brought before the local courts. Richard Partridge "exerted his growing influence with London's merchants and with his fellow Quakers" to help ensure that his brother-in-law, Jonathan Belcher, was appointed governor of Massachusetts and New Hampshire by King George II in 1729. Belcher valued his Quaker brother-in-law, who served as a colonial agent for Massachusetts as well as Rhode Island, because of his "great Freedom of Access to the King's ministers, and all the Publick offices" and for his standing in the Society of Friends, "which Body of men have at this Day a great interest at Court." To placate the Quakers on the tithe issue, Governor Belcher pressed the Massachusetts legislature to pass a relief bill, in 1731, for "the People among us called Quakers, who think themselves under so great Hardships from some of the Laws of this Province." The Quakers, who were the Congregationalists' fellow dissenters from the Church of England, finally found themselves enjoying a more favorable arrangement in Massachusetts than that experienced by Friends in England. After signing the bill into law, Belcher reported to Partridge that the Quakers "never had a Govr so much of their friend as the present."[37]

Governor Belcher reminded the General Court in Massachusetts: "One of the shining Graces of His Majesty's Reign" was "that Dissenters of all Denominations in Great Britain, enjoy the Toleration in its full Ease and Extent." The governor warned that Massachusetts should "imitate the Royal Indulgence" and take care "lest it pass laws that may carry in them a Spirit of Rigour or Severity to those who may conscientiously differ from us in the Modes of Divine Worship." When Belcher later seemed in danger of being replaced as governor, Partridge had no difficulty in mustering English support for his brother-in-law. In 1737 the London Friends appointed a committee "to write Letters up and down the Kingdom in behalf of the Governor and to engage all their good offices for his Service." Partridge wrote to the Quakers of Coventry and Sussex urging them to write "a Suitable letter to your Members of Parliament" and advising them to "meet with ye proper Persons in Authority in behalf of Governor Belcher."

The status of Massachusetts Quakers was elevated by their close connections with politically powerful Rhode Island Friends, as their sectarian network superseded colonial divisions. When the Quaker governor John

Wanton, of Newport, Rhode Island, for example, wrote a letter in 1735 to his colonial agent Richard Partridge (the son of Lieutenant Governor William Partridge of New Hampshire) in London, he suggested, "When You send any Packet again on the Colony's Affairs of any Bigness (Postage now running very high) We desire You'l put it under Cover to Mr. Benjamin Bagnell Watchmaker in Boston who will take Care and transmit it here by some private Hand, there being always Oportunities from thence for such a purpose." Benjamin Bagnall was a trusted fellow member of the Society of Friends, and the Boston host of numerous visiting Quaker preachers, from Mary Weston in 1750 to Rachel Wilson in 1769.[38]

In seventeenth-century Massachusetts, Quakers had been used as symbols of the alien, linked to other satanic agents, like witches, Indians, and papists, by the Puritan clergy to unify the orthodox community. They had been described as "wicked and dangerous seducers" and "malignant & assiduous promoters of doctrines directly tending to subvert both our churches & state." But the dire predictions regarding the impact the presence of Quakers would have on the colony had not materialized after a half-century. The negative images had been largely undermined by the successful Quaker colonization efforts in Pennsylvania and West Jersey. By the 1690s, non-Quakers in Massachusetts might attend Quaker meetings not to disrupt but to sit in respectful silence, although Friends continued to be viewed as outsiders, as the sect emphasized its sense of separateness by observing distinctive testimonies. The eighteenth-century Congregationalist establishment in Massachusetts felt more directly threatened by the possibility of replacement by an Anglican establishment than by the specter of Quakerism. A sign of Friends' growing respectability was the increasing attendance of Quaker weddings by members of the larger community as the century progressed. The 1737 union of two wealthy Boston Quakers was held in the First Church Congregationalist meeting-house because "the vast Concourse of People of all Perswasions who came to see the Solemnity" could not be accommodated in the sect's own edifice, according to the *Boston Evening Post*, August 8, 1737.[39]

In colonial Virginia, some substantial families, like the Walkers, the Pleasants, and the Jordans, had converted early to Quakerism, but eighteenth-century Friends continued to be penalized under the Anglican establishment for their refusal to pay tithes, swear oaths, and participate in military service. The passage of the Toleration Act of 1689 in England, however, had significantly altered the persecutions that had plagued earlier

Quakers in the colony, since royal officials had to recognize the right of liberty of worship of Protestant dissenter citizens. The English preacher Thomas Story, travelling in America, noted in his journal an intriguing visit in 1705 with Colonel Francis Nicholson, Virginia's acting governor, who treated the itinerant Quaker minister "with various sorts of choice wines, and fruits, and much respect." A close friend of William Penn, Thomas Story lived for some years in America, serving in Pennsylvania government as a councillor, a commissioner of property, and a recorder of the City of Philadelphia. Story had already visited the governor of North Carolina, en route to the Virginia Yearly Meeting, and had discussed matters of government, informing him of the methods used by some other governors regarding Quakers. After Story's attendance at the yearly meeting, Francis Nicholson (1655–1728), defender of the Church of England in his capacity as governor of Virginia, invited Story, as well as the travelling Quaker preachers Esther Palmer of Long Island and Mary Lawson of Pennsylvania, to visit the new seat of the capitol, Williamsburg. The kind treatment included the governor's order to the president of the college, the Reverend James Blair, to give the Quakers a tour of the College of William and Mary, founded almost a decade before. Thomas Story wrote that their distinguished guide, Blair, was in "a pleasant natural temper." When the Friends were ready to depart, "he [the Governour] had ordered several sorts of portable fruits, as cocanuts, lemons, etc, for us to take with us."[40]

The Church of England commissary James Blair probably had entertained the Quaker visitors somewhat grudgingly. Blair had proposed to strengthen the Virginia clergy by examining each incoming cleric and insisting that each discourse against "popery, Quakerism, or any other prevailing heresey." Commissary James Blair had, by the time of the Quakers' visit, successfully lobbied to have Governor Nicholson removed from office (the disputatious Blair also succeeded at getting several other Virginia governors removed). Over a year before Nicholson hosted the Quaker preachers, the Reverend James Blair had formally presented, before the Board of Trade on March 30, 1704, the petition asking for Nicholson's removal. Prominent in the affidavits relating to the maladministration of Governor Nicholson was the allegation that the governor had said, in response to the request of a clergyman, recently turned out of his parish by some leading men of the vestry, for another parish which had been vacated by a minister's death: "What do you . . . talk to me of this and the other minister being dead? I wish there were forty of you dead. The Quakers are in the right, you are all hirelings." Nicholson apparently had been angered by the avarice, and, perhaps, less than exemplary lives of some of the Anglican priests in Virginia. In the bitter Blair-Nicholson feud over control of Virginia, however, nearly all the colony's clergy took the governor's side, praising Nicholson as a patron of the church. Whatever sympathy Nicholson may have felt at times with Quaker stances, he remained Anglican all his life, and at his death left the bulk of his estate to the Anglican missionary society, the Society for the Propagation of the Gospel in Foreign Parts.[41]

Even critics of Quakerism had to acknowledge certain of their virtues—industry, frugality, cleanliness, and orderliness—that made them valuable citizens. Colonel William Byrd of Westover, Virginia, wrote: "Thus much I may truly say in their Praise, that by Diligence and Frugality, For which this Harmless Sect is remarkable, and by having no Vices but such as are Private, they have in a few Years made Pensilvania a very fine Country." Patrick Henry gave the thriving colony of Pennsylvania as an example, in contrast to Virginia, where industrious immigrants were free to worship according to their consciences, as an argument for the economic value of religious toleration: "A general toleration of Religion appears to be the best means of peopling our country, and enabling our people to procure those necessarys among themselves, the purchase of which from abroad has so nearly ruined a colony, enjoying from nature and time, the means of becoming the most prosperous on the continent. . . . The free exercise of religion hath stocked the Northern part of the continent with inhabitants." Henry argued that those who felt penalized in Europe for religious differences did not choose to immigrate to Virginia, where the penalties were felt "perhaps in a (greater degree)." Henry hoped to attract hardworking immigrants to Virginia by offering religious toleration. With the assistance of Patrick Henry, a law was passed in Virginia in 1766 that released Quakers from the general requirement of military service (on her 1769 visit, Rachel Wilson described Henry as "a man of great moderation who had appeared in Friends favor"). In the South, the shortage of ordained clergy, the lack of a colonial bishop, and the distance between settlements created a weakened Anglican establishment, and evangelical revivals of competing religious groups tried to fill the gaps. Dissenters from the Church of England, like the Presbyterians (including Patrick Henry's family), Baptists, and Quakers, increasingly found that they were allies in the struggle for liberty of conscience.[42]

In the eighteenth century, legislation still exacted penalties for dissenters from the established church in various colonies, but the former attitude toward Quakers, as deservedly persecuted lunatics and heretics, had softened. "Stingy narrow notions of Christianity which reigned too much in the first beginnings of this country" were being rejected by those, like Governor Jonathan Belcher, who had to live and work with citizens of a variety of faiths. Many colonists had Quaker business associates, and through these connections were introduced to Friends' religious leaders. Henry Laurens, for example, one of the wealthiest merchants of Charleston, South Carolina, relied upon Quaker mercantile correspondents at various ports, including Philadelphia and Bristol, England, in his trade. Laurens, of French Huguenot ancestry, was "a religious man but broadly tolerant of various doctrinal beliefs." He handled a bill for the Quaker preacher Sophia Hume when she visited Charleston in 1767–68. When Rachel Wilson was en route to Charleston in 1769, one of Laurens's Philadelphia business correspondents, Quaker merchant William Fisher, alerted Laurens to the intended visit of the Quaker preacher to his area. In response, Henry Laurens wrote to William Fisher on February 11, 1769, about Rachel Wilson and her Quaker travel companions: "When they were coming toward Town I was on a Journey to Mepkin Plantation [Henry Laurens's plantation on the Cooper River above Charleston] & met them at 10 Miles distance. I was mindful of your recommendation & from the habit of the People [the Quakers were conspicuous by their plain style of dress] concluded those were your friends. I spoke to them & told them they were expected in Charles Town & that I should return & wait upon them in two or three days." He continued, "At my return I immediately called upon them, received much satisfaction indeed in conversation with them. Mrs. Laurens & my Son were equally pleased."[43]

Henry Laurens attended Rachel Wilson's meetings and heard her pray at mealtime. He was deeply moved by the spiritual counsel of the Quaker female preacher. In another letter, Laurens noted, "My good friend Mr. Manigault [probably Gabriel Manigault, a merchant of French Huguenot ancestry who served as the colony's public treasurer, and the father of Peter Manigault, Speaker of the South Carolina Assembly] after asking me some Questions said that altho he had not been in a Quaker Meeting for 50 Years past he would go to hear Mrs. Wilson & I am persuaded that he would have asked her & her friends to his House, a House of Piety, Peace, & Happiness, but they left Charles Town that very Morning." Henry Laurens had altered from performing an obligation for his Philadelphia business associate to a personal appreciation of the Quaker visitors: "Your friends & I beg leave to call them my friends too, Mrs. Rachael Wilson, Mr. Samuel Moreton, & a Lady who accompanied them from Virginia or Maryland have been in Charles Town. Their stay was very short . . . We were all sorry to part with them so soon & so was a great number of People in Charles Town. I have not known Strangers, at any time come among us, meet a more Cordial reception, nor do I remember to have parted from any with more regret." Laurens regretted having not hosted the visitors himself, assuming that the Charleston Quakers had a special arrangement to host the travellers, and "fearful of giving offence if I should interfere beyond common Civility to your friends & the Offer of Money, &ca., otherwise those good people should not have gone beyond my House for Lodgings if they would have accepted such as the House affords." Laurens was focussed on more spiritual topics in the wake of Wilson's visit and was uncharacteristically reluctant to discuss business in his letter to William Fisher: "My mind being bent upon a subject quite different from Merchandize I am not at all disposed to say much about the latter, I shall therefore barely observe that Rice is at 55/." Although, as a young man, Henry Laurens had traded in slaves, he later became the first man of prominence in the lower South to declare his abhorrence of slavery. In 1776, he declared his intention to manumit his slaves, perhaps having been influenced by his Quaker acquaintances (Wilson preached against the slave trade on her American tour).[44]

Enlightenment ideals influenced the American population, as well, and religious toleration was gradually seen as a virtue in itself. The use of reason was commended over prejudice and fanaticism. By the 1720s, the previous century's intolerance, including the death sentence on Quakers, had become an embarrassment in Massachusetts. John Adams, the Congregationalist lawyer, and later, president, acknowledged in his diary that "the Executions of the Quakers . . . anciently" had been a "foul . . . Stain upon this Country." By 1774, when the Continental Congress met, no participant wanted to be accused of bigotry. As the Continental Congress gathered, it was suggested that the meeting be opened with prayer, but the members were so divided in sentiments, ranging from Episcopalian to Quaker, that they had difficulty deciding how they could join in the same act of worship. Samuel Adams arose and said "he was no Bigot, and could hear a Prayer from a Gentleman of Piety and Virtue." More and more, people were judged on the basis of a virtuous life rather than on theological distinctions. As the novelist H. H. Brackenridge, in *Modern Chivalry,* suggested of Quaker and Baptist preachers without theological training: "They do a great deal of good, and that is the first object of preaching."[45]

The Great Awakening, which had swept through New England and the Middle Colonies between approximately 1739 and 1745, was an important part of this attitudinal change toward toleration. Many areas were thrown into a state of turmoil in the 1740s, and church separations occurred as a result of George Whitefield's preaching "raids" and the visits of other itinerant preachers. According to one description, "Agitated souls cried out or moaned loudly during the worship service, and . . . rather emotional Separatist meetings . . . took place in town." The newly converted inhabitants of a town sometimes turned against the incumbent minister as the evangelical fervor, emphasizing the need for a "New Birth" through God's grace, divided the orthodox Christian community into antirevivalist Old Lights and pro-revivalist New Lights, among the Congregationalists, and Old Side and New Side, among the Presbyterians. This splintering of the orthodox Christians led to the eventual disintegration of the state-supported church system, since one faction could not be privileged over another by taxation. Confronted by the plethora of religious choices offered by itinerant ministries, colonists were increasingly making their own decisions regarding their mode of worship rather than automatically affiliating with the established local church.[46]

As a result of the Awakening, audiences were often more willing to listen to itinerants in spite of their minister's opposition and were perhaps more skeptical about the qualifications afforded by scholarship. College education and formal ordination were considered irrelevant by many "New Lights" who believed that true ministers were called to work by the influence of the Holy Spirit. When Mary Weston, the travelling Quaker preacher, appointed a meeting in Connecticut in the early 1750s, the gathering was disturbed by a Yale alumnus. But others in attendance told the man, "Mr. Curtis, you blame us for adhering to & regarding a Woman; you are a wise Man and had your Education at College; if you will preach us as good a Sermon as this Woman has done, we will hear you with as much Attention and be thankful for it." On Long Island, in the 1760s, Rachel Wilson stepped into a non-Quaker place of worship after a church service had ended, and desired liberty to utter a few sentences. Her request was granted until the pastor realized that Wilson was going to assert her right to the ministry. Then he asked her to be silent. When Wilson persisted, the minister walked out of the church, "his hearers Desiring him [to leave] as thay wanted to hear me out [so] that I had ful opertunity to clear my Self & after a solem[n] season in prayr the pepol after bid[d]ing us farwel[farewell] in an afectionat maner one of Em in Viting [inviting] us into his hous to take some Refreshment."[47]

The new religious intensity had unified as much as it had divided, by fracturing barriers between religious groups. In the Great Awakening's rekindling of religious zeal, denominational differences became secondary to one's identification as pro- or antirevivalist, whether one was focussed on the importance of spiritual rebirth or not. The Awakening familiarized colonists with extra-institutional ministering. Although some ministers were convinced that evangelists like George Whitefield were trying to displace the resident clergy, others invited revivalistic ministers of any persuasion into their pulpits to spark their congregations' spiritual regeneration. George Whitefield, the leading preacher of the Awakening, was nominally an Anglican but spoke from the pulpits of a variety of dissenting churches. The ecumenicalism generated by the Awakening likely fostered the new willingness of diverse denominations to share their meeting-houses with Quaker itinerant preachers. Samuel Fothergill, the English Quaker minister, who visited America from 1754 to 1756, noticed the change from 1737 when his father, John Fothergill, also a Quaker preacher, had visited the colonies. In Elizabethtown, New Jersey, a largely Calvinist community of transplanted New Englanders, the younger Fothergill had a meeting and commented on his warm reception: "I could not pass by this circumstance, as in that town, i.e. Elizabeth Town, our dear and worthy father met with bitter opposition when last here, from the former priest, and with difficulty, got a meeting in the place; and such is the change, that the present priest voluntarily offered me, in his terms 'his pulpit.' I did not ascend his rostrum, but, as no place could be procured equally large for the reception of the people, accepted the house."[48]

The College of New Jersey students' ecumenical request to hear Rachel Wilson in 1769 was a by-product of the Awakening, the college itself a legacy of the intercolonial evangelical movement. Founded by New Side Presbyterians for the instruction of prospective ministers, the college offered education to "those of every religious Denomination," but the bulk of its students "favored heart religion over ecclesiastical precision and . . . incorporated revival into their theological positions." The father of Samuel Stanhope Smith, a student at the time of Rachel Wilson's visit (class of 1769), had been converted under George Whitefield's preaching. Smith later became a Presbyterian minister opposed to sectarian religious strife and dogmatic intolerance. Dr. John Witherspoon, the college president in 1769, had a reputation as a friend of religious freedom. Despite significant differences, Quakers and revivalists shared certain attitudes: a dissatisfaction with hollow formalities of the established church, a belief that God's grace superseded university learning, and the desire for a regenerated clergy. Evangelicals also shared the Quakers' interest in a stricter morality. George Whitefield alienated Alexander Garden, the bishop of London's Commissary for South Carolina, when he asked Garden why he had not spoken out against the assemblies and balls in Charleston. Sophia Hume's *An Exhortation to the Inhabitants of the Province of South-Carolina* (1748) similarly warned against the fashionable extravagance of balls and other worldly behavior. Non-Quaker audiences, especially those who were pro-revivalist, would have found much of the content of Rachel Wilson's extemporaneous deliveries familiar (although those of a Calvinist bent would have objected to her advocacy of universal redemption). Wilson preached: "The grace of God in Jesus Christ is universally manifest, he would not that any should perish, but that all should come to the knowledge of the truth and be saved, and witness repentance to the amendment of life; so that they may know a being converted and born again of the Word of Eternal Life, and witness a being regenerated in their minds and affections." George Whitefield himself had been deeply impressed by Rachel Wilson's ministry when he attended one of the public meetings she held in 1764 in Bristol, England.[49]

By the mid-eighteenth century, in the aftermath of the Great Awakening's reduction of denominational barriers, listening to sermons, which had always been a form of entertainment, intellectual stimulation, and religious edification for the colonists, encompassed the religious meetings of the heterodox. A South Carolina society lady, like Ann Manigault, of Charleston, the wife of Gabriel Manigault, one of the colony's wealthiest merchants, could record in her diary on February 14, 1755, "Went to hear a Quaker preacher" (probably Samuel Fothergill, who arrived in Charles Town on February 12, 1755, accompanied by Israel Pemberton Jr. of Philadelphia) and, only a few weeks later, note her attendance at a sermon given by George Whitefield. The diaries of eighteenth-century colonists reveal that they often went to hear preachers of diverse denominations. Ezra Stiles, a clergyman himself, had a professional interest in hearing others preach; he attended the Jewish synagogue, the Baptist meeting, and the Moravian meeting in Newport, Rhode Island, as well as several Quaker meetings (particularly when there was a minister visiting from overseas, like Samuel Neale, the widower of Irish Quaker preacher Mary Peisley). Ezra Stiles noted that on January 9, 1772, "A.M. went to Friends Meeting and heard Mr. Neal an English [*sic*] Friend: present 500 [attenders]."

While in Philadelphia for the Continental Congress in 1774, John Adams attended a Presbyterian service, a Baptist service, a Methodist meeting, a Catholic mass, and a Moravian meeting, as well as a Quaker meeting. Skillful preachers of any denomination were complimented, while sermons and styles of delivery, as well as the different modes of worship, were comparatively critiqued. For example, Adams described a Baptist preacher as having "Not the least Idea of Grace in his Motions, or Elegance in his Style. His Voice was vociferous and boisterous, and his Composition almost destitute of Ingenuity." Many people went to hear any stranger that entered the neighborhood, regardless of the principles espoused by the itinerant preacher. Samuel Neale, on his journey around the colonies, noted in 1770, "It happens when a stranger travels, the intelligence becomes so universal, that the public assembles, and those who seldom attend any place of worship then come."[50]

Changes within Quakerism

Changes within the Society of Friends, in addition to the political influence and economic success achieved by eighteenth-century Quakers, contributed to the alteration in attitude toward Friends. The individualistic Quakers of the 1650s differed substantially from eighteenth-century members of the organized, well-disciplined Society. Early Quakers had often been strident and aggressive, interrupting court sessions and church services to protest unjust laws and hollow forms of worship. They were known for dramatic symbolism (appearing in sackcloth and ashes, for example), and fits of ecstatic religious experience. After the development of an organizational structure, such "enthusiastic" tendencies were down-played. William Penn tried to distance Quakers from the negative connotations of "enthusiasm" by portraying the Inward Light as compatible with the conclusions of natural reason, although the emphasis was still on the immediate inspiration of the Holy Spirit. In 1748, in a religious tract directed to non-Quakers, the preacher Sophia Hume took great pains to distinguish her book from "the Production of a distemper'd and enthusiastick Brain." Hume examined "by the Divine Light" if her actions were consistent with God's honor or Scriptures, but claimed to make "a rational conclusion," no doubt mindful of an eighteenth-century readership that increasingly venerated reason.[51]

Eighteenth-century Quaker worship actually was free of most of the emotional outbursts of religious revivalism: the groans, swoonings, and screamings that accompanied the Methodist movement and Moravian assemblies. Charles Chauncy (1705–87), a Congregationalist minister in Boston, Massachusetts, commented on this behavioral change of Friends when he was cautioning American colonists against the extravagant enthusiasm of the Great Awakening in 1742: "Sometimes it affects their bodies, throws them into convulsions and distortions, into quakings and tremblings. This was *formerly* common among the people called Quakers. I was myself, when a Lad, an eye witness to such violent agitations and foamings, in a boisterous female speaker, as I could not behold but with surprize and wonder."[52] But the quietest trend in the eighteenth-century Quaker ministry stressed introspection, discouraging impetuosity and disorder.

The Quakers, once considered among the most extreme "enthusiasts" and disrupters of civil order, were no longer perceived to be a dire threat. The Society of Friends was now a respectable, if heterodox, group. As the Puritans had denounced Quakers in the seventeenth century, Congregationalist ministers accused New Light radicals (like the Separate Baptists) of ranting, disorderly exhorting, and the madness of "enthusiasm" in the eighteenth century. The contrasting journal entries of Isaac Backus (1724–1806), an itinerant minister and important spokesman for the Separate Baptists, and Rachel Wilson, the Quaker preacher, regarding their experiences in the same Massachusetts town reveal the changing status of these religious groups. In Plymouth, Massachusetts, where Rachel Wilson was well received, the Baptist leader Isaac Backus met only with closed doors. The Plymouth courthouse was opened for Rachel Wilson in the summer of 1769, and she wrote in her travel journal: "Had the meet[in]g in the Court hous[e] the pepol Behav[e]d Remarkable well truth favour[in]g to the astonishment of some and Edefication of others in pure Gospel Love the meet[in]g End[ed] with pray[e]r and praisis my mind Being much Rel[i]eved from that he[a]vy Load." In January 1770, about six months after Rachel Wilson's visit, Isaac Backus complained in his diary: "Went to Plymouth [Mass.], where several have sent their requests for my preaching, yet as the minister appears against it, the people were so much afraid of him, and of one another that they durst not open their doors, and tho' much pains were taken to get the court house doors open, yet it could not be obtained, tho' they were opened last summer for a Quaker woman to preach in: and finally I had no meeting."[53]

Quakers and revivalists frequently competed for the same audiences, but Friends differed from eighteenth-century "New Lights" on several major points. The absence of sacraments and the official recognition of women as preachers had separated Quakers from the Christian orthodoxy. But Friends' period of silent waiting for immediate revelation distinguished them from revivalists as well. "Enthusiasm," for a Friend, was self-generated energy, or the assertion of self, instead of waiting to "speak in the Light." While travelling in Hanover County, Virginia (site of Presbyterian revivals in the 1740s and a Baptist evangelical movement in the 1760s), in December 1768, Rachel Wilson found, to her surprise, at the Quaker meeting-house, "that frds had given way for 2 Baptists to preach thair that day which at first afected my Mind prety Much. . . ." The Baptists, James Child and Christopher Clark, offered her some money, which she refused. They then drew the people into the meeting-house and the Quaker female preacher dryly observed that the Baptist itinerant, "the same Man that oferd me Mony," was now upon his knees "with a good deal of Zeal or fire to me Seemd to be of his own Raising." In marked contrast to eighteenth-century Quaker introversion and orderliness, the Baptists drew people "with a vociferous style of preaching that went beyond the word into shouts and drones, hand clapping, ecstatic twisting and jerking of body." After a period of listening to the Baptist itinerant, Rachel Wilson asked to speak. She pointed out to the crowd the necessity of waiting in silence before "we could Learn Christ Jesus aRight" and that the Baptists were inconsistent in citing Scripture before they had knowledge of it experientially.[54]

Revivalists concentrated on the conversion experience, seeking to bring the sinner to a change of heart through emotional preaching. But Quakers believed that emotions could be just as delusive as reasonings. By preaching only at the guidance of the Holy Spirit, Quakers attempted to reach the spiritual "witness" (as distinguished from the emotions) in every person. "The passionate preacher hath affected the passionate hearer—both have been in raptures and neither of them profited," Samuel Fothergill cautioned another Quaker travelling minister, Susanna Hatton, in 1760, "the emotions of thy mind are sometimes strong and animated, mistake not the warmth of passion for the Gospel authority." To a great extent, the eighteenth-century Quaker ministry was the antithesis of an evangelical ministry, since Friends believed they could preach or travel on religious service only when the Spirit inspired them. Audiences were disappointed when a visiting Quaker preacher sat in silence for the entire meeting. Mary Weston recalled that in Rhode Island, "Many people of Note came with Desire to hear an English woman, but were disappointed, we having a silent Meeting . . . after which great Enquiry was made whether I was ill, or what was the Matter I would not preach, to which it was answer'd according to our principles." Often, Mary Weston was not inspired to preach when she felt that the crowd's "Expectations [were] . . . too much outward." Catharine Payton and Mary Peisley, visiting the American colonies from 1753 to 1756, labored for "the discouragement of a ministry in words, which was not accompanied with the power of Truth, wherewith some of the people were amused, but not profitably fed, and the truly sensible were distressed. In divers places we were mostly or wholly silent, in large mixed meetings [with non-Quakers], perhaps for examples to these forward spirits. It raised the displeasure of some against us. . . ." The Quaker minister's goal was to turn people inward to their own relationship with the Divine, "to bring every one to their own Teacher in themselves," decreasing their dependence on external aids like God's "messengers." Rachel Wilson wrote, "I see such flockings to Meetings, with people of all denominations, and their expectation too much upon the instrument [or preacher]." The non-Quaker audience's desire for a rivetting spectacle of preaching was thwarted, at times, by the quietist Quaker minister's refusal to provide a performance.[55]

Eighteenth-century Quaker women preachers were drawing crowds to their meetings in the colonies, but revivalists' more emotional preaching, with dramatic appeals to the senses, was far more accessible to the public than Quaker quietism. Revivalists were outstripping the Quakers, gaining adherents to Presbyterianism in Pennsylvania, New Jersey, New England, and the South. The Baptists were on their way to becoming a major religious group in the southern colonies. The Methodists were emerging as a force as well on the eve of the American Revolution.

In Great Britain, although Friends at times attracted audiences of two thousand or more, they were not substantially winning converts. John Kelsall, the Quaker clerk at an iron forge, observed in 1731: "Though we have large meetings in many places, and the people seem affected with what they hear, yet I find little or no convincement follows, which makes me think that the manner and way that Truth is now published to the people is not as formerly it was when many were gathered to the church." Kelsall continued, "The government and people of the better sort are very kind and civil to Friends, and they have respect and interest with them. Yea, the very priests in diverse places are seemingly at least loving to friends, and they [Friends] being unwilling to give them offense—as they call it—are too easy towards them in respect to religious matters." The Quakers had gained toleration by nearly eliminating confrontational public witnessing. But Kelsall believed that this conservatism, an unwillingness "to testify openly against the reigning wicked practices in the great and the lifeless superstitious ministry of the priests," was one reason fewer were being converted.[56]

Friends, in the eighteenth century, left to others, like John Wesley, "the task of popular revivalism, wherein they themselves had laboured so fervently in the days of their founder." With the passage of the Toleration Act of 1689, Quakers had sought to emphasize their "peaceable" and "inoffensive" spirit as loyal subjects, hoping to preserve their tolerated status and extend their privileges regarding tithes and the swearing of oaths, as well as gain exemption from military service. In the eighteenth century, Quakers tried to live "at peace with our neighbors of all religions," not inveighing against others' religion, and not meddling, practicing the principles of quietude. Attempting to prove that they were not threatening to authority, Quakers had labored at public relations. Respectful addresses from the Society of Friends to the king or his royal representatives in the colonies furthered their reputation as an orderly, obedient people. They found a kind of middle-class respectability, by achieving economic success and a reputation for thrift, industry, and integrity. The poet Matthew Green (d. 1737) wrote of the Quakers in England: "They, who have lands, and a safe bank stock, / With faith so founded on a rock, / May give a rich invention ease / And construe scripture how they please." No longer scandalous, Friends were singular, but praiseworthy, becoming known for their humanitarian efforts, such as the establishment of almshouses, hospitals, and charity schools.[57]

Changes in the descriptive terms applied to Quakers in the press show the results of the enormous reshaping of their image. Considered heretical and seditious fanatics in the seventeenth century, eighteenth-century Friends were exemplars in the Age of Reason, associated with virtue and moderation, good sense and toleration. The public image of the Quaker female changed dramatically as well: from the socially disruptive "enthusiast" of the previous century to the "pretty Quakeress" of the eighteenth century. The descriptive terms newly applied to Quaker women included "sensible," "modest," and "neatly dressed." Quaker women began appearing in eighteenth-century publications as either virtuous maidens preaching divine benevolence or as loyal, industrious subjects with domestic skills. The *Gentleman's Magazine* of December 1734 recorded, for instance, that Mary Harris, "a faithful Subject . . . and one of those called Quakers, (a People who have distinguished themselves by their Love to . . . [the royal] Family)," presented to the royal princess two linen caps adorned with verses in needlework which the sixty-four-year-old Mrs. Harris had devotedly wrought "with her own hands." In July 1765, the *Gentleman's Magazine* reported that "Seven female quakers, very neatly dressed, being desirous of seeing their Majesties come to court, were admitted into the royal apartments; when her Majesty was so condescending as to order the lady in waiting to compliment each of them; which they returned in a very sensible and modest manner." Mary Knowles (1733–1807), famed for her conversation and needlework, was known as "the ingenious Quaker lady." Queen Charlotte commissioned her to do a needlework portrait of King George III. A dialogue that Mary Knowles had with the author Samuel Johnson regarding the Society of Friends' principles was published in the *Gentleman's Magazine* for June 1791 in which Knowles's "mild fortitude of modest Truth" was contrasted with Dr. Johnson's "boisterous violence of bigoted Sophistry."[58]

Quakers continued to defend themselves against misrepresentations: "We (Quakers) are Believers in God, in Christ, and of his Church, and consequently not Deists, Enthusiasts, Hereticks, or Schismatics," wrote a Friend to the *Gentleman's Magazine* in June 1732. In the English legislative battle over whether Quaker tithes were due to the national church in 1736, Friends were accused by some ill-informed (or ill-intentioned) people of being Jesuits in disguise, controlled by Rome. When Quaker ideals came into conflict with the larger culture's need for war, much antagonism was expressed toward Friends. And, increasingly, eighteenth-century Quakers were criticized for their apparently hypocritical zeal in the accumulation of wealth (Thomas Paine wrote, in 1776, "In the very instant that they are exclaiming against the mammon of this world, [they] are nevertheless, hunting after it with a step as steady as Time, and an appetite as keen as Death"). The observations made by John Adams, the Massachusetts Congregationalist, of Philadelphia Friends' luxurious living, during his attendance at the Continental Congress in 1774, give some merit to this view. Adams used the term "plain" ironically: "Dined with Mr. Miers Fisher, a young Quaker and a Lawyer. We saw his Library, which is clever. But this plain Friend, and his plain, tho pretty Wife, with her Thee's and Thou's, had provided us the most Costly Entertainment—Ducks, Hams, Chickens, Beef, Pigg, Tarts, Creams, Custards, Gellies, fools, Trifles, floating Islands, Beer, Porter, Punch, Wine and a long &c." Yet Quakers had largely transformed their public image (although prejudice against them still existed), achieving respectability, and occasionally admiration, in the British Isles and the American colonies by the middle decades of the eighteenth century.[59]

The Role of Gender

When Quakers as a religious group had established a more respectable reputation, Quaker women benefitted as well. But in Quaker women's public activity as ministers, their gender also importantly influenced the responses they received. Both male and female Quaker missionaries had been persecuted by Massachusetts Bay authorities in the seventeenth century, but only the women were examined for witches' marks. Some early audiences would listen to male Quaker preachers espousing Friends' tenets but not to similar words spoken by a female preacher. Quaker men who preached could still be "gentlemen of sense," but most Christians of the era had believed, on the basis of Apostle Paul's epistles, that women were forbidden to speak in church. In 1706, Samuel Bownas, an English

Quaker minister, observed the reactions of the general public in Newbury, Massachusetts, to a Quaker woman's preaching: "Then stood up one Lydia Norton, a famous Minister, none more so of that Country, and indeed She had an excellent Gift . . . but all this did not avail, the People grew worse and worse in their Behaviour," including "calling for a Dram [a small drink of liquor]" so loudly that Norton could not be heard. Bownas reported that "A good comely Gentleman-like Man, in Excuse for the Behaviour of the People said, Sir, as for Womens Preaching we hold it unlawful, because St. Paul hath forbid it, therefore we think it not proper to give them a hearing . . . but you Seem to be a Gentleman of Sense, and we will hear you."[60]

Friends, such as John Rutty and Josiah Martin, author of *A Vindication of Women's Preaching* (1717), continued to publish defenses of women's preaching in the eighteenth century. In Congregationalist Connecticut, the colony most averse to the practice, several residents of Windham, where no Quaker meetings had ever been held, refused to allow their homes to be used as a site for Mary Weston's meeting in the 1750s, "on acc[oun]t. of my being a Woman preacher, whereupon proposed to our Landlord [innkeeper], the having it in one of his Rooms, but he was against it for the same reason, telling me he was not clear in his Judgment that Women ought to preach tho' he was one call'd a Separatist." Weston did eventually prevail, holding a meeting at his inn. Popular prejudice remained, particularly among those with no knowledge of the Society of Friends' tenets. When Catharine Payton and Mary Peisley encountered inhabitants of the Carolina backcountry who were not familiar with Quakerism, they looked "strangely at us, because they understood not the lawfulness of women's preaching, having never heard any: thus did we pass for a sign and wonder; some would say, when invited to meeting, that we were women who ran from our country for some ill act."[61]

By the middle decades of the eighteenth century, however, in many parts of the British empire there was a noticeable shift not only in the general attitude toward Quakers, but specifically in the reception of Quaker women as preachers. The *Boston Gazette, or Country Journal*'s description, in 1769, of Rachel Wilson as an "eminent preacher" addressing "a large audience" was nearly identical to an assessment of a male Quaker minister (another English Quaker, Samuel Fothergill, who had visited Boston earlier, in 1755). The *Boston Gazette, or Country Journal* had reported of Fothergill's visit: "Last Week, upon Application made to our Selectmen, by some of the People called *Quakers,* they gave Leave that *Faneuil-Hall* might be opened for them to have a Meeting in, which was done on Friday at 4 O'Clock in the Afternoon, when Mr. Samuel Fothergill, a noted Preacher, of that Friendly Society, delivered an excellent Discourse to a very crowded and polite Auditory, and to the Satisfaction of People of all Denominations." Rachel Wilson was compared to the non-Quaker evangelist George Whitefield in terms of eloquence, on her American visit in 1768–69. Newspaper accounts of George Whitefield's itinerant ministry, in 1739, were not distinguishable by gender (omitting names and pronouns) from descriptions of Rachel Wilson's itinerant ministry in 1768:

> On Friday last, the Rev. Mr. Whitefield arrived here with his Friends from New-York, where he preach'd eight Times; and on his Return hither preach'd at Elizabeth Town, Brunswick, Maidenhead, Trenton, Neshaminy, and Abingdon. He has preach'd twice every Day in the Church to great Crowds.

> Mrs. Rachel Wilson, an eminent preacher among the Friends, who lately arrived here in Capt. Falconer, from England, set out by land for South Carolina. She preached several times in this province and New Jersey, to the great satisfaction of thousands of well disposed people of all denominations.[62]

Without waging a battle over women's proper sphere of activity, Quaker women had received recognition as acknowledged preachers among the Friends, or religious leaders, by the larger culture. The shift, which legitimized a public role for women in society, was an inadvertent consequence of the advent of religious toleration. When Friends won their struggle for toleration, legalizing their distinctive mode of worship, those designated as ministers by the sect were obligated to be tolerated as well. Another episode with Mary Weston in mid-eighteenth-century Connecticut illustrates this societal change. Weston's public meeting in Woodbury was disrupted by a man objecting that it was "an unlawful Assembly." Weston, well aware of the legal standing that Quakers had achieved, stressed that under English law (Toleration Act of 1689) "they would find it a punishable Act to molest us, or any religious Congregation of People tolerated by the Govt, & allowed to worship God in the way of Conscience we believe acceptable to Him; & said I apprehended they were subject to the same Law; which was immediately backed by 1 of their Deacons." The disputatious man's friend, according to Weston, then stated that "we were not authoriz'd to hold Meetings without being Licens'd preachers." (The excesses of the Great Awakening had provoked legislation against itinerancy in some colonies. In 1742, Connecticut had passed an act requiring all ministers to be licensed.) Weston recalled, in her journal: "I told him, I was one [meaning a licensed preacher], and could produce a Certificate thereof to proper Persons whenever by them in a fit manner required. The License I meant was my Certificate of the Unity of my Friends with me in the Work of the Ministry, which was allowed by them to be sufficient." This anecdote reveals the victory the Quaker female preachers had achieved: Mary Weston's certificate to travel in the ministry, granted by the legally tolerated group, the Society of Friends, could be accepted as equivalent to the license of any clergyman by the general public. Earlier, when the theological definition of a ministry had been preeminent in a society with one established church, women were excluded from recognition as preachers by the orthodox Christian community. But the change to a legal definition of a ministry, in a society of multiple religious denominations, had solidified the Quaker women's position; the Quakers were a group whose right to worship according to their unique tenets was legally protected by the government.[63]

Representatives of royal authority, upholders of this law, were respectful in their treatment of the women ministers. In Albany, New York, where no Quakers lived (and Ann Moore, the Maryland preacher, believed no Quakers had ever visited before), Moore was readily granted a meeting with the earl of Loudoun, who had only recently arrived in the colonies as the commander-in-chief of all His Majesty's Forces in North America. In November 1756, Moore met with Loudoun, delivering religious advice to the commander-in-chief: "And a sweet time it was. He was put in mind who was the preserver of all mankind to which he readily agreed to returning us thanks which I know through divine mercy belongs to God only." Moore preached on a topic they could agree upon, God as the preserver of humankind, but her objective was to emphasize that people should not, therefore, rely upon warfare and physical weapons. Moore was distressed that anyone acquainted with the peaceable government of Jesus Christ should engage in war, and had travelled to New York to testify against the military preparations for the French and Indian War (1754–63). Moore's mission had been prompted by a vision she had seen as she walked up the hill to the Quaker meeting-house in Oblong, New York: "I seemed translated into heavenly joys and seemed as if I saw myself standing in Albany just by the army and heard the general when he saw us command his army to shout for joy and give glory to the God of heaven who has remembered us."

Ann Moore returned to Albany in February 1758, the Quaker female preacher having obtained permission from General James Abercromby, second-in-command of British military forces in North America, to hold a meeting for worship among the soldiers in the fort there. Moore then went between several forts on the frontier line—Fort George, Fort Edward, and the fort at Stillwater—appointing meetings at each place. Having seen Captain Gordon, the son of Patrick Gordon, a former governor of Pennsylvania, at Fort George the day before, where "he showed himself very kind at which place we had a large and solid meeting," Moore "was invited to come to drink tea with the colonel [the garrison at Fort Edward was under the command of Lieutenant Colonel Haviland] and Captain Gordon with diverse other officers," when she arrived at Fort Edward. "Now we coming in [at Fort Edward] they all rose up paying their compliments to us," upon which Moore asked, if it was no offense, that they sit for a few minutes, because she had a few words to deliver to them. Captain Gordon answered, "It is no offense in the least. We are willing to hear what you have to say." Later Ann Moore and her travel companions went out of Fort Edward onto a nearby island where four companies of Rangers were quartered. They held a meeting with about five hundred people. After the meeting, several officers and others spoke kindly to them, including Major Rogers, who was preparing to undertake a military expedition against the French. The major "very kindly invited us to his dining room where he provided tea, chocolate, and other things to treat us with and provided us lodging and accompanied us thereunto and ordered his waitingman to see that we had anything . . . we wanted." The next day Moore returned to Fort Edward, breakfasting with Captain Gordon and several others. Although she tried to arrange a meeting in the fort, she only received permission to hold one in the officers' room. Moore felt that their meeting was too much in secret, when it ought to have been in the middle of the fort. As a result, several "hungry souls" were not allowed an opportunity to come to meeting. One "tenderhearted Man" in the fort said "there was many in that fort which would be glad to hear the gospel preached."[64] Commonly, during the French and Indian War, sermons were preached to soldiers by orthodox clergymen at the request of the commander, before marching against the enemy, in order to give the troops courage and convince them of the religious necessity of the undertaking (the preservation of a Protestant North America from Catholic designs was the typical justification). But, in the case of the Quaker preacher, although the military officers treated Moore with courtesy (as befit a representative of a religious group tolerated by the government), some probably feared she would promote a pacifist message among the common soldiers.

Nevertheless, Ann Moore and her companions revisited Fort George, where they were treated very well and held a meeting, and then journeyed to the fort at Stillwater, where the captain "welcomed us to the place treating us with wine and ordered us dinner and behaved very kind. And after dinner we mentioned our business and desired to have a meeting with them and where it would be best to hold it. He said, in his room, and called in the Soldiers." Moore acknowledged the kind reception, as the room was filled with standing soldiers, to which the captain answered, "We were heartily welcome its only our duty." Later Moore mentioned that the rough inhabitants of northern New York, particularly the religious leaders who tried to prevent them from holding meetings, were less welcoming to them than the army. When the priest and deacons of Esopus, New York, in 1758 objected to Ann Moore holding a meeting in the town courthouse (which the sheriff had readily granted to the Quakers), a colonel in charge of soldiers there "seemed to be surprised to think that any should be against our having the court house and said it could be offense to none unless they are Bigots." For those who accepted the legal and philosophical justifications regarding religious toleration, the issue had become freedom of worship, not Moore's gender.

Those potentially most threatened by the Quaker women's activities, of course, were the clergy of other denominations. First, the women's preaching raised the topic of what qualified a person for the ministry. The typical clergyman's own qualifications, of university training and ordination, were challenged by the ministering of women lacking such acquirements. Not only did these men interpret the Scriptures as prohibiting women's preaching, but the Quakers' message struck at their very livelihood. Ann Moore, for example, invited the people at her meeting to come "to Christ the true and living way and not give their money for that which was not bread and their labor for that which satisfyth not . . . and not to be so weak as to hire such as were worse than themselves to direct them in the way of life and peace." Hearing the Quaker woman emphasize that the Gospel ministry was not to be paid for, a Presbyterian minister who had been in the audience angrily accosted Ann Moore after the meeting, saying, "Ah, money is the case. You knew I was a minister and intended it for me." Moore, who, like other Quaker ministers, consistently spoke against a "hireling ministry" ("freely ye have received, freely give," Matt. 10:8), denied having had any knowledge of the clergyman's presence at the gathering.[65]

In the American colonies, the travelling Quaker female preachers were often welcomed as substitutes for an absent male clergy (particularly when priests had not found a parish prosperous enough to maintain them); the women's function, preaching the Gospel, more important than their gender. In 1745, Elizabeth Hudson and her travel companion were given lodgings by a kind Baptist woman. When they offered to reimburse her, "She absolutely refused Saying that all the pay She desired was that when any of Our ffrds Came that way we would dirict them to her House And was anxious we Should have a meeting their [there] telling us that their Minester had left them for Some time And they had none to preach the word to them." Catharine Payton recalled, in the Carolinas, "We found a few seeking people in these back settlements, who had very little, even of what they esteem, instrumental help, in this wilderness country; which appears too poor for priestcraft to thrive in." The eighteenth-century women also benefitted from people's anticlericalism. Mary Peisley, travelling in the Carolinas in 1754, found that "many of the people showed a love and esteem for Friends, and a dislike to the priests. We were often kindly entertained, according to their ability, at the houses of those not of our Society."[66]

In spite of this rivalry, many clergymen who accepted the legitimacy of the Society of Friends as a religious group, or simply valued godliness wherever it was found, treated eighteenth-century Quaker women ministers as "professional" colleagues. Anthony William Boehm (1678–1722), a chaplain in the courts of Queen Anne and King George I, with liberal religious opinions, began a correspondence on Christianity with the Quaker minister Elizabeth Webb after she made a religious tour of England in 1710. Boehm shared Webb's letter describing her religious experiences with his friends who wanted to transcribe it for their edification. While travelling in Great Britain, Jane Fenn recorded in her journal "a Conference about sev-

eral points of Religion . . . to good Satisfaction" with a priest who had
attended her meeting. They discussed the ordinances of baptism and communion. She concluded, "We parted Loving and as he afterwards Declared
was mightily pleas'd I gave him the Opportunity, He Came next Day to the
Meeting." In Boston, Mary Weston "had a meeting began about Ten, to
which most of the highest Rank in the town came, both Priests and People,
several Justices, Lawyers, Presbyterian & Episcopalian Teachers, who
generally speak well of the Meeting." Weston held a meeting in South Carolina at a Baptist meeting-house, having been offered the site by the Baptist
preacher: "The Teacher, one Hayward, not only giving Leave but came
himself and most of his Hearers." In 1753, in Norwich, England, when
Mary Peisley felt "called" to visit "a large congregation of the people called
Methodists at their place of worship . . . their speaker left the assembly to
us, sat quietly by us all the time, and bid us act according to our freedom."
During Rachel Wilson's American journey, she frequently noticed ministers of other denominations in attendance. Near Bedford, New York,
"Some hundreds attended in the afternown . . . in a Barn wear [were]
many Pepol gathered of short notis," including a Baptist preacher who
"attended Both thes[e] Meetings and took the pains to inform his nay-
bours."[67]

Abiah Darby, the English Quaker preacher, was well acquainted with
her neighboring Methodist minister, John Fletcher of Madeley, a protégé of
John Wesley and Selina, countess of Huntingdon. Fletcher and Abiah
Darby engaged in religious arguments but agreed on certain theological
points and encouraged each other's work. At times, Abiah preached in his
Methodist assemblies and lent Fletcher books on Quaker doctrine. The
prominent evangelist George Whitefield was "deeply impressed" by
Rachel Wilson's ministry when he heard her preach in Bristol in 1764, and
he asked "to be introduced to this very extraordinary woman." When they
met, Whitefield informed Wilson that he had "been present at her last
public-meeting, and had sat with great pleasure under her ministry."
Rachel Wilson "expressed much satisfaction" but attributed her efforts "to
the goodness of Him, who alone can give the ability." Whitefield acknowledged some envy of Quaker preachers "for the exclusive advantage they
have, of *silently waiting upon God,* before they minister . . . but, according
to our forms, as soon as I am in the pulpit, I am expected to begin, and
must begin with something . . . sometimes, after long labor of this sort,

[God] is graciously pleased to assist me with his holy spirit." Wilson was gratified to hear "a declaration so unexpected, from one who been educated for the priesthood of the National Church." They "parted with mutual expressions of regard, and best wishes for each others welfare."[68]

Since the clergy had formed the largest obstacle to attendance at Quaker meetings in the past, warning that it was a dangerous sin to even be present, with the liberalization of clerical attitudes the public increasingly flocked to meetings. Some, of course, were convinced of the women's "divine calling." Thomas Story had suggested, while travelling earlier in New England, in 1704, that a number of women ministers were simply so effective in their preaching, impressing listeners with their evident sincerity and piety, that they were treated respectfully. Story had described Esther Palmer and Susanna Freeborn as "living ministers," and since their testimonies reached people "all objections were removed at once against women preaching, without the labour of dispute or hurt of contention or jar about it." Even in Connecticut, with its strong prejudice against women preachers, and its history of strict laws against Quakers, some attenders at Mary Weston's meeting in Woodbury told her "they believed the Lord had sent me, & hoped I would not be discouraged at what I met with from without."[69]

But, in a reversal of previous attitudes, non-Quaker audiences eventually seemed to prefer the exceptionalness of Quaker women's preaching to the more ordinary experience of a Quaker man ministering. Eighteenth-century Quaker women could be more enthusiastically received than their Quaker male colleagues. In Massachusetts, where almost fifty years earlier Lydia Norton had been shouted down, Mary Weston observed that, "In the Afternoon there was a mighty Company of People not of our Profession gather'd before the Meeting Doors were open, more than would fill the House." When "the service of the meeting" fell on a male Quaker preacher (he was "inspired" to preach during the meeting), rather than on Weston (she was silent), "there was much grumbling afterwards amongst all Sorts of People at their great Disappointment," even though Weston thought that the man had preached well. That evening, many "of what they call the top sort" came to visit Weston, showing her "Abundance of Respect," hoping that she would have another meeting with them. Again, in another part of the colonies, Mary Weston described the intense interest aroused by the Quaker women ministers in eighteenth-century America: "In the Evening, many People came to our Quarters, wanting they said to hear me preach, our Landlord having given them a good Account of the Morning Meeting, but I had not Freedom to have a Meeting there . . . tho' they generally press'd me to preach, saying they had never heard a Woman &c." On another occasion, Weston "had a considerable large Meeting, being mostly made up of Presbyterians, whose Expectations [of hearing a woman preach for the first time] were so raised by flying Reports, that it very much blocked up my way among them." The unusual sight of women speaking in public drew large numbers of people of other religious affiliations. Catharine Payton wrote about the North Carolina backcountry: "No women ministers had visited part of this country before us, so that the people were probably excited by curiosity to attend some of the meetings we appointed."[70]

One Quaker observer had described the ministry of Catharine Payton and Rachel Wilson as superseding their Quaker male colleagues in this respect: "best calculated for claiming, & gratifying the attention of the multitudes. . . ." Frances Henshaw attracted attention as a preacher to such an extent that she feared the applause from "friends and the great people" was detrimental to her spiritual humility. The response to the eighteenth-century female preachers, in both the British Isles and the American colonies, was such that a male Quaker minister had to caution the women against seeking popular acclaim by appointing meetings for the general public in courthouses, a practice which tended to draw great crowds. Samuel Fothergill wrote to Catharine Payton: "Bear thy testimony against haughtiness and luxury, by a humble, watchful conduct; be not led by them out of the leadings of truth, in the appointment of large meetings in *court houses,* &c., for, in this respect, I am sensible there is some danger, unless, really, the very burden of the word be upon thee, and I would by no means have the faithful labourer in that ability discouraged."[71]

By the mid-eighteenth century, even in areas without a significant Quaker population, many women preachers were treated more as visiting celebrities than as "troublesome women" to be silenced. The reputations of the British visiting ministers especially preceded them in the colonies, as inhabitants hearing reports from their neighbors or reading newspaper accounts were moved to attend. On Mary Weston's visit to Charleston, South Carolina, in the early 1750s, the entire colonial legislature adjourned to attend the English Quaker woman's meeting: "The Assembly sitting at the same time, they adjourned the House, and came to Meeting, both the Counsel, Chief Justice Speaker and the Generality of the Assembly." Henry Laurens, a South Carolina assemblyman for many years, and, later, president of the Continental Congress, had noted that, in Charleston, Rachel Wilson was "attended both in private & Public by many of the best Inhabitants." As a result of her ministerial tour, Rachel Wilson counted many of the leading Americans of the period among her acquaintances. When Benjamin Franklin visited his friends in Westmorland, England, in 1772, he reencountered the English Quaker woman he had met during her religious journey around the American colonies, and wrote to his wife in America: "Rachel Wilson sent her Love to you and our Children." Morris Birkbeck, a nephew of Rachel Wilson, travelled to America in 1773, and paid a visit to "Counceller Stockton" (Richard Stockton, a provincial councillor, College of New Jersey trustee, and, later, delegate to the Continental Congress) and his wife (Annis Boudinot, a talented poet). Neither had forgotten their meeting with Rachel Wilson four years earlier. According to Birkbeck, Stockton [who had Quaker ancestors but was not a current member of the Society of Friends] "particularly enquired after Mrs. Wilson, his wife also, he is a solid, sensible Man, & might be a Friend if he would, they sent their compliments . . . I came away by Brunswick, Woodbridge, Raway, Elizabeth Town, & Newark, all which I suppose Aunt remembers."[72]

Novelty, combined with a decrease in the potency of theological objection to the practice (only the most devout, orthodox Christians, or the most bigoted, would refuse to attend an appearance by a noted visitor), helps explain the Quaker female preachers' popularity. Enlightenment rationalism had diminished fears of witchcraft in the eighteenth century. (In 1736, witchcraft ceased to be a capital offense in England.) Yet the stereotype of females as irrational, receptive beings (prone by temperament to be instruments of divine inspiration) continued to impress eighteenth-century audiences, who still held a providential worldview. Female preaching could be appreciated within the traditional framework of women as mediums, as prophetesses, and as mystics. The Quaker preacher May Drummond, for example, was compared to the sixteenth-century Catholic mystic Saint Teresa of Avila: both women were apparently moved by larger supernatural forces. As late as 1830, an "inspired" woman (still associated in the public's mind with Quakers) could evoke awe of the supernatural in a previously hostile crowd, as an episode involving Methodist itinerant preachers, one male and one female, demonstrated: "A crowd had gathered to throw things, but when the ringleader saw her [the Methodist woman] dressed in the characteristic garb of a Friend [Quaker] he was overawed and said, 'None of you shall touch that woman.' "[73]

But the eighteenth-century Quaker female preachers could also be seen as part of a new trend: of women asserting their own abilities in increasingly public roles. The presence of Catharine Macaulay (not a Quaker) in the audience at the Quaker meeting where Sarah Morris preached was an indication of the changes since the seventeenth century. Macaulay's authorship and that of other female "wits," although still exceptional, reflected some broadening of women's roles. A number of women with intellectual ambitions, "bluestockings" such as Lady Mary Wortley Montagu, championed female education. The expanding market of female readers encouraged female authorship as new periodicals were established, such as *The Ladies' Mercury* (1693), *Female Tatler* (1709), and *Female Spectator* (1744–46). By the eighteenth century, the Quaker female preacher was no longer exclusively perceived as a "divine instrument" but had also become a symbol of women's capabilities. A poem commemorating the "celebrated Quaker Mrs. Drummond," in the *Gentleman's Magazine* of 1735, first compared her to the traditional female figure of the mystic Saint Teresa, then continued in a more politically challenging vein:

> Too long indeed our sex has been deny'd,
> And ridicul'd by men's malignant pride;
> Who fearful of a just return forbore,
> And made it criminal to teach us more.
> That woman had no soul, was their pretence,
> And womans spelling, past for woman sense.
> 'Till you most generous heroine stood forth,
> And shew'd your sex's aptitude and worth.
> Were there no more, yet you bright maid alone
> Might for a world of vanity atone.
> Redeem the coming age, and set us free
> From that false brand of Incapacity.

The poem had originally been written to celebrate the pioneer feminist Mary Astell but the tribute was transferred to a Quaker female preacher when May Drummond's name was inserted in this later version.[74]

Ironically, those who did not believe that the Quaker women were "divinely-led" were particularly likely to be impressed by their natural talents. Even critics, who believed that giving females the liberty to preach was a religious error, often acknowledged the Quaker women's skill. The author of a pamphlet criticizing May Drummond for preaching admitted that she acted "so admirably well the Part of a Preacher. . . ."[75] Those who could not theologically agree with the idea that God utilized women, as well as men, in preaching the Gospel, were insidiously led into greater respect for the women's independent accomplishments. Sophia Hume was described as a "celebrated writer and preacher," Mary Peisley was noted for her "remarkable . . . accomplishments," and Rachel Wilson was complimented on her sermon's "singular penetration" by the non-Quaker press.

Disputes over women's abilities and their role in public life continued throughout the eighteenth century. Widespread prejudice still existed against women as preachers. Like many members of eighteenth-century Anglo-American society, Dr. John Byrom made a distinction between his tolerant interest in attending the assemblies of other sects and the approval of a female friend's conversion to Quakerism (Frances Henshaw, later Dodshon): "I told [her] I hoped I should never hear of her preaching in a Quaker meeting, calling it an indecent thing." Frances Dodshon did, however, later become an acclaimed preacher. Although Dr. Samuel Johnson was acquainted with a number of female authors (including Catharine Macaulay, the historian), he still maintained the belief that "Publick practice of any art . . . is very indelicate in a female." James Boswell's visit to a Quaker meeting in 1763 had prompted Samuel Johnson's notorious remark, "Sir, a woman's preaching is like a dog's walking on his hind legs. It is not done well; but you are surprised to find it done at all." Nevertheless, Quaker female ministers achieved a public prominence in eighteenth-century England and in America. Religious toleration had enabled women to gain a new legal acceptance by the larger society in the public role of Quaker minister. In a dramatic change from the seventeenth century, these religious leaders of a tolerated sect were written about respectfully and listened to, at times, by attentive, orderly crowds. Never before had so many women spoken in public before audiences composed of both sexes. Of course, many non-Quakers did not theologically recognize the Quaker religious leaders as ministers equivalent to their own ordained clergymen who delivered prepared sermons. Yet the advocacy of liberty of conscience in religious worship had promoted the toleration of Quaker preachers, and female involvement in this role had expanded women's sphere of influence, demonstrating women's capacities in a new way.[76]

The Ending of an Era

Quaker female missionaries in the mid-seventeenth century had represented a scorned group on the fringes of society. But eighteenth-century Quaker female ministers, who still sought out an unconverted public, were allied with powerful Quaker politicians and merchants, creating a peak period for the women ministers as public figures in the non-Quaker culture, particularly in America. With the organization of the Society of Friends, passage of the Toleration Act of 1689, and the founding of Pennsylvania, attitudes toward the Quakers had shifted from fear, outrage, and prejudice to grudging toleration, and, eventually, in some cases, to admiration. Enlightenment thought confirmed the value of liberty of conscience and Quaker reputability. Revivalistic ecumenicalism further contributed to the advent of religious toleration so important for Quaker women. Since the Society had not eliminated its ministerial role for women in its movement toward respectability, the increasing "normalization" of Quakers had resulted in a new visibility of their spiritually "gifted" females. Heightened Quaker secular power in the eighteenth century provided a unique opening for female leadership, as Quaker women ministers advised assemblymen and preached at treaty conferences. The level of visibility experienced by Quaker women ministers during the pre-Revolutionary War era, however, appears to have been short-lived.

Ironically, during the same period that non-Quakers were crowding in to hear visiting Quaker preachers, many members of the Society of Friends were becoming spiritually "lukewarm" and apathetic. As Quakers won toleration of their principles and prospered materially, religious zeal was diminishing within the Society. Even as Voltaire was discovering and admiring the Friends in England in 1733, he already perceived that "their children whom the industry of their parents has enrich'd, are desirous of enjoying honours, of wearing buttons and ruffles; and quite asham'd of being call'd Quakers, they become converts to the Church of England, merely to be in the fashion." Thomas Story, visiting Bristol, England, noticed "traditionalists," the children of faithful Friends who had earlier suffered for Truth. For a time, these "birthright" Quakers had continued their parents' manner of worship, but as adults "being only in their natural state," without any personal spiritual experience, many had been "taken by the lust of the eye with the vain and sinful fashions, customs, and notions of the world, and become, some deists, some free-thinkers, others profane libertines, and others atheists; denying all revealed religion as contained in the Holy Scriptures."[77]

As Rachel Wilson had noted, "The Danger Seemed more in Fawning [flattering] than Frowning" for Quakers in the eighteenth century. Instead of being persecuted, Friends were being observed by a curious world. But exactly at the time the larger culture was perceiving the Quakers' virtues (as exemplars of ideals that few could practice), fewer Quakers were actually living up to Friends' rigorous standards. In the American colonies, in such places as Philadelphia and Newport, Friends had developed into well-to-do elites who dominated the political and economic life of their areas. As Quakers had become more accepted by the world, they were becoming more like the world. Friends' intermixing with worldly culture, through political officeholding and commercial dealings, presented temptations that made it increasingly difficult to maintain the distinctive Quaker testimonies. Precisely that which created a peak period of visibility for the Quaker women preachers in the larger culture, Friends' worldly assimilation, was viewed, eventually, as jeopardizing the survival of the religious society. Mary Peisley and Catharine Payton, travelling through the colonies in 1754, had found that the common presence of non-Quakers at the Friends' meetings for discipline "rendered it difficult for us to discharge our duties."[78]

Devout members of the Society reacted to the weakening of Quaker principles by reasserting the boundaries between Friends and the world. The radical reformation, initiated in the mid-eighteenth century by Quaker ministers, led to a more rigidly enforced discipline, the withdrawal of many Quakers from political office, and a sharply decreased membership in the Society. While Rachel Wilson was receiving popular acclaim among non-Quakers in Charleston, South Carolina (as Henry Laurens noted, "I have not known Strangers, at any time come among us, meet a more Cordial reception"), she could not help but observe the scanty number of actual Quakers in Charleston: "thears few that Bear our Name. . . ." While non-Quakers, such as Henry Laurens, were eager to accommodate the celebrated visitor, Wilson noted that in the small Quaker community, ironically, "thair no one that had a bed to spair among Em. . . ."[79]

In addition to the Society of Friends' attempts to distinguish its membership from the "world's" people, external events further estranged Quakers from American culture only a few years after Rachel Wilson had successfully toured the colonies. Ezra Stiles, who had found Rachel Wilson to be "a pious sensible woman" in 1769, was darkly suspicious by 1774 when another English Quaker preacher, Mary Leaver, visited Rhode Island. With tensions increasing between Britain and its colonies, Ezra Stiles wondered about the real mission of Mary Leaver, on a religious tour of America, and John Pemberton, the Quaker minister from Philadelphia accompanying her. When the itinerant Quaker preachers arrived in Rhode Island, near the end of 1774, Ezra Stiles noted in his diary that John Pemberton and "an English Quakeress, Speakers, are travelling here among Friends at this late Season & I suppose upon very particular Business."[80]

The Philadelphia Yearly Meeting of Friends had released a general epistle to American Quakers recommending that they not join other colonists in their opposition to Parliament, after the Continental Congress's issuance of a letter, in September 1774, to all the colonies recommending union in the American resistance to the late Acts of the British Parliament. Ezra Stiles did not see this yearly meeting epistle as evidence of the Quaker religious principle of pacifism but rather as proof of the influence of the English government upon the Quakers (whom he felt were dictated to by the London Yearly Meeting), designing to divide the colonists. Stiles believed that the "true Reason" for the Quaker ministers' journey to New England was to support this general epistle, interpreted by Stiles as designed to "detach the whole Quaker Interest from the rest of America in the present Conflict . . . & so in effect to contravene & nullify the Letter of the Congress with respect to the Friends—and so to conform to the Wishes of the Ministry to divide us." He especially feared John Pemberton's influence as "an eminent Speaker among Friends & Brother to Israel Pemberton of Phila." Stiles concluded that "to enforce this Epistle, I suppose, is the true Reason that the Philada. Meetg. sent off so considerable & principal a Quaker as Mr. Pemberton at this late Season of the year. This I suppose to be his Errand hither."[81]

The pacifist Friends with their close connections to England were viewed with growing suspicion by revolutionary patriots. Quaker ministers Mary Leaver and John Pemberton were escorted by Moses Brown (from the prominent mercantile family of Providence, Rhode Island) on their religious visit through New England, and Brown was publicly a Quaker neutral. But, formerly, as a Baptist in the late 1760s he had been one of Rhode Island's most active organizers of resistance to taxation by the British Parliament. After Brown's conversion to Quakerism, although he privately sympathized with the American cause, he advocated reconciliation until early 1776, in a principled stance against war. But when Philadelphia Friends called on all Americans to reject the revolutionary government and to remain loyal to the established government in England, Brown wrote, disapprovingly, in a letter of March 1776 to John Pemberton, that it would have been better to remain neutral, not addressing the people in general, but only the Quakers. Brown feared that the public was being given the impression the Society of Friends was meddling beyond and contrary to their religious profession.[82]

During the American Revolution, many people considered the neutralism of the Quakers merely a cover for loyalist sympathies, although Moses Brown's strict neutralism and his selfless efforts to help innocent war victims regardless of their political affiliation diminished the criticism of Quakers in New England. But Joseph Wanton, the Quaker governor of Rhode Island during Rachel Wilson's visit in 1769, was removed from office in November 1775 when he refused to sanction treasonous acts against the British government. When the British evacuated Newport in 1776, Wanton accompanied them to New York. Thomas Paine severely criticized the Quakers in an appendix, "an Address to the People called QUAKERS," to *Common Sense* (published in 1776) for acting not as a religious group but as a political body. Paine argued that Friends were not practicing neutrality, but were objecting only to the warfare engaged in by the American side: "If ye really preach from conscience, and mean not to make a political hobbyhorse of your religion, convince the world thereof, by proclaiming your doctrine to our enemies, *for they likewise bear ARMS.* Give us proof of your sincerity by publishing it at St. James's. . . . Had ye the honest soul of [Robert] *Barclay* ye would preach repentance to *your* king; Ye would tell the Royal Wretch his sins, and warn him of eternal ruin."[83] Quakers did advocate wisdom to the king, as the female preacher, Frances Dodshon, had addressed King George III in the *Gentleman's Magazine,* advising him to "prevent the effusion of blood, the rending of a potent empire." English Friends Dr. John Fothergill and David Barclay had attempted to negotiate a peace between the colonists and the English government. But Paine's accusation that the Quakers did not adhere to their own principles, mistaking "party" for "conscience" and dabbling in matters that their professed quietude instructed them not to, made a deep impression on the general public.

Meanwhile, the Society of Friends itself was wracked with internal divisions about appropriate loyalties. Friends who chose to fight in the Revolutionary War were disowned, increasing the diminution of the Quaker membership already begun with the mid-eighteenth-century reformation. In turn, many of the prominent leaders of the eighteenth-century Society of Friends, men who had been pivotal in supporting the transatlantic Quaker ministry, were arrested as Tory sympathizers and exiled to Winchester, Virginia, in 1777. Israel Pemberton Jr. and his brothers John and James, two members of the Fisher family (merchant shipowners who had served as Rachel Wilson's companions on her travels), and John Hunt, former member of the Meeting for Sufferings (London Yearly Meeting), were among the Quakers arrested on the general charge of opposing and discouraging the American cause as General Sir William Howe and the British army approached Philadelphia. Although the Friends were released in spring 1778 (John Hunt died in exile), antipathy toward Quakers remained after the American Revolutionary War. In 1784, Moses Brown thought that the American public would not support an organization started by a Quaker. Friends regained status with their humanitarian efforts, but they had been significantly out of step with the political direction of the new nation.[84]

Quaker accumulation of worldly power, the acquisition of wealth and political office, had created a spiritual crisis within the Society; and war in the larger culture had brought Quakers into conflict with the world. The severing of the transatlantic British empire in which the Quakers had wielded influence by their lobbying of the imperial government at London, along with the united strength of their coreligionists dispersed throughout the English Atlantic world, dramatically altered the circumstances for the Society and their travelling preachers. In addition, American Quaker withdrawal from government, in order to uphold Quaker principles, had moved Friends from the center of society to its peripheries, reducing the celebrity of the Quaker female preachers and their ability to influence Quakers in public office, although they still had impact on the general Quaker population. The decrease in the membership of the Society of Friends resulting from the radical reformation as well as the Quaker decline, proportionally, in comparison to other religious groups in America (increasing in membership through revivalism and immigration) had also lessened Friends' secular power. As the peak Quaker period receded, Quaker women preachers, as well as Friends generally, continued to influence the larger society with their principled idealism, but in private philanthropies and social reform movements such as abolitionism. Quakers' reassertion of boundaries between their religious society and worldly culture strengthened their commitment to Quaker values, but reduced the visibility of Quaker women as public figures in their preaching role, resulting in a closer confinement of the female ministry to the cloistered meetings of a "peculiar people."[85]

AFTERWORD

R E S I D I N G in a fieldstone house amidst the beautiful, rolling
countryside of the Brandywine Valley, Elizabeth Webb (1663–1727)
was, in many respects, like other colonial American white women whether
Puritan, Anglican, or Quaker (the three leading religious affiliations during
Webb's lifetime, among those of European descent). As the wife of Richard
Webb, a moderately prosperous farmer, Elizabeth lived on a large tract of
land between "the great Birmingham road" and Brandywine Creek in
Chester County, Pennsylvania. She gave birth to ten children over approximately two decades. The estate inventory, taken after her husband's death,
included cows, pigs, sheep, wheat, flax, malt, and hops. These items suggest the chores that Elizabeth engaged in to maintain the farm household:
dairying, with the attendant production of cheese and butter; the curing of
meat and rendering of fat for lard; baking bread; brewing beer; and spin-
ning wool into yarn for clothing the family. Yet the eighteenth-century
rural woman experienced not only a world of farm chores and child care—
Elizabeth saw a world where the supernatural was everywhere. After she
had "made a public confession to the goodness of God," she "was in love
with the whole creation of God" and "saw everything to be good in its
place . . . as it was in the outward, so it ought to be in the inward and new
creation." Every living thing preached God's goodness to her. As the Pennsylvania farmwife and mother of ten recalled, even "the very fragrant
herbs . . . had a speaking voice in them to my soul."[1]

   The Webbs lived more comfortably than some colonists, with a few luxury items, such as looking glasses, books, and a feather bed, in addition to

their more commonplace flock beds. But Elizabeth, as a "feme covert," shared the legal status of other eighteenth-century wives, unable to own property. During her "coverture," the duration of her marriage, Elizabeth could not execute contracts, initiate suits, or convey property without her husband's consent. Richard Webb was the legally recognized head of the household. His name alone appeared on the community list of ratepayers (landholders assessed for taxes). Elizabeth was subsumed within her husband's legal and political identity. Only he could vote or hold governmental office. Dependent upon Richard Webb for her economic status, lacking political rights of her own, subordinate to her husband's authority under law, Elizabeth felt many of the constraints of eighteenth-century womanhood. A closer examination of Elizabeth Webb's biography, however, complicates this portrayal of a "voiceless" woman, confined to the domestic sphere, in a male-controlled society. Elizabeth's spiritual experiences, including having "certain manifestations of many things in dreams, which did come to pass according to their significations" and being drawn "to call to others sometimes, to come and taste and see how good the Lord is" or "to warn people, that they should not provoke the Lord by disobedience," were formally recognized by the Quaker community as the "divinely inspired gifts" of a minister. Elizabeth's public role as a Quaker preacher altered her life as an eighteenth-century woman in significant ways.[2]

The ministerial role changed the boundaries of Elizabeth Webb's world, which, traditionally, for a woman, encompassed the dwelling house and its adjacent parts—the washhouse, the garden, and the milkyard. The demarcation of Elizabeth's world eventually encircled the British Isles and the American colonies, as she followed her "inward leadings" on journeys approved by the Quaker meeting. She was likely the first member of her family to see the New World. Following her religious visit to America from 1697 to 1699, the Webbs emigrated from Gloucestershire, England, to Pennsylvania in 1700. The impressions gleaned by Elizabeth during her travels probably provided the impetus for their relocation. She was also likely the first one in her family to see a black person. Travelling in Virginia, witnessing "great numbers of black people who were in slavery," Elizabeth had a dream "that the call of God was to the black as well as to the white." Elizabeth saw the fulfilling of this vision, in part, before she returned to England in 1699. She preached to blacks at a Friend's house in New England. One young man "was so reached by the love of God . . . the tears ran down like rain"; thereafter, he and his family attended Quaker worship.[3]

Instead of being isolated by her domestic circle of cares, Elizabeth spent months journeying with other female preachers. She travelled from North Carolina to New Hampshire with Mary Rogers in 1697–99. She accompanied Sarah Clements through New England in 1701–1702. In 1704, Elizabeth visited Maryland, Virginia, and North Carolina, escorted by Mary Lawson. From 1710 to 1712, she toured the British Isles with various English women ministers, sailing back to America with Ann Chapman. In 1724, Elizabeth revisited New England with her Chester County neighbor Jane Brinton. Through the ministry, Elizabeth formed connections with Quaker women in every region, visiting them, hosting them, and encountering them at yearly meetings.[4] Her rich social network included Quaker men, particularly preachers, such as John Richardson, Thomas Lightfoot, and Thomas Chalkley, whom she also met at meetings or travelled with part of the way on the same routes.

An eighteenth-century woman was seen "chiefly as an adjunct of her husband," since her identity was not dissociated from her function in the family. But because Elizabeth had a public role as a minister, her spiritual talents as an individual were recognized. The Quaker minister Thomas Chalkley observed Elizabeth in 1699 when they sailed across the Atlantic together: "It was my lot once to cross the sea from America to Europe with this servant of Jesus, and her conversation and deportment had a tendency to draw people's minds toward God. Heavenly things it was her practice to speak, read and write, so that her conversation seemed to us to be in heaven whilst she was on earth. I have blessed the Lord that I was acquainted with her." After Irish Friends heard her preaching, they wrote, "The said Elizabeth was a Woman Extraordinarily gifted & (it may be said) thoroughly furnished for the work of the Gospel in the deep & weighty things of Gods Kingdom." Although the influence of women of this era, "as wholly domestic beings," tended to be "confined to their immediate families," Elizabeth affected a range of people in the British Isles and the American colonies. Chalkley asserted that "she preached the gospel of God our Savior with power and clearness . . . divers[e] being really convinced of the truth of the gospel through her ministry."[5]

The literacy required to read the Bible and express her religious inspiration gave Elizabeth further entry into transatlantic culture, as she corresponded with far-flung acquaintances. Her preaching evolved naturally into authorship. Eighteenth-century females usually "understood that men controlled their society, that in all areas of public and private life men's

This was the home of Elizabeth Webb's Quaker neighbor and travel companion, Jane Brinton. Sitting room, first floor, Brinton 1704 House, Birmingham Township, Delaware County (formerly part of Chester County), Pennsylvania. Photograph by Theodore B. Hetzel. *Courtesy Chester County Historical Society, West Chester, Pennsylvania*

opinions and activities were deemed more important than theirs." But Elizabeth had recognized spiritual authority as a preacher; her pronouncements in Quaker meetings were respectfully heard. Her written interpretations of the Book of Revelation were copied by Thomas Chalkley, and approved by the Quaker overseers of the press for publication.[6]

Richard Webb formally spoke for his wife in the legal and political realms. But it was to Elizabeth, as an authority on Quaker matters, after her travel through the colonies, that William Penn was directed by a Philadelphia man: "I referr thee to her for a more perticul[e]r acco[unt] of the Affaires of Truth & Condicion of Friends in America." Traditionally, men also spoke in public for the community as a whole. But it was Elizabeth, rather than her husband, who publicly represented the Quaker inhabitants of Birmingham in a proposal to the Concord Monthly Men's Meeting, although Richard Webb held public offices in civil government (provincial assemblyman 1705, county assessor 1709–10, and justice of the peace, 1711–20). Elizabeth held a type of public authority, a recognized "gift" in the ministry, which her husband did not possess. Her request, made in conjunction with John Bennett, that a meeting for worship be held at Bennett's house in the winter because of the neighbors' distance from the Concord meeting-house, was approved.[7]

Elizabeth's spiritual identity was not subsumed in that of her husband. Disciplinary action by the Quaker meeting against Richard Webb had further accentuated the contrast in their religious standings. When the Webbs relocated from Philadelphia to Chester County, after their immigration to America, the Philadelphia Monthly Meeting had sent a removal certificate, in 1704, recommending Elizabeth to Concord Monthly Meeting, but omitting mention of her husband. The meeting's reluctance to grant a joint certificate stemmed from disturbing reports that Richard had persuaded a woman to drink too much rum. Richard Webb's disciplinary problem, however, did not affect his wife's spiritual status in the community. Elizabeth was granted a certificate to travel in the ministry to the southern colonies during the period her husband was under investigation. But Elizabeth's observations on the matter were deemed so important that the Philadelphia Monthly Men's Meeting elected to wait for her return from the ministerial visit before making a final decision on Richard Webb's removal certificate. Not until 1710, when Richard condemned his wrongful behavior, did the onetime Pennsylvania assemblyman receive full membership in the Quaker meeting. After his repentance, Richard was appointed a trustee of the meeting's burial ground in 1712 and served as a representative to Chester Quarterly Meeting.[8]

In her role as "Public Friend," Elizabeth Webb held spiritual authority recognized even beyond the Quaker community, as she represented the Society of Friends to the world, interpreting Quaker tenets. Anthony William Boehm, the chaplain to Prince George of Denmark (consort of Queen Anne of England), admiringly began a correspondence with Elizabeth Webb during her religious journey to the British Isles in 1710–12. Writing to Boehm, Elizabeth explained Quaker beliefs: "The principle that we make profession of, is the very Truth, viz. Christ in the male and female, the hope of glory: and Christ, thou knowest, is the Way, the Truth, and the Life, and none comes to God but by him." The Pennsylvania farmwife exchanged letters with the Anglican chaplain, as if they were "professional" colleagues, discussing forms of religion and elucidating Christian principles. She gave an account of her own religious experience ("what my soul hath tasted of the good word of life") and sent him a copy of his letter with her annotations. Boehm answered her in a letter, dated 1712, "Your letter hath been read with great satisfaction by myself and many of my friends . . . Some have even desired to transcribe it for their edification." Boehm concluded, in spiritual fellowship with the colonial American mother of ten, "how welcome it is to me to meet with a fellow-pilgrim traveling to the city adorned with twelve pearls, which is to receive all such who have made up the family of God in this wicked generation." The Londoner requested of the traveller, "If you will be pleased to correspond with me, even after you return[,] from America, I shall always be ready to answer your kindness."[9]

Elizabeth Webb's authority, founded on her strong spirituality (the Lord "having been pleased to furnish her w[i]th wisdome, holy zeale, . . . dilligence, & Patience"), inevitably flowed into other parts of life in the Quaker community that, more than many other Christian societies, refused to segregate religious values from other activities. When Richard Webb died in 1720, Elizabeth was named by him to be sole executor of his estate. Richard bequeathed all of his property to his ministerial wife except for one-pound legacies to each of their children. A year after her husband's death, Elizabeth conveyed to the Quaker meeting an acre of land, upon which was then built the first Birmingham Friends' meeting-house.[10]

A letter written during Elizabeth Webb's widowhood displayed her remarkable mixture of a minister's "heavenly conversation," a farmwife's pragmatism, and a seasoned traveller's knowledge. She revealed an astute eye for livestock, as well as a firm grasp of the vagaries of colonial currency. On her religious visit to Newport, Rhode Island, in 1724, Elizabeth wrote to her companion's thirty-two-year-old son, Joseph Brinton, giving him spiritual counsel, reminding him of "the love ministered daily to thy Soul, by him who is the fountain of it; to sweeten thy passage through this troublesome world and to draw thy mind heavenward." Elizabeth then explained to the Pennsylvania man that she had found a Quaker who had several young horses to sell, of good kind and good colors, "but the generality of such creatures are very mean on the island." She informed Brinton that she had purchased a horse for him, apparently at his request: "I have agreed with a friend . . . for a young mare, a natural pacer 2 years old . . . if thee hast a mind for any more than one thou may bring money with thee." She warned Brinton about the payment necessary for this transaction in another colony: "Our paper money will not do, and if thou get some changed it should be for whole pieces of Gold for that which is cut will pass but at 6 lbs . . . So I have given thee the best information that I can."[11]

As a ministerial mother, Elizabeth requested that Brinton be "fatherly" to her children in her absence, relying on the extended Quaker "family of faith" while she travelled "in the service of Truth." The Quaker appreciation of the value of her "gospel labours" had created a community willingness to release Elizabeth, at times, from her household tasks. A conscientious Quaker mother, Elizabeth demonstrated, by example, obedience to the Lord and wrote narratives of her religious experiences for her children. She asked Joseph Brinton to gather her children together, and read a letter she had written specifically to them: "My tender, motherly love is to you all. . . ." Elizabeth exhorted them to read the Scriptures, advised them to submit to God's will ("as a tender mother, I show you the way by which my Saviour hath led my soul to rest and peace with him"), and committed them to God's care, "although I love you dearly, yet I know the love of God, your heavenly father, far exceeds mine."[12]

Hidden within the traditional outlines of Elizabeth Webb's life, as an eighteenth-century farmwife and mother, were public activities of preaching and authorship, extensive travel, and a striking amount of authority. Elizabeth's story illustrates the degree to which the Quaker ministerial role reshaped women's lives. Her position in the community, based on her spiritual "gifts," differed markedly from her legal and political status. Inclusion in the Quaker ministry, a possibility for both men and women, was particularly significant for eighteenth-century females constrained by disabilities in worldly affairs.

The theological basis for Quaker women's ministerial activity was the power of God to use any "instrument," however weak, for His purposes. But the effects of women's participation in this role were more complicated than this religious justification. As the Protestant Reformation had destroyed old cultural patterns and reshaped social behavior, Quaker belief in universal access to the Inward Light dramatically altered traditional gender roles and spheres of activity. Virtuous women, traditionally silent in public and confined to the domestic sphere, gave public testimonies and travelled to spread the message of "Truth." The repercussions of these changes became obvious in the nineteenth century, as Quaker women, habituated to public speaking and influence, were prominent in social reform movements such as abolition, temperance, prison reform, and woman's rights. Lucretia Mott, a Quaker preacher, rejected as a delegate to the World Anti-Slavery Convention in 1840 because she was female, helped begin the woman's rights movement in America.[13]

Less well known is the religious diversity of the British colonies in North America that included this alternative Quaker female tradition. In every area of the British empire with Quaker populations (including New Hampshire, Massachusetts, New York, New Jersey, Pennsylvania, Maryland, Virginia, and the Carolinas), eighteenth-century women were recognized as preachers and travelled on religious service. The dominance of the New England Puritan model in colonial American history has concealed the existence of this public, authoritative role for women. In the pre-Revolutionary War transatlantic culture, women like Elizabeth Webb, Esther Palmer, Ann Moore, and Susanna Hatton crisscrossed the colonies and the British Isles, preaching, advising, shaping attitudes, and influencing behavior: promoting religious toleration, pacifism, integrity, among other ideals. Quaker female preachers were particularly visible in colonial America, where Quakers formed the third largest religious group, and Friends' political officeholding created a peak of Quaker secular influence in the first half of the eighteenth century. The women offered spiritual wisdom to government and military leaders, as well as to poor farmers on the frontier. Every Quaker woman potentially could participate in this role. Even those women without such a "gift" might accompany a minister on her travels. The female preachers' example shaped Quaker women's expectations, providing a model of female behavior. Approximately thirteen hundred to fifteen hundred women ministered in the colonies and the British Isles as part of the Quaker transatlantic culture. These women were religious leaders of a significant Anglo-American group, and their activities enlarge our conception of eighteenth-century women's opportunities.

Eighteenth-century Quakerism was conservative in its strict oversight of members' dress, language, and behavior, and often patriarchal in its organizational structure. But the Society of Friends' valuing of individual religious experience performed a crucial, liberating function for eighteenth-century women who became convinced of their personal access to the divine authority. Eighteenth-century Quaker women's conviction of their direct connection to God empowered them; not only allowing them to surmount the physical barriers of mountains and oceans, expanding the geographical boundaries of their world, but enabling them to overcome the conceptual barriers of traditional gender roles and perceived limitations of women's capacities, expanding their life possibilities. As Elizabeth Webb wrote to her companion's adult son who remained behind in Pennsylvania during their religious journey to Rhode Island in 1724: "Thy mother is become very courageous in riding thru deep waters and over rocky mountains beyond what I could expect. She says fear is taken away from her and that she is born up by a secret hand, which I am very glad of and thankful . . . to the Lord for."[14]

Appendix 1

INDIVIDUAL DESCRIPTIONS
OF THE TRANSATLANTIC MINISTERS

Alice (Burton) Alderson (1678–1766): of Dent, Yorkshire, England; father's occupation unknown; Anglican parents; convinced in her youth; her brother John Burton also became a Quaker minister; she became a minister in 1706, age twenty-eight, at first with just a few words, but her gift grew: "though she had not much human learning, she was frequently furnished with copious expressions well adapted to the matter she had to deliver, deep and weighty in her delivery, and enabled to speak feelingly to the state of meetings and individuals"; "a grave Elderly Matron" when she visited Ireland in 1743; married 1717 to Ralph Alderson (d. 1772), a yeoman of Nathwaite, Ravenstonedale, Westmorland, England; he was active in MM, appointed as representative to QM;* Alice was the mother of four children.

Elizabeth (Sampson) (?) (Sullivan) Ashbridge (1713–1755): born in Middlewich, Cheshire, England; father was a ship's surgeon; Anglican parents; after a tumultuous life of elopement, indentured servitude, and abuse by a non-Quaker husband, Ashbridge visited Quaker relatives in Pennsylvania, converting to Quakerism against the wishes of her husband; after she was widowed, supported herself as seamstress and schoolmistress while active as a Quaker preacher; a minister by at least age twenty-seven, in 1740; she was a clerk of women's MM; "She was a Woman of an excellent Natural Understanding. In her conversation She was cheerful; yet solid; grave & instructive; She felt the Afflictions of others with a tender Sympathy, & bore her own with Patience & resignation. As a minister—She was deep in Travail, clear in her openings, plain and pertinent in her Expression; solid and awful in her deportment, & attended with that Baptizing Power, which is the evidence of a living Ministry"; she married (1) a non-Quaker stocking weaver who died five

*MM (monthly meeting); QM (quarterly meeting).

months later; (2) Mr. Sullivan, a non-Quaker impoverished schoolmaster, excessive drinker (d. ca. 1740), left her in debt; she married at age thirty-three in 1746 to (3) widower Aaron Ashbridge (d. 1776) of Goshen, Chester County, Pennsylvania, a well-to-do Quaker farmer, third out of sixty-eight on tax list for Goshen in 1747; he took an active part in public affairs; he was clerk of men's MM, overseer, and representative to QM; Elizabeth had no children.

Sarah (Payton) (Clarke) Baker (1669–1714): born Dudley, Worcestershire, England; the Paytons were nailmakers; her father was a Quaker minister; she was a minister at twenty-one in 1690; she "did freely & frequently, in large & lesser Assemblies, Preach & Teach, the things concerning the Kingdom of God . . . She had also good Service in womens meetings, being well qualified for an helpmeet in Government"; "She was a mournful & bowed down woman and often waded through great & deep Exercises not only for her own Sake but for the Sake of others . . . behaving herself in her family with much discretion and meekness having a godly care upon her heart for the good of her Children & Servants that they might be Educated and Nurtured up in the fear of God and out of light and frothy discourse & behaviour that tended to vanity"; travelled with her brother Henry Payton, a minister, on religious service to America; married 1694 (1) John Clarke, yeoman, of Tarperley, Cheshire, England, who died five months later leaving her with one child; he left his wife 150 pounds from his estate; she married 1699 (2) widower Samuel Baker (1660–1720), tallow chandler of Dublin, Ireland; he was an elder who often accompanied ministers on religious service; "Being Endowed with Worldly Substance he was Liberal to the Poor"; Sarah had four more children with her second husband.

Mary (Hogsflesh) Bannister (fl. 1703): of Spitalfields, London, England; her family background and when she became a minister are unknown; married 1669 to Charles Bannister (d. 1704, age sixty-five), a mariner, then chandler of London; he did some MM business; he died while Mary was on a religious visit to America; as a widow, she borrowed ten pounds from MM "in order to providing for her self by way of a Lively hood"; Mary was the mother of at least seven children, possibly more.

Barbara Bevan (1682–1705): born Treverigg, Glamorganshire, Wales; immigrated, in 1683, with her childhood family to Haverford, Pennsylvania; a minister at age sixteen in 1698; her testimony was "closely pressing Friends to beware of covetousness, and learn to be men as to the things of God, but children as to evil etc. She seemed very sensible and lively, and came to the state of the meeting very fully though through hard exercise"; travelled in the ministry with her father, John Bevan, a wealthy Quaker preacher and leading promoter of Welsh settlement of Pennsylvania; he had the highest tax rate for Haverford and was a Pennsylvania assemblyman; she died unmarried at age twenty-three.

Jane (Boid) (Atkinson) Biles (d. 1709): born Yorkshire, England; her family background is unknown; already a minister when she immigrated with her family to New Jersey in 1682; she "was unusually well educated for a woman of her time . . . is said to have had an eminent public testimony"; she was temporarily a supporter of George Keith in the Keithian schism but later wrote a testimony against him; married 1678 (1) Thomas Atkinson (d. 1687) of Adingham, Yorkshire, England; he was a Quaker preacher, representative to YM;* his "worldly fortunes were not prosperous" partly because of poor health—MM assisted him because he was "in want as to his outward concerns"; he owned land but was unable to pay for all of it before his death; Jane married 1688 to (2) widower William Biles (d. 1710), a Quaker preacher and prominent merchant/landholder; in the 1690s his taxable property ranked him among the five richest men of Bucks County, Pennsylvania; he served in Pennsylvania Assembly and Provincial Council, also in many county and local political offices; he was a representative to QM and YM, very active in MM (which met at his house for several years); but considered a difficult man, disciplined by the meeting for selling rum to the Indians; Jane was mother to three children and eight stepchildren.

Esther (Palmer) Champion (1678–1714): born Flushing, Long Island; father's occupation unknown; her family active in MM; a minister by at least age twenty-six, in 1704; "she was a virtuous woman, of a sound judgment, and very quick understanding, abounding in true love and zeal for the Lord and his truth; solid and grave, yet of a cheerful disposition"; on a religious visit to England she married in 1711/12 widower Richard Champion (d. 1748, age seventy-two), of Bristol, England, prosperous soapmaker, merchant, leading partner in the Bristol Brass and Wire Company; he gave financial assistance to Abraham Darby at Coalbrookdale; he was active in MM, representative to London YM; Esther was the mother of two children and two stepchildren; she died of smallpox.

Esther (Peacock) Clare (ca. 1675–1742): of Wilton, Cheshire, England; father's occupation unknown; she was a minister by at least 1714; concerned "to stir up Friends to their Duty in seeking unto & waiting upon the Lord, with Advice to Love him above all & one another freely"; married in 1703 to William Clare (d. ca. 1741), a shoemaker of Northwich, Cheshire, England, later cordwainer of Philadelphia, "an improving man in religious things . . . although not ranking amongst the rich or great in civil society"; Esther immigrated with her family to Philadelphia in 1714; she was the mother of seven children.

Comfort (Stanyan) (Hoag) Collins (1711–1816): of Hampton, New Hampshire; daughter of Ann Stanyan, who was a minister and representative to QM, and James Stanyan, representative to QM; Comfort was a minister by at least 1750; set sail for England but when the ship sprang a leak and turned back, she found herself released from that religious visit; lived to be 105 years old; married 1733 (1) Jonathan Hoag of Stratham, New Hampshire; Comfort Hoag's husband and children were in difficult financial straits while she was away on a religious visit and a wealthy Quaker aided the family anonymously; married 1777 (2) widower Tristram Collins; his

*YM (yearly meeting).

cousin Zaccheus Collins was a "weighty Friend" and fifth wealthiest man of Lynn, Massachusetts; Comfort was the mother of seven children.

Hannah (Dent) Cooper (d. 1754): of Wensleydale, North Yorkshire, England; her parents were in financial difficulties in 1734 in Yorkshire; her mother and sister were preachers; Hannah was a minister since at least 1721; she was described with a companion as "brave sensible women deep in the mysteries of the Kingdom and very notable in Deliverance"; after her religious visit in America, she married in 1735 widower Joseph Cooper Jr. (1691–1749), of Newton, Gloucester County, New Jersey; he was a wealthy landowner, on West Jersey Council of Proprietors, an assemblyman, very active in local government, clerk of men's MM and QM, frequent representative to YM; Hannah had no children of her own, but one stepchild.

Margaret Copeland (1684–1759): born Kendal, Westmorland, England; her father was a glazier; she was a minister at twenty-two in 1706; "her Ministry . . . was to the Comfort and Edification of the Heritage of God, and the whole of her Conduct correspondent therewith"; she never married.

Ruth (Trueman) Courtney (1684–1762): of Lurgan, County Armagh, northern Ireland; supposedly her father was a wealthy Quaker preacher who "gave his daughter a superior education indoctrinating her in the cardinal principles of the Gospel"; a minister in 1722; she travelled to America with her maid, Susanna Hudson (later Lightfoot), another preacher: "Ruth Courtney & Susy (her maid) . . . are two good women & well respected—I think Susy wou'd make a considerable minister were she from her mistress, & rid of some bad habits she has got in her delivery"; married 1702 Thomas Courtney of Grange, County Antrim, Ireland, occupation unknown; his father was described as an affluent property-owner; Ruth was the mother of three children.

Jane (Rowlandson) Crosfield (1712–1784): born Cartmel, Lancashire, England; the MM may have been held on her father's property, and he may have been disowned and then reinstated when Jane was fourteen, if meeting records were referring to same person; she was a minister at twenty in 1732, representative to QM; "a pious young Woman" when she visited Ireland in 1743; "suitably opened in Councell to Parents of Children &c. & advised Friends to plainness of Speech, Behaviour & Apparell"; she married in 1747 George Crosfield (1705–1784), a yeoman farmer, independent but not affluent, of Low Park, Preston Richard, Westmorland, England; he was very active in meeting business, regularly appointed as representative to QM; Jane was the mother of five children.

Phebe (Willets) (Mott) Dodge (1699–1782): born Jericho, Long Island; her grandfather was a New York proprietor; her grandmother was a preacher; the MM was held alternately at her grandmother's and her mother's homes; Phebe was a minister in 1723; married 1731 (1) Adam Mott (1672–1738) of Cowneck, Hempstead, Queens County, Long Island; his maternal grandfather was one of the first patentees of Mamaroneck; his grandmother directed in her will that her bequest to him should be the last paid "because his needs are less than the others"; his elder half-brother, a farmer, had more taxable property than any of his neighbors in 1680; Adam Mott did some meeting business; Phebe married 1741 (2) Tristram Dodge (d. 1760) of Long Island; he left to his widow "the negro girl, Rachel" in his will; he was an overseer, representative to QM, member of M&E.* Phebe Dodge, in 1776, having "for some years been under a concern of mind on account of holding negroes in bondage," declared it to be her "duty, as well as a Christian act," to set Rachel at liberty and manumitted her; Phebe was the mother of three children.

Mary (?) Ellerton (d. 1736): of York, Yorkshire, England; became a minister when young; known for her prophecies and warnings during her Pennsylvania visit; "had an excellent Searching Gift in the Ministry . . . wonderfully opened, & powerfully concerned in verbal Testimony, not only concerning the goodness of God . . . also to tell her own Experience, & the Steps she had trodden, where she had mist it (when she was young) by letting Slipp her testimony in Speaking Truth's Language"; married before 1695 to Ruben Ellerton (1670–1723), occupation unknown, a minister; in 1719, during her marriage, the meeting gave her money to assist in religious travel because "the Circumstances she is under as to Outward things are but Low"; Mary was the mother of one child.

Margaret Ellis (d. 1765 in old age): born Wales; Anglican parents; appeared in ministry ca. 1730; "a sincere-hearted woman, diligent in the exercise of her gift, which was in much plainness and simplicity"; immigrated ca. 1730 to Pennsylvania; resided in the household of Margaret Lewis's parents, elders of Radnor MM; she never married.

Elizabeth (Hoyle) (Robinson) Gibson (1729–1804): born Burnside, Lancashire, England; appeared as minister at age twenty-three in 1752; "emenently [sic] clothed with dignifying authority, when the power of Gospel Ministry rose baptizingly into dominion"; described by James Jenkins as dictatorial; married in 1754 (1) Joshua Robinson (1714–1775) of Countersett, Wensleydale, Yorkshire, England; he was a yeoman; he inherited his uncle's farm, which he remodelled with style; in 1759 he was sixth out of fourteen on land tax return for Countersett; he was regular representative to MM and QM; his brother was a minister; his grandfather was the first convinced Quaker of Wensleydale, Yorkshire, and the first Quaker meetings were held at his home; Elizabeth married 1778 (2) widower George Gibson (b. 1732) of Saffron Walden, Essex, England; he was an upholsterer and a minister since 1772; Elizabeth had several stepchildren.

Alice (Featherstone) Hall (1708–1762): born Allendale, Northumberland, England; her grandfather was imprisoned for Quaker testimonies; she was a minister in 1730 at age twenty-two, representative to QM; her cousin Hannah Harris was a minister and travel companion; married 1743 Isaac Hall (1720–1787), a farmer, of Little Broughton, Cumberland, England; he was an elder in 1764, regularly appointed representative to QM; Alice died while on a religious visit to America; "in her mar-

*M&E (Ministers and Elders).

ried State she still above all cared for the best things . . . truly concern'd for the good cause, & its Promotion"; Alice was the mother of five children.

Eliphal (Smith) (Perry) Harper (d. 1747): of Sandwich, Massachusetts; her family background is unknown; according to an English Quaker, "the American is a good, honest, old-fashioned preacher, a prudent woman"; a minister at least since 1729, representative to YM and appointed to write epistles to YM; married 1705 (1) Edward Perry Jr. (ca. 1673–d. before 1728) of Sandwich; he was clerk of QM, his father had been Quaker preacher/author of substantial estate; his maternal grandfather was the vice-governor of Plymouth Colony; his sisters Dorcas Easton and Mary Wing were New England ministers; Eliphal had five children with him; she married 1728 (2) Stephen Harper (d. ca. 1739) of Falmouth, Barnstable County, Massachusetts; he was overseer, representative to YM; his father was Robert Harper "of a family of famous Quaker preachers"; Eliphal moved in 1742 to Pennsylvania.

Hannah (Featherstone) Harris (1708–1786): probably born in Northumberland, England; her grandfather was imprisoned for his Quaker testimonies; her cousin Alice Hall was a preacher; she was a minister in 1726 at age eighteen, representative to QM; "large in testimony weighty & deep"; married between 1737 and 1743 to John Harris (1702–1785), a yeoman, of Oldfield, Greysouthen, Brigham, Cumberland, England; he was an elder in 1755, regularly a representative to QM; no children listed in records.

Rebecca (Owen) (Minshall) Harvey (b. 1687–fl. 1751): born in Welsh Tract, Pennsylvania; daughter of Dr. Griffith Owen, Welsh Quaker community leader, preacher, overseer of press, and physician, who served many years in the Assembly and Provincial Council; Rebecca was recommended as minister in 1729; described with Mary Lewis as "Women well gifted in the Ministry and divided the Word aright, speaking plain & home to the disobedient . . . but tender over the Seed of God in any"; married 1707 (1) Isaac Minshall (ca. 1685–1731), a yeoman of Providence, Chester County, Pennsylvania; he was an elder; Nether Providence Quaker meeting was established at his father's house and built on his land; in 1715 Isaac was the highest taxpayer of eleven of Lower Providence, second out of twenty-nine in Providence taxes; she married in 1739 (2) widower Job Harvey (d. 1751), cloth-worker of Darby, Chester County; he was seventh out of forty-eight in 1747 for Lower Darby tax rate; Rebecca was the mother of seven children.

Jane (Fenn) Hoskins (1694–1764): born London, England; Anglican parents; immigrated to Pennsylvania at age nineteen as an indentured servant in 1712; after appearance in the ministry ca. 1715, became a housekeeper to David Lloyd family in Chester, Pennsylvania; "a middle aged Woman & unmarryed . . . had a living ministry & good Utterance & close in Testimony suitable to the States of Friends . . . also had divers Meetings on acct. of others not of our Society . . . also in a Prophetick manner Spoke of a distressing time in general, a Winnowing time, & that some should be concerned to go over & preach the Gospel in the dark Countrys where Popery abounded . . . & that the great Whore of Babylon should drink one draft more of the blood of the Saints, & then should tumble down," when she visited Ireland in 1728; she married in 1738 Joseph Hoskins (d. 1773), a "fairly wealthy" Quaker minister of Chester, Pennsylvania; he was fourteenth out of 68 in 1739 and sixth out of 102 in 1766 for Chester tax assessment; Jane was childless.

Sophia (Wigington) Hume (1702–1774): born Charleston, South Carolina; granddaughter of early Quaker preachers Mary Fisher and William Bayley; daughter of a prosperous Anglican landowner and colony official; married Robert Hume of Charleston, an Anglican lawyer, landowner, public official; after being widowed, she moved to London, England, ca. 1741, converted to Quakerism and renounced her fashionable lifestyle; appeared in ministry 1747; "a well-meaning woman, but . . . had about her too much Church-buckram, reproving, with severity, the young people for what she deemed improper with respect to dress"; well-known author of several religious books advocating Quaker principles; mother of two children who lived to adulthood.

Mary (Goodwin) James (d. ca. 1776): born Llandewi-Brefi, Cardiganshire, Wales; immigrated with childhood family in 1708 to Edgmont, Chester County, Pennsylvania; her father was probably a farmer; all four siblings were ministers; she was recognized as a minister in 1718 or 1737, was also overseer, representative to QM; she married in 1712 Thomas James (d. 1752), a yeoman of Willis Town, Chester County, Pennsylvania; in 1715 he was eighth out of thirteen, and in 1740 he was thirty-second out of fifty-seven on Willis Town tax list; he was overseer, representative to QM; Mary was the mother of seven children.

Elizabeth (?) Kay (d. 1713): of Newton, West New Jersey; father's occupation unknown; unknown when she became minister; a preacher "with whom Frds. were much Comforted"; "a true Orthodox preacher in Gift & Conduct"; she was possibly clerk of women's MM, representative to QM; she married ca. 1683 John Kay (1656–1742) of Newton, New Jersey; he was born in Yorkshire, England, and emigrated by 1684; he was a farmer and mill owner, West Jersey proprietor and assemblyman; Elizabeth was the mother of nine children.

Mary (Ransome) Kirby (1709–1779): born Southrepps, Norfolk, England; a minister since at least 1739, age thirty; married in 1731 Samuel Kirby (d. 1737), a worsted weaver of Lammas, Norfolk, England; he or his father appointed to attend QM, otherwise not much meeting activity; she was widowed after six years of marriage; mother of three children; "[she was] the happiest woman I ever knew, and I was favoured to experience a good share of that sweetness in which she dwells."

Lydia (Rawlinson) Lancaster (1683–1761): born Graithwaite, Lancashire, England; her father, previously styled a "Gentleman," was banished from his father's house because of his Quaker conversion; he became an early Quaker missionary; her brother was a minister; she was a preacher in 1707, age twenty-four; "in a powerful manner was not only concerned in a common way of Testimony but in a prophetical way told us, that she believed & yt. it was in her mind the Lord would try, Sift & Winnow his People to the blowing away the Chaff . . . that she had heard a rattling Noise of Mortality to be both among us & other People"; she was clerk of women's MM, representative to QM; married in 1706 at age twenty-three to Bryan Lancaster (d. 1747), of Kendal, Westmorland, later moved to Lancaster, Lancashire; his occupation was unknown; his grandfather was a tanner and left him a legacy; in 1721, he was disowned by Quaker meeting for excessive drinking and running into debt, later gave paper of acknowledgment desiring reinstatement; "she had a large experience in affliction being deeply tried therewith in her nearest temporal conexion"; Lydia was childless.

Mary (Payne) Leaver (1720–1789): born Newhill Hall, Yorkshire, England; great-grandfather was early Quaker missionary; she was a minister in 1753 at age thirty-three, overseer, representative to QM; "she was endowed with a good natural Capacity, her ministry lively and edifying, she was frequently concerned to stir up the lukewarm to religious duty & to make a right use of their time & Talents received"; married in 1755 John Leaver (1711–1794) of Nottingham, England, prosperous grazier, landlord; he was a minister, elder, overseer, trustee of meeting-house and burial ground, representative to QM; Mary was the mother of three children.

Margaret (Thomas) Lewis (1712–1789): born Radnor, Pennsylvania; her parents were elders of Radnor MM; father was a miller and an assemblyman; her grandmother Margaret Miles was a wealthy minister; she was a preacher in 1744, age thirty-two; "Says but Little and yt is pritty well Approved off, . . . she has behaved with Prudence & humbleness . . . not too forward neither in Conversation nor in Meetings"; married at eighteen in 1731 Nathan Lewis (d. 1788) of Newtown, Chester County, Pennsylvania; he was fifth out of thirty-seven in 1739, third out of forty-one in 1762 on Newtown tax list; his Welsh grandfather had been chief organizer of Newtown Quaker meeting and freeholder of large plantation in Haverford, Pennsylvania; he was disciplined by meeting for excessive drinking but continued a member; Margaret was the mother of ten children.

Susanna (Hudson) (Hatton) Lightfoot (1720–1781): born Grange, County Antrim, Ireland; from an impoverished family; her mother was a minister; she was placed out as a maid to Ruth Courtney at thirteen; a minister at age seventeen in 1737; married in 1742 (1) Joseph Hatton (d. 1759), a Quaker linen weaver of Lisburn, northern Ireland; Quakers collected money for them to open a huckster's shop but it failed; he had some words in public testimony, disowned for bankruptcy in 1747 but later reinstated with paper of acknowledgment; in 1754 Ulster Quakers raised money by subscription for support of Hatton family, and they removed to Waterford where Friends agreed to aid them financially; she married (2) in 1763 Thomas Lightfoot of Pikeland, Chester County, Pennsylvania, farmer, owner of a sawmill, second out of seventy-seven in 1766 for Pikeland taxes; he became a minister after her death, overseer, elder, clerk of men's MM, representative to QM; Susanna was the mother of nine children.

Ann (Herbert) Moore (1710–1783): of Byberry, Pennsylvania; "her Mother dying when very Young, She was placed amongst Friends"; "a faithful Labourer in the

Church of Christ"; appeared in ministry in 1738, age twenty-eight; married (sometime previous to her recognition as minister) Walter Moore (1693–1782), a Quaker schoolmaster, who was disowned in 1753 for "drinking Strong liquer to Excess"; the family moved frequently, settled in Pennsylvania, Virginia, and, eventually, Maryland; the last years of her life she lived in Baltimore, Maryland; Ann was the mother of six children.

Elizabeth (Roberts) Morgan (1688–1777): born Llangower, Wales; her father, Robert Cadwalader, was a Welsh farmer, originally Anglican; immigrated to Gwynedd, Pennsylvania, with her family ca. 1698; her brother Rowland Roberts was a Quaker minister; she was a minister by 1730, representative to QM; married at age twenty-nine in 1718 Daniel Morgan (1691–1773) of Gwynedd, Pennsylvania, a yeoman; he was a minister, representative to QM; Elizabeth was the mother of two children.

Elizabeth (Hudson) Morris (1722–1783): born Philadelphia, Pennsylvania; heiress, granddaughter of William Hudson I, who was a member of Pennsylvania Governor's Council and Philadelphia mayor; she was a minister at twenty-one, in 1743; she married at age thirty in 1752 widower Anthony Morris (1705–1780) of Philadelphia, gentleman, the son and grandson of Philadelphia mayors, partner in brewing business, substantial property-owner, wealthy philanthropist, city assessor, overseer of public school; in 1755 he signed address against paying taxes for military purposes; his grandfather, Anthony Morris, and his aunt, Sarah Morris, were Quaker preachers; Elizabeth was the mother of three children and six stepchildren.

Sarah Morris (1703–1775): born Philadelphia, Pennsylvania; daughter of Anthony Morris (1654–1721), a Philadelphia brewer, wealthy merchant; he was a prominent Quaker minister, clerk of men's MM and YM, YM treasurer, overseer of press; he was very active in provincial and local politics, a Philadelphia mayor; her brother was also a leader of men's MM; Sarah was a minister at forty-three in 1746, clerk of women's MM; "She is generally most favored in the largest assemblies . . . [she] lifted up her voice like a trumpet, to the rousing of us all"; Sarah never married.

Susanna (Heath) Morris (1682–1755): born Teen, Staffordshire, England; immigrated with childhood family in 1701 to Abington, Pennsylvania; her three sisters were preachers; she appeared in ministry by 1711; "a prophetic minister who testified against use of tobacco, liquor, and the use of 'you' for the single person"; married in 1703 Morris Morris (1677–1764), yeoman, "one of the earliest and most extensive land owners of Richland Township [Pennsylvania], as well as one of the most prominent figures in the settlement of the township, an assemblyman"; he was born in Wales and immigrated with family to Pennsylvania in 1690; he was elder, overseer of MM, representative to YM, donated site of meeting-house, left legacy to establish a meeting school; Susanna was the mother of thirteen children.

Mary (Peisley) Neale (1717–1757): born Ballymore, County Kildare, Ireland; her Quaker father was imprisoned for debt and cautioned by the meeting; she worked as a domestic servant; a minister at twenty-seven, in 1744; an extreme quietist, "perhaps more than any other of these eighteenth-century Friends she let every detail of her life and service be dictated by direct Divine influence"; avid reformer, encouraged strict adherence to the discipline; married at age thirty-nine in 1757 to another minister, Samuel Neale (1729–1792), of Ireland, merchant; "having an independent property, he had money at his own disposal" from inheritance; Mary fell ill and died three days after her marriage.

Sarah (Clements) Owen (fl. 1703): of East Smithfield, London, England; father was a mariner of Chatham, England; she boarded with sister and brother-in-law, a haberdasher, before marrying; unknown when she became a minister; was one that "lived near the Kingdom"; visited America on religious service in 1699 with William Penn; she signed the birth certificate of Penn's son in 1700 in Pennsylvania; in 1703 she married Thomas Owen, of Sevenoaks, Kent, England; he was a mercer, no information on his Quaker activity; it is unknown whether Sarah had children.

Ann (Chapman) Parsons (1676–1732): born Stangah, Skelton, Yorkshire, England; immigrated with childhood family in 1684 to Wrightstown, Bucks County, Pennsylvania; her brothers, Abraham and Joseph, held important public positions in county and province; the Quaker MM was held at Abraham's house and he served as clerk of MM; both brothers were representatives to QM and elders; Ann appeared in the ministry in 1699, age twenty-three, and was representative to QM; she preached "with much Labour of Love for the Restoration of Backsliders warning them to prize time . . . to make a right Use of it . . . while the Lord in Mercy did Call . . . to provoke all to love & good Works, & to Reality & Sincerity more than an outward Shew of formality"; "She appeared a plain and innocent woman truly concerned for the prosperity of truth everywhere"; married in 1717 John Parsons, of Pennsylvania, occupation unknown; he was representative to QM, but later disowned in 1731 for adultery; Ann was childless.

Mary (Morgan) Pennell (1678–1764): of Radnorshire, Wales; Anglican parents; she was convinced at about age thirteen; her sister also became a Quaker and was mother of the minister John Griffith; Mary, at age sixteen, in 1694, went to live with a Quaker family in Pennsylvania; in 1722 she became a minister; "spoke of a trying day she had seen coming on this Nation, advising all to prepare for it" on a 1733 visit in Ireland; described by an English Quaker "as a notable good woman . . . from Pennsylvania"; married 1703 John Pennell (d. 1764) of Concord, later East Caln, Pennsylvania; he was a yeoman; in 1747 was forty-sixth out of fifty, in 1756 was fifty-second out of sixty-eight in Concord tax assessment; Mary was the mother of six children.

Catharine (Payton) Phillips (1726–1794): born Dudley, Worcestershire, England; her father, Henry Payton, was a travelling minister and iron merchant, who later fell into financial difficulty; her aunt Sarah was also a preacher; Catharine was a minister at twenty-two, representative to QM; "She was rather tall of stature, had a wide mouth, with masculine features . . . of a high and domineering disposition . . . she was an extraordinary woman who possessed no common gift in the ministerial allotment, as well as of natural abilities"; deferred marriage until she was forty-five; married in 1772 widower William Phillips (d. 1785) of Redruth, Cornwall; he was an agent to a Cornwall copper company, often accompanied travelling ministers and announced appointed meetings; Catharine was author of several treatises; she was childless but stepmother to two children, including James Phillips, the primary Quaker printer for London YM.

Elizabeth (Beck) Rawlinson (1670–1750): of Swarthmore, Lancashire, England; daughter of Dorothy (Mackreth) Beck, a minister, and William Beck, a preacher, representative to QM; her father was a skinner and glover; she was a preacher in 1687 at seventeen, representative to QM; she had "a brave Testimony for his Name & Truth, & against Untruth, labouring much to Stir up the pure mind in all . . . Also a pretty great Concern was on her to Caution all to take Care of the World & Spirit of it, Calling it a bewitching World, & to young People to Seek & fear the Lord"; in 1696, at age twenty-six, she married Abraham Rawlinson (1666–1737) of Rusland, Lancashire, a gentleman; he was representative to QM; his father was one of the first Quaker missionaries, his sister was the minister Lydia Lancaster; Elizabeth was the mother of seven children.

Ann (Lewis) (Williams) (Bennett) Roberts (1678–1750): born in Wales; Anglican parents; after her convincement, she immigrated to Haverford, Pennsylvania, ca. 1699; a minister at twenty-two in 1700; Ann predicted the appearance of new preachers at a meeting: "about that time our meeting was favoured with heavenly visitations . . . thereby was verified what she had declared at our meeting . . . though it seemed improbable, when spoken, and many doubted the accomplishment of it"; she married in 1699 (1) James Williams (d. 1707) of Haverford, Pennsylvania, yeoman, blacksmith; in 1708 (2) Henry Bennett (d. 1714) of Abington, Pennsylvania, husbandman; he was representative to QM; in 1719 (3) Rowland Roberts (1685–1749) of Gwynedd, Pennsylvania; he was a minister, yeoman, innkeeper; he suffered financial losses; "she met with great difficulties in respect to her outward circumstances"; Ann had three children.

Mary (Wheeler) Rogers (d. 1699): born Witney, Oxfordshire, England; Quaker parents; her father's occupation unknown; unknown when she became a minister; she married 1685 Joseph Rogers of East Markham, Nottinghamshire, England; his occupation unknown; he registered his home as a Quaker meeting-house; he was representative to QM and YM; he may have been a minister; it is unknown whether Mary had children; she died on a religious visit in the West Indies.

Elizabeth (Levis) Shipley (1690–1777): born Springfield, Chester County, Pennsylvania; daughter of Samuel Levis, a wealthy Quaker Pennsylvania assemblyman, justice of peace, member of Provincial Council; she was a minister at twenty-seven in 1717; she married at about thirty-seven, in 1728, widower William Shipley (d. 1768, age seventy-five) of Ridley, Pennsylvania; they relocated in 1735 and he became the virtual founder of Wilmington, Delaware, the town's first burgess; he helped introduce various industries to the town, "a wealthy and enterprising man"; he was disciplined by MM for minor dispute; Elizabeth's dream vision prompted the family's move to Wilmington; she was the mother of three children.

Ann (Waln) (Dillworth) Sibthorp (1654–1710): born Burnholme, Yorkshire, England; her parents were among earliest converts to Quakerism in Yorkshire; she was a minister by at least 1689, representative to YM; her brother was Nicholas Waln, a Pennsylvania assemblyman and Quaker minister; she married 1680 (1) James Dillworth (ca. 1658–1699) of Thornley, Lancashire, England, a husbandman; they immigrated in 1682 to Neshaminy, Pennsylvania, bought a thousand acres from William Penn; Dillworth was a minister, representative to QM; Quaker meeting was held at his home; he was a Pennsylvania assemblyman; she married 1701 (2) widower Christopher Sibthorp (d. 1707) of Philadelphia; he was "a large landholder in the Northern Liberties"; although he held no office, he was an important leader in the MM; Ann was the mother of eight children.

Elizabeth Smith (1724–1772): born Burlington, New Jersey; her father was a West Jersey assemblyman, wealthy merchant, and proprietor; her brothers, including Samuel, a historian, treasurer of the province, and John, a founder of Pennsylvania Hospital, were also assemblymen prominent in political and religious activities; she began preaching at twenty-one in 1745; she wrote epistles to women's meetings; member of New Jersey Society for Helping the Indians; *Pennsylvania Gazette* obituary described her as "deep in council, sound in judgment . . . She was from a child of unusual steadiness and composure of deportment and character"; Elizabeth never married.

Margaret (Paine) Stones (d. 1740): of Dunstable, Bedfordshire, England; father's occupation unknown; she was a minister since at least 1709; "was concerned to shew the goodness of the Lord to mankind in three respects, first by sending forth his messengers to warn you, secondly by the privelege of the holy Exhortations, counsels etc, in the Scriptures, and lastly by the inspeakings of His Holy Spirit etc, all which she pressed Friends to prize and to walk answerable thereto"; she married 1725 John Stones (d. 1756) of York, England; he was a mariner and a minister; no children listed in records.

Rebecca (England) Turner (d. 1721): born Carnabee, Yorkshire, England; father's occupation is unknown; she was a minister since at least 1699; married 1683 Robert Turner (d. 1723) of Hastrup, near Kirbymoorside, Yorkshire; his occupation is unknown; he was a minister; Rebecca was the mother of twelve children.

Mary (Hayes) (Lewis) Waln (d. 1753): born Marple, Chester County, Pennsylvania; father was wealthy landowner and Pennsylvania assemblyman; he was relatively inactive in the meeting in early years but later he was overseer, representative to QM; she was recommended as minister in 1723; married 1705 (1) Evan Lewis (d. 1735) of Newtown, Pennsylvania, a yeoman; son of chief organizer of Newtown Quaker meeting, local meetings for worship were held at his home; he was overseer, representative to QM and YM; he had extensive landholdings; he was consistently assessed the highest tax rate in Newtown from 1715 to 1734; he was justice of the peace and a Pennsylvania assemblyman; Mary's husband died while she was travelling in Ireland "being willing to return home as soon as Could . . . which Exercise was heavy on her"; she married 1739 (2) widower Richard Waln (1678–1756) of Norrington, Philadelphia County; he was a yeoman and a minister, later disowned for excessive drinking; he was son of Nicholas Waln (a minister and First Purchaser of a thousand acres in Pennsylvania); Mary was the mother of eight children.

Mary (Pace) (Weston) Waring (1712–1766): born Southwark, England; her father had a prosperous linen drapery business; he was not very active in the meeting in early years but was later a MM treasurer; she was a minister since at least 1735, age twenty-three; a representative to QM; "She was a Woman of an open, generous, & charitable Disposition, a lover of Truth, & the Friends of it, & was much beloved by them"; she married at age twenty-nine in 1741 (1) Daniel Weston (1707–1755) of London; he was a cooper and wealthy merchant; he was representative to YM, an elder, member of Meeting for Sufferings; she married 1765 (2) Jeremiah Waring (1715/16–1791) of Wandsworth, Surrey; he was independently wealthy; "having a competence for his own limited desires, he never embarked in trade on his own accounts"; he was an elder, clerk of London YM, 1754, 1759, 1769; Mary gave birth to five children, but only one survived to adulthood.

Abigail (Craven) (Boles) Watson (1684–1752): born Limerick, Ireland; father's occupation unknown; she had "more learning than some others of our sex"; a minister since 1712, age twenty-eight; "many were Comforted and edified by her Ministry, which was not with the enticing Words of Mans Wisdom, but in the demonstration of the power; in which she was made as a Sharp Threshing Instrument against all undue Liberty, yet Comfortable to the Mourners in Zion & heavy hearted"; "One of the few nurceing Mothers that Our Israel is favoured wth . . . I Esteem'd her one of Our first rank female warriors"; she married at age thirty-five in 1719 (1) widower John Boles (1661–1731) of Woodhouse, near Cashel, County Tipperary, Ireland; he was a substantial property-owner and landlord; he was clerk of Cashel meeting, which was held at his house; she married 1735 (2) widower Samuel Watson (1685–1762) of Killconner, County Carlow, Ireland; he was a gentleman landowner, "his Circomstances it being very Considerable in ye world"; he was an elder; Abigail was childless but a stepmother to at least twelve children.

Elizabeth (?) Webb (1663–1727): of Gloucestershire, England; Anglican parents; father's occupation unknown; she was convinced at age nineteen; unknown when she became a minister, but since at least 1697; "was concerned that all might see to the exercise of their minds, how the same was employed in shewing how that man's mind in Paradise before the Fall was exercised only on heavenly things, and the same exercise should all be found in who come to the regeneration by Jesus Christ . . . She was exceedingly notable in prayer"; "a Woman Extraordinarily gifted & . . . thoroughly furnished for the Work of the Gospel"; she married Richard Webb (1656–1720) (formerly of Gloucestershire, England, then Birmingham, Pennsylvania); they immigrated with their family to Pennsylvania in 1700 after her religious visit to America; he was a yeoman and prospered moderately; he was a Pennsylvania assemblyman, county assessor, justice of the peace; he was disciplined by MM for minor misbehavior but served as representative to QM and trustee of meeting burial ground; Elizabeth was the mother of ten children.

Elizabeth (Duckworth) Whartnaby (d. 1734): of Southwark, England; her father was a carpenter; she kept a shop in London, England; a minister since at least 1700; she was "an Elderly Woman, & Widow . . . weakly & afflicted with lameness & Rheumatism . . . was Sound & lively in Testimony" when she visited Ireland in 1728; married 1712 Edward Whartnaby (d. ca. 1715) of London; he was a joiner and merchant; they immigrated to Pennsylvania ca. 1712; Elizabeth, as a widow in Philadelphia, "kept a small shop in Market street, for a living" advertising "genuine Spirit of Venice Treacle, truly and only prepared by her" for sale; she was childless.

Esther (Canby) (Stapler) White (1700–1777): born Abington, Pennsylvania; her father moved the family to Solebury, Bucks County; he was in the milling business; he was also a justice of the peace and Pennsylvania assemblyman as well as a minister, clerk of MM, overseer, and elder; she was a minister in 1732, representative to QM, appointed to write epistles to YM; she married 1720 (1) John Stapler (d. 1734) of Bucks County, Pennsylvania; he was disciplined for excessive drinking but made acknowledgment, did little meeting activity; she married 1735 (2) John White (d. ca. 1768); he was a minister, representative to QM; they moved to Wilmington, Delaware; Esther was the mother of eight children.

Elizabeth (Scot) Wilkinson (1712–1771): born Use-bridge-end, Cumberland, England; father's occupation unknown; her parents died when she was young, and she was brought up by Quakers; she was a minister in 1760; married 1750 Jonathan Wilkinson (1703–1779) of Cockermouth, Cumberland, England; his occupation is unknown; he was an elder and was regularly appointed as representative to QM; Elizabeth was the mother of three children.

Rachel (Wilson) Wilson (1720–1775): born Kendal, Westmorland, England; her grandfather and father were tanners; a family "long highly respectable amongst Friends"; her mother was a preacher; her father was active in MM and QM; she was a minister at age eighteen, in 1738; "To a fine figure, and striking presence, she was gifted with a clear, distinct voice, and all the pathos of pure, unstudied eloquence"; her preaching was admired by George Whitefield and people of all classes; she married 1740 Isaac Wilson (1714/15–1785) of Kendal; he was a shearman-dyer and "founded the woollen business in Kendal about 1740"; he was an elder, a minister late in life, clerk of London YM 1778; he was appointed to London YM committee in 1761 to visit meetings throughout England; Rachel was the mother of ten children.

Sarah (Goodwin) Worrell (d. 1755): born Llandewi-Brefi, Cardiganshire, Wales; immigrated with her childhood family in 1708 to settle in Edgmont, Chester County, Pennsylvania; father was probably a farmer; her four siblings were ministers; she was a preacher in 1723; Sarah "was an Ancient Friend" when she visited Ireland in 1753 and "was very unwell mostly since she came"; she died there in 1755; she married 1714 widower John Worrell (1655–1745) of Middletown, later Edgmont, Pennsylvania; he was a yeoman and had the highest tax rate for his community between 1715 and 1740; he was county assessor, town constable, a Pennsylvania assemblyman; he was disciplined several times by MM but still was active; Sarah was the mother of eight children and was granted her certificate to visit the British Isles, "having the Consent of her children."

SOURCES: Among the sources consulted were the Chester County Tax Records, 1715–1800, Chester County Archives and Record Services, West Chester, Pennsylvania; (London Yearly Meeting) Testimonies concerning Deceased Ministers, vols. 1–3, LRSF; Irish Yearly Meeting Testimonies, FHLD; Cork, Ireland, Ministers' Visits, 1708–1877, FHLD; DQB; "Record of Friends Travelling in Ireland, 1656–1765," *JFHS* 10 (October 1913); Heiss, *Quaker Biographical Sketches; Piety Promoted;* vols. 2 and 3; Jenkins, *The Records and Recollections of James Jenkins;* "John Kelsall Diary," LRSF; Devonshire House (England) Monthly Meeting minutes, vol. 3, 1707–1727, LRSF; Tabitha Hornor to Abigail Watson, 5mo.23.1737, and 9mo.20.1741, Tabitha Hornor to Samuel Watson, 6mo.24.1733, Portfolio 3.B40, FHLD; "Diary of Deborah Morris, 1772," FHLSC; "Testimony of Gunpowder Monthly Meeting," in Ann Moore, "MS Journal of visits to Meetings, from Md. to Pa., N.Y. & N.E., 1756–1758; in Md. and Va., 1760; to Gt. Britain, 1760–1762; to Pa. & N.Y., 1778," FHLSC; Chester (Pennsylvania) Monthly Meeting minutes, 1681–1760, FHLSC; Yorkshire (England) Quarterly Meeting minutes, 1698–1733, microfilm, FHLSC; Mary Weston to Israel Pemberton Jr., 8mo.25.1752, Pemberton Papers, 8: 70–71, HSP; James Bowden, *The history of the Society of Friends in America* (London, 1850–54), vol. 2; Rev. John Douglas Brixton, *Memoir of the late Mrs. Julia Adelaide C. Duncan of Portglenone, Ireland* (London, 1890); Grubb, *Quakers in Ireland 1654–1800;* Hallowell, ed., *James and Lucretia Mott, Life and Letters;* Jordan, ed., *Colonial Families of Philadelphia,* vols. 1 and 2; Leadbeater, *Biographical Notices of Members of the Society of Friends, who were Resident in Ireland;* Norman Penney, ed., *Pen Pictures of London Yearly Meeting, 1789–1833, Being Extracts from the Notes of Richard Cockin, James Jenkins, and others* (London, 1930); Rev. Calbraith Bourn Perry, *The Perrys of Rhode Island and Tales of Silver Creek* (New York, 1913); Clarence V. Roberts, *Early Friends Families of Upper Bucks* (Philadelphia, 1925); *Genealogies of Pennsylvania Families: From the Pennsylvania Magazine of History and Biography* (Baltimore, 1981); Soderlund, "Women's Authority in Pennsylvania and New Jersey Quaker Meetings, 1680–1760," *WMQ,* 3d ser., vol. 44 (1987); John Somervell, ed., *Some Westmorland Wills, 1686–1738* (Kendal, England, 1928).

Appendix 2

PARTIAL LIST OF COLONIAL AMERICAN QUAKER WOMEN MINISTERS ACTIVE 1700–1775

NAME	HUSBAND	BIRTH/DEATH	FLOURISHED	MEETING LOCATION	BIRTHPLACE
Anderson, Margaret	William Anderson	d. 1770		Pa.	
Anthony, Alice			1708	R.I.	
Anthony, Patience			1724	R.I.	
Ashbridge, Elizabeth* née **Sampson**	(1)? (2)? Sullivan (3) Aaron Ashbridge	1713–1755		N.J., Pa.	England
Ashton, Mary		d. 1759		Pa.	
Austin, Sarah			1708	N.H.	
Austin, Sarah née **Field**	Nicholas Austin	d. 1764		Pa.	
Baker, Keziah			1743	N.Y.	
Baker, Phebe			1702	N.J. or Pa.	
Ball, Catharine née **Lester**	John Ball	ca. 1691–1764		Pa.	Pa.
Ballinger, Hannah			1748	Va.	
Barker, Patience			1742	N.J.	
Benezet, Joyce née **Marriott**	Anthony Benezet	d. 1786		Pa., Del.	
Bennett, Rebecca née **Fincher**	Joseph Bennett	1708–1757		Pa.	Pa.
Berry, Mary	James Berry	1731–1806		Md.	Pa.

NAME	HUSBAND	BIRTH/ DEATH	FLOURISHED	MEETING LOCATION	BIRTHPLACE
Bevan, Barbara*	unmarried	1682–1705		Pa.	Wales
Bevan, Eleanor	widow	d. 1744		Pa.	
Biles, Jane* née **Boid**	(1) Thomas Atkinson (2) William Biles	d. 1709		Pa.	England
Blunstone, Phebe		1666–1749		Pa.	England
Bolton, Elizabeth née **Jones**	Everard Bolton	d. 1707		Pa.	England
Bolton, Sarah			1754	Pa.	
Boone, Deborah née **Howell**	George Boone	1691–1759		Pa.	Pa.
Borden, Hope			1707	R.I.	
Brayton, Patience[†] née **Greene**	Preserved Brayton	1734–1794		Mass.	R.I.
Brientnall, Jane née **Blanchard**	David Brientnall	ca. 1656–1725		Pa.	England
Brooke, Mary née **Matthews**	Roger Brooke	1734–1808		Md.	Md.
Brown, Deborah			1745	Mass.	
Brown, Elizabeth			1764	Pa.	
Brown, Mary			1779	N.J.	
Brown, Rachel née **Needham**		1728–1780		Pa.	Del.
Brown, Susanna née **Churchman**	William Brown	1701–1790		Pa.	Pa.
Bryan, Rebecca née **Collins**	Thomas Bryan	d. 1747		N.J.	
Buckman, Agnes			1728	Pa.	
Buffin[g]ton, Isabel	Benjamin Buffin[g]ton		1756	Mass.	
Bull, Ann[‡] née **Cleaton**	(1) Governor Nicholas Easton (2) Governor Henry Bull	1647–1728		R.I.	England
Bunting, Alice	John Bunting	1696–1755		N.J.	
Bunting, Rachel			1702	N.J.	
Burdsall, Elizabeth		d. 1772		N.J.	
Burley, Elizabeth			1751	Va.	
Burr, Jane			1757	N.J.	
Buzby, Hannah			1775	N.J.	
Caldwell, Betty née **Pierce**	Vincent Caldwell	1680–1757		Pa., Del.	England
Cannon, Mary	Jeremiah Cannon	d. 1760		N.C.	

NAME	HUSBAND	BIRTH/ DEATH	FLOURISHED	MEETING LOCATION	BIRTHPLACE
Carleton, Hannah née **Howell**	(1) Robert Roberts (2) Thomas Carleton	1689–1758		Pa.	Pa.
Carpenter, Hannah née **Hardiman**	Samuel Carpenter	ca. 1645–1728		Pa.	Wales
Cary, Sarah			1751	Pa.	
Chace, Hannah			1756	Mass.	
Chace, Sarah			1730	Mass.	
Chalkley, Martha née **Betterton**	Thomas Chalkley	ca. 1677–1712		Pa.	England
Champion, Esther* née **Palmer**	Richard Champion	1678–1714		N.Y.	N.Y.
Chandler, Ann			1766	Pa.	
Chase, Mary			1756	N.Y.	
Churchman, Margaret née **Brown**	John Churchman	1707–1770		Pa.	Pa.
Clare, Esther* née **Peacock**	William Clare	ca. 1675–1742		Pa.	England
Clark, Mary			1724	R.I.	
Clemens, Abigail			1723	N.Y.	
Cocke, Sarah			1740	N.Y.	
Coggeshall, Martha née **Sankee**	(1) Daniel Medlicott (2) James Kite (3) Jonathan Coggeshall	ca. 1660–1734		Pa.	England
Collins, Comfort* née **Stanyan**	(1) Jonathan Hoag (2) Tristram Collins	1711–1816		N.H.	N.H.
Comley, Mary			1767	Md.	
Cook, Charity† née **Wright**	Isaac Cook	1745–1822		S.C.	Md.
Cook (Cock), Hannah			1743	N.Y.	
Cook, Margaret née **Williams**	Stephen Cook	1734–1822		Pa.	Md.
Cooper, Esther	James Cooper	d. 1706		Pa.	
Cooper, Hannah* née **Dent**	Joseph Cooper Jr.	d. 1754		N.J.	England
Coperthwaite, Sarah	John Coperthwaite		1712	N.J.	
Cowgell, Rachel			pre-1770	Del.	
Cox, Mary	William Cox	ca. 1721–1790		Md.	England
Croasdale, Grace née **Heaton**	Jeremiah Croasdale	1703–1769		Pa.	Pa.
Daniel, Elizabeth	James Daniel	1709–1760		N.J.	

NAME	HUSBAND	BIRTH/DEATH	FLOURISHED	MEETING LOCATION	BIRTHPLACE
Daves, Priscilla née **Thomas**	Abraham Daves	ca. 1726–1772		Pa.	Pa.
David, Eleanor	Meredith David	d. 1734		Pa.	
Daws, Sarah			1725	Pa.	
Day, Elizabeth	John Day		pre-1762	N.J.	
Dean, Lydia née **Gilpin**	William Dean	1699–1750		Pa., Del.	Pa.
Dennis, Ruth			1730	N.J.	
Dodge, Phebe* née **Willets**	(1) Adam Mott (2) Tristram Dodge	1699–1782		N.Y.	N.Y.
Dow, Mary			1720	N.H.	
Downing, Jane née **Albin**	Thomas Downing		1756	Pa.	
Dunghill, Sarah			1760	Pa.	
Durborough, Elizabeth née **Taylor**	Hugh Durborough	ca. 1660–1722		Pa.	England
Easton, Dorcas née **Perry**	John Easton Jr.		1735	R.I.	Mass.
Eavitt (Ezets), Ann			1739	Pa.	
Ellis, Jane née **Hughes**	Thomas Ellis	1683–1772		Pa.	Wales
Ellis, Margaret*	unmarried	d. 1765		Pa.	Wales
Ellis, Sage		1678–1761		Pa.	Wales
Elwall, Jane			1735	Pa.	
Ely, Phebe née **Canby**	(1) Robert Smith (2) Hugh Ely	1699–1774		Pa.	Pa.
Emlen, Mary née **Heath**	George Emlen	ca. 1692–1777		Pa.	England
Estaugh, Mary née **Lawson**	James Estaugh		1707	Pa., Del.	England
Estes, Patience			1757	Mass.	
Evans, Elizabeth	William Evans	d. 1748		N.J.	
Evans, Emme	Daniel Evans		1724	Pa.	
Evans, Hannah née **Nicholls (Nicholas)**	William Evans	d. 1747		Pa.	Ireland
Evans, Mary	Owen Evans	ca. 1695–1769		Pa.	Pa.
Evans, Ruth née **Morgan**	Nathan Evans		1760	Pa., Del.	Pa.
Farquhar, Rachel née **Wright**	William Farquhar Jr.	1737–1777		Md.	Ireland

NAME	HUSBAND	BIRTH/ DEATH	FLOURISHED	MEETING LOCATION	BIRTHPLACE
Farrington, Kezia			1768	N.Y.	
Ffell, Elizabeth			1731	Pa.	
Ferris, Phebe née **Beecher**	Benjamin Ferris	b. 1708	1756	N.Y.	
Fish, Ruth			1724	R.I.	
Fisher, Grace	(1) Samuel Mason (2) John Fisher		1747	N.J., Pa.	
Foster, Hannah née **Core**	William Foster	1710–1777		N.J.	N.J.
Foulke, Ann née **Williams**	Hugh Foulke	1693–1773		Pa.	Wales
Freeborn, Susanna			1704	R.I.	
Fry, Ruth	unmarried	d. 1733		R.I.	
Galloway, Ann	Samuel Galloway		1699	Md.	
Garrett, Ann			1762	Pa.	
Garrett, Jane	Samuel Garrett	d. 1736		Pa.	
Garrett, Sarah			1750	Pa.	
Gaunt, Ann née **Ridgway**	Hananiah Gauntt	b. 1710	1787	N.J.	N.J.
Gibbons, Ann née **Pierce**	James Gibbons	1686–1753		Pa.	Pa.
Gibbons, Jane née **Sheward**	James Gibbons	ca. 1702–1798		Pa.	England
Gidley, Elizabeth			1750	Mass.	
Gifford, Susanna			1745	Mass.	
Goodson, Sarah			1702	Pa. or N.J.	
Gould, Lydia			1722	New Eng.	
Gray, Naomi née **Walley**	(1) ? Berry (2) George Gray	d. 1709		Md., Pa.	England
Green, Mary			1750	N.H.	
Griffin, Mary née **Palmer**	(1) William Moore (2) ? Griffin	ca. 1710–1810		N.Y.	Ct.
Griffith, Alice	Hugh Griffith	d. 1749		Pa.	
Griffith, Elizabeth			1702	Pa. or N.J.	
Hadly, Phebe		d. 1769		Pa. or N.J.	
Haig, Mary née **Masters**	William Haig	ca. 1679–1718		Antigua, N.C.	
Hales, Susanna née **Greenwood**	(1) John Halliday (2) Joseph Hales	ca. 1704–1753		Del.	Del.

NAME	HUSBAND	BIRTH/ DEATH	FLOURISHED	MEETING LOCATION	BIRTHPLACE
Hall, Mary n-e **Brown**	William Hall		1734	N.H., R.I.	
Hallowell, Margaret			1743	Pa.	
Hammons, Lowry née **Lewis**	William Hammons		1738	Pa., Del.	
Hammons, Lydia née **Roberts**	(1) Benjamin Mendenhall Jr. (2) William Hammons	ca. 1694–1752		Pa., Del.	Wales
Hardiman, Rebecca			1702	Pa. or N.J.	
Harker, Grace	Adam Harker	1669–1747		Pa.	England
Harper, Eliphal* née **Smith**	(1) Edward Perry Jr. (2) Stephen Harper	d. 1747		Mass., Pa., Del.	
Harris, Martha			1758	Va., Pa.	
Harrison, Hannah née **Norris**		d. 1774		Pa.	
Harvey, Ann			1758	Pa. or N.J.	
Harvey, Elizabeth née **Woolman**	(1) Nathaniel Payne (2) Robert Hunt (3) John Harvey	1685–1755		N.J.	N.J.
Harvey, Rebecca* née **Owen**	(1) Isaac Minshall (2) Job Harvey	b. 1687	1751	Pa.	Pa.
Hathaway, Hepzibah			1717	New Eng.	
Haydock, Elizabeth	James Haydock	ca. 1737–1763		N.J.	
Hearne, Sarah		d. 1727		Pa.	
Henny, Sarah			1731	N.H.	
Hibberd, Mary			1755	Pa.	
Hill, Hannah née **Lloyd**	(1) John Delavall (2) Richard Hill	1666–1727		Pa.	Wales
Hinton, Susanna née **Beal**	William Hinton		1749	Del., Pa.	
Hoag, Hannah		d. 1759		N.H.	
Holland, Mary			1733	Pa.	
Holland, Ruth	Richard Holland		1774	Va., Md.	
Hooton, Elizabeth			1714	Pa.	
Hopkins, Sarah			1750	N.J.	
Horne, Elizabeth	Edward Horne		1723	Pa.	England
Hornor, Mary	Isaac Hornor	1736–1776	N.J.	N.J.	
Hoskins, Jane* née **Fenn**	Joseph Hoskins	1694–1764		Pa.	England
Humphreys, Hannah		d. 1750		Pa.	

NAME	HUSBAND	BIRTH/ DEATH	FLOURISHED	MEETING LOCATION	BIRTHPLACE
Hunt, Esther			1775	N.C.	
Hurford, Hannah	(1) ? Serman	1690–1763		Pa.	England
née **Heath**	(2) Samuel Hurford				
Iden, Hannah	John Iden		1726	Pa.	
née **Simcock**					
Ireland, Ruth		1699–1757		N.J.	
Jackson, Elizabeth	(1) Isaac Ricketts	d. 1704		Pa.	England
née **Palmer**	(2) Ralph Jackson				
Jacobs, Mary		d. 1730		N.J.	
James, Dinah	(1) ? Brown	1699–1766		Pa.	Pa.
née **Churchman**	(2) Mordecai James				
James, Mary*	Thomas James	d. ca. 1776		Pa.	Wales
née **Goodwin**					
Janney, Elizabeth		d. 1770		Del.	
Janney, Sarah			1768	Va.	
Jenkins, Abigail	Stephen Jenkins	1679–1750		Pa.	England
née **Pemberton**					
Jenkins, Mehitabel[†]	Elijah Jenkins	1731–1815		N.H.	(now
née **Weymouth**					Maine)
Jenkins, Sarah			1772	N.H.	
Jenkinson, Hannah			1742	Md., Pa.	England
Jennings, Ann	Samuel Jennings		1702	N.J.	
Jerman, Margaret	John Jerman	d. 1740		Pa.	
Jessup, Ann[†]			1775	N.C.	
Jones, Elizabeth			1750	Pa.	
Jones, Hannah		d. 1738		Pa.	
Jones, Margaret	(1) ? Hillborn	d. 1743		Pa.	
	(2) John Jones				
Jones, Mary	Edward Jones	d. 1726		Pa.	
Jones, Rebecca[†]	unmarried	1739–1817		Pa.	Pa.
Jones, Ruth			1730	Pa.	
Kay (Key), Elizabeth*	John Kay	d. 1713		N.J.	
Kinsman, Hannah	John Kinsman	1660–1718		Pa.	England
née **Simcock**					
Kirby, Abigail			1742	Mass.	
Kirk, Mary		d. 1773		Va.	
Knight, Mary	Isaac Knight Sr.	1682–1769		Pa.	Pa.
née **Carver**					

NAME	HUSBAND	BIRTH/ DEATH	FLOURISHED	MEETING LOCATION	BIRTHPLACE
Knowles, Sarah née **Lee**	Francis Knowles	ca. 1684–1735		Pa.	England
Knox, Sarah			1765	Del.	
Lapham, Hannah	Joshua Lapham		1763	R.I.	
Lay, Sarah	Benjamin Lay	ca. 1677–1735		Pa.	England
Lea, Hannah née **Webb**	John Lea		1714	Pa.	England
Lee, Eleanor			1766	Pa.	
Levis, Elizabeth née **Reed**	William Levis	ca. 1694–1775		Pa., Del.	
Lewis, Margaret* née **Thomas**	Nathan Lewis	1712–1789		Pa.	Pa.
Lewis, Sarah	Thomas Lewis		1753	Pa.	
Lightfoot, Katherine			1764	Pa.	
Lightfoot, Mary			1757	Pa.	
Lightfoot, Susanna* née **Hudson**	(1) Joseph Hatton (2) Thomas Lightfoot	1720–1781		Pa.	Ireland
Lippincott, Elizabeth née **Wills**	Freedom Lippincott	1697–1740		N.J.	N.J.
Lippincott, Rachel		1699–1779		N.J.	
McVaugh, Sarah	James McVaugh	d. 1738		Pa.	
Marriott, Mary	(1) Cadwallader Foulke (2) Thomas Marriott	d. 1747		Pa.	
Marshall, Mary née **Hunt**	Abraham Marshall	d. 1769		Pa.	
Mather, Elizabeth	Joseph Mather	d. 1730		Pa.	
Mendenhall, Charity née **Beeson**	Mordecai Mendenhall		1735	Pa., Va.	
Mendenhall, Martha		1713–1794		Md.	
Mifflin, Mary née **Pusey**	(1) Joseph Husband[s] (2) Daniel Mifflin	ca. 1743–1823		Pa., Va., Md.	Pa.
Miles, Margaret	Samuel Miles		1715	Pa.	
Milhouse, Sarah	Thomas Milhouse	ca. 1701–1775		Pa.	
Miller, Catharine née **Lightfoot**	James Miller	d. 1729		Pa.	Ireland
Miller, Margaret	Samuel Miller	1683–1765		Pa.	Ireland
Miller, Phebe née **Massey**	George Miller		1760	Pa.	

NAME	HUSBAND	BIRTH/ DEATH	FLOURISHED	MEETING LOCATION	BIRTHPLACE
Millner, Sarah née **Baker**	? Millner	ca. 1673–1715		Pa.	England
Mitchell, Mary née **Callender**	Joseph Mitchell	1732–1810		R.I., Mass.	R.I.
Mitchenor, Ann			1775	Pa.	
Moore, Ann* née **Herbert**	Walter Moore	1710–1783		Pa., Va., Md.	Pa.
Moore, Ann née **Starr**	James Moore	1718–1761		Pa.	Pa.
Moore, Mary née **Wildman**	(1) Thomas Atkinson (2) James Moore	1720–1766		Pa.	Pa.
Moore, Rebecca			1770	Pa.	
Morgan, Elizabeth* née **Roberts**	Daniel Morgan	1688–1777		Pa.	Wales
Morris, Elizabeth* née **Hudson**	Anthony Morris	1722–1783		Pa.	Pa.
Morris, Sarah*	unmarried	1703/4–1775		Pa.	Pa.
Morris, Susanna* née **Heath**	Morris Morris	1682–1755		Pa.	England
Mott, Elizabeth		d. 1770		N.J.	
Mott, Johanna	Jacob Mott	d. 1728		R.I.	
Murfin, Sarah née **Bunting**	William Murfin	ca. 1686–1762		N.J.	
Newcom[b]e, Mary	Richard Newcom[b]e		1706	N.J.	England
Newlin, Ann			1761	Pa.	
Nichols, Mary	Thomas Nichols	ca. 1680–1770		Pa., Del.	England
Nixon, Elizabeth née **Toms**	Zachary Nixon		1768	N.C.	
Norton, Elizabeth			1765	N.C.	
Norton, Lydia			1723	N.H.	
Norton, Sarah			1723	N.H.	
Nutt, Elizabeth			1768	Pa.	
Pancoast, Hannah née **Scattergood**	William Pancoast		1726	N.J.	
Parsons, Ann			1702	Pa. or N.J.	
Parsons, Ann née **Chapman**	John Parsons	1676–1732		Pa.	England
Paxon, Abigail née **Pownall**	William Paxon	1675–1747		Pa.	

NAME	HUSBAND	BIRTH/ DEATH	FLOURISHED	MEETING LOCATION	BIRTHPLACE
Paxon, Mary			1740	Pa.	
Peaslee, Mary			1766	N.H.	
Peirce, Ann		d. 1747		Pa., Del.	
Pennell, Alice			1727	Pa.	
Pennell, Mary* née **Morgan**	John Pennell	1678–1764		Pa.	Wales
Pennock, Elizabeth née **Widdowfield**	Samuel Pennock	ca. 1710–1755		Pa.	Pa.
Penquite, Agnes née **Sharp**	John Penquite	d. 1758		Pa.	England
Petell, Martha			1733	Mass.	
Phipps, Ann	John Phipps	1681–1743		Pa.	England
Phipps, Sarah née **Binfield?**	Joseph Phipps	1643–1725		Pa.	England
Pierce, Mary			1728	Pa.	
Pike, Abigail née **Overman**	John Pike	b. 1709	1765	Va., N.C.	N.C.
Pleasants, Jane	(1) Samuel Tucker (2) John Pleasants	d. 1708		Va.	
Porter, Margaret			1773	Pa.	
Potts, Joan		d. ca. 1740		Pa.	
Potts, Rachel	Thomas Potts	ca. 1695–1758		Pa., N.J.	
Powel, Gwin			1702	Pa. or N.J.	
Preston, Margaret née **Burton**	(1) Josiah Langdale (2) Samuel Preston	ca. 1684–1742		Pa.	England
Prior (Pryor), Mary			1736	N.Y.	
Proud, Hannah			1734	R.I.	
Pyle, Ann née **Webb**	Nicholas Pyle		1718	Pa.	
Pyle, Sarah			1736	Pa.	
Rasin, Mary			1729	Md.	
Redman, Mercy née **Davis**	Thomas Redman	1722–1778		N.J.	N.J.
Reed, Deborah			1740		
Reese, Rebecca	Edward Reese	d. 1733		Pa.	Wales
Reeve, Hannah			1768	N.J.	
Richardson, Ann			1716	R.I.	

NAME	HUSBAND	BIRTH/ DEATH	FLOURISHED	MEETING LOCATION	BIRTHPLACE
Richardson, Elizabeth			1721	Pa.	
Ridgway, Phebe	Thomas Ridgway	d. 1752		N.J.	
Rigbie, Sarah			1766	Pa.	
Roberts, Ann* née Lewis	(1) James Williams (2) Henry Bennett (3) Rowland Roberts	1678–1750		Pa.	Wales
Roberts, Martha née Foulke	(1) William Edwards (2) John Roberts	1716–1781		Pa.	Pa.
Roberts, Rebekah			1775	N.J.	
Rodman, Hannah			1724	R.I.	
Rodman, Patience			1724	R.I.	
Rutledge, Mary	William Rutledge	d. 1725		Pa.	England
Schofield (Scholefield), Ann			1750	Pa.	
Seaman (Simmons), Rachel	Nathaniel Seaman		1718	N.Y.	
Seaton, Jane	unmarried	d. 1738		N.J.	Ireland
Sharp, Mary			1762	N.J.	
Shipley, Elizabeth* née Levis	William Shipley	1690–1777		Pa., Del.	Pa.
Shotwell, Elizabeth	(1) Joseph Parker (2) ? Shotwell	1677–1759		N.J.	N.J.
Shotwell, Sarah	Joseph Shotwell	1715–1759		N.J.	N.Y.
Shove, Lydia			1733	Mass.	
Sibthorp, Ann* née Waln	(1) James Dillworth (2) Christopher Sibthorp	1654–1710		Pa.	England
Simcock, Jane			1746	N.J., Pa.	
Simcock, Mary née Waln	John Simcock	d. 1771		N.J., Pa.	
Simpkins, Mary		d. 1770		N.J.	
Sirkite (Sizquite), Sarah			1700	N.J. or Pa.	
Slade, Mary			1733	New Eng.	
Slocum, Mary			1704	New Eng.	
Small, Elizabeth née Bettson	Benjamin Small	1666–1717		Va.	Va.
Smith, Eleanor née Dolby	John Smith	1653–1708		Pa.	England
Smith, Elizabeth		1699–1747		N.J.	
Smith, Elizabeth*	unmarried	1724–1772		N.J.	N.J.
Smith, Hannah née Logan	John Smith	1720–1761		N.J., Pa.	Pa.
Smith, Margaret			1775	R.I.	

NAME	HUSBAND	BIRTH/ DEATH	FLOURISHED	MEETING LOCATION	BIRTHPLACE
Smith, Mary née **Murfin**	Daniel Smith	1674–1746		N.J.	England
Smith, Ruth			1709	Mass.	
Sole (Soule), Lydia			1738	N.Y.	
Somers, Hannah	John Somers	ca. 1667–1738		N.J.	England
Southwick, Elizabeth			1771	R.I.	
Southworth, Lydia			1761	New Eng.	
Speakman, Phebe[†] née **Schofield**	(1) Nathan Yarnall (2) Micajah Speakman	1739–1828		Pa.	Pa.
Stanyan, Ann	James Stanyan		1717	N.H.	
Starbuck, Mary née **Coffin**	Nathaniel Starbuck Jr.	1645–1718		Mass.	Mass.
Starr, Eunice			1773	Pa.	
Stedham, Mary			1768	S.C.	
Stevens, Elizabeth née **Johns**	John Stevens	1694–1772		Md., Pa.	Md.
Stevenson, Mary		ca. 1730–1788		N.J.	
Stockdale, Phebe	William Stockdale	d. 1738		Pa.	
Swett, Hannah			1750	N.H.	
Swett, Mary[†]	Benjamin Swett		1775	N.J.	
Sykes, Joanna née **Murfen**	John Sykes	ca. 1683–1772		N.J.	N.J.
Teague, Elizabeth née **Janney**	Pentecost Teague	d. 1728		Pa.	England
Test, Elizabeth	Francis Test	ca. 1708–1772		N.J.	N.J.
Thatcher, Sarah			1775	Pa.	
Thomas, Phebe née **Wardell**	(1) Thomas Lancaster (2) Samuel Thomas		1754	Pa.	Wales
Thurston, Amy			1771	New Eng.	
Tibbets, Rose		d. 1755		N.H.	
Toms (Tombs), Rebecca	Francis Toms	d. 1754		N.C.	
Townsend, Elizabeth			1726	Pa.	
Townsend, Millicent née **Somers**	Richard Townsend	1685–1762		N.J.	Pa.
Trimble, Phebe	William Trimble	ca. 1717–1784		Pa.	
Tucker, Ruth			1706	Pa.	
Tyson, Sarah	John Tyson	d. 1768		Pa.	

NAME	HUSBAND	BIRTH/ DEATH	FLOURISHED	MEETING LOCATION	BIRTHPLACE
Vandewoestyne, Katharine		d. 1704		Pa.	Holland
Varman, Abigail née Sandwith	Hattil Varman	1689–1760		Pa.	Ireland
Waln, Ann née Heath	Richard Waln		1715	Pa.	England
Waln, Mary* née Hayes	(1) Evan Lewis (2) Richard Waln	d. 1753		Pa.	Pa.
Walmsley, Ruth née Miller	(1) Elisha Kirk (2) Thomas Walmsley	1752–1798		Pa.	Md.
Way, Phebe née Titus	John Way		1758	N.Y.	
Webb, Elizabeth*	Richard Webb	1663–1727		Pa.	England
Webster, Ann née Smith	William Webster	1730–1769		Pa.	Pa.
West, Hannah			1767	Del.	
Whartnaby, Elizabeth* née Duckworth	Edward Whartnaby	d. 1734		Pa.	England
White, Esther* née Canby	(1) John Stapler (2) John White	1700–1777		Pa., Del.	Pa.
Widdowfield, Ann			1746	Pa.	
Wildman, Alice			1714	New Eng.	
Wiley, Abigail née Lightfoot	Joseph Wiley	1694–1767		Pa.	Ireland
Wilkins, Mary	Thomas Wilkins	d. 1749		N.J.	
Wilkins, Susannah		d. 1731/32		N.J.	
Willets, Rachel	Thomas Willets		1761	Pa.	
Williams, Elinor	Edward Williams	d. 1749		Pa.	
Williams, Joanna	George Williams	d. 1728		N.J.	
Williams, Mary	George Williams	d. 1739		N.J.	
Williamson, Sarah	John Williamson		1735	Pa.	
Willis, Jane			1771	N.Y.	
Willits, Margaret			1749	N.Y.	
Willitts, Mary		d. 1713		N.Y.	
Wilson, Grace			1736	Pa.	
Wilson, Hannah			1775	Pa.	
Wing, Mary née Perry			1729	Mass.	Mass.
Wood, Keziah			1757	N.Y.	

NAME	HUSBAND	BIRTH/ DEATH	FLOURISHED	MEETING LOCATION	BIRTHPLACE
Wood, Martha née **Lloyd**	Thomas Wood	ca. 1688–1735		Pa.	Wales
Wood, Peace			1735	New Eng.	
Worrell, Sarah* née **Goodwin**	John Worrell	d. 1755		Pa.	Wales
Wright, Rachel			1768	S.C.	
Wright, Rebecca†	Nathan Wright	ca. 1737–1811		N.J.	
Wyatt, Elizabeth née **Tomlinson**	Bartholomew Wyatt	1706–1749/50		N.J., Pa.	
Yarnall (Yarnell), Dorothy			fl. 1727	Pa.	
Yarnall, Sarah		1711–1795		Pa.	

*One of the transatlantic ministers, 1700–1775.

†A minister who travelled across the Atlantic on religious service after 1775.

‡An English Quaker missionary to America before 1700.

SOURCES: Among the sources consulted were the "Dictionary of Quaker Biography"; Heiss, *Quaker Biographical Sketches;* John Smith, *The Lives of the Ministers of the Gospel among the People called Quakers;* Philadelphia Yearly Meeting of Ministers and Elders minutes, New England Yearly Meeting of Ministers and Elders minutes, and some New Hampshire, Massachusetts, Rhode Island, New York, New Jersey, Pennsylvania, Virginia, and South Carolina monthly meeting records; lists of ministers visiting New England Yearly Meeting, or Nantucket; "A List of Friends' Names Eminent for their Piety and Virtue Since the First Settlement in America"; and ministers' journals.

Note: This is a partial list of colonial American female preachers: forty-eight of the sixty-eight American monthly meeting records were not examined, including those for Maryland, Delaware, and North Carolina, as well as others in the above-mentioned colonies.

Appendix 3

THE NUMBER OF DEATHS OF
QUAKER MINISTERS IN LONDON YEARLY MEETING,
COMPILED BY CHARLES HOYLAND

TEN-YEAR PERIODS	MEN	WOMEN	TOTAL
1700–1709	144	43	187
1710–1719	192	73	265
1720–1729	205	108	313
1730–1739	159	88	247
1740–1749	155	102	257
1750–1759	116	102	218
1760–1769	123	95	218
1770–1779	93	95	188
1780–1789	80	73	153
1790–1799	51	55	106
1800–1809	47	47	94
1810–1819	33	61	94

Printed in John S. Rowntree's *Life and Work*
(London, 1908), 252.

Abbreviations

DQB	"Dictionary of Quaker Biography," typescript, at Quaker Collection, Haverford College, and at Library of the Religious Society of Friends, London
FHLD	Friends Historical Library, Dublin
FHLSC	Friends Historical Library, Swarthmore College
FL	William Evans and Thomas Evans, eds., *The Friends' Library Comprising Journals, Doctrinal Treatises, and other Writings of Members of the Religious Society of Friends,* 14 vols. (Philadelphia, 1837–50)
HSP	Historical Society of Pennsylvania, Philadelphia
JFHS	*Journal of the Friends' Historical Society*
LRSF	Library of the Religious Society of Friends, London
PMHB	*Pennsylvania Magazine of History and Biography*
QCHC	Quaker Collection, Haverford College
WMQ	*William and Mary Quarterly*

Notes

Until 1752, Great Britain and the American colonies operated under the Julian calendar. Before the change to the currently used Gregorian calendar, February was the twelfth month and March was the first month of the year. In the endnotes, the Quaker dating will follow the original numbering system. To assist the reader, all dates in the body of the text were converted to their modern equivalents.

INTRODUCTION

1. Sarah Kemble Knight, *The Journal of Madam Knight* (1st ed. 1825; reprint, Boston, 1972), 2. See also Wendy Martin, ed., *Colonial American Travel Narratives* (New York, 1994), 336.

2. Mary Beth Norton, "The Evolution of White Women's Experience in Early America," *American Historical Review* 89 (1984): 593–619, for example, described Quaker women's meetings but omitted mention of their ministerial role. While the existence of eighteenth-century Quaker women ministers has been noted in recent scholarship, discussion of these women typically has been designated as an area for future research or relegated to a chapter of a study on another topic. For example, see Joan M. Jensen, *Loosening the Bonds: Mid-Atlantic Farm Women 1750–1850* (New Haven, Conn., 1986), 145–66; Margaret Hope Bacon, *Mothers of Feminism: The Story of Quaker Women in America* (San Francisco, 1986), 24–41; and Barry Levy, *Quakers and the American Family: British Settlement in the Delaware Valley* (New York, 1988), 193–230. Work on eighteenth-century Quaker women includes excellent articles by Mary Maples Dunn, "Women of Light," in *Women of America: A History,* ed. Carol Ruth Berkin and Mary Beth Norton (Boston, 1979), 114–36; "Saints and Sisters: Congregational and Quaker Women in the Early Colonial Period," in *Women in American Religion,* ed. Janet Wilson James (Philadelphia, 1980), 27–46; and Jean R. Soderlund, "Women's Authority in Pennsylvania and New Jersey Quaker Meetings, 1680–1760," *WMQ,* 3d ser., vol. 44 (1987): 722–49. Mary Maples Dunn pointed to the need for further examination in "The Eighteenth

Century: Latest Light on Women of Light," in *Witnesses for Change: Quaker Women over Three Centuries,* ed. Elisabeth Potts Brown and Susan Mosher Stuard (New Brunswick, N.J., 1989). The creation of a conceptual bridge between seventeenth-century Quaker ecstatic visionaries and Friends' prominence as nineteenth-century reformers, particularly as activists for women's rights, may be aided by an increased awareness of eighteenth-century Quaker female preachers.

3. "The Journals of Esther Palmer, 1704," *JFHS* 6 (1909):139.

4. "A Letter from Elizabeth Webb to Anthony William Boehm," *FL,* 13:171.

5. "Journals of Esther Palmer," 68, 135, 139. For the location of the Indian village of Askiminikansen, see *Handbook of North American Indians,* ed. William C. Sturtevant et al. (Washington, D.C., 1978), 15:241. Thomas Story, a Quaker preacher who was travelling with the women for a few days after they had attended the Virginia Yearly Meeting, described this episode with Governor Nicholson in his journal: see Emily E. Moore, *Travelling with Thomas Story: The Life and Travels of an Eighteenth-Century Quaker* (Letchworth, Eng., 1947), 86–87.

6. Sydney E. Ahlstrom, *A Religious History of the American People* (New Haven, 1972), 209. Recent historians of American religion have suggested "that we attach less importance to Puritanism as the major force in shaping religion in America and more importance to the religious eclecticism that has long been prominent." See Jon Butler, *Awash in a Sea of Faith: Christianizing the American People* (Cambridge, Mass., 1990), 2.

7. "Memoirs of the Life of Catharine Phillips," *FL,* 11:267. The practice of recording the names of those whose ministry was acceptable to their meetings was discontinued by Friends of London Yearly Meeting in 1924. In the eighteenth century, acknowledged ministers met in select meetings with elders (those appointed to assist in the spiritual oversight of preachers). The spoken ministry in meetings for worship was given almost entirely by those whose "gift" had been recorded. "The importance of the influence of ministers and elders in the Society in the eighteenth and early nineteenth centuries can hardly be overemphasised . . ."; but in the twentieth century the ministry came to be more widely shared, and the practice of recording ministers was deemed "anomalous and unnecessary." It was found that the presence of a recorded minister might hinder others from speaking and lay an undue burden on the person. See L. Hugh Doncaster, *Quaker Organisation and Business Meetings* (London, 1958), 22, 52. There are a variety of practices among American Friends, in the wake of nineteenth-century divisions. Yearly meetings belonging to Friends General Conference have either discontinued the practice of recording ministers or left it optional. The Book of Discipline of Baltimore Yearly Meeting, 1962 edition, for example, stated: "We do not set anyone apart whose special duty is to supply the spoken words in our meetings." The orthodox/Gurneyite division of American Friends, however, has adopted the pastoral system in which a pastor is set aside to give whole or part-time service with special responsibility for the conduct of worship. See Seth B. Hinshaw, *The Spoken Ministry Among Friends:*

Three Centuries of Progress and Development (North Carolina Yearly Meeting, 1987), 60, 107.

8. "Elegiac Reflections to the Memory of Rachel Wilson," Row MSS, Book 1, LRSF. The ministers' gallery has been described in many books. The *Guide to the Records of Philadelphia Yearly Meeting*, compiled by Jack Eckert (1989), pointed out that, in most Quaker meeting-houses, there are "slightly raised 'facing' benches at the front; in earlier times, this is where ministers and elders sat," x. J. William Frost, *The Quaker Family in Colonial America: A Portrait of the Society of Friends* (New York, 1973), observed that "normally there was a raised platform or gallery at the front with a bench where the ministers and elders could sit facing the congregation," 36. Richard Bauman, *Let Your Words Be Few: Symbolism of Speaking and Silence among Seventeenth-Century Quakers* (Cambridge, Eng., 1983), 147, suggested that the ministers' gallery, "a long raised platform facing the assembly at the front of the meeting on which the ministers were seated," had its origin in the earlier constructions of "a convenient place for Friends to stand on to minister" in the meeting-house.

9. Although Quakers had been the third largest religious group in 1750, the Society of Friends ranked a distant ninth, by 1850, in comparison of size with other American religious groups, having been weakened by internal schisms and outpaced by the growth of other denominations, such as Methodism. See Edwin Scott Gaustad, *Historical Atlas of Religion in America* (New York, 1962), 160-61. Rufus M. Jones, assisted by Isaac Sharpless and Amelia M. Gummere, *The Quakers in the American Colonies* (London, 1911), described Quakers' participation in the colonial governments of Pennsylvania, Rhode Island, New Jersey, and North Carolina. About one-third of the New Jersey assemblymen were Quaker (between 1722 and 1776); see Jean R. Soderlund, *Quakers and Slavery: A Divided Spirit* (Princeton, N.J., 1985), 41. Howard II. Brinton, a Quaker historian, characterized the period between 1700 and 1740 as "The Golden Age of Quakerism in America," in *Friends for 300 Years* (Wallingford, Pa., 1964), 183. Quakers had made a complete exodus from American government by the Revolutionary War.

10. *Boston-Gazette, or Country Journal,* no. 744, July 10, 1769.

11. Quoted in Butler, *Awash in a Sea of Faith*, 64.

12. Historian John Nelson quoted in John Frederick Woolverton, *Colonial Anglicanism in North America* (Detroit, 1984), 168-69. See Jones, *The Quakers in the American Colonies*, for a detailed description of the beginnings and strength of Quakerism in each colony.

13. Levy, *Quakers and the American Family*, 21-22.

14. Ian K. Steele, *The English Atlantic 1675-1740: An Exploration of Communication and Community* (New York, 1986), 263.

15. Voltaire praised William Penn's "holy experiment" of Pennsylvania as a utopia of reasonable laws in his *Letters Concerning the English Nation* (1733). See Edith Philips, *The Good Quaker in French Legend* (Philadelphia, 1932), for further discussion of the *philosophes'* view of Quakers.

16. Gaustad, *Historical Atlas of Religion in America,* 161. By 1773, the southernmost Quaker meeting was in Wrightsborough, Georgia. In 1772, even after a mid-eighteenth-century internal reformation had decreased the Society's membership, New England Yearly Meeting had 13 monthly meetings (47 local meetings), New York Yearly Meeting had 4 monthly meetings (20 particular meetings), Pennsylvania and New Jersey Yearly Meeting had 35 monthly meetings (103 local meetings), Maryland Yearly Meeting had 4 monthly meetings (20 particular meetings), Virginia Yearly Meeting had 5 monthly meetings (26 local meetings), and North Carolina Yearly Meeting had 7 monthly meetings (23 particular meetings). Eighteenth-century Quakers kept no formal membership lists; in addition, according to Steele, *The English Atlantic,* 263, the Friends in British North America "escaped careful numbering because Pennsylvania never had a colonial census and religion was not usually distinguished in other censuses." Hugh Barbour and J. William Frost, *The Quakers* (New York, 1988), 154, give an estimate of fifty thousand to sixty thousand colonial American Quakers in 1760.

17. Bernard Bailyn argued that "American culture in this early period becomes most fully comprehensible when seen as the exotic far western periphery . . . of the metropolitan European culture system," *The Peopling of British North America: An Introduction* (New York, 1986), 112. Frederick B. Tolles, *Quakers and the Atlantic Culture* (New York, 1960), pointed to a Quaker transatlantic culture. No eighteenth-century religious group "had closer transatlantic ties than . . . the Quakers," according to Michael Kraus, *The Atlantic Civilization: Eighteenth-Century Origins,* quoted in Tolles, x. Many historians have described the Quakers' strong transatlantic links, including Steele, *The English Atlantic,* 264–65: "The Quaker Atlantic community was a religious, political, and economic fraternity that demonstrated a level of communication between migrants and their English brethren that had been quite impossible for migrating dissenters half a century earlier." Alison Gilbert Olson, *Making the Empire Work: London and American Interest Groups 1690–1790* (Cambridge, Mass., 1992), revealed the extensive political lobbying undertaken by Quakers on behalf of their coreligionists across the Atlantic, for example: "By 1716 the London-American Quaker lobby . . . had become one of the most sophisticated of the metropolitan-provincial lobbies," 70.

18. *Piety Promoted, in a Collection of Dying Sayings of Many of the People Called Quakers* (Philadelphia, 1854), 2:95, 98. For Quaker contributions to the Industrial Revolution, see Arthur Raistrick, *Quakers in Science and Industry* (London, 1950).

19. Norton, "The Evolution of White Women's Experience in Early America," 616.

20. Benjamin Marshall to Hugh Forbes, October 18, 1763, in Robert C. Moon, *The Morris Family of Philadelphia, Descendants of Anthony Morris 1654–1721* (Philadelphia, 1898), 1:156.

21. Martin, ed., *Colonial American Travel Narratives,* 50 (first quotation). Even a New England midwife might label herself a "gadder," as a woman who left home fre-

quently; see Laurel Thatcher Ulrich, *A Midwife's Tale: The Life of Martha Ballard, Based on Her Diary, 1785–1812* (New York, 1990), 220. For an extended examination of the Puritan woman's experience in the colonies, see Laurel Thatcher Ulrich, *Good Wives: Image and Reality in the Lives of Women in Northern New England 1650–1750* (New York, 1980).

22. Frederick B. Tolles, *Meeting House and Counting House: The Quaker Merchants of Colonial Philadelphia 1682–1763* (New York, 1963), 4 (first quotation). Jack Marietta, *The Reformation of American Quakerism 1748–1783* (Philadelphia, 1984), 148, also suggested that because Quakers did not limit spiritual oversight to a religious realm segregated from other activities, religious equality legitimized many possibilities for Quaker women. [William Smith], *A Letter from a Gentleman in London to his Friend in Pennsylvania; with a Satire Containing Some Characteristical Strokes Upon the Manners and Principles of the Quakers* (London, 1756), 17 (second quotation).

23. *Virginia Gazette,* July 6, 1767, cited in Julia Cherry Spruill, *Women's Life and Work in the Southern Colonies* (1st ed. 1938; reprint, New York, 1972), 253. Norton asserted, in "The Evolution of White Women's Experience in Early America," 608, that "the literacy skill normally acquired by women was passive (receiving the thoughts of others through reading) whereas the active skill, writing (conveying one's thoughts to others) was available primarily to men."

CHAPTER ONE: BEGINNINGS

1. George Fox, *The Woman Learning in Silence, or the Mystery of the Woman's Subjection to Her Husband* [1656], in *The Works of George Fox* (Philadelphia, 1831), 4:108.

2. Quoted in David J. Latt's introduction to Margaret Fell, *Womens Speaking Justified* [1667] (reprint of 2d ed., Los Angeles, 1979), xi.

3. John Vicars, *The Schismatick Sifted: Or, A Picture of Independents Freshly and Fairly Washt over Again* (1646); and a petition of January 16, 1646, to the House of Lords, quoted in Ethyn Morgan Williams, "Women Preachers in the Civil War," *Journal of Modern History* 1 (1929): 563–64. For a detailed examination of these sects and movements, see Christopher Hill, *The World Turned Upside Down: Radical Ideas during the English Revolution* (New York, 1972).

4. A petition of February 1642 to the House of Commons, quoted in Patricia Higgins, "The Reactions of Women, with special reference to women petitioners," in *Politics, Religion, and the English Civil War* (London, 1973), ed. Brian Manning, 187 (first quotation); Samuel Butler, *Hudibras,* ed. A. R. Waller (Cambridge, Eng., 1905), 42 (second quotation); John Milton, *Complete Poems and Major Prose,* ed. Merritt Y. Hughes (Indianapolis, 1957), 641 (third quotation).

5. Hugh Ormsby-Lennon observed that the Tower of Babel was an important

linguistic metaphor of the period, "The Dialect of Those Fanatick Times: Language Communities and English Poetry from 1580 to 1660" (Ph.D. diss., University of Pennsylvania, 1977), 305.

6. Barry Reay, *The Quakers and the English Revolution* (London, 1985), 7; George Fox, *The Journal of George Fox,* ed. John L. Nickalls (Philadelphia, 1985), 11.

7. George Fox, quoted in Ernest E. Taylor, *The Valiant Sixty* (York, Eng., 1947), 17.

8. Robert Barclay, *An Apology for the True Christian Divinity being an Explanation and Vindication of the Principles and Doctrines of the People Called Quakers* (Philadelphia, 1908), x, 302.

9. Fox quoted in Taylor, *The Valiant Sixty,* 13, 17; *Journal of George Fox,* ed. Nickalls, 24.

10. Francis Higginson, *The Irreligion of the Northern Quakers* (London, 1653), reprinted in *Early Quaker Writings,* ed. Hugh Barbour and Arthur O. Roberts (Grand Rapids, Mich., 1973), 71. See also Phyllis Mack, *Visionary Women: Ecstatic Prophecy in Seventeenth-Century England* (Berkeley, Calif., 1992), 135–36, 151–55.

11. See William C. Braithwaite, *The Beginnings of Quakerism,* 2d ed. (Cambridge, Eng., 1955), 57–58, 131–32, for the origins of the term "Quaker." Braithwaite asserted that there was no real inconsistency between Fox's account that Justice Bennett had given the nickname because Fox had told him to tremble at the name of the Lord, and Barclay's account that "the name came from the trembling of Friends under the powerful working of the Holy Ghost."

12. Barclay, *Apology,* x, 32. Quakers distinguished their ministry from that of the world's religions in terms that correspond to Max Weber's prototypes of legitimate authority in *On Charisma and Institution Building* (Chicago, 1968). The Quaker prophet was legitimized by "charismatic" authority (personally "called" by the Holy Spirit) in contrast to the priest's acquisition of "traditional" authority.

13. Tolles, *Meeting House and Counting House,* 7.

14. This section is based on discussions in Bonnie S. Anderson and Judith P. Zinsser, *A History of Their Own: Women in Europe from Prehistory to the Present* (New York, 1988), vol. 1, and Mary Maples Dunn, "Women of Light," in *Women of America.* Anderson and Zinsser additionally mentioned that women's periodic "uncleanness," or menstruation, was thought to be contaminating—another reason for women's exclusion from a priestly position, 80.

15. Milton D. Speizman and Jane C. Kronick, "A Seventeenth-Century Quaker Women's Declaration," *Signs* 1 (1975): 231–45. Sarah Fell, Margaret's daughter and clerk of the Lancashire Women's Quarterly Meeting, wrote this important epistle (ca. 1675) directed to Quaker women's meetings everywhere. Fell, *Womens Speaking Justified,* 3.

16. George Fox, *A Collection of Many Select and Christian Epistles, Letters, and*

Testimonies (London, 1698), 2:323–24. See Phyllis Mack's discussion in "Gender and Spirituality in Early English Quakerism, 1650–1665," in *Witnesses for Change*, 37–39. Barclay, *Apology*, 17.

17. Fell, *Womens Speaking Justified*, 9.

18. Richard Farnsworth quoted in David Latt's introduction to *Womens Speaking Justified*, xii; Edward Burrough quoted in Mack, "Gender and Spirituality in Early English Quakerism," 48–49.

19. Fell, *Womens Speaking Justified*, 16–17.

20. Anderson and Zinsser, *A History of Their Own*, 238. Fell, *Womens Speaking Justified*, 4, 9, 11, 16.

21. George Fox quoted in Taylor, *The Valiant Sixty*, 9.

22. George Fox quoted in Bauman, *Let Your Words Be Few*, 33.

23. Edward Burrough quoted in Bauman, *Let Your Words Be Few*, 33.

24. See Kenneth L. Carroll, "Early Quakers and 'Going Naked as a Sign,' " *Quaker History* 67 (1978): 69–87.

25. George Fox quoted in Tolles, *Quakers and the Atlantic Culture*, 22; Jones, *The Quakers in the American Colonies*, 267 (second quotation).

26. Quoted in Sydney V. James, *A People Among Peoples: Quaker Benevolence in Eighteenth-Century America* (Cambridge, Mass., 1963), 99.

27. Mack, *Visionary Women*, 247.

28. For further information on the earliest Quaker female preachers, see Hugh Barbour, "Quaker Prophetesses and Mothers in Israel," in *Seeking the Light: Essays in Quaker History in Honor of Edwin B. Bronner*, ed. J. William Frost and John M. Moore (Wallingford, Pa., 1986); Taylor, *The Valiant Sixty;* Phyllis Mack, "Women as Prophets During the English Civil War," *Feminist Studies* 8 (1982): 19–45; and Mack, *Visionary Women*.

29. David S. Lovejoy, *Religious Enthusiasm in the New World: Heresy to Revolution* (Cambridge, Mass., 1985), 12.

30. Quoted in Bauman, *Let Your Words Be Few*, 51, 66.

31. Quoted in Keith Thomas, "Women and the Civil War Sects," *Past and Present* 13 (1958): 46. See Carla Gardina Pestana, "The City upon a Hill under Siege: The Puritan Perception of the Quaker Threat to Massachusetts Bay, 1656–1661," *New England Quarterly* 56 (1983): 323–53.

32. William C. Braithwaite, *The Second Period of Quakerism*, 2d ed. (Cambridge, Eng., 1961), 114–15.

33. Quoted in Reay, *The Quakers and the English Revolution*, 122.

34. Braithwaite, *The Beginnings of Quakerism*, 151.

35. Quoted in Bauman, *Let Your Words Be Few*, 143–44.

36. Quoted in William Beck and T. Frederick Ball, *The London Friends' Meetings: Showing the Rise of The Society of Friends in London; . . . Their History and General Associations* (London, 1869), 42–43, 347. See Irene L. Edwards, "The

Women Friends of London: The Two-Weeks and Box Meetings," *JFHS* 67 (1955): 3. For a more detailed study of Margaret Fell, see Bonnelyn Young Kunze, "The Family, Social and Religious Life of Margaret Fell" (Ph.D. diss., University of Rochester, 1986).

37. See Arnold Lloyd, *Quaker Social History 1669–1738* (London, 1950), 50. George Fox wrote that "the Lord opened to me . . . how I must order and establish Men's and Women's Monthly and Quarterly Meetings in all the nation, and write to other nations, where I came not, to do the same," quoted in Edwin B. Bronner, "Quaker Discipline and Order, 1680–1720: Philadelphia Yearly Meeting and London Yearly Meeting," in *The World of William Penn*, ed. Richard S. Dunn and Mary Maples Dunn (Philadelphia, 1986), 324. Kunze cites evidence of Fell's influence in the establishment of women's meetings, "The Family, Social and Religious Life of Margaret Fell," chapter 4.

38. George Fox, Epistle 320, *The Works of George Fox*, 8:95, 114.

39. Braithwaite, *The Second Period of Quakerism*, 292; William Mather quoted in Mack, *Visionary Women*, 296–97.

40. Rosemary Radford Ruether, "Prophets and Humanists: Types of Religious Feminism in Stuart England," *Journal of Religion* 70 (1990): 3; George Keith, *The Woman Preacher of Samaria* (London, 1674), 27–28; Fox, Epistle 320, *The Works of George Fox*, 8:96–97; William Mather quoted in Mack, *Visionary Women*, 296.

41. Quoted in Mack, *Visionary Women*, 288. Phyllis Mack suggested that the basis for the authority of women's meetings was the extension of women's traditional gendered roles into the public sphere. Fox, Epistle 320, *The Works of George Fox*, 8:93.

42. On women's status under English common law, see Marylynn Salmon, "Equality or Submersion? Feme Covert Status in Early Pennsylvania," in *Women of America*, 94. Judith Boulbie wrote the epistle of 3mo.22.1693 in Yorkshire (England) Women's Quarterly Meeting Minutes, 1678–1745, microfilm, FHLSC.

43. Quoted in Beatrice Carre, "Early Quaker Women in Lancaster and Lancashire," in *Early Lancaster Friends*, ed. Michael Mullen (Leeds, Eng., 1978), 44.

44. Quoted in Barbour, "Quaker Prophetesses and Mothers in Israel," 55; William Braithwaite hypothesized that women's want of business training precluded their admission to the executive body, but Arnold Lloyd remained unconvinced by this view—citing the account books kept by the London Women's Meeting (the Box and Two Weeks Meeting of women Friends). See Braithwaite, *The Second Period of Quakerism*, 286, and Lloyd, *Quaker Social History*, 120, n. 36, 157, and chapter 8. The inclusion of women in the London Six Weeks Meeting, begun in 1671 as a court of final appeal for all monthly meetings of the city, makes the absence of a London Yearly Meeting of women Friends even more conspicuous. Beck and Ball argued that their inclusion in the Six Weeks Meeting showed "how important was the position early assigned to women Friends in the arrangements of the Society, their duties in this case . . . requiring more of an administrative and legislative

nature than the care over the poor that had still earlier been committed to them," *The London Friends' Meeting,* 93. See Doncaster, *Quaker Organisation and Business Meetings,* 17; Carre, "Early Quaker Women in Lancaster and Lancashire"; Dunn, "Women of Light"; and Soderlund, "Women's Authority in Pennsylvania and New Jersey Quaker Meetings, 1680–1760." Marietta, *The Reformation of American Quakerism,* 28–29, noted that in Bucks Quarter of Philadelphia Yearly Meeting, women's meetings had full jurisdiction over their disciplinary cases since they did not submit them to the men's meetings for review. See also Bacon, *Mothers of Feminism,* 44.

45. Craig W. Horle, "Changing Quaker Attitudes toward Legal Defense: The George Fox Case, 1673–75, and the Establishment of Meeting for Sufferings," in *Seeking the Light,* 18, 36. See also Reay, *The Quakers and the English Revolution,* 105, 121.

46. Horle, "Changing Quaker Attitudes toward Legal Defense," 36.

47. Bauman, *Let Your Words Be Few,* 137–38. Mack, *Visionary Women,* 275, 290, noted that Quaker evolution was distinctive because Fox and his party, the proponents of structure, continued to affirm the importance of the prophetic ministry.

48. Quoted in Bauman, *Let Your Words Be Few,* 146.

49. Kunze, "The Family, Social and Religious Life of Margaret Fell," 183. Braithwaite, *Second Period of Quakerism,* 281.

50. Second Day's Morning Meeting minutes, 6mo.9.1703, LRSF. See Patricia Crawford, "Appendix 1: Provisional Checklist of Women's Published Writings, 1600–1700," in *Women in English Society 1500–1800,* ed. Mary Prior (London, 1985). Luella M. Wright, *The Literary Life of Early Friends, 1650–1725* (New York, 1932), 106.

51. Quoted in Braithwaite, *The Second Period of Quakerism,* 180; Second Day's Morning Meeting Minutes, 9mo.11.1700, LRSF.

52. Samuel Carpenter to William Penn, November 9, 1698, in *The Papers of William Penn,* ed. Richard S. Dunn et al. (Philadelphia, 1986), 3:559.

53. Second Day's Morning Meeting Minutes, 1mo.4.1700, LRSF (first quotation); "From the Yearly Meeting of Ministering friends held by Adjournment the first of ye 4th mo 1702 in London . . . A brief memorial of some Ne[ce]ssary Things Recommended only to Ministers . . . ," written in back of Lurgan (Ireland) Monthly Meeting Minutes, 1710–1752, microfilm, FHLD (second quotation); "Memoirs of the Life of Catharine Phillips," 234 (third quotation).

54. Quoted in Jones, *The Quakers in the American Colonies,* 341, 346, n. 1.

55. Quoted in Jones, *The Quakers in the American Colonies,* 314.

56. Jones, *The Quakers in the American Colonies,* 438, and George Fox quoted in the same book, 78; *Extracts from the Minutes and Advices of the Yearly Meeting of Friends Held in London* (1st ed. 1802; reprint, London, 1822), 20–25, no. 13.

57. Thomas Chalkley, Israel Pemberton Jr., and William Penn quoted in Tolles, *Meeting House and Counting House,* 56, 55, 53.

58. William Gordon quoted in Jones, *The Quakers in the American Colonies,* 351.

CHAPTER TWO: "CHOSEN INSTRUMENTS"

1. Amelia Mott Gummere, *The Quaker: A Study in Costume* (1st ed. 1901, reprint; New York, 1968), discussed the green aprons that had become "almost the badge of Quakerism," 133–35. Plainness did not, at this period, refer to the uniform, drab-colored dress of the later Quakers: Tolles, *Meeting House and Counting House,* 126. It was interpreted to mean the ordinary dress of the day stripped of superfluous ornaments and useless fripperies like lace and ribbons. Although adherence to the plainness "testimony" varied according to region, level of wealth, and degree of devoutness, an identifiable Quaker appearance did develop, as evidenced by this minute from Dublin (Ireland) Monthly Meeting, FHLD, 10mo.24.1745: "Some Strangers under the Habit of Friends having lately been observed in this City . . . the Committee of the Poor are desired to speak to & advise them to apply to the respective Meetings from whence they came for Certificates. . . ."

2. This description of a Quaker preaching was written by Peter Kalm, a Swedish traveller, when he visited the Bank Meeting House in Philadelphia, December 7, 1750. He observed that either a man or a woman might first rise to speak, after a long period of the meeting waiting in silence for "promptings of the Spirit." Kalm noted that "The women who hope to preach [ministers] and therefore sit in a special pew generally keep their heads bowed, or hold a handkerchief with both hands over their eyes." Peter Kalm, *Peter Kalm's Travels in North America: The English Version of 1770,* ed. Adolph B. Benson (New York, 1966), 2:649–51.

3. A Testimony from Lancaster Monthly Meeting concerning Lydia Lancaster, (London Yearly Meeting) Testimonies Concerning Deceased Ministers, 1758–1774, 2:149, LRSF. "That eminent minister, Benjamina Padley, of Swansea" was remembered as standing up with one hand in her pocket, according to James Jenkins, *The Records and Recollections of James Jenkins,* ed. J. William Frost (New York, 1984), 67.

4. "Lydia Lanchester's [*sic*] Farewel Sermon at Gracious-street, Dec. 17, 1738, concerning the Great Love of God, in sending Christ into the World to redeem and save it," *Sermons of several of the people called Quakers. Taken in Short-Hand, as they were spoken in their Meeting-Houses, and made publick to prevent the Clamour and Misunderstanding of many People, about their Manner and Method of Preaching,* ed. Joseph Ady (London, 1738). The preface by Joseph Ady approvingly described the Quaker method of preaching "not with enticing Words of Man's Wisdom, but in the Demonstration of the Spirit and Power, that their Faith might not stand in the Wisdom of Man, but in the Power of God," iv–v.

5. A Testimony of Lancaster Monthly Meeting concerning Lydia Lancaster, 149. "Her Prayer after Sermon, verbatem," in *Sermons of several of the people called Quakers,* ed. Ady.

6. Henry Gouldney to Sir John Rodes, 2mo.6.1714, in Mrs. Godfrey Locker Lampson, ed., *A Quaker Post-Bag: Letters to Sir John Rodes of Barlbrough Hall, in*

the County of Derby, Baronet, and to John Gratton of Monyash 1693–1742 (London, 1910), 98.

7. See Appendixes 1–3. In New England, for example, Lydia Norton was "a famous Minister [among the Quakers], none more so of that Country, and indeed she had an excellent Gift," according to Samuel Bownas, *An Account of the Life, Travels, and Christian Experiences in the Work of the Ministry of Samuel Bownas* (London, 1756), 101. In the Patuxent River area of Maryland, Ann Galloway was "the only ministring Friend at that time in all those parts—a very honest, innocent, lively and honourable Friend in the Truth and everywhere acceptable in her Services," *Travelling with Thomas Story*, 58.

8. "The Life of that Faithful Servant of Christ, Jane Hoskens [*sic*], A Minister of the Gospel, Among the People Called Quakers," *FL*, 1:467. Although Jane Fenn had previously spoken in meetings, while residing in Plymouth and Haverford, I have found no formal recognition of her as a minister, in the meeting records, until she moved within the compass of Chester Monthly Meeting. Haverford Friends, according to her account, called her a preacher and, therefore, were unwilling to part with her when she moved to Chester. I wish to acknowledge Jean Soderlund for her extracts from the Chester (Pennsylvania) Monthly Meeting Minutes, 1681–1760, and Chester (Pennsylvania) Women's Monthly Meeting Minutes, 1695–1760, FHLSC.

9. "The Life of that Faithful Servant of Christ, Jane Hoskens," 467–68.

10. "The Life of that Faithful Servant of Christ, Jane Hoskens," 460–61.

11. "The Life of that Faithful Servant of Christ, Jane Hoskens," 462–64.

12. "The Life of that Faithful Servant of Christ, Jane Hoskens," 466, 468, 471. Willard Heiss, ed., *Quaker Biographical Sketches of Ministers and Elders, and other Concerned Members of the Yearly Meeting of Philadelphia* (Indianapolis, 1972), 245. Note that the spelling is "Hoskins" in the relevant wills and other original documents. See also Roy N. Lokken, *David Lloyd: Colonial Lawmaker* (Seattle, 1959). Jane Fenn's selectivity of employers while she was an indentured, and then hired, domestic servant, and her subsequent upward social mobility (becoming the house-keeper for the wealthiest family in Chester) were in marked contrast to the experiences of many young women who immigrated to Pennsylvania as indentured servants. Sharon V. Salinger, " 'Send No More Women': Female Servants in Eighteenth-Century Philadelphia," *PMHB* 108 (1983), found that, for female indentured servants, "once on the bottom of the economic ladder in Philadelphia, upward movement was virtually impossible," 46. The typical eighteenth-century female indentured servant arrived in Pennsylvania, served her time, and ended up in "the poor house sick, destitute, totally without resources," 47. Jane Fenn's independence of thought in determining her life choices despite her menial position apparently stemmed from her belief that she received direct divine communications. The Quaker meeting's recognition of her spiritual "gifts" also enlarged her social network and resources.

13. "Memoirs of the Life of Catharine Phillips," 189.

14. "Memoirs of the Life of Catharine Phillips," 207, 191.

15. "Memoirs of the Life of Catharine Phillips," 189, 190.

16. "Memoirs of the Life of Catharine Phillips," 190–93.

17. Jenkins, *The Records and Recollections of James Jenkins*, 118–19, 260.

18. Catharine Phillips, *Considerations on the Causes of the High Price of Grain, and Other Articles of Provision, for a Number of Years Back; and Propositions for Reducing Them: with Occasional Remarks* (London, 1792), i. Jenkins, *The Records and Recollections of James Jenkins*, 262.

19. Robert Jordan to Abigail Boles, 9mo.27.1729, Portfolio 3.B40, FHLD.

20. Abigail Watson (formerly Boles) to Mary Peisley, 12mo.3.1745, Portfolio 4.40, FHLD.

21. Abigail Boles to Barnaby Rallins, n.d., Portfolio 3.B40, FHLD; Abigail Watson to Mary Peisley, 12mo.3.1745, Portfolio 4.40, FHLD.

22. Henry Gouldney to John Boles, 7mo.15.1722, Watson MSS, LRSF.

23. Grace Lloyd to Abigail Boles, 7mo.26.1727, Watson MSS, LRSF. In the same letter, Grace Lloyd wrote of the difficulty she had in parting with her housekeeper and friend, the minister Jane Fenn, bound for religious service in Ireland: "The parting w[i]th. Thee & poor Jane [Fenn] been very hard to Mee as parting w[i]th. Jane was harder than usuall So I have wanted her More then Ever tho[ugh] I Never Murmerd being truly desirous Shee should faithfuly Serve her Great Master . . . Lett me have a full Ac[coun]t. of your Voige [voyage] & how poor dear Jane gott along among fr[ien]ds. . . ." Ellin Evans, an elder of Gwynedd Monthly Meeting, also wrote to Abigail from Pennsylvania, "My dear and Tender Love Salutes thee, for thou often In my remembrance Sinse thy Visitt hear [here] and hearawayes. . . ." (Ellin Evans to Abigail Boles, 3mo.1726, Watson MSS, LRSF), as did the preacher Michael Lightfoot and many others. The Farringtons of New Jersey wrote a letter several years after Abigail's American visit, "The relish whereof is not forgotten by us, & by many more . . . thou art as an Epistle written in our hearts," Abraham and Phebe Farrington to Abigail Boles, 7mo.25.1735, Portfolio 17.29, LRSF.

24. Mary Weston, "Journal of her visits in Great Britain, 1735–1747, and in America, 1750–1752," LRSF, 3. Mary Weston to Abigail Watson, 9mo.25.1749, Watson MSS, LRSF. Mary Weston to Abigail Watson, 1mo.6.1749/50, Portfolio 3.B40, FHLD.

25. Elizabeth Hudson, "An Abstract of the Travels w[i]th. Some other Remarks of Eliza. Hudson from 22d. of 1st mo. 1743," QCHC, 7mo.12.1748.

26. Mary Peisley to Abigail Watson, 1mo.6.1745/6, Watson MSS, LRSF. Catharine Payton, Mary Peisley's companion on several religious journeys, also corresponded with Abigail. See "Memoirs of the Life of Catharine Phillips," 197.

27. John Boles, postscript to letter, Abigail Boles to Benjamin Hornor,

6mo.24.1728, Watson MSS, LRSF; Elizabeth Hudson, "An Abstract of the Travels," 7mo.12.1748; Mary Leadbeater, *Biographical Notices of Members of the Society of Friends, who were Resident in Ireland* (London, 1823), 249–50.

28. Abigail Boles to John Boles Jr., 3mo.31.1723, Portfolio 3.B40, FHLD; Abigail Watson to Mary Peisley, 12mo.3.1745, Portfolio 4.40, FHLD.

29. Tabitha Hornor to Abigail Watson, 7mo.17.1737, Portfolio 3.B40, FHLD. Heiss, *Quaker Biographical Sketches,* 191. Susanna Lightfoot remembered that when she was young, attending a London meeting, "she perceived the Spirit of prayer to move from one end of the Gallery to the other before any one would give up to it," 3mo.3.1781, "Some Account of the last Illness and Expressions of that eminent Instrument and useful Handmaid of the Lord, Susannah [sic] Lightfoot," Portfolio 2.A6, FHLD.

30. "Memoirs of the Life of Catharine Phillips," 267. Jenkins, *The Records and Recollections of James Jenkins,* 172.

31. Bauman, *Let Your Words Be Few,* 130. A Friend described Sarah Baker's preaching: "That which crowned her service was the Lord was with her and gave her Testimony an Entrance into many hearts . . ." Dublin (Ireland) Monthly Meeting Family Lists, 1655–1699, 176 [341], FHLD.

32. Philadelphia Yearly Meeting of Ministers and Elders Minutes, 7mo.1700, microfilm, FHLSC; "From the Yearly Meeting of Ministering friends held by Adjournment the first of ye 4th mo 1702 in London . . . A brief memorial of Some Ne[ce]ssary Things recommended only to Ministers"; Elizabeth Hudson, "An Abstract of the Travels . . . ," 5mo.2.1750.

33. John Scarbrough was disciplined on 12mo.6.1700, Middletown (Pennsylvania) Monthly Meeting Minutes, FHLSC. Conversely, good conduct helped legitimize a ministry. Quakers described a minister's religious visit by noting that "her Life and Conversation hath been Circumspect Weighty and Blameless Whereby her Ministry was Confirmed," Second Day's Morning Meeting Minutes, 6mo.1699, LRSF.

34. Margaret Ellis, "Diary of travels in the ministry in both America and England, 1739–1752," QCHC, 3, 8.

35. Bauman, *Let Your Words Be Few,* 149. Samuel Bownas described the Quaker theory of preaching: "We who apprehend ourselves called into this publick Station of Preaching, ought closely to wait on our Guide, to put us forth in the Work . . . carefully mind our Openings, & go on as we are led by the Spirit; for if we over-run our Guide & Openings, we shall be confused, not knowing where, or how to conclude: But if we begin & go on with the Spirit, we shall conclude so, that all who are truly spiritual will sensibly feel that we are right: Thus will our Ministry edify them that hear it," Bownas, *An Account of the Life, Travels, and Christian Experiences in the Work of the Ministry,* 54.

36. For an introductory look at the numbers of Quaker women ministers active

during this period, see Appendix 2 for colonial American female preachers and Appendix 3 for British female preachers.

37. Bownas, *An Account of the Life, Travels, and Christian Experiences in the Work of the Ministry,* 161. Heiss, *Quaker Biographical Sketches,* 179.

38. An eighteenth-century British Quaker observed in the 1780s: "The war with America being ended . . . in the course of this year, we received the religious visits of many American Friends . . . The gifts of some of these were so small, as to be a matter of surprise to, not a few Friends, that they should have felt a concern, (and their American friends concurred therewith) to 'put their small sickles into so large, and distant harvest field' . . . ," Jenkins, *The Records and Recollections of James Jenkins,* 171–72.

39. See Appendix 1 for individual descriptions of the fifty-seven transatlantic ministers. Of these women who received certificates of unity with their "concerns" to travel abroad, two women did not complete the transatlantic journey (although they had travelled extensively regionally). Elizabeth Smith of Burlington, New Jersey, died before she could embark on her transatlantic visit. Comfort Hoag of Hampton, New Hampshire, set out in a ship that sprang a leak. When the ship returned for repairs, Hoag decided that "the will had been taken for the deed" and gave up the trip.

40. Richard T. Vann, *The Social Development of English Quakerism, 1655–1755* (Cambridge, Mass., 1969), 166–67, 174–76.

41. "Thomas Rawlinson" entry in DQB. Lydia Lancaster, Sophia Hume, and Mary Leaver were the three descendants of "The Valiant Sixty."

42. Dublin (Ireland) Monthly Meeting Minutes, 8mo.1.1745, FHLD. There may have been more "weighty" Friends among these women's parents and siblings; the meeting activities of nine women's parents were not traced because of incomplete meeting records and other reasons.

43. Mary Weston, "Journal of her visits," 1.

44. Heiss, *Quaker Biographical Sketches,* 174. Susan S. Forbes, "Quaker Tribalism," in *Friends and Neighbors: Group Life in America's First Plural Society,* ed. Michael Zuckerman (Philadelphia, 1982) concluded that "the meeting could determine an individual's potential for activism from the family that raised him," and that "the family conferred status as well as membership in the meeting," 156–66. Quaker family activism, rather than wealth and political officeholding, most closely correlated with the members most frequently assigned meeting duties in Forbes's study. But Forbes examined those who performed committee assignments in meetings for business rather than those who were recognized as ministers. It appears that the ministers were a more disparate group because their status rested on the demonstration of individual "charismatic" gifts.

45. Poem by Zebulon Ferris, in "The Journal of Ann Moore 1756–1762," transcribed by Rosalie B. Douglas, FHLSC, 24. An extract from James Gough's MS journal printed in "Life of Joseph Oxley," *FL,* 2:460.

46. "From the Yearly Meeting of Ministering friends held by Adjournment the first of ye 4th mo 1702 in London . . . A brief memorial of Some Ne[ce]ssary Things recommended only to Ministers" (first quotation); "The Life of that Faithful Servant of Christ, Jane Hoskens," 471 (second quotation); Heiss, *Quaker Biographical Sketches,* 126 (third quotation).

47. Markyate/Dunstable (Bedfordshire, England) Monthly Meeting Minutes, 2mo.2.1725, LRSF.

48. Quoted in Amelia Mott Gummere, *Friends in Burlington* (Philadelphia, 1884), 57.

49. Mary Weston, "Journal of her visits," 1. A study of English Quakers found that "the most striking difference between Friends and the rest of society . . . is the virtually complete absence, not only of paupers, but also of persons called only 'labourers,' " 73; Richard T. Vann and David Eversley, *Friends in Life and Death: The British and Irish Quakers in the Demographic Transition, 1650–1900* (Cambridge, Eng., 1992). Eighteenth-century Quakers formed a greater number of the wealthy families in Philadelphia than their proportion of the population would warrant, although poor and middle-class Friends also lived in the city. Friends also dominated the top tax bracket in Chester County, Pennsylvania. Lack of data on the socioeconomic level of the transatlantic ministers makes a conclusive generalization impossible, but enough information was available on thirty women's families to assign them to three categories (wealthy, moderate, poor) as rough standards by which to compare financial status across regions and at different periods of time. Although wealthy members were often appointed as elders, it appears that those who served as transatlantic ministers were from a variety of backgrounds. Frost, *The Quaker Family in Colonial America,* 40, mentioned that, while overseers and elders were often the older and wealthier members, "neither age nor riches were of much consideration in the ministry." Soderlund, "Women's Authority in Pennsylvania and New Jersey Quaker Meetings, 1680–1760," 735, also found that ministers "were a somewhat more disparate group than the elders" in terms of wealth.

50. See "William Beck" entry in DQB.

51. An extract from James Gough's MS journal printed in "Life of Joseph Oxley," 460 (first quotation); "Some Account of the Life and Religious Exercises of Mary Neale," *FL,* 11:74–75 (second quotation); "Some Account of the Life of Elizabeth Ashbridge," *FL,* 4:13 (third quotation).

52. The source material may create an impression of greater uniformity in the group's spiritual development than truly existed, since Quaker memoirists primarily wrote their autobiographies to illustrate Quaker principles. In the words of Luella M. Wright, *The Literary Life of Early Friends, 1650–1725,* 156, "the Quaker autobiographer was a Friend first, and an individual penning his memoirs second." In addition, much of the information for this analysis is from published sources which passed through a Quaker editorial committee. Overseers of the press tended to minimize

personal, idiosyncratic details, while emphasizing those conforming to the group experience. See George J. Willauer Jr., "Editorial Practices in Eighteenth-Century Philadelphia: The Journal of Thomas Chalkley in Manuscript and Print," *PMHB* 107 (1983): 217–34. However, information acquired through unpublished sources (such as private correspondence) was thematically consistent with published accounts, indicating a commonality in the way the women conceptualized their experiences. The memoirs of the transatlantic female ministers conformed to the categories described by Howard H. Brinton, "Stages in Spiritual Development As Recorded in Quaker Journals," in *Children of Light: In Honor of Rufus M. Jones*, ed. Howard H. Brinton (New York, 1938). Brinton's study of one hundred early Quaker (male and female) ministers' autobiographies found that their lives divided into common stages: an experience of divine revelation in childhood, compunction over youthful frivolity, search and conflict, convincement, and conversion. J. William Frost has pointed out that Quakers rarely used the word "conversion" and referred to "convincement" when an outsider became a Friend. Frost added that "in more traditional theological terms, what the journalists were undergoing can be described as conviction of sin and the realization of the failure of good works to save, justification, and progression toward sanctification," *The Quaker Family in Colonial America*, 32–33.

53. "Memoirs of the Life of Catharine Phillips," 189; *Piety Promoted*, 2:25; "Some Account of the Life of Elizabeth Ashbridge," 11; "A Letter from Elizabeth Webb to Anthony William Boehm," 171.

54. "Some Account of the Life and Religious Exercises of Mary Neale," 73; Margaret Ellis, "Diary of travels in the ministry," 1; Sophia Hume, *Remarks on the Practice of Inoculation for the Small Pox*, 2d ed. (London, 1767), 34.

55. Mary Weston, "Journal of her visits," 1; "Memoir of Sarah Morris," *FL*, 6:478.

56. "A Letter from Elizabeth Webb to Anthony William Boehm," 165; Heiss, *Quaker Biographical Sketches*, 194.

57. "A Letter from Elizabeth Webb to Anthony William Boehm," 166; Sophia Hume, *An Exhortation to the Inhabitants of the Province of South-Carolina*, 2d ed. (Bristol, Eng., 1751), 24.

58. "Memoir of Sarah Morris," 478; "A Letter from Elizabeth Webb to Anthony William Boehm," 168. It is unlikely that the women's conversion experiences correlated with the onset of menarche, since the women usually referred to a specific illness or accident in conjunction with their spiritual crisis.

59. The response to Elizabeth Ashbridge's change was described in Elizabeth Hudson, "An Abstract of the Travels," 8mo.10.1745; Hume, *An Exhortation to the Inhabitants of the Province of South-Carolina*, 58.

60. Margaret Ellis, "Diary of travels in the ministry," 2–3.

61. "Some Account of the Life of Elizabeth Ashbridge," 19–20. Nancy F. Cott has suggested in a different context that "conversion set up a direct relation to God that allowed female converts to denigrate or bypass men's authority—to defy man—for

God." See "Young Women in the Second Great Awakening in New England," *Feminist Studies 3* (1975): 15–29.

62. "Memoir of Sarah Morris," 478; Bauman, *Let Your Words Be Few,* 139.

63. "Some Account of the last Illness and Expressions of that eminent Instrument and useful Handmaid of the Lord, Susannah Lightfoot," 4mo.6.1782; Sophia Hume to Hannah Hyam, 6mo.1.1748, Letter 57, in John Kendall, ed., *Letters on Religious Subjects Written by Divers Friends Deceased,* in *Friends' Family Library* (Philadelphia, 1831) 2:160; Margaret Ellis, "Diary of travels in the ministry," 9.

64. Testimony of Lancaster Monthly Meeting concerning Lydia Lancaster, 148; Elizabeth Hudson, "An Abstract of the Travels," 1mo.22.1743.

65. "The Life of that Faithful Servant of Christ, Jane Hoskens," 465.

66. Mary Rogers's testimony in Nottinghamshire and Mansfield (England) Women's Quarterly Meeting Minutes, 1mo.30.1691, Nottinghamshire Record Office, Nottingham, England. Elizabeth Hudson, "An Abstract of the Travels" (following), 3mo.10.1753. Margaret Ellis, "Diary of travels in the ministry," 9. The ministerial "gift" was considered to be a lifelong one: ministers often described knowing that they were nearing the end of their lives when they felt no more religious "concerns." Abigail Watson's husband wrote, "About a year before she died she was sensible her departure drew nigh; for she found no Engagement on her Mind to Travel abroad, as she frequently had done . . . but said, she found her Work was done, & nothing in her way . . . ," 107, Irish Yearly Meeting Testimonies, FHLD.

67. Ashbridge heard the woman preach at a Quaker meeting in Boston, "Some Account of the Life of Elizabeth Ashbridge," 14. See Benjamin Ferris of Oblong, "Religious Visits in the year 1750 & later, MS journal 1708–1775 & Religious Testimony," FHLSC.

68. "Some Account of the Life of Elizabeth Ashbridge," 17.

69. "Some Account of the Life of Elizabeth Ashbridge," 20; Sophia Hume to Hannah Hyam, 6mo.1.1748, Letter 57, in John Kendall, ed., *Letters on Religious Subjects,* 159–60.

70. "A Letter from Elizabeth Webb to Anthony William Boehm," 169–70.

71. Elizabeth Hudson, "An Abstract of the Travels," 4mo.6.1747; Elizabeth Wilkinson, "Journal of a Religious Visit to Friends in America, 1761–1763," QCHC, 40, 122.

72. Abigail Watson to Mary Peisley, 12mo.3.1745, Portfolio 4.40, FHLD; Jenkins, *The Records and Recollections of James Jenkins,* 52.

73. "Some Account of the Life and Religious Exercises of Mary Neale," 76.

74. Levy, *Quakers and the American Family,* 218; Margaret Ellis, "Diary of travels in the ministry," 10–11.

75. "The Life of that Faithful Servant of Christ, Jane Hoskens," 465. Margaret Ellis, "Diary of travels in the ministry," 11.

76. Heiss, *Quaker Biographical Sketches,* 174; Ann Roberts to John Kinsey, 6mo.13.1739, Henry S. Drinker Papers, HSP.

77. A Testimony from Monthly Meeting of Sedbergh concerning Alice Alderson (London Yearly Meeting) Testimonies Concerning Deceased Ministers, 1758–74, 2:275, LRSF; Mary Ellerton letter in "Diary of Abiah Darby, ca. 1744–1769," LRSF, 16. Generally, in western Europe and the American colonies, "literacy rates were biased in favor of the upper classes, males, and urban dwellers." Higher literacy has also been associated with Protestant areas because of the stress on lay reading in religious devotion. Even so, evidence has shown that the literacy rate of women typically lagged behind that of men because "high-status and male occupations demanded literacy more than did the jobs open to the poor and women," Carl F. Kaestle et al., *Literacy in the United States: Readers and Reading since 1880* (New Haven, 1991), 3, 4, 13. According to Kenneth A. Lockridge, "Literacy in early America 1650–1800," in *Literacy and Social Development in the West: A Reader,* ed. Harvey J. Graff (Cambridge, Eng., 1981), less than 50 percent of New England women were literate in the eighteenth century. Joel Perlmann and Dennis Shirley, "When Did New England Women Acquire Literacy?" *WMQ,* 3d ser., vol. 48 (1991): 50–67, suggested that Lockridge may have understated female literacy in New England.

78. Quoted in Tolles, *Meeting House and Counting House,* 153–54; Elizabeth Hudson, "An Abstract of the Travels," 1mo.22.1743; Tolles suggested that Quakers insisted upon an ideal of universal elementary education for their children, 149. Many monthly meetings collected copies of Quaker books, such as Fox's *Journal* and Barclay's *Apology,* and functioned as lending libraries for members. Raistrick, *Quakers in Science and Industry,* 33, "The net effect of the Quaker concern for education was that the whole Society was literate, and was accustomed to reading and study." Vann and Eversley, *Friends in Life and Death,* 54, assumed a "virtually universal literacy" among eighteenth-century Quakers. The strategic use of writing skills and publication had ensured the Society of Friends' survival. An embittered former Friend commented, "Who hath wrote more than the Quakers?" (quoted in Wright, *The Literary Life of Early Friends 1650–1725,* 8, 79).

79. "From the Yearly Meeting of Ministering friends held by Adjournment the first of ye 4th mo 1702 in London . . . A brief memorial of Some Ne[ce]ssary Things recommended only to Ministers."

80. "A Letter from Elizabeth Webb to Anthony William Boehm," 166; "Some Account of the Life of Elizabeth Ashbridge," 16.

81. Heiss, *Quaker Biographical Sketches,* 182; *Diary and Autobiography of John Adams,* ed. L. H. Butterfield et al. (Cambridge, Mass., 1961), 2:133, September 12, 1774, entry; Elizabeth Hudson, "An Abstract of the Travels," 1mo.1744, 1mo.22.1743.

82. Israel Pemberton Sr. to Isaac Greenleafe, 8mo.22.1748, Pemberton Papers, 4:146, HSP; "The Journal of Ann Moore 1756–1762," 118.

83. "It is clear that members of the select meetings [ministers and elders] were regarded as the significant leaders of the Society. Their importance was because God had called them for a particular service, and should have had nothing to do

with 'status,' but nonetheless a status they acquired," Doncaster, *Quaker Organisation and Business Meetings*, 92.

84. Levy, *Quakers and the American Family*, 222, "No similar body of literature exists for any other colonial women, none is nearly comparable."

85. An extract from James Gough's MS journal printed in "Life of Joseph Oxley," 460.

CHAPTER THREE: "LOVE YT [THAT] MANY
WATERS CANNOT QUENCH"

1. See accounts of the shipwreck in Dublin (Ireland) Monthly Meeting Removals, 1682–1754, 58, and Cork, Ireland, Ministers' Visits, 1708–1877, 53, FHLD. Joseph Taylor's remembrance of the disaster was given in the introduction to "Journal of the Life and Travels of Susanna Morris," in *Friends' Miscellany*, ed. John and Isaac Comly (Philadelphia, 1834), 1:146. A recent edition of Susanna Morris's journal has been published in Margaret Hope Bacon, ed., *Wilt Thou Go On My Errand? Three Eighteenth-Century Journals of Quaker Women Ministers: Susanna Morris 1682–1755, Elizabeth Hudson 1722–1783, Ann Moore 1710–1783* (Wallingford, Pa., 1994).

2. "Journal of the Life and Travels of Susanna Morris," 146, 156.

3. Dublin (Ireland) Monthly Meeting Removals, 1682–1754, 58.

4. (London Yearly Meeting) Meeting for Sufferings Minutes, 1709–1775, LRSF.

5. Lurgan (Ireland) Monthly Meeting Minutes, 1710–1752, microfilm, FHLD.

6. County Tipperary (Ireland) Monthly Meeting Accounts, 1717–1800, FHLD; Yorkshire (England) Quarterly Meeting Minutes, 1698–1733, microfilm, FHLSC.

7. Tabitha Hornor to Abigail Watson, 7mo.17.1737, Portfolio 3.B40, FHLD.

8. Thomas Gent, *The Life of Thomas Gent, Printer, of York, Written by himself* (London, 1837), 158–59.

9. See (London Yearly Meeting) Testimonies Concerning Deceased Ministers, vols. 1–2, 1728–1774, LRSF.

10. See Philadelphia Monthly Meeting Minutes, 1682–1775, and Philadelphia Women's Monthly Meeting Minutes, 1686–1775, microfilm, FHLSC.

11. The total number of female preachers travelling in this sample of nine meetings (including Philadelphia Monthly Meeting, between 1698 and 1767, with twenty-four women) was eighty-eight (six of the women had resided in more than one of the monthly meetings, so their duplicate appearances were subtracted). Hampton (New Hampshire) Monthly Meeting records are at the Archives of the New England Yearly Meeting, Rhode Island Historical Society, Providence, Rhode Island. The other meeting minutes are at FHLSC.

12. The directives of seventeenth-century conduct books were quoted in Mary

Prior, ed., *Women in English Society 1500–1800* (London, 1985), 200; Abigail Adams to Isaac Smith Jr., April 20, 1771, in L. H. Butterfield et al., eds., *The Book of Abigail and John: Selected Letters of the Adams Family 1762–1784* (Cambridge, Mass., 1975), 50.

13. Captain Peter Reeve to James Pemberton, March 18.1750/1, Pemberton Papers, 7:19, HSP.

14. "Journal of the Life and Travels of Susanna Morris," 154.

15. London Yearly Meeting Epistles Sent, vol. 1, 1683–1703, 5mo.24.1694, LRSF (first quotation); Mary Peisley quoted in "Memoirs of the Life of Catharine Phillips," 204.

16. Elizabeth Hudson, "An Abstract of the Travels," 4mo.6.1747.

17. London Yearly Meeting Epistles Sent, vol. 1, 1683–1703, 6mo.2.1703; London Yearly Meeting epistle, 3mo.13–17.1695, quoted in London Yearly Meeting Minutes, vol. 2, 1693–1701, LRSF.

18. Quoted from London Yearly Meeting Epistles Sent to Maryland Yearly Meeting in 3mo.20–24.1700 and 4mo.9–12.1701. The Virginia Quaker was quoted in Tolles, *Quakers and the Atlantic Culture,* 139.

19. "A Letter from Elizabeth Webb to Anthony William Boehm," 171.

20. Lydia Norton's horse hire was mentioned in Hampton (New Hampshire) Monthly Meeting Minutes, 7mo.21.1710. Such expenses occur throughout eighteenth-century Quaker meeting records. Province Men's Meeting, Cork (Ireland), 10mo.10.1739, FHLD, paid the expense of horse hire from Cork to Dublin for Irish women ministers returning from a religious visit to America. They charged it to the national stock when the account was settled. For Ann Dillworth's ship passage, see Bristol Men's Meeting Minutes, 3mo.6.1700 and 5mo.1.1700, in Russell Mortimer, ed., *Minute Book of the Men's Meeting of the Society of Friends in Bristol, 1686–1704* (Gateshead, Eng., 1977), 164, 167. Steele, *The English Atlantic,* 274–75, detailed the different durations of Atlantic crossings.

21. Michael Lightfoot to Abigail Boles, 8mo.30.1730, Watson MSS, LRSF.

22. John Hunt to James Pemberton, 3mo(May).5.1750, Pemberton Papers, 6:162, HSP.

23. Rachel Wilson to Isaac Wilson, 8mo.17.1768, LRSF.

24. Steele, *The English Atlantic,* 92–93.

25. "An Account of Rachel Wilson's Religious Visit to Friends in America, carefully transcribed from her Manuscript for the Information and Benefit of her Children and near Relations by Deborah Braithwaite," 5, LRSF; "Some Account of the Life and Religious Exercises of Mary Neale," 103; (London Yearly Meeting) Meeting for Sufferings, 9mo.1753.

26. Catharine Payton, on her passage to America, recorded that she and Peisley held religious meetings with the sailors and steerage passengers. She criticized a priest who read prayers only to the cabin passengers without taking care of the

others on board. "The captain offered us the cabin to meet in," Payton recalled, "but we rather chose to go to them in steerage; from which the priest would have dissuaded us, by telling us, they would be likely to insult us; but, on our sending a message to the sailors . . . they returned for answer . . . they should be glad to hear the word of God . . . ," in "Memoirs of the Life of Catharine Phillips," 206. Rachel Wilson to Isaac Wilson, 8mo.2.1768, LRSF. Introduction, 2, to "An Account of Rachel Wilson's Religious Visit to Friends in America, 1768–1769" (a different transcript from that of Deborah Braithwaite; all subsequent citations will be from this QCHC copy), QCHC, 15.

27. "An Account of Rachel Wilson's Religious Visit," 10.

28. "An Account of Rachel Wilson's Religious Visit," 8. Thomas Chalkley to Elizabeth Levis and Jane Fenn, 12mo.1.1724/5, printed in "The Life of that Faithful Servant of Christ, Jane Hoskens," 470.

29. Margaret Ellis, "Diary of travels in the ministry," 24–26.

30. Jane Fenn, "Journal 1727–1729," 4mo.4.1727 entry, FHLSC.

31. Elizabeth Hudson, "An Abstract of the Travels," 12mo.1747 (February 1748).

32. Jane Crosfield, "Diary, 1760–1761," 1, FHLSC; "The Journal of Ann Moore 1756–1762," 89–92.

33. "The Journal of Ann Moore 1756–1762," 88–108.

34. "A Letter from Elizabeth Webb to Anthony William Boehm," 171.

35. "The Journal of Ann Moore 1756–1762," 29.

36. "An Account of Rachel Wilson's Religious Visit," 36, chapter 11:15.

37. See Jones, *The Quakers in the American Colonies*, as well as Barbour and Frost, *The Quakers*, for estimates of colonial American Quaker populations.

38. Elizabeth Webb, "A Short Account of My Viage into America with Mary Rogers My Companion," QCHC, 12.

39. Mary Weston to Abigail Watson, 9mo.30.1752, Portfolio 3.B40, FHLD.

40. "The Journal of Ann Moore 1756–1762," 32–33.

41. See Isabel Grubb, *Quakers in Ireland 1654–1900* (London, 1927), for an estimate of the Irish Quaker population. William C. Braithwaite, *The Second Period of Quakerism,* 459, estimated that there were fifty thousand Quakers in England by 1680. Braithwaite believed that the number remained stationary for some time, with emigration balancing the increase through births.

42. Mary Weston to Daniel Weston, 10mo.3.1750, inserted at 71, in Mary Weston, "Journal of her visits"; "Memoirs of the Life of Catharine Phillips," 210; "Some Account of the Life and Religious Exercises of Mary Neale," 80–81.

43. "The Journal of Thomas Chalkley, A Minister of the Gospel in the Society of Friends," *FL,* 6:18, 49.

44. "An Account of Rachel Wilson's Religious Visit," 40–41, 45; Mary Weston to Daniel Weston, 6mo.3.1750, inserted at 45, in Mary Weston, "Journal of her visits."

45. "Journals of Esther Palmer," 67–69.

46. "The Journal of Thomas Chalkley," 16.

47. Elizabeth Hudson, "An Abstract of the Travels," 11mo.15.1749.

48. "Some Account of the Life and Religious Exercises of Mary Neale," 112–13; "Some Account of the Life of Elizabeth Ashbridge," 22–23.

49. Dublin (Ireland) Monthly Meeting Minutes, 7mo.6.1743, FHLD; Philadelphia Quarterly Meeting Minutes, 4mo.7.1703, microfilm, FHLSC.

50. "Journals of Esther Palmer," 64–65; Elizabeth Webb, "A Short Account of My Viage," 18; "Journal of the Life and Travels of Susanna Morris," 151.

51. Elizabeth Hudson, "An Abstract of the Travels," 8mo.10.1745.

52. Mary Weston, "Journal of her visits," 51–52.

53. Mack Thompson, *Moses Brown: Reluctant Reformer* (Chapel Hill, N.C., 1962), 80.

54. "The Journal of Ann Moore 1756–1762," 4; Mary Weston, "Journal of her visits," 51–52.

55. "Diary of Deborah Morris, 1772," FHLSC.

56. "Journal of the Life and Travels of Susanna Morris," 166; Mary Pemberton to John Pemberton, 6mo.3.1750, Pemberton Papers, 6:80, HSP.

57. Samuel Fothergill to Susanna Hatton, 6mo.27.1760, Grubb Collection, FHLD; "An Account of Rachel Wilson's Religious Visit," 16.

58. "An Account of Rachel Wilson's Religious Visit," 33; "Memoirs of the Life of Catharine Phillips," 214–15.

59. Mary Weston to Peter Peisley, 9mo.10.1749, Portfolio 4.49, FHLD; Lydia Lancaster to Samuel Fothergill, 12mo.4.1757, LRSF.

60. Elizabeth Wilkinson, "Journal of a Religious Visit," 3; Jane Fenn, "Journal 1727–1729," 4mo.27.1727 entry; "The Journal of Ann Moore 1756–1762," 110.

61. "From the Yearly Meeting of Ministering friends held by Adjournment the first of ye 4th mo 1702 in London . . . A brief memorial of Some Ne[ce]ssary Things recommended only to Ministers"; Rachel Labouchere, *Abiah Darby of Coalbrookdale* (York, Eng., 1988), 262; Tolles, *Meeting House and Counting House,* 135.

62. Tolles, *Meeting House and Counting House,* 136, n. 72; Elizabeth Wilkinson, "Journal of a Religious Visit," 69; Elizabeth Wilkinson to [Nurse] Grace Buchanan, 2mo.8.1763, referring to Sally Smith, with whom she corresponded several times; see Wilkinson/Smith letters in Howland Collection, QCHC.

63. Mary Weston to Daniel Weston, 6mo.3.1750, inserted at 45, in Mary Weston, "Journal of her visits"; "Memoirs of the Life of Catharine Phillips," 219; "An Account of Rachel Wilson's Religious Visit," 29; see Labouchere, *Abiah Darby of Coalbrookdale.*

64. London Yearly Meeting Epistle Sent to Maryland Friends, 2mo.17.1697, LRSF; Mary Weston, "Journal of her visits," 97.

65. "Some Account of the Life and Religious Exercises of Mary Neale," 80–81, 106–7; "Journals of Esther Palmer," 136.

66. "The Journal of Ann Moore 1756–1762," 57; Mary Weston, "Journal of her visits," 102.

67. "An Account of Rachel Wilson's Religious Visit," 54.

68. Daniel Weston to Israel Pemberton Jr., 6mo.22.1750, Pemberton Papers, 6:90, HSP; Mary Weston to Israel Pemberton Jr., 8mo.7.1750, Pemberton Papers, 6:115, HSP.

69. Daniel Weston to James Pemberton, 3mo.30.1750, Pemberton Papers, 6:34, HSP; John Sinclair to James Pemberton, March 18, 1750/1, Pemberton Papers, 7:18, HSP.

70. Yorkshire (England) Quarterly Meeting Minutes, 10mo.29–30.1714; County Tipperary (Ireland) Monthly Meeting Accounts, 1717–1800, 7mo.5.1726.

71. Margaret Ellis, "Diary of travels in the ministry," 11–12.

72. Mary Weston, "Journal of her visits," 46.

73. John Pemberton to Israel Pemberton Jr., 11mo.15.1750, Pemberton Papers, 6:155, HSP; Mary Weston to Daniel Weston, 6mo.3.1750, inserted at 45, in Mary Weston, "Journal of her visits"; "The Journal of Ann Moore 1756–1762," 46.

74. Jane Fenn, "Journal 1727–1729," 7mo.1–5.1728 entries.

75. "Memoirs of the Life of Catharine Phillips," 231.

76. "From the Yearly Meeting of Ministering friends held by Adjournment the first of ye 4th mo 1702 in London . . . A brief memorial of Some Ne[ce]ssary Things recommended only to Ministers" (first quotation); Cork, Ireland, Ministers' Visits, 1708–1877, 72.

77. "Some Account of the Life and Religious Exercises of Mary Neale," 112–19.

78. "A Letter from Elizabeth Webb to Anthony William Boehm," 172; Elizabeth Wilkinson, "Journal of a Religious Visit," 33.

79. "The Journal of Ann Moore 1756–1762," 95; "Diary of Deborah Morris, 1772," quoted in Moon, *The Morris Family of Philadelphia*, 1:285.

80. Catharine Phillips, *Considerations on the Causes of the High Price of Grain, and Other Articles of Provision, for a Number of Years Back; and Propositions for Reducing Them*, 58.

81. Tabitha Hornor to Abigail Boles, 5mo.28.1733, Portfolio 3.B40, FHLD; Will of Sarah Morris, 1775, at Philadelphia Register of Wills.

CHAPTER FOUR: "DUTIFUL WIVES, TENDER MOTHERS"

1. Mary Weston to Israel Pemberton Jr., 3mo.8.1753, Pemberton Papers, 8:141; Mary Weston to Israel Pemberton Jr., 8mo.25.1752, Pemberton Papers, 8:70–71, HSP.

2. Mary Weston to Israel Pemberton Jr., 8mo.25.1752, Pemberton Papers, 8:70–71, HSP; Margaret Ellis, "Diary of travels in the ministry," 32; Margaret Ellis to Rachel Pemberton, 2mo.10.1753, Pemberton Papers, 8:129, HSP.

3. Mary Weston to Israel Pemberton Jr., 3mo.8.1753, Pemberton Papers, 8:141, HSP; Goshen (Pennsylvania) Monthly Meeting, Certificates of Removal Received 1721–1757, FHLSC.

4. Samuel Willard, *A Compleat Body of Divinity* (Boston, 1726), 125.

5. Abigail Watson to Mary Peisley, 12mo.3.1745, Portfolio 4.40, FHLD; "Memoirs of the Life of Catharine Phillips," 253; "Some Account of the Life and Religious Exercises of Mary Neale," 100; Levy, *Quakers and the American Family,* 133.

6. See Robert V. Wells, "Quaker Marriage Patterns in a Colonial Perspective," *WMQ,* 3d ser., vol. 39 (1972): 415–42; Vann and Eversley, *Friends in Life and Death,* 89. The ministerial pattern of late marriage seemed to supersede regional differences. After the mid-eighteenth century, the general Quaker pattern became more like this ministerial group, although perhaps for different reasons: a diminishment in the number of Quakers resulted in a limited number of marital partners. Friends' withdrawal from the world may have increased their desire to limit family size and hoard family resources in order to keep their children from "the world's ways." A number of studies found that Quaker women after 1750 increasingly married at older ages.

7. "Some Account of the Life and Religious Exercises of Mary Neale," 76.

8. "Memoirs of the Life of Catharine Phillips," 254–55.

9. "John Alderson" entry in DQB (first quotation); Jenkins, *The Records and Recollections of James Jenkins,* 467. Jenkins's story may not be accurate, since the American Revolution was under way at the time of Mary Fyfield's marriage, and no Friends visited during the war.

10. "Some Account of the last Illness and Expressions of that eminent Instrument and useful Handmaid of the Lord, Susannah Lightfoot," 3mo.6.1781; "Memoirs of the Life of Catharine Phillips," 254.

11. "Some Account of the Life and Religious Labours of Samuel Neale," *FL,* 11:17–20.

12. Levy, *Quakers and the American Family,* 228–29; "Some Account of the Life and Religious Labours of Samuel Neale," 21.

13. Aaron Ashbridge, "A Wedding Invitation," *PMHB* 31 (1907): 376; "Memoirs of the Life of Catharine Phillips," 253; Abigail Boles to Benjamin Hornor, 6mo.24.1728, Watson MSS, LRSF.

14. William Redwood to John Pemberton, 7mo.(Sept.)4.1749, Pemberton Papers, 5:156, HSP; "Memoirs of the Life of Catharine Phillips," 220.

15. Heiss, *Quaker Biographical Sketches,* 182.

16. An extract from James Gough's MS journal printed in "Life of Joseph Oxley," 460; John Boles, postscript to letter, Abigail Boles to Benjamin Hornor, 6mo.24.1728, Watson MSS, LRSF.

17. *Piety Promoted,* 4:397; Heiss, *Quaker Biographical Sketches,* 167.

18. Abington (Pennsylvania) Monthly Meeting Minutes, 10mo.29.1753; A Testimony of Lancaster Monthly Meeting concerning Lydia Lancaster, 149.

19. Sandwich (Massachusetts) Monthly Meeting Marriage Records, 124, Archives of the New England Yearly Meeting, Rhode Island Historical Society, Providence, Rhode Island.

20. George Keith, *The Woman Preacher of Samaria* (London, 1674), 11 (first quotation); Philadelphia Yearly Meeting of Ministers and Elders Minutes, 7mo.15.1700, microfilm, FHLSC.

21. Cotton Mather, *Ornaments for the Daughters of Zion, or the Character and Happiness of a Woman*, 3d ed. (Boston, 1741), 95. On women's status under English common law, see Marylynn Salmon, "Equality or Submersion? Feme Covert Status in Early Pennsylvania," in *Women of America,* 94.

22. Gwynedd (Pennsylvania) Monthly Meeting of Ministers and Elders Minutes, 10mo.27.1760, 1mo.26.1761, FHLSC; Devonshire House (England) Monthly Meeting Adjourned Minutes, 2mo.14.1703, 6mo.11.1703, 8mo.13.1703, LRSF.

23. Middletown (Pennsylvania) Monthly Meeting Minutes, 7mo.2.1708, FHLSC; (London Yearly Meeting) Testimonies Concerning Deceased Ministers, 3:295.

24. Joseph Hatton to Benjamin Grubb, 5mo.26.1755, Grubb Collection, FHLD; Jane Crosfield to George Crosfield, 10mo.24.1751, in Notes for a chapter in a Family record, compiled by John D. Crosfield, 1900, at FHLSC; Isaac Hall to Alice Hall, 5mo.26.1747, in *Genealogical Notes on the families of Hall, Featherston, . . . etc.,* compiled by John Hall Shield (Allendale, Eng., 1915), 35a–37.

25. "Memoirs of the Life of Catharine Phillips," 208, 247.

26. Elizabeth Hudson, "An Abstract of the Travels," 8mo.1751.

27. Rachel Wilson to Isaac Wilson, 8mo.17.1768; Rachel Wilson to Isaac Wilson, 5mo.25.1769, LRSF.

28. Henry Gouldney to John Boles, 7mo.15.1722, Watson MSS, LRSF.

29. "Memoirs of the Life of Catharine Phillips," 525.

30. Cork, Ireland, Ministers' Visits, 1708–1877, 10mo.1735; "Some Account of the Life of Elizabeth Ashbridge," 22.

31. John W. Jordan, ed., *Colonial Families of Philadelphia* (New York, 1911), 2:1291.

32. George Fox, Epistle 320, *The Works of George Fox,* 8:93.

33. Will of John Boles of Woodhouse, 1731, Registry of Deeds, Dublin, Ireland. County Tipperary Six Weeks Meeting Minutes, 1mo.5.1731/2, Clonmel, Ireland, FHLD, noted the misbehavior of Ann Boles's nephew.

34. Will of James Dillworth of Bristol, 1700, Philadelphia Register of Wills; Will and Inventory of Christopher Sibthorp of Philadelphia, 1707, Philadelphia Register of Wills; Will of Abraham Rawlinson of Hornby, 1737, Lancashire Record Office, Preston, England.

35. Will of John Leaver of Nottingham, 1794, Nottinghamshire Record Office, Nottingham, England.

36. See Marylynn Salmon, *Women and the Law of Property in Early America* (Chapel Hill, N.C., 1986). Will and Inventory of Mary Waln of Norrington, 1753,

Philadelphia Register of Wills; Will and Inventory of Evan Lewis of Newtown, 1735, Chester County Archives and Records Services, West Chester, Pennsylvania.

37. Will, Inventory and Administration of Estate of Job Harvey of Darby, 1750/1, Chester County Archives.

38. Isaac Hall to Alice Hall, 5mo.26.1747, in *Genealogical Notes on the families of Hall, Featherston, . . . etc.*

39. Jones, *The Quakers in the American Colonies,* 69, n. 3; Braithwaite, *The Beginnings of Quakerism,* 236–37.

40. The Box Meeting epistle is cited in Mack, *Visionary Women,* 367; Jane Crosfield to George Crosfield, 10mo.24.1751, in Notes for a chapter in a Family record.

41. Pardshaw (Cumberland, England) Women's Monthly Meeting Minutes, 3mo.19.1747, Cumbria Record Office, Carlisle, England.

42. Vann and Eversley, *Friends in Life and Death,* 147; Wells, "Quaker Marriage Patterns," 441.

43. "An Account of part of the Travels of Susanna Morris," HSP; Mary Weston to Israel Pemberton Jr., 8mo.25.1752, Pemberton Papers, 8:70–71; John Pemberton to Israel senior and Rachel Pemberton, 2mo.17.1753, Pemberton Papers, 8:133, HSP.

44. George Fox to Friends in Bucks County, Pennsylvania, 3mo.20.1685, printed in *PMHB* 29 (1905):106.

45. Goshen (Pennsylvania) Monthly Meeting, Certificates of Removal Received 1721–1757, 115–16; "Diary of Abiah Darby, Ca. 1744–1769," 41, LRSF.

46. Dublin (Ireland) Monthly Meeting Minutes, 11mo.27.1707; Hume, *An Exhortation to the Inhabitants of the Province of South-Carolina,* 89.

47. Abraham and Phebe Farrington to Abigail Boles, 7mo.25.1735, Portfolio 17.29, LRSF (first quotation); "The Journal of Ann Moore 1756–1762," 83.

48. Isaac Hall to Alice Hall, 5mo.26.1747, in *Genealogical Notes on the families of Hall, Featherston, . . . etc.*

49. John F. Crosfield, *The Crosfield Family* (Cambridge, Eng., 1980), 24; Elizabeth Webb, "A Short Account of My Viage," 27–28.

50. "A Brief Testimony concerning our Dear Friend and Brother Samuel Baker . . . ," Dublin (Ireland) Monthly Meeting Family Lists, 1655–1699, 178 [344], FHLD. For Phebe Dodge, see Anna Davis Hallowell, ed., *James and Lucretia Mott, Life and Letters* (Boston, 1884), 2–5.

51. Robert Barclay quoted in Frost, *The Quaker Family in Colonial America,* 64–65 (first quotation). "Ruth Seaman" entry in DQB. Ruth Seaman joined the Wilson household after the deaths of her husband and only child.

52. The meeting's responsibility for the Quaker child is detailed in Frost, *The Quaker Family in Colonial America.*

53. Waterford (Ireland) Six Weeks Meeting Minutes, 9mo.26.1760, 3mo.13.1761; Dublin (Ireland) Monthly Meeting Certificates of Removal, 1754–1776, 111–12.

54. (London Yearly Meeting) Testimonies Concerning Deceased Ministers, 2:89.

55. Mary Leaver epistle to her daughters, printed in *The British Friend* (4mo.1848); 89–90; Susanna Morris to her family, dated Manchester, 1745, in "An Account of part of the Travels of Susanna Morris," HSP.

56. See Catherine M. Scholten, *Childbearing in American Society: 1650–1850* (New York, 1985). Scholten argued that motherhood was a newly self-conscious occupation in the nineteenth century. As part of relying on the extended Quaker community for assistance in child rearing, Friends expected the Quaker masters to whom they apprenticed their children to provide not only child care but religious instruction. See Vann, *The Social Development of English Quakerism*, 180.

57. William Wordsworth, "Ode: Intimations of Immortality from Recollections of Early Childhood," in *Major British Writers*, ed. G. B. Harrison et al. (New York, 1954), 2:243.

58. See Vann's discussion of the "reconstruction" of the Quaker family, *The Social Development of English Quakerism*, 167–79.

59. Quoted in Frost, *The Quaker Family in Colonial America*, 64–66.

60. "The Testimony of Samuel Baker concerning his dear wife," Dublin (Ireland) Monthly Meeting Family Lists, 1655–1699, 176 [341], FHLD; London Yearly Meeting advice quoted in Philip Greven, *The Protestant Temperament: Patterns of Child-Rearing, Religious Experience, and the Self in Early America* (New York, 1977), 166–67.

61. Mary Leaver epistle to her daughters, printed in *The British Friend* (4mo.1848).

62. Heiss, *Quaker Biographical Sketches*, 122; Mary Doe [Dow] letter to her children, printed in "The Journal of Thomas Chalkley," 17–18.

63. "Memoirs of the Life of Catharine Phillips," 232; in Phillips's case, the struggle was to leave behind her dear and aged mother, instead of a child; Mary Weston to Daniel Weston, 10mo.3.1750, inserted at 71, in Mary Weston, "Journal of her visits"; "An Account of Rachel Wilson's Religious Visit," 72.

64. Rachel Wilson to Isaac Wilson, 5mo.17.1769, and 2mo.4.1769, LRSF.

65. *Piety Promoted*, 2:393.

66. "The Journal of Ann Moore 1756–1762," 108–9.

67. Mary Smith to her son, 8mo.2.1728, printed in Heiss, *Quaker Biographical Sketches*, 160.

CHAPTER FIVE: "IN THE SERVICE OF TRUTH"

1. "Diary of Ann (Cooper) Whitall, 1760–1762 (with additional entries from other years)," transcribed by Michael C. Osborne, QCHC, B-71–72, 92, 124; *Ann C. Whitall, the Heroine of Red Bank* (Gloucester County Historical Society, Woodbury, N.J., 1904). Fort Mercer was built in the Whitalls' apple orchard during the Revolutionary War.

2. "Diary of Ann (Cooper) Whitall, 1760–1762," B-57, 60–61, 71–72, 107–8.

3. Richard Partridge was described by Belcher in a letter of November 1731, quoted in Michael C. Batinski, *Jonathan Belcher, Colonial Governor* (Lexington, Ky., 1996), 96; Margaret Ellis, "Diary of travels in the ministry," 2, 4. "The substance of the foregoing Relation of Margt. Ellis was taken down from her own Mouth in a Journey from London into Wales & wrote [by] Richd: Partridge in the Year 1752," 14.

4. "John Kelsall Diary," 1:127–28, 135–37, LRSF. See Raistrick, *Quakers in Science and Industry,* for the British Quaker contributions to the iron industry.

5. "Diary of Ann (Cooper) Whitall, 1760–1762," B-76.

6. Mary Weston, "Journal of her visits," 50; Henry Gouldney to John Boles, 7mo.15.1722, Watson MSS, LRSF.

7. Elizabeth Wilkinson, "Journal of a Religious Visit," 14, 89.

8. See Benjamin Ferris of Oblong, "Religious Visits in 1750 & later, MS journal 1708–1775."

9. Mary Weston, "Journal of her visits," 49. Often crowds of both Quakers and others flocked to hear the visiting Englishwomen. In Newport, at another time, Mary Weston "declared the gospel" at the largest meeting she had ever seen: "It was generally concluded there were many more people than at any of their Yearly Meetings, or that had ever been at the place considerably above 4,000 in number," 62. "An Account of Rachel Wilson's Religious Visit," 39.

10. Quoted in Heiss, *Quaker Biographical Sketches,* 200.

11. Philadelphia Monthly Meeting Minutes, 10mo.29.1710; for Jacob epistle, see Carla Gardina Pestana, *Quakers and Baptists in Colonial Massachusetts* (Cambridge, Eng., 1991), 78–79.

12. "Prophecies of Mary Ellerton a Friend on a Visit to America from Europe," Parrish Collection, Pemberton Papers, HSP; Cork, Ireland, Ministers' Visits, 1708–1877, 12.

13. "Record of Friends Travelling in Ireland, 1656–1765," *JFHS* 10 (Oct. 1913).

14. Mary Weston to Peter Peisley, 9mo.10.1749, Portfolio 4.49, LRSF.

15. *Gentleman's Magazine* 20 (1750): 86, and "Verses to Mary Peisley," Row MSS, Collection of poems by various people, 105–7, LRSF; "On the Death of Jane Hoskins," by Hannah Griffitts, Library Company of Philadelphia.

16. Jenkins, *The Records and Recollections of James Jenkins,* 260.

17. "John Griffith's account of Susanna Morris" in "Journal of the Life and Travels of Susanna Morris," 144; "Some Account of the Life and Religious Exercises of Mary Neale," 98.

18. Richard Partridge to John Kinsey, 4mo.11.1745, Pemberton Papers, 3:167, HSP.

19. John Hunt to Israel Pemberton Sr., 6mo.30.1746, Pemberton Papers, 4:41, HSP.

20. "Journal of the Life and Travels of Susanna Morris," 152; "Some Account of the Life and Religious Exercises of Mary Neale," 99, 73–74.

21. "Some Account of the Life and Religious Exercises of Mary Neale," 78–79.

22. Heiss, *Quaker Biographical Sketches,* 139, 141.

23. Ibid., 267.

24. Margaret Ellis to Sampson Lloyd II, 11mo.27.1755, and 10mo.9.1757, Lloyd MSS, LRSF.

25. Cork, Ireland, Ministers' Visits, 1708–1877, 6mo.19.1711; George Keith quoted in Henry J. Cadbury, "Intercolonial Solidarity of Quakerism," *PMHB* 60 (1936): 365; "Some Account of the Life and Religious Exercises of Mary Neale," 89; "Journal of the Life and Travels of Susanna Morris," 165; Mary Weston, "Journal of her visits," 62; quoted in Heiss, *Quaker Biographical Sketches,* 200.

26. Dublin (Ireland) Monthly Meeting Minutes, 2mo.1.1746, FHLD; Barclay, *Apology,* Proposition 15, sec. 9; see, for example, Abiah Darby, *An Exhortation in Christian Love, to all who frequent Horse-racing, Cock-fighting, Throwing at Cocks, Gaming, Plays, Dancing, Musical Entertainments, or any other Vain Diversions,* 3d ed. (Newcastle, Eng., 1770).

27. Mary Weston, "Journal of her visits," 6; Jean Pierre Brissot de Warville quoted in Tolles, *Meeting House and Counting House,* 61. Tolles noted that the Quaker spirit of order "was essential for success in a 'rationalized' capitalist economy in which the pursuit of gain was regarded as a continuous and intensive activity based upon the expectation of regular production, markets, and profits." Heiss, *Quaker Biographical Sketches,* 200, 264.

28. Dublin (Ireland) Monthly Meeting Minutes, 8mo.13.1691, FHLD; Tolles, *Meeting House and Counting House,* viii; Heiss, *Quaker Biographical Sketches,* 263.

29. Dublin (Ireland) Monthly Meeting Minutes, 8mo.13.1691, FHLD; Raistrick, *Quakers in Science and Industry,* 142: "The Darby families, both men and women, were able to combine in a striking fashion, the duties of the [iron]works and of the Society of Friends, and for several generations they maintained a most healthy balance of activities. . . . Abiah Darby took the occasion at her table, often, to speak a few words of ministry or advice or pleading, to the visitors who had come to the works solely on business. . . ."

30. *Journal of George Fox,* ed. Nickalls, 11; Barclay, *Apology,* 314.

31. *The Quakers in the American Colonies,* 204; Ann Roberts to John Kinsey, 6mo.13.1739, Henry S. Drinker Papers, HSP; Arthur J. Mekeel, "The Founding Years, 1681–1789," in *Friends in the Delaware Valley: Philadelphia Yearly Meeting 1681–1981,* ed. John M. Moore (Haverford, Pa., 1981), 35. John Kinsey (1693–1750) became the Speaker of the Pennsylvania Assembly in 1739.

32. "Some Account of the Life and Religious Exercises of Mary Neale," 81; Elizabeth Hudson, "An Abstract of the Travels," 8mo.11.1749.

33. Elizabeth Wilkinson, "Journal of a Religious Visit," 18, 41, 53, 48, 46, 84–85, 123, 89, 130.

34. "An Account of Rachel Wilson's Religious Visit," chapter 11:16, 18.

35. Moses Brown quoted in John Somervell, *Isaac and Rachel Wilson, Quakers of*

Kendal, 1714–1785 (London, 1924), 62–63; "An Account of Rachel Wilson's Religious Visit," chapter 11:18.

36. Margaret Ellis, "Diary of travels in the ministry," 13.

37. "Journal of the Life and Travels of Susanna Morris," 160–61, described "where there were two places that Friends met in; the old adversary, that strives to break unity amongst people, having, instead of love, sowed discord."

38. Jenkins, *The Records and Recollections of James Jenkins,* 37, 134, 257; "An Account of Rachel Wilson's Religious Visit," chapter 13:37; Waterford (Ireland) Six Weeks Meeting Minutes, 4mo.29.1760.

39. Elizabeth Wilkinson, "Journal of a Religious Visit," 125–26, 129.

40. "Some Account of the Life and Religious Exercises of Mary Neale," 81.

41. "Some Account of the Life and Religious Exercises of Mary Neale," 98–99.

42. Heiss, *Quaker Biographical Sketches,* 192. As early as 1750, Susanna Morris was preaching against the too frequent use of strong drink and tobacco, "Journal of the Life and Travels of Susanna Morris," 184.

43. Susanna Morris to Israel Pemberton Jr., 1mo.26.1752, Pemberton Papers, 7:158, HSP.

44. Mary Weston to Israel Pemberton Jr., 5mo.23.1752, Pemberton Papers, 8:32, and 8mo.25.1752, Pemberton Papers, 8:70–71, HSP.

45. Heiss, *Quaker Biographical Sketches,* 192, 318; *The Journal of John Woolman and A Plea for the Poor* (Secaucus, N.J., 1961), 43; "Elizabeth Levis" entry in DQB; Marietta, *The Reformation of American Quakerism,* 107–8.

46. Mary Weston, "Journal of her visits," 89–90; quoted in Tolles, *Meeting House and Counting House,* 48; Tolles noted: "The list of attenders at this meeting, situated in the heart of the trading and financial district, reads like a bead-roll of the most important banking and commercial families of England: it includes the Barclays, Gurneys, Hanburys, Lloyds . . . to name only some of the most famous."

47. "Some Account of the Life and Religious Exercises of Mary Neale," 92; Joseph White quoted in Marietta, *The Reformation of American Quakerism,* 162.

48. Samuel Fothergill quoted in Marietta, *The Reformation of American Quakerism,* 40–41.

49. The number of delinquency cases are from Marietta, *The Reformation of American Quakerism,* 46–47, 58 (quotation).

50. "Some Account of the Life and Religious Exercises of Mary Neale," 86.

51. Dr. John Rutty, *Spiritual Diary and Soliloquies* (London, 1776); Elizabeth Ashbridge quoted in Irish Yearly Meeting Testimonies, FHLD, 108.

52. Marietta, *The Reformation of American Quakerism,* xii.

53. See Marietta, *The Reformation of American Quakerism,* 34, for the reform efforts of John Churchman; "Some Account of the Life and Religious Exercises of Mary Neale," 87.

54. "Some Account of the Life and Religious Exercises of Mary Neale," 90–91;

Mary Weston to Abigail Watson (formerly Boles), 9mo.25.1749, Watson MSS, LRSF.

55. Marietta, *The Reformation of American Quakerism,* 34, "Some Account of the Life and Religious Labours of Samuel Neale," 4.

56. John Pemberton to Israel senior and Rachel Pemberton, 6mo.20.1752, Pemberton Papers, 8:47, HSP. In another letter to his parents, Pemberton noted that they had met with more substantial Quakers in the south than in the north of Ireland, "tho those for the far greater part among the females . . . unto whom Our Souls have been & Still are united in fellowship & have had to Sympathizingly to mourn in Communion under a Sence of the prevailing degeneracy [of the Society] . . . ," John Pemberton to Israel senior and Rachel Pemberton, 9mo.29.1752, Pemberton Papers, 8:80, HSP.

57. Mary Weston, "Journal of her visits," 61.

58. Mary Weston to Abigail Watson, 9mo.30.1752, Portfolio 3.B40, FHLD; Mary Weston, "Journal of her visits," 59, 113; Marietta, *The Reformation of American Quakerism,* 44, details Israel Pemberton Jr.'s change.

59. Mary Weston to Israel Pemberton Jr., 11mo.25.1750, Pemberton Papers, 6:159, HSP.

60. Marietta, *The Reformation of American Quakerism,* 41; "Some Account of the Life and Religious Exercises of Mary Neale," 117–18.

61. "Some Account of the Life and Religious Exercises of Mary Neale," 105–6.

62. Ibid., 106–9, 111; "Memoirs of the Life of Catharine Phillips," 222.

63. "Some Account of the Life and Religious Exercises of Mary Neale," 115.

64. Marietta, *The Reformation of American Quakerism,* 54.

65. See Margaret Hope Bacon, "A Widening Path: Women in the Philadelphia Yearly Meeting Move Toward Equality, 1681–1929," in *Friends in the Delaware Valley,* ed. Moore; "Some Account of the Life and Religious Exercises of Mary Neale," 113.

66. Marietta, *The Reformation of American Quakerism,* 55–56.

67. "Some Account of the Life and Religious Exercises of Mary Neale," 113.

68. "Memoirs of the Life of Catharine Phillips," 230.

69. Quoted in Marietta, *The Reformation of American Quakerism,* 148–49.

70. "Some Account of the Life and Religious Exercises of Mary Neale," 113–14.

71. Marietta, *The Reformation of American Quakerism,* 153–55 (quotation).

72. Samuel Fothergill quoted in Marietta, *The Reformation of American Quakerism,* 155, 119.

73. Marietta, *The Reformation of American Quakerism,* 156 (first quotation); Mary Weston, "Journal of her visits," 51–52.

74. Marietta, *The Reformation of American Quakerism,* 158.

75. "Some Account of the Life and Religious Exercises of Mary Neale," 115; Ellen Evans to Ann Fothergill, 6mo.1756, in *Memoirs of the Life and Gospel Labours of*

Samuel Fothergill, with Selections from his Correspondence. Also An Account of The Life and Travels of his Father, John Fothergill, And Notices of Some of His Descendants, ed. George Crosfield (New York, 1844), 260.

76. Marietta, *The Reformation of American Quakerism,* 61, 297, n. 32. According to Amelia Mott Gummere, ed., *The Journal and Essays of John Woolman* (New York, 1922), 544, the eminent Quaker minister Rebecca Jones "was led to join the Society largely through the influence of Catharine Payton, an English Friend who visited Philadelphia on a preaching tour in 1754."

77. John Fothergill quoted in Marietta, *The Reformation of American Quakerism,* 163.

78. Quoted in Marietta, *The Reformation of American Quakerism,* 159–62.

79. This section is largely based on the chapter "Perfecting Pacifism, 1756–1758" in Marietta, *The Reformation of American Quakerism* (quotation, 172).

80. Quoted in Marietta, *The Reformation of American Quakerism,* 179.

81. Ibid., 185; Soderlund, "Women's Authority in Pennsylvania and New Jersey Quaker Meetings, 1680–1760," 749.

82. "Some Account of the Life and Religious Exercises of Mary Neale," 107; Soderlund, *Quakers and Slavery: A Divided Spirit,* and J. William Frost, "The Origins of the Quaker Crusade against Slavery: A Review of Recent Literature," *Quaker History* 67 (1978), found that some reformers, such as John Woolman and Anthony Benezet, focussed more on eliminating slavery than on the strict enforcement of Quaker discipline, while others, like Peisley and Payton, were more concerned about upholding Quaker testimonies. But "while each group had its particular focus, each supported the other type of reform," Soderlund, 170–71.

83. John Churchman quoted in Marietta, *The Reformation of American Quakerism,* 119; 111–14, 121.

84. Elizabeth Wilkinson, "Journal of a Religious Visit," 12; "An Account of Rachel Wilson's Religious Visit," 60.

85. Marietta, *The Reformation of American Quakerism,* 157–58, 187–89.

86. "Memoirs of the Life of Catharine Phillips," 230; Amos W. Butler, ed., "Documents: A Visit to Easton," *Indiana Magazine of History* 32 (1936): 268–69.

87. Elizabeth Wilkinson, "Journal of a Religious Visit," 44, 71, 28, 22.

88. Ibid., 78–79; Marietta, *The Reformation of American Quakerism,* 63–67.

89. "Some Account of the Life and Religious Exercises of Mary Neale," 111.

90. Elizabeth Wilkinson, "Journal of a Religious Visit," 79; "Diary of Ann (Cooper) Whitall, 1760–1762," B-97, 25.

91. Elizabeth Wilkinson, "Journal of a Religious Visit," 74–75.

92. Marietta, *The Reformation of American Quakerism,* 66.

93. Elizabeth Wilkinson, "Journal of a Religious Visit," 78; Marietta, *The Reformation of American Quakerism,* 85–86. See Tolles, *Meeting House and Counting House,* 239: "In less than a century Philadelphia Quakerism had come full circle." As Friends increasingly tried to wall off the destructive influences of "the world,"

and no longer contended for political office, they isolated themselves "from the main currents of American life."

94. Mary Weston, "Journal of her visits," 106.

95. John Churchman to Margaret Churchman, 9mo.11.1750, Henry H. Albertson Collection, QCHC.

96. John Pemberton to Israel Pemberton Jr., 6mo.11.1750, Pemberton Papers, 6:83, HSP.

97. John Griffith to John Pemberton, 2mo.17.1753, Pemberton Papers, 8:134, HSP.

98. Heiss, *Quaker Biographical Sketches,* 192; "Some Account of the Life and Religious Labours of Samuel Neale," 13.

99. Marietta, *The Reformation of American Quakerism,* 38-39. During Susanna Morris's travel in England, in 1752, she noted, "I was grieved to see that a wrong spirit had got in amongst some of the elders, and in others a disbelief that the Lord required females to labour in the gospel. . . . but I may say, the Lord so filled me with his goodness, that I seemed to get the victory over all the wrong spirits, and, had some good service amongst them . . . ," in "Journal of the Life and Travels of Susanna Morris," 187-88.

100. Mary Weston to John Churchman, 8mo.17.1755, Henry H. Albertson Collection, QCHC; Philadelphia Yearly Meeting quoted in Soderlund, "Women's Authority in Pennsylvania and New Jersey Quaker Meetings, 1680-1760," 748.

101. Quoted in Janet Scott, "Women in the Society of Friends," in *A Quaker Miscellany for Edward H. Milligan,* ed. David Blamires, Jeremy Greenwood, and Alex Kerr (Manchester, Eng., 1985), 129. See also Margaret Hope Bacon, "A Widening Path: Women in the Philadelphia Yearly Meeting Move Toward Equality, 1681-1929," in *Friends in the Delaware Valley,* ed. Moore, and Doncaster, *Quaker Organization and Business Meetings,* 36.

102. Marietta, *The Reformation of American Quakerism,* 202. The Quaker men's abdication of political office had increased the authority of ministers, many of whom were women, in the Society of Friends. "The great figures of that period in Philadelphia Quakerism were to be ministers rather than political leaders; most of them—Friends like Thomas Scattergood, George Dillwyn, Rebecca Jones, and William Savery—had come of age in the years following the withdrawal from political life," see Tolles, *Meeting House and Counting House,* 239.

CHAPTER SIX: FROM "WITCHES"
TO "CELEBRATED PREACHERS"

1. Quoted in Justin Windsor, ed., *The Memorial History of Boston* (Boston, 1880), 1:180. This story has been told in many places; see Jones, *The Quakers in the American Colonies,* 27, 40, 70, 76. Carla Gardina Pestana extensively discusses the

context of this episode in "The City upon a Hill under Siege: The Puritan Perception of the Quaker Threat to Massachusetts Bay, 1656–1661," *New England Quarterly* 56, no. 3 (September 1983). In 1656, the first law was passed against Quakers in the Massachusetts Bay Colony. Ship captains who brought Quakers into the colony paid a fine of one hundred pounds. Further laws in 1657 provided for a fine of forty shillings for every hour a Quaker was entertained by a colony resident, and whippings, cropped ears, and tongues bored with a hot iron for returning Quakers. William Robinson and Marmaduke Stephenson were hanged in 1659, Mary Dyer in 1660, and William Leddra in 1661.

2. The *Boston-Gazette, or Country Journal,* no. 744, July 10, 1769. The same article appeared in the *Massachusetts Gazette,* no. 394, July 6, 1769.

3. "An Account of Rachel Wilson's Religious Visit," chapter 12:21–22, 24–25.

4. In 1699, the English Quaker preacher Thomas Story stopped in New Haven: "After using endeavours to have a meeting in this place, but without success, the magistrate not favouring it, we proceeded on our journey to Rhode Island . . . ," William Alexander, ed. *The Life of Thomas Story,* abridged by John Kendall (York, Eng., 1832), 222. See Moore, *Travelling with Thomas Story,* 60–62.

5. According to "The Records of the Quakers in Charles Town," ed. Mabel L. Webber, *The South Carolina Historical and Genealogical Magazine* 28 (July 1927): 181, on February 3, 1769, Wilson preached at the Quaker meeting-house, and on February 5 Wilson held two meetings in the Baptist meeting-house. See "An Account of Rachel Wilson's Religious Visit," 54; *Country Journal,* February 7, 1769; *General Gazette,* February 13, 1769; *The Papers of Henry Laurens,* ed. George C. Rogers Jr. et al. (Columbia, S.C., 1970), 6:269, n.2.

6. "We came to Burdentown (19th.) whear the Meetghous was quite too Smal to Contain the pepol that many stood out in the Rain and not finding my Self Clear a Metg was appointed at 4 the Baptists ofering thair Meetg hous as more Conveneant it Being such hevey Rain we acceptaed of it and a memorabl one we had in it," chapter 10:2, 4, "An Account of Rachel Wilson's Religious Visit."

7. "An Account of Rachel Wilson's Religious Visit," chapter 10:2–3; chapter 11:13; Request from the Students of Nassau Hall in New Jersey, May 20, 1769, to Mrs. Rachel Wilson, Friends' Autographs, 3:85, LRSF; *The Literary Diary of Ezra Stiles, D.D., L.L.D.,* ed. Franklin Bowditch Dexter (New York, 1901), 1:14.

8. "An Account of Rachel Wilson's Religious Visit," 67–68, 70.

9. Jenkins, *The Records and Recollections of James Jenkins,* 52; Thomas Story to James Logan, 12mo.20.1735/6, quoted in Moore, *Travelling with Thomas Story,* 255; Stephen Hobhouse, *William Law and Eighteenth-Century Quakerism* (London, 1927), 73.

10. Elizabeth Hudson, "An Abstract of the Travels," 5mo.10.1748, and 5mo.28.1748; "Some Account of the Life and Religious Exercises of Mary Neale," 80; Jenkins, *The Records and Recollections of James Jenkins,* 51–52; *Memoirs of the Life and Gospel Labours of Samuel Fothergill,* ed. Crosfield, 91.

11. "Diary of Deborah Morris, 1772," 28; John Adams corresponded with Catharine Macaulay, *Diary of John Adams*, 1:360, August 9, 1770, entry. Macaulay's multi-volume *History of England, from the Accession of James I to That of the Brunswick Line* (London, 1763–83) "was for a time a kind of Bible for political radicals in England and America," 361, n. 1.

12. "The Life of that Faithful Servant of Christ, Jane Hoskens," 471–72; Elizabeth Hudson, "An Abstract of the Travels," 8mo.12.1745; "Memoirs of the Life of Catharine Phillips," 222, 231.

13. Margaret Ellis, "Diary of travels in the ministry," 19–20; Amos W. Butler, ed., "Documents: A Visit to Easton," *Indiana Magazine of History* 32 (1936): 268; Julian P. Boyd, ed., *The Susquehannah Company Papers 1756–1767* (Ithaca, N.Y., 1930–71), 2:118.

14. Israel Pemberton Sr. to Isaac Greenleafe, 8mo.22.1748, Pemberton Papers, 4:146, HSP; Frances Dodshon asserted in her published letter: "Infinite Wisdom will work by such instruments as he sees meet, and his powerful word has been as a fire within me, so that I dare not any longer keep silence, but, in humble and awful fear of obedience, offer these weighty things, O King, to thy serious consideration, imploring Divine Goodness to . . . endue thee with wisdom . . . to act for . . . the preservation of peace . . . throughout thy extensive dominions," 275–76, *Gentleman's Magazine* 45 (June 1775).

15. *Gentleman's Magazine* 5 (1735): 555, and *Gentleman's Magazine* 20 (1750): 86; quoted in Hobhouse, *William Law and Eighteenth-Century Quakerism*, 74, 165 n., and Lloyd, *Quaker Social History 1669–1738*, 128.

16. *Gentleman's Magazine* 23 (June 1753): 292; *Gentleman's Magazine* 25 (April 1755): 186; *Gentleman's Magazine* 52 (August 1782): 406; Lydia Pocock's obituary appeared in the *Virginia Gazette,* January 30, 1772. Hobhouse, *William Law and Eighteenth-Century Quakerism,* 182, gives a contradictory death date, August 1, 1793, for the preacher Frances Dodshon.

17. Quoted in Hobhouse, *William Law and Eighteenth-Century Quakerism,* 75; Mack, *Visionary Women,* 409. Other eighteenth-century Quakers published vindications of women's preaching, including Josiah Martin (1683-1747), a Quaker writing-master who had introduced Quaker readers to the French quietists through his translations of the works of Madam Guion and Fénelon, and wrote a reply to Voltaire's admiring, but somewhat misleading, account of Quakers in his *Letters Concerning the English Nation* (1733). Martin authored *A Letter to the Author of Some Brief Observations on the Paraphrase and Notes of the Judicious John Locke, Relating to the Women's Exercising their Spiritual Gifts in the Church* (1716) and *A Vindication of Women's Preaching* (1717).

18. [William Smith], *A Letter from a Gentleman in London to his Friend in Pennsylvania, with a Satire Containing Some Characteristical Strokes Upon the Manners and Principles of the Quakers* (London, 1756), 17. Benjamin Franklin quoted in John Frederick Woolverton, *Colonial Anglicanism in North America* (Detroit, 1984),

211–12. See, for example, *The Ceremonies and religious customs of the various nations of the known world . . . Written originally in French [by J. F. Bernard]. . . . Faithfully translated into English, by a gentleman some time since of St. John's College in Oxford* (London, 1733–39), 7:118–19, which described Quaker meetings: "This Variety of Behaviour is caused as they pretend, by the Impression of the *Spirit,* which often dictates to the *Man* or *Woman Preacher,* Sermons two or three Hours long, after a deep and sullen Silence of an equal Duration has stupified those Enthusiasts. . . . If the other Customs and tenets of the Quakers were not more singular or blame-worthy, 'twere almost to be wished all the World might turn *Quakers.*"

19. H. H. Brackenridge, *Modern Chivalry: Containing the Adventures of Captain John Farrago, And Teague O'Regan, His Servant* (Philadelphia, 1792), introduction by Lewis Leary (reprint, New Haven, 1965), 2:126–27.

20. Voltaire, *Letters Concerning the English Nation* (1733), introduction by Charles Whibley (reprint, London, 1926), 27.

21. Byrom quoted in Hobhouse, *William Law and Eighteenth-Century Quakerism,* 112, 115. Boswell's experience apparently prompted Samuel Johnson's famous remark, "Sir, a woman's preaching is like a dog's walking on his hind legs. . . ." See James Boswell, *The Life of Samuel Johnson, L.L.D. [1791]* (New York, 1931), 279. Peter Quennell, *Caroline of England; an Augustan portrait* (New York, 1940), 134–35. The queen's attitude of inquiry was evident in an account of May Drummond's interview with Queen Caroline: "She hath also been to wait on the Queen, and was more than an hour in her presence. At her first coming in the Queen soon began and asked her many questions which May was not very forward to answer, but after some little pawce she began and had a good [religious] opportunity for near half an hour . . . To speake to the Queen the Princesses and some Ladys of honour . . . which she and those three friends who accompanied her had good reason to think was very much to all their satisfaction . . . ," quoted in Gummere, *The Quaker: A Study in Costume,* 135. Catharine Macaulay was "liberal in her attitude to other religious sects. Her close friendships with Dissenters and others of diverse affiliations make this clear . . . ," 149–50, Bridget Hill, *The Republican Virago: The Life and Times of Catharine Macaulay, Historian* (Oxford, Eng., 1992). She was a defender of Quakerism; see J. P. Brissot de Warville, *New Travels in the United States of America 1788,* ed. Durand Echevarria (Cambridge, Mass., 1964), 311. Hannah More to Horace Walpole, September 1790, *Horace Walpole's Correspondence,* ed. W. S. Lewis et al. (New Haven, 1961), 31:350–51; Horace Walpole to Sir Horace Mann, April 17, 1780, *Horace Walpole's Correspondence,* ed. W. S. Lewis et al. (New Haven, 1971), 25:40.

22. Quoted in Robert K. Massie, *Peter the Great: His Life and World* (New York, 1980), 211; see *Travelling with Thomas Story,* 43–44, 154–55; Faujas de St. Fond quoted in Rosamond Bayne-Powell, *Travellers in Eighteenth-Century England* (1st ed. London, 1951; reissued New York, 1972), 159.

23. Voltaire, *Letters Concerning the English Nation* (1733), 2, 9–10, 22–23.

24. Raistrick, *Quakers in Science and Industry; The Papers of Benjamin Franklin,* ed. William B. Willcox et al. (New Haven, 1978), 21:361–62; *The Correspondence of Edmund Burke,* ed. Thomas W. Copeland (Cambridge, Eng., 1958), 1:xvi, 90–91; "Some Account of the Life and Religious Exercises of Mary Neale," 98, n.

25. Batinski, *Jonathan Belcher,* 65–66, 128; *The Literary Diary of Ezra Stiles,* 1:496; *The Papers of Benjamin Franklin,* 21:360–65.

26. Lloyd, *Quaker Social History,* 101; Moore, *Travelling with Thomas Story,* 146.

27. Moore, *Travelling with Thomas Story,* 42, 165, 197–99, 211–12, 220, 298.

28. The conversion of an Anglican woman to Quakerism often distressed her immediate relatives and friends. Hobhouse, *William Law and Eighteenth-Century Quakerism,* gives an extensive account of the "convincement" of Frances Henshaw (later Dodshon) against the opposition of her family. Her family encouraged William Law, author of *A Serious Call to a Devout and Holy Life, adapted to the state and condition of all orders of Christians* (1729), to correspond with the young woman (twenty-three years of age when she became a Quaker) to turn her away from Quakerism. Dr. Samuel Johnson was enraged when a young heiress and acquaintance of his, twenty-year-old Jane Harry, converted to Quakerism. In a dialogue between Johnson and Mrs. Knowles, a Quaker friend, published in the *Gentleman's Magazine* 61 (June 1791): 500–502, regarding the incident, Mrs. Knowles defended Jane Harry's right to examine and change her religious tenets, arguing that she was "an accountable creature" and "a moral agent." Dr. Johnson responded, "Pshaw! Pshaw!—an accountable creature!—girls accountable creatures!—It was her duty to remain with the Church wherein she was educated; she had no business to leave it . . . I hate the arrogance of the wench, in supposing herself a more competent judge of religion than those who educated her . . . she ought not to have presumed to determine for herself in so important an affair." Moore, *Travelling with Thomas Story,* 249–50, 254.

29. Moore, *Travelling with Thomas Story,* 255, 248; Hobhouse, *William Law and Eighteenth-Century Quakerism,* 159.

30. Moore, *Travelling with Thomas Story,* 274–75.

31. Ibid., 224, 227, 233–35, 240. "By 1730 Quakers were generally being treated with respect. Under the Whig Government, which brought in the Hanoverian Kings, they were in considerable favour with politicians and even with some of the bishops, and secured important legislative concessions," Hobhouse, *William Law and Eighteenth-Century Quakerism,* 200.

32. Gertrude S. Kimball, *Providence in Colonial Times* (New York, 1972), 204; Mary Weston, "Journal of her visits," 48.

33. "An Account of Rachel Wilson's Religious Visit," chapter 12:26.

34. "Memoirs of the Life of Catharine Phillips," 230; Richard Peters quoted in

The Papers of Benjamin Franklin, ed. Leonard W. Labaree et al. (New Haven, 1963), 6:457, n.; Benjamin Marshall to Hugh Forbes, October 18, 1763, in Moon, *The Morris Family of Philadelphia, Descendants of Anthony Morris 1654-1721,* 1:156.

35. Batinski, *Jonathan Belcher,* 152-53; John Hunt to Israel Pemberton Sr., 6mo.30.1746, Pemberton Papers, 4:41, HSP; *Memoirs of the Life and Gospel Labours of Samuel Fothergill,* ed. Crosfield, 254.

36. The Reverend Mr. John Blair quoted in Woolverton, *Colonial Anglicanism in North America,* 170; Mary Weston, "Journal of her visits," 86-87; see "The Records of the Quakers in Charles Town," ed. Mabel L. Webber, *The South Carolina Historical and Genealogical Magazine* 28 (January 1927): 22-43.

37. Carla Gardina Pestana, *Quakers and Baptists in Colonial Massachusetts* (Cambridge, Eng., 1991), 137; Carl Bridenbaugh, *Mitre and Sceptre: Transatlantic Faiths, Ideas, Personalities, and Politics, 1689-1775* (New York, 1962), 65; Batinski, *Jonathan Belcher,* 50, 65-66, 96.

38. Batinski, *Jonathan Belcher,* 26, 63-65, 128-29; *The Correspondence of the Colonial Governors of Rhode Island 1723-1775,* ed. Gertrude Selwyn Kimball (1st ed. 1902-03, reprint, Freeport, N.Y., 1969), 1:75, Governor Wanton to Richard Partridge, December 1, 1735.

39. Pestana, *Quakers and Baptists in Colonial Massachusetts,* 138-41, 147-49.

40. Moore, *Travelling with Thomas Story,* 86-87; "The Journals of Esther Palmer, 1704," *JFHS* 6 (1909): 139. It is not known whether the Quaker women were included in the tour of the college, but they reported in their journal that they were hosted by the Virginia governor in Williamsburg "at his Request." The female preachers had been at the Virginia Yearly Meeting with Thomas Story and were with him at this stage of their trip.

41. Parke Rouse Jr., *James Blair of Virginia* (Chapel Hill, N.C., 1971), 144-48; *Historical Collections Relating to the American Colonial Church,* ed. William Stevens Perry (1st ed. 1870-78; reprint, New York, 1969), 1: 87-133.

42. *The Writings of "Colonel William Byrd of Westover in Virginia Esqr.,"* ed. John Spencer Bassett (New York, 1901), 20. William Wirt Henry, *Patrick Henry: Life, Correspondence, and Speeches* (New York, 1891), 1:115-16. Although Patrick Henry proposed a multiple church establishment, rather than a total separation of church and state, in 1776 the Virginia state legislature adopted the Bill of Rights (with a section drafted by Henry), which recognized the priority of conscience in matters of faith, formally ending civil discrimination against dissenters. "An Account of Rachel Wilson's Religious Visit," 70.

43. Batinski, *Jonathan Belcher,* 63-65; *The Papers of Henry Laurens,* ed. Philip M. Hamer et al. (Columbia, S.C., 1970), 1:xxii; 5:556; Henry Laurens to William Fisher, February 11, 1769, in 6:273-75.

44. *The Papers of Henry Laurens,* 6:273-75.

45. Batinski, *Jonathan Belcher,* 26; *Diary of John Adams,* 2:79, March 5, 1773, entry; *The Book of Abigail and John,* 76; Brackenridge, *Modern Chivalry,* 1:61.

Patrick Henry, writing on ministers and religious toleration, argued, "A good life is the best lecture," Henry, *Patrick Henry: Life, Correspondence, and Speeches,* 112.

46. *The Diary of Ebenezer Parkman 1703-82,* ed. Francis G. Walett (Worcester, Mass., 1974), 1:xi. Some historians date the revival from as early as 1730, but most identify the intercolonial fervor with George Whitefield's arrival in America in 1739. See *The Great Awakening: Event and Exegesis,* ed. Darrett B. Rutman (New York, 1970), 1, and Alan Heimert, *Religion and the American Mind: From the Great Awakening to the Revolution* (Cambridge, Mass., 1966), 2.

47. Mary Weston, "Journal of her visits," 122; "An Account of Rachel Wilson's Religious Visit," chapter 10:7.

48. *Memoirs of the Life and Gospel Labours of Samuel Fothergill,* ed. Crosfield, 254.

49. Mark Noll, *Princeton and the Republic, 1768-1822: The Search for Christian Enlightenment in the era of Samuel Stanhope Smith* (Princeton, 1989), 17, 31-32; "A Sermon preached by Rachel Wilson at Stourbridge [England] the 1st of 9th mo. 1765," inserted in "An Account of Rachel Wilson's Religious Visit to Friends in America, 1768-1769," LRSF; Heimert, *Religion and the American Mind,* 36; on Whitefield and Wilson, see Jenkins, *The Records and Recollections of James Jenkins,* 208-10.

50. Pestana, *Quakers and Baptists in Colonial Massachusetts,* 141 42; "Extracts from the Journal of Mrs. Ann Manigault 1754-1781," *The South Carolina Historical and Genealogical Magazine* 20 (January 1919): 59; *The Literary Diary of Ezra Stiles,* 200, n.; *The Book of Abigail and John,* 149; "Some Account of the Life and Religious Labours of Samuel Neale," 54.

51. Margaret Brewster, a Quaker missionary who journeyed from Barbados in 1677 to interrupt a sermon in Boston, her face blackened with ashes to demonstrate God's judgment upon the misguided Puritans, was the last woman to receive punishment for that kind of offense in Massachusetts. Lovejoy, *Religious Enthusiasm in the New World: Heresy to Revolution,* 131. Sophia Hume, *An Exhortation to the Inhabitants of the Province of South-Carolina,* 4, 11.

52. Charles Chauncy, *Enthusiasm Described and Caution'd Against* (1742), in *The Great Awakening: Event and Exegesis,* ed. Rutman, 55.

53. "An Account of Rachel Wilson's Religious Visit," chapter 12:21; *The Diary of Isaac Backus,* ed. William G. McLoughlin (Providence, R.I., 1979), 2:751, January 18, 1770, entry.

54. "An Account of Rachel Wilson's Religious Visit," 41-42; Henry Mayer, *A Son of Thunder: Patrick Henry and the American Republic* (New York, 1986): 157.

55. Samuel Fothergill to Susanna Hatton, 6mo.27.1760, Grubb Collection, FHLD; Mary Weston, "Journal of her visits," 58, 61; "Memoirs of the Life of Catharine Phillips," 222; George Fox quoted in Lovejoy, *Religious Enthusiasm in the New World: Heresy to Revolution,* 133; Rachel Wilson quoted in Somervell, *Isaac and Rachel Wilson, Quakers, of Kendal, 1714-1785,* 76.

56. John Kelsall's Diary quoted in Raistrick, *Quakers in Science and Industry,* 127. Christine Leigh Heyrman, *Southern Cross: The Beginnings of the Bible Belt* (New York, 1997), 13, noted the evangelicals' vigorous rates of growth in the southern colonies between about 1750 and 1776. In part, the number of "new evangelical churches formed before the American Revolution" was the result of Scots-Irish Presbyterian migration into the region.

57. Quoted in G. M. Trevelyan, *English Social History: The Eighteenth Century* (London, 1951), 3:68–69.

58. In the eighteenth century, many non-Quakers commented on the aesthetic appeal of the Quaker women's neatness of appearance. When May Drummond arrived for her interview with Queen Caroline of England, "The Queen seemed much pleased with her plain dress, and green apron, and often said she thought it exceedingly neat and becoming," quoted in Gummere, *The Quaker: A Study in Costume,* 135. When Thomas Story dined with the countess of Kildare and some other people of rank in Ireland, "this lady and the rest commended the plain dress of our women as the most decent and comely, wishing it were in fashion among them," quoted in Moore, *Travelling with Thomas Story,* 164. *Gentleman's Magazine* 4 (December 1734): 702; *Gentleman's Magazine* 35 (July 1765): 344; "An interesting DIALOGUE between the late Dr. SAMUEL JOHNSON and Mrs. KNOWLES," *Gentleman's Magazine* 61 (June 1791): 500–502.

59. *Gentleman's Magazine* 2 (June 1732); Thomas Paine, *Common Sense [1776] and the Crisis* (reprint, Garden City, N.Y., 1960), 63; *Diary of John Adams,* 2:126–27, entry for September 7, 1774.

60. Bownas, *An Account of the Life, Travels, and Christian Experiences in the Work of the Ministry,* 101–2.

61. Mary Weston, "Journal of her visits," 125; "Some Account of the Life and Religious Exercises of Mary Neale," 107.

62. Samuel Fothergill's sermon, reported in the *Boston Gazette, or Country Journal,* no. 18, August 4, 1755; see Jenkins, *The Records and Recollections of James Jenkins,* 54, n. 3; *Virginia Gazette,* January 11–18, 1739, and December 8–15, 1768.

63. Mary Weston, "Journal of her visits," 121–22.

64. "The Journal of Ann Moore 1756–1762," 11–12, 9, 49–52.

65. "The Journal of Ann Moore 1756–1762," 53, 42, 34, 36.

66. Elizabeth Hudson, "An Abstract of the Travels," 8mo.18.1745; "Memoirs of the Life of Catharine Phillips," 214; "Some Account of the Life and Religious Exercises of Mary Neale," 107. Heyrman, *Southern Cross,* noted that "the besetting sin of the Anglican clergy was the lackluster vice of sloth, which caused them to neglect the needs of men and women in those remote areas . . . ," so itinerant preachers (in this case, evangelical Presbyterians, Baptists, and Methodists) trained their energies on these backcountry districts, 12–13.

67. Jane Fenn, "Journal, 1727–1729," 9mo.2.1728 entry; Mary Weston, "Journal of

her visits," 54, 87; "Some Account of the Life and Religious Exercises of Mary Neale," 102; "An Account of Rachel Wilson's Religious Visit," chapter 12:30.

68. See Labouchere, *Abiah Darby of Coalbrookdale,* xii; Jenkins, *The Records and Recollections of James Jenkins,* 208–10. Although George Whitefield admired Pennsylvania's toleration and certain aspects of the Quakers, he felt that they mistakenly equated conscience with the Holy Spirit and taught an inward Christ at the expense of the historical, external Christ. Whitefield also felt that denying the Calvinist belief in election dishonored God by making salvation dependent not on God's free grace but on man's free will. Whitefield helped sinners prepare for God's act of grace should He choose to manifest it. See Lovejoy, *Religious Enthusiasm in the New World: Heresy to Revolution,* 149, 165. Quaker minister Samuel Fothergill, on his way to Georgia, wrote that "George Whitefield passed through this town a few days ago, for Georgia, having travelled very hard from Philadelphia, to get to his flock before we came amongst them," *Memoirs of the Life and Gospel Labours of Samuel Fothergill,* ed. Crosfield, 174.

69. Moore, *Travelling with Thomas Story,* 84; Mary Weston, "Journal of her visits," 122.

70. Mary Weston, "Journal of her visits," 47, 50–51, 57; at one of her meetings, Weston "was told that every person of Note in & about the [Massachusetts] Town which was very considerable was present; it was judged about Two thousand in Number, a part of the Meeting House broke down with the Throng . . ."; "Memoirs of the Life of Catharine Phillips," 214.

71. Jenkins, *The Records and Recollections of James Jenkins,* 51–52. Frances Henshaw wrote that after "the gift of the ministry" had been committed to her, and she had been "led" to visit different parts of England, "the opposer of all good [Satan], who secretly envies the growth of truth . . . sought to exalt [me] and cause many to think of me more highly than they ought to think. . . . And in the midst of popularity and applause [I] found my mind secretly called down to humility and retirement . . . nor do I know that I joined at all with the tempter, in his presentations in myself to lift me up, or took pleasure in hearing the satisfaction [that] friends and the great people expressed concerning my ministry," quoted in Hobhouse, *William Law and Eighteenth-Century Quakerism,* 159; *Memoirs of the Life and Gospel Labours of Samuel Fothergill,* ed. Crosfield, 124.

72. Mary Weston, "Journal of her visits," 86; *The Papers of Henry Laurens,* 6:273–75; Benjamin Franklin to Deborah Franklin, July 14, 1772, *The Papers of Benjamin Franklin,* ed. William B. Willcox et al. (New Haven, 1975), 19:207; Morris Birkbeck to Isaac Wilson, 10mo.16.1773, Gibson 1:37, LRSF.

73. Quote from Wade Hampton Lagrone, "Ecstasy and Innovation: The Female Itinerant Preachers of English Methodism, 1785–1850" (B.A. thesis, Harvard University, 1990), 48–49. John Wesley originally approved only of ministers ordained by the Anglican church but out of necessity later used lay preachers. Wesley was

horrified by the Quaker practice of regular female preaching, which he found to be scripturally unsupportable. Wesley advised a woman in 1769: "Even in public you may properly enough intermix short exhortations with prayer, but keep as far from what is called preaching as you can: therefore never take a text, never speak in a continued discourse without some break, about four or five minutes," quoted in Lagrone, 41. See also Deborah M. Valenze, *Prophetic Sons and Daughters: Female Preaching and Popular Religion in Industrial England* (Princeton, N.J., 1985). Methodist women preached on an unofficial, ad hoc basis. After Wesley's death, the leaders of official Methodism strictly ordered the end of women's preaching. Sectarian Methodists broke away from Wesleyan Methodism to preserve their local forms, which included camp meetings and female preaching. By the 1830s, even the sectarians discouraged women's ministry as they made the transition from evangelicalism to "respectable" pastoralism. In contrast, the Quaker practice was engaged in not as a temporary expediency but as a result of Friends' theological principles—which gave women an official commission to preach, on equal terms with men.

74. *Gentleman's Magazine* 5 (September 1735): 555. The original poem was addressed to Mary Astell and entitled "To Almystrea, on her Divine Works" (1722) by the English poet Elizabeth Thomas (1675–1731). Thomas "found encouragement in the claims of the early feminist Mary Astell for the independent dignity, intellectual self-respect, and moral autonomy of women." See Roger Lonsdale, ed., *Eighteenth Century Women Poets: An Oxford Anthology* (Oxford, Eng., 1989), xxii, 43.

75. *A dissertation upon the liberty of preaching granted to women by the people call'd Quakers. In a letter to the famous itinerant preacher Mrs. M. Dromond* [sic] . . . *By a traveller* (Dublin, 1738).

76. Byrom quoted in Hobhouse, *William Law and Eighteenth-Century Quakerism*, 127; Boswell, *The Life of Samuel Johnson, L.L.D.* [1791], 279, 534.

77. Voltaire, *Letters Concerning the English Nation* (1733), 25–26; Moore, *Travelling with Thomas Story*, 256.

78. "An Account of Rachel Wilson's Religious Visit," 74; see also Rachel Wilson to Isaac Wilson, 4mo.29.1769, LRSF, describing her American travels, "pepol of all persuations Flocking to Meetgs—yt [that] we never want Numbers to preach to . . ."; "Some Account of the Life and Religious Exercises of Mary Neale," 109. According to Pestana, *Quakers and Baptists in Colonial Massachusetts*, 184, "The Great Awakening indirectly contributed to the Quaker reformation in that it fractured the orthodox community and furthered contact across religious boundaries." The Great Awakening may have promoted a greater toleration of Quaker female preachers by non-Friends and increased their visibility among different denominations, but this intermixing helped lead to the Society's reaction of reasserting the boundaries between Friends and the world.

79. *The Papers of Henry Laurens*, 6:273–75; "An Account of Rachel Wilson's Religious Visit," 57.

80. *The Literary Diary of Ezra Stiles,* 1:492.

81. Ibid., 1:492–96.

82. Thompson, *Moses Brown,* 108–9, 130.

83. Paine, *Common Sense,* 62–63.

84. Thompson, *Moses Brown,* 183, 295. The war raised serious problems for the Society of Friends, both from without and from within. For example, Quakers agreed that all members should pay taxes for the support of civil government, but Friends were divided over tax obligations during wartime. Israel Pemberton Jr. defined neutrality as continuing to support the old British government and refusing to support the revolutionary government. Timothy Davis of Sandwich Monthly Meeting on Cape Cod believed that Quakers should pay taxes to the revolutionary government in Massachusetts. When Davis published his views without the permission of the Society, he was disowned. "At one time Friends had been of great importance to Rhode Island politics but after the Revolution, except in isolated instances, they exerted only an indirect influence," Thompson, *Moses Brown,* 239.

85. Tolles, *Meeting House and Counting House,* 239. By the Revolutionary War, the Quakers "in erecting barriers against the 'world,' thus strengthening their group solidarity and isolating themselves from the main currents of American life," increasingly adopted "a pattern of behavior characteristic of sects like the Mennonites, whom in many particulars they now came more and more to resemble." Although nineteenth-century Quaker female preachers, like Elizabeth Fry and Lucretia Mott, were very prominent in reform movements—prison reform, abolitionism, and women's rights—they were primarily visible as social reformers rather than as preachers in the non-Quaker culture.

AFTERWORD

1. Richard Webb, a yeoman, resided on 415 acres in Birmingham township. Chester County tax returns for Birmingham in 1715 rank him the sixth highest taxpayer. He owned additional property in Caln and Uwchlan townships. Will and Inventory of Richard Webb, 1720, Chester County Archives and Records Services, West Chester, Pennsylvania. Clement Biddle, "The Early Settlers of Birmingham" (Local History, Chester County Historical Society Library). "A Letter from Elizabeth Webb to Anthony William Boehm," 170.

2. See Salmon, *Women and the Law of Property in Early America,* and Ulrich, *Good Wives,* 7. "A Letter from Elizabeth Webb to Anthony William Boehm," 170–71.

3. Ulrich, *Good Wives,* 13; "A Letter from Elizabeth Webb to Anthony William Boehm," 172; quoted in Biddle, "The Early Settlers of Birmingham," 3.

4. Although Jane Brinton served as a travel companion for Elizabeth Webb, Brinton was not a minister herself. All of the other women mentioned were recognized Quaker preachers.

5. Norton, "The Evolution of White Women's Experience in Early America," 600; quoted in Biddle, "The Early Settlers of Birmingham," 3–4; "Record of Friends Travelling in Ireland, 1656–1765," *JFHS* 10 (October 1913); Mary Beth Norton, *Liberty's Daughters: The Revolutionary Experience of American Women, 1750–1800* (Boston, 1980), 616.

6. *The Journal of Esther Edwards Burr 1754–1757*, ed. Carol F. Karlsen and Laurie Crumpacker (New Haven, 1984), 37; Heiss, *Quaker Biographical Sketches,* 101, n.

7. Samuel Carpenter to William Penn, 9mo.19.1698, *The Papers of William Penn,* 3:559; Concord (Pennsylvania) Monthly Meeting Minutes, 8mo.1704.

8. Philadelphia (Pennsylvania) Monthly Meeting Minutes, 12mo.1703, 2mo.1704, 3mo.26.1704, and 1mo.1710.

9. "A Letter from Elizabeth Webb to Anthony William Boehm," 164, 169, 173.

10. Samuel Carpenter to William Penn, 9mo.19.1698, *The Papers of William Penn,* 3:559.

11. Elizabeth Webb to Joseph Brinton, 6mo.24.1724, printed in Gilbert Cope, *The Brinton Genealogy: A History of William Brinton . . . and of His Descendants,* ed. Janetta W. Schoonover (Trenton, N.J., 1925), 140–43.

12. Elizabeth Webb to her children, 6mo.24.1724, printed in *The Friend* (May 1856), 132.

13. Four of the five women who planned "the world's first woman's rights convention" at Seneca Falls, New York, in 1848 were Quakers, although Friends formed a small proportion of the American population at this time; see Bacon, *Mothers of Feminism,* 1. Susan B. Anthony, who joined the woman's rights movement in 1852, and Alice Paul, the twentieth-century author of the Equal Rights Amendment, were both Quakers. Quakers comprised 40 percent of female abolitionists, 19 percent of feminists born before 1830, and 15 percent of suffragists born before 1830, according to Mary Maples Dunn, "Women of Light," in *Women of America: A History,* 132.

14. Elizabeth Webb to Joseph Brinton, 6mo.24.1724, printed in *The Brinton Genealogy,* ed. Schoonover, 140–43.

Acknowledgments

This project has evolved from a Ph.D. dissertation completed at Harvard University. I am deeply grateful to Bernard Bailyn, my dissertation advisor, in whose seminar on Anglo-American history the earliest version of this work emerged. The History of American Civilization program at Harvard and the Charles Warren Center for Studies in American History provided travel grants, enabling me to accomplish essential archival research in the British Isles and in Pennsylvania. A Library Company of Philadelphia / Historical Society of Pennsylvania summer fellowship made it possible for me to peruse their rich resources. A Philadelphia Center for Early American Studies Dissertation Fellowship provided invaluable support that permitted a year-long research sojourn in Pennsylvania. I also benefitted from the Woodrow Wilson National Fellowship Foundation, which funded a year of dissertation writing.

I wish to express my appreciation to many individuals, named and unnamed, who contributed information and assisted in other ways on this project. I particularly thank Kenneth Carroll, J. William Frost, Jean Soderlund, Richard Dunn, Mary Maples Dunn, Craig Horle, Albert Fowler, Phyllis Mack, Wayne Bodle, and Kenneth Morgan. The staff at many libraries and record offices provided invaluable help, including Elisabeth Potts Brown and Eva Myer at the Quaker Collection, Haverford College; Mary Ellen Chijioke, Pat O'Donnell, and Nancy Speers at the Friends Historical Library, Swarthmore College; Malcolm Thomas, Sylvia Carlyle, and the staff of the Library of the Religious Society of Friends in London; Stephen Tabor at the William Andrews Clark Memorial Library, University of California, Los Angeles; and the staff of the Library Company of Philadelphia, the Historical Society of Pennsylvania (particularly Pamela Webster), and the Chester County Historical Society in Pennsylvania. I am especially grateful to Rosalind Wiggins of the New England Yearly Meeting Archives at the Rhode Island Historical Society, Providence, Rhode Island, and Mary Shackleton of the Friends Historical Library in Dublin, Ireland, for not only assisting me with archival materials but providing meals and lodging as well. My thanks to Cathy Wood; to Lyn and Pat Kelly of Swanbrook House, Dublin; and to the staff of the Penn Club in London, especially to

Alison Boyce. I also wish to thank Jane Garrett of Alfred A. Knopf for her generosity and encouragement. My gratitude to my family, particularly my mother, my grandmother, Emma Andreas, my sister, Diana Boltz, and my brother-in-law, Ray Boltz, is inexpressible: this project would not have been possible without their inspiration, care, and support.

Index

A NOTE ABOUT THE AUTHOR

Rebecca Larson was born in Palo Alto, California. She received a B.A. from the University of California, Santa Barbara, in 1984. From Harvard University she received an M.A. in history in 1987, and a Ph.D. in the history of American civilization in 1993. She was awarded the Charlotte W. Newcombe Dissertation Fellowship. In addition, she has been the recipient of fellowships and research grants from the Philadelphia Center for Early American Studies, the Library Company of Philadelphia, and the Charles Warren Center for Studies in American History, Harvard University. She is a writer currently living in Santa Barbara. *Daughters of Light* is her first book.

A NOTE ON THE TYPE

This book was set in a typeface called Bulmer. This distinguished letter is a replica of a type long famous in the history of English printing which was designed and cut by William Martin about 1790 for William Bulmer of the Shakespeare Press. In design, it is all but a modern face, with vertical stress, sharp differentiation between the thick and thin strokes, and nearly flat serifs. The decorative italic shows the influence of Baskerville, as Martin was a pupil of John Baskerville's.

Composed by North Market Street Graphics, Lancaster, Pennsylvania

Printed and bound by Quebecor Printing, Fairfield, Pennsylvania

Maps by Mark Stein Studios

Designed by Iris Weinstein